EXPLODING
THE MYTHS OF
MODERN
ARCHITECTURE

EXPLODING
THE MYTHS OF
MODERN ARCHITECTURE

MALCOLM MILLAIS

FRANCES LINCOLN LIMITED
PUBLISHERS

Frances Lincoln Limited
4 Torriano Mews
Torriano Avenue
London NW5 2RZ
www.franceslincoln.com

First Frances Lincoln edition 2009

A catalogue record for this book is available
from the British Library.

978-0-7112-2974-7

Printed and bound in Singapore

1 2 3 4 5 6 7 8 9

Acknowledgements

This book was written with the help of many people and it is a pleasure to record my gratitude to all of them. The book started, rather unsteadily, with some 'essays' that I sent to Michael Barclay, and it was with his encouragement that these 'essays' became this book. Sadly Michael did not live to see the book completed.

Over the years a number of people took the time and trouble to read, comment and correct what I was writing. For doing this I would like to thank Michael Bussell, Judith Catchpole, Gavin Hill, Jan Macaig, Andrew Mackeith (who also coined the name The Corbuncle), John O'Connor, Maria do Carmo Paço d'Arcos, Miranda Pythian-Adams, Vera d'Almeida Ribeiro, Nikos Salingaros and Tim Uden: all of whom improved the book in different ways.

Many people generously gave me permission to use their photos and drawings. I am particularly grateful to Bill Risebero, who gave me permission to use any of his drawings that beautifully illustrate his books listed in the bibliography, and to Louis Hellman, who gave me permission to use a number of his brilliant cartoons.

I would like to thank Michael Bussell, Maria Charalambous, Laura Gray, Anna Millais, Rhona Millais, Bruce Sutherland and Malcolm Wood for taking photos specifically for the book.

I am grateful to Michael Bussell, Jenny McLellan, David Owen, Jill Pearlman, Andrew Saint, Nikos Salingaros, Tim Uden and Malcolm Wood for sending me useful information.

The book was meticulously edited by Chris Fagg, who improved the language, the content and most of all the internal logic. My publisher, John Nicoll of Frances Lincoln Ltd., was continuously supportive. It was a pleasure to work with Maria Charalambous on the design of the book.

MALCOLM MILLAIS

Contents

Modern architecture
is like Esperanto, an
attempt to invent and
impose a common
"rational" language
and succeeding only
in being
incomprehensible
and alien to the
majority of people.

Louis Hellman 1986

Introduction

What myths are there about modern architecture that need to be, and should be exploded? How can it be possible that something that has come to be so much part of today's world is founded on myth and deceit? In addressing these questions this book examines both the absurd pretensions in which modern architecture has clothed itself and the highly suspect manner of its derivation.

But, before the myths about modern architecture can be identified, it has to be asked if there is something that can be defined as 'architecture', as opposed to mere building; equally, a meaning has to be given to the adjective 'modern'. All pretty simple? Indeed, some might say 'it's perfectly obvious'. Well, whatever architecture may be is not as obvious as all that, but there are some forms of architecture by which buildings are designed with an intellectual dimension, or perhaps intellectual intent. Some might say that this 'intellectual intent' is what distinguishes architecture from building.

When the term 'modern architecture' is used it usually means buildings designed by architects who consider themselves, or can be considered, as part of the Modern Movement – and in this book this is what it does mean. This is a style of architecture that had its roots before World War I, but is generally considered to have flowered in the 1920s. This architectural genre often, but not always, resulted in plain flat-roofed boxes.

Modern Movement architecture as a plain, flat-roofed box

1

Other shapes were possible, including apparently quite randomly-curved buildings. And there could be an intermediate stage, where things were curved and straight at the same time! These often ended up being a bit wonky.

Modern Movement architecture as a randomly-curved building

Modern movement architecture as something a bit wonky

And the Modern Movement also came with a set of edicts, which included:

- Buildings must be designed on the basis of functionality.
- Decorating buildings is wrong.
- All previous designs are of no value.
- All roofs have to be flat.
- Walls must have extensive glazing or be fully glazed.
- Structures must be built of concrete or steel.
- The difference between the inside and the outside of a building must be abolished.
- Floor plans must be flexible, allowing users to do what they want.
- Materials must be used honestly.
- The building's structure must be on view, be expressed.
- Buildings must use modern technology.

At face value, some of these requirements seem quite reasonable, such as the need for architecture to be functional and to incorporate modern technology: others seem quite arbitrary, such as the blanket dismissal of decoration and previous design styles. But perhaps there were compelling reasons for the less obvious edicts, and when these are understood they all make sense. Perhaps these assumptions would lead to a new, modern, architecture, which would be functional and rational and based on science and modern technology – perhaps exactly what the modern world wanted and needed.

If a 'new' architecture were needed (and in fact there was no special reason to think so), what architecture would these assumptions produce? Would it be efficient and economical and work much better than what went before? In which case, aesthetics aside, there would be obvious advantages following such edicts, and the basic myth (as propounded by the architectural ghetto) is that this is the case. But this is not the case, as Modern Movement buildings were neither efficient nor economical, nor do they work better than those that went before. Flat roofs for example; virtually all roofs that have been built in the world are pitched, so what's better about flat ones? Well not much in Milton Keynes at any rate, 'Around 25% of all homes could have been built with faulty roofs ... some 3,450 homes have now been identified ... the common factor is that every one was built with a flat roof.'[1]

Or flexible floor plans? 'The first architectural work he [Alain Sarfati] ever did was to knock down the walls of his own three-roomed flat and create the fashionable open plan of the 1960s. That proved disastrous: it helped the break up of his marriage, by destroying the privacy of the family. Now he tries to do the opposite ...'.[2]

Or using a lot of glass? 'Because there's so much glass it gets very hot in summer and cold in winter. But it's also that you can't open any windows. Part of people being happy where they work is that they can control their environment, but you can't do that at all. And because it gets so hot and people shut their blinds, we have a problem with there not being enough light'.[3]

It's easy to find more examples, and many more are given throughout the book, but the problem is much deeper than just a few 'mistakes'. The whole Modern Movement approach is based on false premises: far from being arrived at by logical analysis, as is inferred by its propagandists, it was driven by pure emotion. Furthermore, because, according to the edicts, all previous ways of designing were obsolete, no lessons could be drawn from them, hence there was no point in knowing or understanding how buildings had been conceived and built before the arrival of the Modern Movement. So everything had to be reinvented from scratch by deliberately ignoring what had previously sufficed; this almost inevitably led to problems. The idea, though never stated, was to make things look different, look functional.

Of course, for buildings to look 'functional', whatever that really means, and to actually be functional, are two very different things. But, believing in the myths, Modern Movement architects couldn't grasp this point. Buildings are literally out in all weathers, with little or no regular maintenance, factors which make extreme demands on the materials used. So the 'functional-looking' buildings would show up any small defect, any cracks or stains, whereas the ornamented ones could hide them.[4] This effect can be readily seen in any modern city.

But not only did this 'new' Modern Movement architecture fail technically and economically, it also failed culturally as most people simply didn't like it. When some Modern Movement houses were built in 1924, the estate agents had to point out that: 'the new look

[1] *Milton Keynes Gazette*, 1985.

[2] Zeldin, 1997, p183.

[3] *Guardian*, 8 February 2006, p12.

[4] Bit like spilling red wine on a white carpet rather than a heavily patterned one.

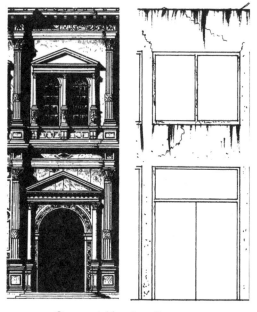

Ornamental functionality versus
lack-of-ornament non-functionality

Not pleasing at first sight?

of this villa may perhaps raise doubts in your minds ... the external appearance is not always pleasing at first sight.'[5]

Over 80 years later nothing had changed. In 2005 a librarian wrote to an architectural magazine to point out that: 'For the majority of people, modern architecture is cold, ugly and alien.'[6] But architects know this. In 1997 architect Vernon Gibberd noted: 'In the first place ordinary people didn't like International Modern (the Modern Movement) very much, and with familiarity seemed to like it less and less.'[7] All this is because, according to Alexander Tzonis, a professor of architectural theory, such buildings '... awaken us to the predicament of (post-war) everyday life; the loss of quotidian joy, the dreariness of work, loneliness of leisure.'[8]

In 1959, some poor people had the chance to be awakened to this predicament when they were put in some concrete boxes in Richmond Park near London. According to architectural pundit Jonathan Glancey, 'Architecturally, if not socially, this is one of the most successful attempts ...'[9] but 'Sadly, few of the middle-class dog walkers who stroll across Richmond Park have much good to say about it ...'.[10]

But can a building succeed 'Architecturally, if not socially'? What is this saying? The people don't like living there but architects like looking at it. This is a constant theme in tracts about modern architecture – great architecture, pity about the building.

Of course what ordinary people like is, according to architects, puerile rubbish '... in all Western countries, a bastardised vernacular remained popular with the general

---

[5] Zeldin, 1997, p176.

[6] *The Architect's Journal*, 12 June 2005, p29.

[7] Gibberd, 1997, p121.

[8] Tzonis, 2001, p160.

[9] Glancey, 2003, p205.

[10] The very un-middle-class Jonathan, has the very un-middle-class job of architectural and design editor for a very un-middle-class newspaper called the *Guardian*.

Where the poor people awakened to their predicament

public.'[11] In 1988, also in Richmond, some bastardised vernacular did get built, which probably pleased the middle-class dog walkers, but pundit Jonathan didn't like it at all – '... an annoying confection of pseudo-Georgian offices and shops ... a fake in the worst sense ... open-plan offices dressed in wannabe Georgian frock coats ...'.[12]

A sop to middle-class dog walkers

So yet another myth appears, which is that although the general public didn't like modern architecture, they would *when* they 'understood it'. Of course they do understand it, which is why they don't like it.

What this book aims to do is to explain how and why this extraordinary situation came about – whereby architects designed buildings based on a set of completely false premises, and so produced buildings that neither worked nor were liked. This totally flawed approach is rarely criticised, and its practitioners are so entrenched in their ghetto that they are unable (or unwilling) to see the deep-seated problem. Any criticism from within the architectural profession of the Modern Movement, past or present, is seen as evidence of eccentricity, if not mental illness, and no criticism can come from outside because outsiders 'simply don't understand'. So on they go, endlessly designing their mostly rectangular, flat-roofed, steel, concrete and glass boxes, whilst often living in Georgian houses in leafy squares.

---

[11] Gibberd, 1997, p151.

[12] Glancey, 2003, p65.

1. What's Architecture then?

It don't mean a thing if it ain't got that swing

When the legendary jazz pianist Thomas 'Fats' Waller (1904–1943) was asked what 'swing' was, he is reputed to have replied 'Lady, if you have to ask you ain't got it!'

Asking what architecture is invites similar put-downs, but this is odd because the word 'architecture' appears with monotonous regularity in the general culture. Daily newspapers have 'architectural correspondents' who write about 'architecture' and if someone says she or he is an architect few people will ask 'and what do you do exactly?' – everyone knows, but do they?

So is it worth bothering to try and define architecture in some way? It is unlikely that a clear definition will emerge, yet if something is to be discussed, some attempt must be made at the outset to clarify what exactly is under discussion. Furthermore, whilst such discussion may not be conclusive, the process may be enlightening in some way.

Probably few people would dispute that a Gothic cathedral,[1] built in the twelfth century, is 'architecture'. But what about a shed in the country? Certainly the cathedral and the shed are both buildings but is one architecture, the cathedral, and the other, the shed, just a building?[2] And if so why? What does a dictionary say:[3]

'**architecture**, the art or science of building; structure; specifically one of the fine arts, the art of designing buildings, style of buildings; structures or buildings collectively.'

Not much help really, unhelpful words like 'art', 'science', 'design' and 'structures' appear. Let's try an encyclopaedia:[4]

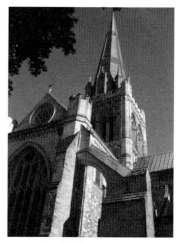

Architecture!

Architecture?

---

[1] According to the greatest 'modern' architect, Le Corbusier, '... a (Gothic) cathedral is not very beautiful.' Le Corbusier, 1927, p32.

[2] According to Nikolaus Pesvner '... a bicycle shed is a building; Lincoln Cathedral is a piece of architecture.' Quoted in *Encyclopaedia Britannica,* Vol. 13, fifteenth edition, 1993, p897.

[3] *The Chambers Dictionary,* Chambers Harrap Publishers Ltd., 1993, p83.

[4] *Encyclopaedia Britannica,* Vol. 1, fifteenth edition, 1993, p530.

'**architecture**, the art and technique of designing and building, as distinguished from the skills associated with construction. As with some other arts, the practice of architecture embraces both aesthetic and utilitarian ends that may be distinguished but not separated, and the relative weight given to each can vary widely from work to work. Thus, at one end of the scale are purely functional structures (that may nonetheless possess certain aesthetic qualities, intended or not), while at the other are purely decorative ones with no genuine practical function at all.'

With this definition both the shed – '... purely functional structures (that may nonetheless possess certain aesthetic qualities, intended or not) ...' and the cathedral – '... purely decorative ones with no genuine practical function at all,'[5] can be defined as architecture. But there is a catch. Who decides and how that a purely functional structure possesses certain aesthetic qualities? And how can it be known if these aesthetic qualities were intended or not? These are difficult questions, but it is no use everyone using the word architecture without there being some agreement on what it is. Let us try a simple test.

If we accept that a cathedral has no genuine practical function at all then, in accordance with the definition, it is purely decorative and therefore architecture. Given that basically a cathedral is one large space, built to accommodate the participants in the religious celebrations, a very large shed would serve for this purpose. One church, built in 1930, certainly looked more like a shed than a church.

Church or shed?   A shed becomes great architecture

Not many passers-by would think that this building was a church or, probably, feel it came under the heading architecture. But what about sheds? In 1952, the 'greatest modern architect', Charles-Édouard Jeanneret, better known as Le Corbusier, designed a shed. This was built in the south of France, and the architect used it as a study. But is it architecture? Well it certainly would be considered to be architecture by his fans – almost exclusively architects and design groupies – and great architecture at that.

In 1965 a factory building, that was basically a shed, was built in Swindon. The architects were called Team 4 and included both Norman Foster and Richard Rogers, both of whom went on to found their own firms, where they achieved great success and international renown, at least amongst architects.

---

[5] 'A medieval cathedral ... never used ... for any recognizably useful purpose'. Dawkins, 2006, p192.

An architect-designed shed-like building

Because this building was designed by architects, who later became well-known, pictures of it appear in numerous books on architecture – so clearly this 'shed' is architecture.[6] So it seems that the function of a building cannot determine whether it is architecture or just building.

Yet another aspect has to be considered – unbuilt architecture. This is part of the metaphysical question about where architecture actually resides – in the mind of the beholder, as a separate physical entity, in the mind of the creator, as a photo or a drawing or in all of these places? Leaving aside the mind's impenetrability and the difficult problem of drawings and photographs of built projects, physical manifestations of unbuilt projects are considered to be architecture by some[7] – 'paper' architecture as it's often called.

These drawings, models and computer simulations of unbuilt projects fall into two distinct categories, those that were to be built but didn't go ahead, a very common situation, and those that were never intended to be built. To see how architecture can be extended into the realms of pure fantasy, only never-to-be-built projects are included.

For architects who want to be noticed, and that's quite a few, producing never-to-be-built projects has huge advantages. Firstly they are cheap, if salaries are neglected as they usually are, secondly tedious technological constraints can be dispensed with, and thirdly they could be whole cities. In fact it is possible to build an entire architectural career on never-to-be-built projects, and many have.

Unbuilt architecture has a long history. Maybe the first example was in the fifteenth century, when Antonio Filarete (c.1400–c.1465) proposed a city called Sforzinda, named after his patron Francesco Sforza, the Duke of Milan. In the eighteenth century, the French architect Claude-Nicolas Ledoux (1736–1806) started, in his fantastic designs, to introduce a technological aspect. This mainly took the form of drawing buildings with impossibly huge domed or even spherical structures.

---

[6] Demolished in 1990, the manager of the company that used it said '... the sooner it comes down the better'. *Guardian*, 19 March 1990, p38.

[7] According to Modern Movement master Le Corbusier: 'When a technical work is drawn up it exists.' Collins, 1979, p51.

Fifteenth century architectural fantasy

A fantastically large spherical structure

The full force of industrialisation was first felt in the nineteenth century. But with relentlessly gathering momentum in the twentieth, fantasy architects became obsessed with technological appearance, if not with technology itself. This gave rise to a number of paper architectural projects that became iconic in the architectural ghetto. The first was the 'New City' drawn by the young Italian Antonio Sant'Elia (1888–1916). His seductive drawings of a futuristic city, based on industrial iconography, are reproduced ad nauseam in architectural tracts.

Illustrated with similar frequency, is a wonky tower designed by the Russian Constructivist Vladimir Tatlin (1885–1953).[8] His tower, naively celebrating the Third International, was intended to be 100 metres higher than the then tallest structure in the world – the Eiffel tower. Furthermore, parts of it were to rotate.

Neither Sant'Elia nor Tatlin were responsible for any substantial built project.[9] This lack of practical experience was commonplace with the 'paper' architects, a group that came to be known as Archigram being a case in point. They emerged in the 1960s producing dynamic sci-fi images, one of which was so dynamic that it showed a city walking.

Paper architecture goes technological

---

[8] Already illustrated on page 2.

[9] Sant'Elia was killed, at the age of 28, in World War I, so he didn't have much opportunity to build anything, but Tatlin, whilst Stalin's demonic purges raged, was ensconced in a 'research' station. Here he studied the flight of cranes to provide him with technical data for the design of his revolutionary 'air bicycle' which was to be powered by humans using their arms. This was a total failure because Tatlin had omitted to notice that the crane's most powerful muscles powered their wings, whereas for humans the biggest muscles powered the legs.

A city passes by   Architecture as a lot of hot air

Also in the 1960s, the American techno-mystic-guru, Richard Buckminster Fuller, was proposing that people would be able to float around the world in one mile diameter hot-air balloon cities. It's quite hard to imagine why anyone would want to spend their life floating around the world in a sphere, but so far no one has had the chance to find out.

In 1998 Willy Maas conceived Metacity/Datatown, which was a city in a video. As Maas explained, 'It is a city described by electronic information, a city without topography, without prescribed ideology, without representation, without context ...'. A population of 241 million inhabitants was predicted. It was divided into 'sectors' and the 'sector of life' was a seemingly endless sea of red cuboids, most of the same height but some of quite different heights.

No doubt, with ever increasing technological facilities, in the future hologramic architecture will be possible and perhaps techniques not yet imagined.

From this range of 'is-it-architecture-or-not?' examples can anything be concluded? Perhaps not, but there do seem to be three categories into which most of these examples can be fitted. Firstly there are buildings, or maybe other structures, that are constructed by people who want to use them. This is not to say they may not decorate them or

Life in a cuboid sea

10

Unpretentious cottages

Huge, but unpretentious

consider their appearance of importance, but that is as far as they want to go. These could be considered unpretentious buildings. Perhaps most buildings in the world would fit into this category.

For a building to be unpretentious it doesn't necessarily have to be small, it can be huge. One of the biggest buildings in the world, NASA's vehicle assembly building, is unpretentious, or '... a functional building designed with little thought for architectural effect'.[10]

And if a building is not unpretentious then it has to be pretentious. Unfortunately, the word pretentious is rarely used to flatter, but here it's meant neither to flatter nor insult, but to categorise buildings that are intended to be more than just functional. That is, non-functional aspects play a major role in their design. This consciously enables them to be cultural symbols – some might say this is architecture.

Consciously cultural

[10] Risebero, 1982, p229.

To be pretentious, or consciously cultural, a building does not have to be large or imposing, it can be quite modest, a weekend house in the country can be terribly cultural – architect Will Bruder designed one in 1994, and noted that 'The sculptural concept of this house is based on the creation of a succession of metaphorical separations that form a type of abstract canyon of concrete blockwork that emerges from the surrounding desert'.[11] That seems pretty cultural.

A house or a succession of metaphorical separations?

Buildings that are not built but only exist, if that's the right word, as drawings, models, videos or computer files, would not be considered to be buildings or architecture by most people – but they could be considered to be imaginary buildings. They cannot be ignored as they have played and continue to play an important role in the secluded world of architectural design.

Yet dividing all known buildings, built or otherwise, into three categories does not lead to any obvious answer as to what the difference is between building and architecture. But one could tentatively propose that those consciously trying to introduce a cultural component into the design of a building are likely to be thinking that they are creating architecture. Whereas, those just wanting a useful building, even if they paint it their favourite colour, probably aren't even thinking about it. Those who are not involved in the design/building process, but are just users or passers-by, have to decide for themselves.

---

[11] Jodidio, 2001, p56.

2. Ways of being Modern

Nowadays more and more people live in the 'modern' world, so it could be thought that this 'modern' world should be built of 'modern' rather than 'traditional' architecture. But this importantly ignores the quite different meanings that the word 'modern' can have. When this emotive adjective is applied to something it is often implied that it is better in some way than things that aren't modern. And if things are not modern, then what are they? Are they old-fashioned, out-of-date, traditional or past it? These descriptions can suggest that they are superseded and ought to be replaced. But the issue is not quite as simple as that, because the word can take several meanings and these different meanings can apply simultaneously. The word modern '... was first recorded in 1585 in the sense "of present or recent times", (and) has travelled through the centuries designating things that inevitably must become old-fashioned as the word itself goes on to the next modern thing'.[1] This may seem to have only one meaning but, actually, modern here can mean one of two things.

Modern can be used in the sense of an irreversible advance. To see how modern means this, one only has to look at the development of fighter aircraft for instance. In less than 60 years these developed from planes made of fabric, wood and wires capable of barely 100 mph, to those made from titanium and carbon-fibre capable of breaking the sound barrier and more.

Fighter planes in 1917 and 1976

But modern can also mean 'in fashion'. How long something is modern, in terms of fashion, is arbitrary and what follows at the end of one 'modern fashion' does not necessarily depend on what went before.

---

[1] See http://dictionary.reference.com/browse/modern

The height of fashion in 1832

What is modern, or fashionable, at any one time, can remain in fashion for an indeterminate length of time. Then what happens to it can vary. It can go out of fashion for ever, come back into fashion or even become the norm.

'Modern' meaning an irreversible alteration – modernity – affects society, often profoundly. For instance, the appearance of gunpowder can be seen to have the effect of modernity. Gunpowder was discovered in China in the ninth century but only arrived in Europe in thirteenth century. It permitted a completely new approach to weapons, with consequent and complete transformation of how wars could be fought, and with far-reaching effects on European society and eventually the world. The essential point about gunpowder, as an example of modernity, is that firearms using gunpowder and the gunpowder itself were continuously improved. As soon as something more effective was developed, the use of gunpowder was dropped – this is how modernity works.

On the other hand, 'modern' applied to fashion does not necessarily change society in general, but usually only influences a small group – the fashionable. Once a majority of a society adopts a new fashion it is no longer fashionable, so the fashionable have to find something new. Fashion is frequently linked to a style of personal appearance, particularly clothes. The term 'fashionable' can be applied to a variety of non-essential activities or objects. The latest fashion is modern but not necessarily modernising. Oddly these two meanings of the word modern, though very different and having very different effects, can become intertwined. When this happens it is difficult to identify how the word applies and what is affecting what.

This can happen when a revolutionary design is used for fashionable ends – the Jeep for example. This was a small World War II vehicle designed for the transport of military personnel over rough terrain. After the war, the chief engineer of the British Rover Car Co. bought one, and used it as a basis for the Land Rover. This vehicle was a huge success, being used worldwide by farmers, contractors, armed services and many others who needed a rugged all-terrain vehicle.

The revolutionary Jeep

A huge success

In 1970, the Rover Company caused a revolution by introducing the Range Rover. It had the technical capabilities of the all-terrain Land Rover but, instead of the spartan appearance and the mimal comfort, all the mod-cons of a normal car had been added; a comfortable ride, a stylish body, a low level of noise and styled interior. Initially, these rather expensive cars were bought by people who had country properties as they might need to go 'off-road' now and then. Gradually they came to denote a certain status and started to appear in cities. Eventually they became a fashionable 'must-have' and spawned the 'sports-utility-vehicle' or SUV. Now they are a commonplace sight in city centres, driven by people who, in the main, need none of the off-road capabilities.[2]

The must-have Land Rover

But how does either of these uses of the word 'modern' operate when the word is used in modern architecture? It could be naively thought, and architects would certainly encourage this, that the word is being used to reflect irreversible advances in the evolution of buildings, but this is far from the case. In fact the word comes from Modernism, the term used to denote the avant-garde arts movements of the early twentieth century and their legacy.[3] To understand how the word modern applies to architecture, the essentials of Modernism need to be understood. Unfortunately, identifying the essentials and understanding them is rather easier said than done as, in common with most 'isms', there are several points of view; however, dictionary definitions can give an initial flavour.

> **Modernism** *n* 'a deliberate philosophical and practical estrangement or divergence from the past in the arts and literature occurring esp. in the course of the twentieth century and taking form in any of various innovative movements and styles.'[4]

or, similarly

> **Modernism** *n* 'The deliberate departure from tradition and the use of innovative forms of expression that distinguish many styles in the arts and literature of the twentieth century.'[5]

It can be seen immediately that this use of the word modern is absolutely specific and can only really be used for one point in time. The questions are: why did it take place only in the twentieth century and what provoked a deliberate estrangement or departure or divergence from what went before? The answer is that Modernism is a product, or by-product, of industrialisation. Industrialisation was made possible by a discovery,

---

[2] And in this case the fashion for SUVs has had an effect on society, by putting on the city streets unnecessarily large and threatening vehicles.

[3] The word Modernism is also used for a late nineteenth-century movement amongst Catholics, which tried to incorporate contemporary thought into the teachings of the church. It was condemned in 1907 by pope Pius X, and its leading members were excommunicated or left the church.

[4] *The Random House Unabridged Dictionary*, © Random House, Inc., 2006.

[5] *The American Heritage Dictionary of the English Language*, Fourth Edition, copyright © Houghton Mifflin, 2006.

Iron smelting in the eighteenth century

by Abraham Darby in 1709, of a smelting method that used coke, derived from coal, to produce iron.

Iron had been smelted since the Iron Age, from about 2500BC, but, before Darby's discovery, iron was an expensive material to produce. Due to the abundance of coal, iron now became a material that was cheap enough to be used on a large scale. And with affordable iron, large machines – steam engines – could be built to produce power that far exceeded that previously provided by humans and domestic animals. The steam engine, already in use in the 1700s, allowed the Industrial Revolution, as Arnold Toynbee termed it, to take place over the next two centuries.

Animal and steam power

While steam power, based on iron components, was to alter the face of Europe, America, and gradually the rest of the world, something else had already happened that would lead to a revolution in the way people thought. Two discoveries initiated this: the differential calculus, simultaneously and independently discovered by Isaac Newton (1643–1727) and Gottfried Wilhelm Leibniz (1646–1716), and Newton's concept of gravitational force (reputedly coming to him after an apple fell on his head). Combining this concept with the new differential calculus, Newton developed a system of theoretical mechanics, now known as Newtonian Mechanics, and showed how it could be used to calculate the behaviour of the solar system. This intellectual breakthrough took place in the seventeenth century, some 50 years before Darby's discovery.

The apple drops

As Newton stated, he could only make his discoveries by standing on the shoulders of giants. However his discoveries were the culmination of what is often called the Scientific Revolution. This meant that physical phenomena could be explained rationally rather than mystically.

Initially, these two revolutions – the Industrial and the Scientific – had little connection, one forging ahead with practical developments to increase productivity and create wealth, for some at least, whilst the other was seen as part of philosophy – natural philosophy. But gradually, and with increasing speed, these two started to intermesh to produce what is now known as Science and Technology. It is this that has produced, amongst thousands, such wonders as the jumbo jet, the hydrogen bomb, organ transplants, the personal computer and decoding the human genome.

The linking of science to practice – technology – produced modernising developments that came thick and fast, changing whole societies and eventually the world.[6] During the nineteenth century and the first years of the twentieth, there were so many of these practical and intellectual developments that it is hard to decide which had most effect – here is a short list:

1839 – First commercial photographic process by Louis Daguerre.
1848 – *The Communist Manifesto* by Karl Marx and Friedrich Engels.
1867 – Dynamite invented by Alfred Nobel.
1873 – James Clerk Maxwell's theory unifies electricity and magnetism.
1874 – First commercial typewriter by Remington & Sons.
1876 – Telephone invented by Alexander Graham Bell.
1879 – Light bulb invented by Thomas Edison.
1885 – Gottlieb Daimler invents the internal combustion engine.
1885 – The Rover 'Safety' bicycle marketed.
1888 – John Dunlop patents the pneumatic tyre.
1899 – Sigmund Freud publishes *The Interpretation of Dreams*.
1901 – Guglielmo Marconi transmits radio waves across the Atlantic.
1903 – Orville & Wilbur Wright perform first aeroplane flight.
1903 – Henry Ford uses an assembly line to make the Model T.
1905 – Albert Einstein publishes the special theory of relativity.
1913 – Niels Bohr presents the quantum model of the atom.[7]

---

[6] One of the most notable alterations due to industrialisation was population increase. In Britain the population was 10 million in 1800, but by 1900 was 40 million.

[7] It would be easy to produce other lists for this period containing equally world-shattering developments.

What this list shows is that, in the space of less than 75 years, the world was changed utterly, both practically and intellectually – in other words, the modern world had arrived.

Inventions and theories were endlessly developed and improved, each development and improvement constantly being rigorously criticised, if they did not show benefits they were rejected.[8] And all these developments had an effect on fashions, because with more efficient manufacture, transport and communications, fashions could be changed much more rapidly and drastically.[9]

Though scientific developments and the associated technology introduced radical changes, they also altered perceptions of time and space for many people. Exact time now intruded into their lives, it became important for travel; railways had to run to time-tables.[10] Being late could mean that you'd miss your train, or lose your job. Trains, ocean liners, then cars and planes supplied totally new experiences of speed and space – the landscape viewed as something detached. In 1829, after the Rainhill Trials,[11] Henry Booth noted that 'perhaps the most striking result produced by the completion of this Railway, is the sudden and marvellous change which has been effected in our ideas of time and space.'[12] And Booth wasn't the only one. When Victor Hugo (1802–1885) took his first train ride in 1841 he was overwhelmed, he entered a different universe writing, 'The flowers at the trackside aren't flowers anymore; they turn into blotches or red and white stripes. The corn is a huge mass of yellow hair ... Towns, steeples and trees dance about in a crazy jumble on the horizon ...'.[13]

Whilst all these radical changes could, and did, bring excitement and material well-being to some, to others it bought despair and alienation – 'the existential angst of an individual in a mass civilisation' as John Carey puts it.[14] Despair and alienation are constant themes in one aspect of modernism; this was really a reaction to the effect of industrialisation.

Many regard Charles Baudelaire (1821–1867) as the first modernist. Though from a middle-class family, he lived as an 'outsider' which is or was an essential stance of modernism. The first line of his 1860 poem *A une passante* (*To a passing woman*) reads

La rue assourdissante autour de moi hurlait
(The deafening street howled around me)

---

[8] There are innumerable examples of this, such as the Wankel engine. This was an alternative design for the internal combustion engine. There were no pistons going up and down in cylinders but a special shaped rotating piston. It seemed to have many advantages over the earlier model, but in spite of much development and a few production models, it just couldn't replace the earlier model so, in the end, was rejected.

[9] For example, the Italian knitwear producer Benetton would produce all its garments in white yarn, so that they could be quickly dyed fashionable colours for any market.

[10] Before the railways, town clocks in Britain were set at 12 noon by the sun, so time for towns which were more easterly or westerly would vary by several minutes. This played havoc with the railways, so Railway Time was introduced. In Great Britain it became law with the 1880 Statutes (Definition of time) Bill.

[11] These were held to choose a locomotive to pull the train on the passenger railway between Manchester and Liverpool. It was won by Stephenson's Rocket.

[12] Marchant, 2003, p61.

[13] Robb, 1997, p206.

[14] Carey, 1992, p107.

The first modernist?

Baudelaire is considered the precursor of the Symbolist poets and, according to AN Wilson, 'Modernism found it roots in the symbolist poets of the 1890s.'[15]

In art, despair and alienation appeared in the paintings of de Chirico (1888–1978), amongst others. For instance his 1913 painting entitled *Melancholy and Mystery of a Street* evokes feelings of loneliness and fear in an almost deserted townscape.

There was, however, another reaction to the achievements of industrialisation – to celebrate it unreservedly. This was the approach adopted by the Italian Futurists under their founder and leader, Filippo Tommaso Emilio Marinetti (1876–1944). From a wealthy background, he was a bilingual man-of-the-world. His chief interest was literature and especially poetry, which he usually wrote in French. But he also had another aim in life and that was to convince people – well, order more like – to embrace the new urban, technological life with enthusiasm. A key communication technique he used (common to many movements of the time) was the manifesto, the first appearing on February 20 1909, on the front page of the most prestigious newspaper in Europe – *Le Figaro*. It was entitled *Le Futurisme*, and the following extract gives the flavour of the self-styled Futurists:

'We will sing of great crowds excited by work, by pleasure ... greedy railway stations that devour smoke-plumed serpents: factories hung from clouds by the crooked lines of their smoke: bridges that stride the rivers like giant gymnasts, flashing in the sun with the glitter of knives ...: deep-chested locomotives whose wheels paw the tracks like the hooves of enormous steel horses bridled by tubing ...'.[16] And so on.

The despair of modernism

The excitement of modernism

---

[15] Wilson, 2006, p43.

[16] From *The Founding and Manifesto of Futurism* of 1909. Tisdall, 1977, p7.

Seductive and exciting as this poetic prose was, it makes no attempt to confront any of the realities of the new industrial life. Marinetti had no understanding of the underlying technology nor, more importantly, did he want any. Immensely rich, full of energy and a master of the media, he quickly attracted painters to his 'cause': to create an artistic equivalent of industrial technology. The idea of many of these paintings was to show the dynamic excitement of technology; Giacomo Balla's (1871–1958) work of 1914 entitled *Abstract Speed + Sound*, for instance.

The first modern battleship built in 1906

It wasn't a big step, from these effusive descriptions of the speed and power of technology to a similar enthusiasm for the mechanical violence that this technology could produce. An example of this mechanical violence was the development of huge armoured battleships with powerful guns.[17]

One modernist who glorified the violence modern technology could bring was Percy Wyndham Lewis (1882–1957). He was a founder member of a group called the Vorticists and during World War I he produced a magazine suitably titled *Blast*.[18]

Thus the Modernist reactions to the reality of the new industrial world were extreme: despair on the one hand and glorification on the other. Neither of these standpoints necessarily led to a deliberate estrangement or departure or divergence from what went before, or determined as to how these reactions were to be represented.

Modernism goes to war

Before the scientific and industrial revolutions, artistic creativity could be thought of as being high art and low or popular art. High art was based to a large extent on religious beliefs, so the great painters and

---

[17] The prototype for this was the 18,420 ton HMS *Dreadnought* built in 1906. This ship, built in only four months, had ten 12 inch guns and steam turbine engines that gave a top speed of 21 knots, out-performing by far all existing warships and triggering an arms race between Great Britain and Germany.

[18] This modernist view of the world led many modern artists, including Lewis, to hold right-wing views and in many cases to enthusiastically support the fascist regimes of the 1920s and 30s.

sculptors worked largely to glorify God (and to offer suitably religious and moral imagery for powerful potentates and princes), as did musicians and composers.[19] Low or popular art took the form of folk music and dancing, popular plays and story-telling (for the almost entirely illiterate audiences), as well as handcrafts and folk artefacts.

High and low art before modernisation

However, starting in eighteenth century, the complex forces that technology was unleashing also caused a cultural upheaval. Many trace this to the writings of Jean-Jacques Rousseau (1712–1778) who called for humanity to throw off the artificial constraints of society, particularly aristocratic society, and seek solace in the beauties of nature. Rousseau proclaimed the importance of the individual and of 'natural' individual human feelings, and in doing so completely reoriented art, literature and music as well as political thought; this is now termed Romanticism. It swept through the nineteenth century at every social and political level, and, for the first time, people felt they could experience art, literature and music directly.

So a painting such as Constable's *The Hay Wain* (actually a very carefully constructed work) of 1821 could be enjoyed as a literal, spontaneous depiction of an everyday country scene. And the values of Romanticism – specifically the importance of the individual and of individual human feeling and romantic love – continue to be, in many ways, the basis for much of the culture enjoyed by a large part of the population. But the Modernists deliberately produced art, literature and music that could not be experienced directly, which alienated the 'masses'.

In 1839, barely two years after Constable's death, the first successful commercial photographic process, the daguerreotype, became available.[20] While the nineteenth-century art critic John Ruskin (1819–1900) could state that '... a photograph is not a work of art ...',[21] the introduction of photography caused a crisis in the art world. All of a sudden,

---

[19] According to Richard Dawkins: 'Sacred music and devotional paintings largely monopolized medieval and Renaissance talent.' Dawkins, 2006, p192.

[20] By the eponymous Louis-Jacques-Mandé Daguerre.

[21] Ruskin, 2001, p318.

A Romantic painting

The first photo

someone with no special skill or training could produce 'photographic realism' by taking a photograph. So, according to philosopher and critic Walter Benjamin (1892–1940), 'With the advent of photography ... art sensed the approaching crisis', thus giving rise to art which 'not only denied any social function of art but any categorizing by subject matter'.[22] The historical purpose of art had been fundamentally challenged.

The development of photography, together with new methods of graphic reproduction and application of industrial manufacturing methods to the decorative arts, caused confusion for artists and craftspeople. How could painters continue to try and accurately portray 'real' things when a photograph could do it 'perfectly'? As the emasculating effect of 'perfect' photos was now everywhere, painters gradually abandoned the idea of depicting things realistically. This started with the work of the Impressionists in the latter part of the nineteenth century. As the word implies, their work tried to capture a fleeting moment, given that life is made up of fleeting moments. The pictures presented were still representational, but no attempt was made at realistic depiction. The pictures were blurred, something seen fleetingly.

Rouen cathedral caught in a fleeting moment

The reward for their efforts was to have their work rejected by the art establishment who refused to give them exhibition space. So they banded together to mount their own exhibition which they pointedly called Le Salon des Refusés. The fact that the establishment had rejected their work showed that, to them at least, they were on the right track. Clearly, as industrialised modernity had forced a rejection of the old rural life, their work couldn't be acceptable to artists who were still clinging to the 'old' way

---

[22] Benjamin, 1936.

Distorted and abstract paintings

of painting, which included painting with consummate skill. In 1907, the most famous modernist of all, Pablo Picasso (1881–1973), painted *Les Demoiselles d'Avignon*. Often considered to be the first Modernist painting, it shows five more or less naked, more or less young, women. The bodies of the women are not attractive, erotic or pornographic, they are simplified geometric. Their faces stare blankly, three directly at the viewer without emotion – the viewer is not invited to make any emotional connection with them. 'Primitive' elements, drawn from African tribal art, were included deliberately subverting the European tradition.[23] As the twentieth century progressed these modernist paintings became more distorted and eventually abstract.

Obviously to some this new art, this 'modern' art, was shocking, but there again the effect of technological progress was also shocking. Imagine how shocking it must have

been to see, for the first time, a 200 ton express steam engine bearing down on you at 100 mph, or a powered flying machine circling above you. It wasn't only physical aspects of this modernity that were shocking – there were intellectual shocks. Sigmund Freud shocked the world with his attempts at analysis of the unconscious mind. Especially shocking was his exposition of 'penis envy' and the 'Oedipus complex' which claimed that sons had sexual desires for their mothers. In 1905, Albert Einstein shocked everybody with his theory of relativity, including those (which was most people) who couldn't understand it.[24] Yes, to be modern was to be shocking.

The shocking Albert Einstein

---

[23] Even so, it was not exhibited publicly until 1916, and then it was considered immoral.

[24] Numerous attempts have been made to explain relativity to the layman, perhaps most notably by Stephen Hawking with his worldwide best-seller *A Brief History of Time*. However the actual predictions of relativity are so far from any ordinary experience that they cannot be explained verbally. The language of relativity is theoretical physics or, more accurately, applied mathematics. The physical results of the predictions can be 'seen', but only by using highly specialised technical equipment.

Some groups deliberately wanted to shock. Not only did the Futurists enthuse over the power of technology, they held shocking views such as, from a 1910 manifesto, '... all forms of imitation must be despised and all forms of originality should be glorified' or '... art criticisms are either useless or harmful.' Another group of shockers were the Dadaists, founded in 1916 in Zurich, its central figure being Tristan Tzara (1896–1963). The Dadaists adopted the slogan of 'destruction is also creation'. Their despair with the world around them – World War I was raging – manifested itself in an attacking nihilistic jollity. But perhaps the most shocking artistic act of all was carried out by Marcel Duchamp (1887–1968) when, in 1917, he placed an ordinary, and at the same time provocative, piece of sanitary-ware, a urinal, in an art gallery, signing it R Mutt and claiming that if he said it was art, then it was.[25]

The artist waiting to take the piss

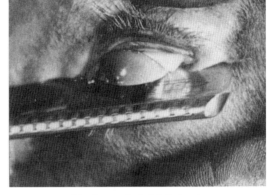
The image that didn't shock

But being shocked is a transitory state, what is shocking at first becomes accepted or ignored, so something more shocking is needed. Unfortunately for modernism, industrial modernity just kept 'shocking' without end or limit – radios, televisions, jet-planes, bombs delivered by rocket, heart transplants, the list just goes on and on. In 1929 Luis Buñuel and Salvador Dali made a short film called *Le chien andalou*. Within the first minutes of the film there is a close-up shot of an eyeball being sliced open with a cut-throat razor.

On the opening night, the audience, made up of the 'hated' bourgeoisie, remained notably unshocked: 'Failure to scandalize disappoints Luis Buñuel and Salvador Dalí' read the headline.[26] Yet from then until now, Modernist artists seem never to have given up their deep need to shock, presenting tins of their shit, sheep cut in half, varnished elephant dung,[27] and bags of crumpled paper as art. In the event this has rarely shocked, becoming newsworthy

---

[25] The original urinal has now disappeared; in 1964 Duchamp had eight replicas made, now each worth 2 million pounds. It was elected the most influential work of art of the twentieth century by a panel of curators. *Guardian Weekly*, 17–23 December 2004, p19. The replicas have twice been attacked by the hammer-wielding French artist Pierre Pinoncelli; for the second attack he was sentenced to three months in prison.

[26] Karney, 1995, p203.

[27] The winner of the 1998 prestigious Turner Prize for (avant-garde) art, Chris Ofili, liked '... introducing things like elephant dung into his work; he enjoys the tension between the beautiful paint surfaces and the perceived ugliness of the dung'.

2. WAYS OF BEING MODERN

only when 'works of modern art' have been inadvertently thrown away as rubbish.[28]

Like Modernist visual art, literature and music, to become Modernist, had to break with the past (the past of stories and tunes) get under the 'surface', create something completely different. Inspired by Freud's revelation that our unconscious thoughts were as important as what we had naïvely thought were, well, our thoughts, Modernist writers tried to tap this new source. This gave rise to a quest for 'automatic' writing whereby the writer tried to write, or type, without consciously thinking what he/she was doing. Words could be written on paper, cut up and reassembled randomly. Attempts were made at writing thoughts as they came into the head – the stream of consciousness.

Obviously this new Modernist literature couldn't make sense to the casual reader; there was no narrative, no plot, and no description. Perhaps equivalent to Picasso's *Les Demoiselles d'Avignon* was the publication, in 1922, of James Joyce's *Ulysses*.[29] Joyce (1882–1941) spent much of the rest of his life working on what he considered to be his masterpiece, the massive, and massively incomprehensible, *Finnegan's Wake* which was finally published in 1939. No-one was very clear whether it was shocking or not, as half the words had been made up by Joyce himself.

> The fall (bababadalgharaghtakamminarronnkonnbronntonner-ronntuonnthunntrovarrhounawnskawntoohoohoordenenthur-nuk!) of a once wallstrait oldparr is retaled early in bed and later on life down through all christian minstrelsy. The great fall of the offwall entailed at such short notice the pftjschute of Finnegan, erse solid man, that the humptyhillhead of himself promptly sends an unquiring one well to the west in quest of his tumptytumtoes: and their upturnpikepointandplace is at the knock out in the park where oranges have been laid to rust upon the green since devlinsfirst loved livvy.

The third paragraph of Joyce's masterpiece

The intellectual approach of the Modernists, blanket rejection of anything that came before Modernism, tinged with despair or, alternatively, uncomprehending worship of the latest technology could perhaps be tolerated for 'art'. But gradually modernism became the touchstone for everything 'creative', everything 'designed'. So this approach became *sine qua non* for what were ostensibly completely inappropriate objects. This spawned, for example 'modern' furniture, which was rarely comfortable to use, or virtually unwearable 'modern' jewellery.

---

[28] Numerous instances have been recorded of gallery cleaning staff throwing away works of art under the impression they were rubbish. One work of art that suffered this fate was a number of plastic bags filled with scrumpled-up paper – hard to blame the cleaners.

[29] The book runs to hundreds of pages, many of which are without any punctuation. The shock value was there, for those who needed to find it like our guardians of morality, as sexual desires are expressed explicitly. It is literature's equivalent of Einstein's theory of relativity – world-famous, but understood by very few – 'More than almost any other twentieth century novel, it is for intellectuals only'. Carey, 1992, p20. In fact, it came third in a survey, carried out in 2007, on books that people buy but never finish.

Modernism diversifies

Clearly architects weren't going to miss out on this bonanza of Modernism. So all those buildings which had endured, or could endure, for centuries, made of brick and stone, built to keep the water out and which often became more beautiful as the years passed, had to be rejected. The uses of buildings had to be re-analysed in the light of modernity. New materials had to be employed and out-of-date concepts like indoors and outdoors had to be done away with.

Modernism comes home

But what were 'the public', the masses, supposed to make of all this? Actually they weren't supposed to make anything of it because, and this is a central point of Modernism, it wasn't for them, it was for the (intellectual) elite. As art historian RH Fuchs pointed out, modern art '... could not be understood by the public, since it was not based on assumptions about art that were shared by the artist and the public'.[30] So, unlike music and painting before modernism, it was no good just turning up at a concert to hear music played on washing machines or entering an art gallery full of pieces of rope and expect to

---

[30] Fuchs, 1986. p175.

enjoy it – no, a lot of demanding homework had to be done first. And this exclusion was not accidental but specific because, as John Carey points out, 'The early twentieth century saw a determined effort, on the part of the European intelligentsia, to exclude the masses from culture.'[31] So what Duchamp was really saying with his 'a urinal is art' sculpture, was piss off if you're not clever enough to understand this.

For most people Modernism is of no consequence whatever, except for one small detail – architecture or 'modern' architecture. One can avoid visiting galleries where putrefying meat is on display, reading books of made-up words, going to plays where the only actor is a mouth, but buildings are not so easy to avoid. According to John Ruskin, '... we are affected by the buildings in which we work, and live or were raised'[32] – or even pass by, might be added. The art establishments are permeated with disciples of Modernism; this includes art schools, museums of modern(!) art, university departments of literature and schools of architecture. This doesn't mean that the only books you can buy, or borrow from a library, are written by James Joyce, or that the only records that are available are of Schoenberg's music;[33] but most architecture you can see, at least that built since World War II, is designed by architects who believe that only Modernist architecture should be designed and built. An icon of the architectural modernism is the Unité d'Habitation, designed by Le Corbusier and built near Marseille in 1952.

As has already been noted on page 4, for Alexander Tzonis, professor of architectural theory, the 'Unité d'Habitation awakens us to the predicament of post-war everyday life; the loss of quotidian joy, the dreariness of work, loneliness of leisure' – unfortunately several thousand people had to live in it.[34]

For many people the result of Modernism, whether modern painting, modern music, modern literature, or anything else that is modern in the sense of Modernism, is boring, or even unpleasant, but this has little effect on any 'loss of quotidian joy'. But when 'modern' is applied to architecture 'loss of quotidian joy' inevitably results.

An icon of architectural modernism

---

[31] Carey, 1992, p16.

[32] Hilton, 2002, pxvi.

[33] Arnold Schoenberg (1874–1951) was one of the most important composers to bring Modernism to music. He is best known for introducing the twelve-tone technique. Unlike tonal music, which uses a key signature, this technique gave equal importance to all the twelve notes in an octave. The resulting music was for many people devoid of recognisable melody or acceptable harmony, perhaps even cacophonous.

[34] Originally designed to house working-class families, who found living there intolerable, the block is now occupied by middle-class families who live there enjoying the cachet attached to the worldwide fame of the building.

3. What's Modern Architecture?

Here we come to the crux of the matter – is there something called modern architecture? Clearly, some people think so, as there is a plethora of books with 'modern architecture' in the title, such as *The Sources of Modern Architecture and Design*[1] or *Modern Architecture and Design*[2] or *An Introduction to Modern Architecture.*[3] But what does the word modern bring when used in modern architecture? Pevsner never got round to trying to define it, the nearest he comes to it is on page 149 (out of 201) when he says '... a piece of design with aesthetic connotations, that is, architecture' – so for him the word modern, when applied to architecture, was obvious in some way. Risebero starts his book at the beginning of the nineteenth century and what is generally construed as modern architecture only appears on page 162 (out of 245) with no attempt to define either modern or architecture, both taken as read. But Richards, writing in 1940, and revised in 1956, is very different, he's an evangelist for the stuff, his opening paragraph is worth quoting in full:

> The words 'modern architecture' are used here to mean something more particular than contemporary architecture. They are used to mean the new kind of architecture that is growing up with this century as this century's own contribution to the art of architecture; the work of those people whose number is happily increasing, who understand that architecture is a social art related to the life of the people it serves, not an academic exercise in applied ornament. The question that immediately arises, whether there is in fact enough difference between people's lives as they were lived in previous centuries to justify a truly 'modern' architecture being very different to that of the past – indeed whether 'modern' architecture is quite as revolutionary as it is supposed to be.

It may seem odd to start with JM Richards, whose architectural career was brief, as he became an architectural journalist after only a few years of architectural practice, and who wrote his book in the 1940s. But actually it can be seen as a turning point – not the book, the 1940s – because although modern architecture, or Modern Movement architecture as it is better described, came from Modernism of the early twentieth century, very little of it was built before World War II.[4] After the war, with Modern Movement architects in influential positions, much of the re-building of the war-time destruction followed Modern

---

[1] Pevsner, 1968.

[2] Risebero, 1982.

[3] Richards, 1940.

[4] Nearly all books on the architecture of the twentieth century give the impression that most buildings that were built in the 1920s and 30s were designed by Modern Movement architects – this is completely untrue.

Movement edicts, so what is usually described as 'modern architecture' is practically only about 50 years old, whereas the edicts themselves were about twice as old.

But to stay with Richards a bit longer, what was he espousing? To cut his fairly short story shorter, it was, in a word, science. That is science in the wider sense of rationality, functionality, technology and industrial progress. Here are a few more quotes from Richards:

... we have no excuse for building unscientifically

One thing which has made modern architecture different in kind from architecture of the past is that it is connected with modern industry

Modern architecture is setting seriously about the task of making something good and coherent out of what science offers

Another way of looking at the lightness and poise so characteristic of modern architecture is this: steel and concrete, as modern scientific materials, lend themselves to exact calculation

... the idea of absolute functionalism ...

So for Richards,[5] and probably for most Modern Movement architects, the basis of modern architecture was the way it was driven relentlessly, almost ruthlessly, by a strict adherence to scientific principles as they applied to the design and construction of buildings. And so, one would have thought, there would have been a steady progress in both the appearance and performance of buildings as there was with cars and fighter aeroplanes for instance – but this didn't happen at all.

As usual, to try and see how it all came about, one has to go back a bit, but not, in fact, as far as Pevsner, Risebero and Richards go (that is, the early ninetenth century): the end of the nineteenth century will do quite nicely.

Most people have some idea of what is meant by traditional architecture – the old stuff – which is what the Modern Movement wanted to replace. Though they wanted, in the spirit of Modernism, to shock with the new, there were some, considered transitional figures by some commentators, whose projects attempted to make a smooth change; sometimes they also acted as mentors to the Modern Movement pioneers. Five are chosen (others, or more could have been), Hendrikus Berlage (1856–1934), Auguste Perret (1874–1954), Frank Lloyd Wright (1869–1950), Peter Behrens (1868–1940) and Tony Garnier (1869–1948). All five tried to confront, in different ways, the new industrial technology and the new uses to which buildings were being put.

---

[5] As an amusing aside, it is interesting to note that Richards' book is peppered with comments about how the general public find modern architecture unacceptable, like: '... connoisseurship of modern architecture is still largely confined to the professional man and the intelligentsia', p102, or '... the next stage of development of modern architecture will be towards its humanisation', p60.

None of the buildings produced by this quintet would seem particularly like 'modern architecture' but all thought, and to some extent built, along new lines, particularly in terms of the use of construction materials. They used some of these in ways that became a Modern Movement edict, which is 'honesty' – 'honesty of materials.' What this actually meant had nothing to do with 'honesty' in the everyday sense of the word; it meant that materials, especially the modern materials steel and concrete, were not hidden from view by plaster, panelling or other devices. At this date, buildings designed by engineers routinely exposed the construction materials, but those designed by architects did not.

In 1887, Berlage won a competition for rebuilding the recently burnt-down Amsterdam Stock Exchange; his design was finally realised in 1903. Berlage had trained at the Polytechnic in Zurich, and was not only a practising architect, but a theorist and teacher which increased his influence. A socialist, his writings are full of 'morality' expressing such views as 'The art of the master-builder lies in this: the creation of space not the sketching of façades' or '… in architecture, decoration and ornament are quite inessential while space-creation and the relationships of masses are its true essentials.'

Berlage shows what it's made of

At the Stock Exchange, internal brick walls were unplastered and the roof structure was of exposed factory steel trusses, supporting a roof with generous areas of glazing. But he couldn't avoid one or two little decorative features. What the Dutch stockbrokers thought of their new, honest, industrial workplace is not recorded, but probably they weren't best pleased.

Perret was quite different, a hard-nosed contractor who had started work for his stonemason father at the age of 14 as a draughtsman; he knew the building business inside out. He had also attended the prestigious, and very traditional, architectural school of the École des Beaux-Arts, but he spent his entire career running a design-and-build company. He was also an enthusiast for the very new structural material reinforced concrete.

Hidden modernity

In 1906, Perret's company[6] built a modest, fairly innocuous-looking block of flats in Paris. But it had several features that became central to Modern Movement mores. What were they? The building was supported by a frame – beams, slabs and columns – that allowed the walls to be infill panels or large windows, it also 'freed-up' planning so internal partitions could be placed at will, rather than be restricted by any vertical load-bearing function. Even more modern was that, instead of a sloping roof, there was a roof garden! For a short period, Perret was something of a father figure to the younger architects of the Modern Movement, but, as he refused to toe the party lines they drew, he was dumped.

Frank Lloyd Wright was an American, of Welsh descent, from the mid-west, and was so extraordinary, as a person, as an architect and designer, that whole books can't do him justice. He oversaw his first project at the age of 19, and he never stopped designing and building until his death at the age of 91.[7] He was as arrogant as he was talented, and

Frank Lloyd Wright tosses off another innovation

considered himself the originator of 'modern' architecture. He had no connection with Modernism or the Modern Movement, and thought that Modern Movement architects were upstarts, and so treated them with utter contempt. But he exerted a considerable influence on the European Modern Movement architects, who held him in awe, as whatever they 'pioneered', he had already done.

It is completely impossible to categorise Wright in any way, he was simply a one-off. His 1906 rebuilding of a Unitarian church was made from concrete left exposed, but for Wright this was not 'honesty to materials' but a way of building within the budget. The next year he was designing houses with overhanging pitched roofs, built economically of wood and plaster.

The 'designed' factory

Behrens, like Berlage and Perret, was only influential for a brief period. Starting life as a painter, in 1907 he was offered, and accepted, the role of designer for the electrical company Allgemeine Elektricitäts Gesellschaft, better known as AEG. The idea that an industrial, commercial

---

[6] Auguste formed a company Perret Frères Entrepreneurs, with his brothers Gustave and Claude.

[7] And even then, some of his projects were built posthumously.

company would have any need for a designer, let alone one who had started life as a painter, was revolutionary, but Behrens rose to the challenge. His role as designer ranged from letterheads to packaging, from cookers to desk lamps. When, in 1909, a huge new turbine factory was needed, he designed that too.

It had mixed reviews: Glancey thinks that the Turbinenfabrik was '... a brilliant attempt to reconcile Classical culture and history with the new reality of industrial commerce and production',[8] whereas for Banham '... the massively rusticated and battered corners make nonsense of the frame-and-fill and glass-and-steel structure of the side ...'.[9] So what was the fuss about? Along the sides, the steel columns projected out through the walls, with the spaces between the columns infilled with brick and glazing. From a practical point of view, having the steel columns appear on the outside makes weather-proofing the building difficult, but it means from a visual point of view the structure has been 'expressed', another piece of 'honesty.' The 'difficulty' lies with the gable. Here concrete is used but, horror of horrors, horizontal grooves appear, aping rusticated stonework – 'dishonest' concrete. And perhaps even worse, above the large window and rusticated concrete corners is another piece of concrete that mimics the entablature of a Greek temple – how unmodern is that? Like Berlage and Perret, Behrens had had his day and was soon passed over by the upcoming young Turks of the Modern Movement.

Garnier was quite different from the others. Like Perret he had attended the École des Beaux-Arts, but unlike Perret, who didn't complete the course, Garnier won the top prize in 1899, the *Grand Prix de Rome*. In Rome, Garnier was supposed to study, measure, and draw the ancient monuments, returning to Paris with immaculate drawings of the ruins plus a major, classically-inspired, design. Garnier did none of this. When he returned, he had immaculate drawings alright, but of a projected industrial city for 35,000 inhabitants, with the buildings to be made from reinforced concrete! His professors weren't enamoured

Immaculate crayon drawing of the future

with his efforts, but Garnier continued to work on it – the *Cité Industrielle* being published in 1917 in the form of 164 drawings plus a short explanatory text. He returned to his native Lyon in 1905, where he practised and taught architecture in relative obscurity until his retirement in 1939.

Garnier's city, which was worked out in great detail was divided into zones, such as residential or industrial. Plans and elevations were made for the buildings together with perspectives. The houses had no decoration and flat roofs, musts for the Modern Movement, but quite normal windows, and the planning (of the houses) was quite conventional.

[8] Glancey, 2003. p34.

[9] Banham, 1960, p83.

A nearly Modern Movement house

Berlage, Perret, Wright, Behrens, Garnier and others of the period were trying to find a pair of corrective spectacles that would adjust the vision of the architectural profession, but this wouldn't do for Modernism. What was wanted was a razor slash across the eyeball, the shock of the new. Two people were up for this: Adolf Loos (1870–1933) and Filippo Marinetti (1876–1944); both were out to shock, which they certainly did.

Loos, who came from a humble background, acted as both architect and writer and caused scandals with both. In 1893 he went to visit the Universal Exhibition in Chicago and ended up staying there three years. This stay had a profound effect on him and he was especially impressed by the skyscrapers that were being built there. Returning to Vienna in 1896, he found work as an interior designer. But in 1908 he got the chance to design a huge shop for Goldman and Salatsch that was to be built opposite the Imperial Palace. Seen through twenty-first century eyes it looks quite ordinary, even nondescript, but the Viennese of the era saw it rather differently – they were scandalised.

Look no eyebrows

Vienna in the 1900s was, for some anyway, a place of pleasure, fantastic cream cakes served in sumptuously decorated cafés eaten by people who loved to dress up and be seen dressed-up. So this building, christened 'The house with no eyebrows', was shocking in its starkness, with its lack of decoration, a bit like going to meet the Emperor wearing working clothes.[10] But Loos could also shock, perhaps more so, with his writing. In 1908 he published an essay called *Ornament und Verbrechen – Ornament and Crime*. Others had already suggested that buildings should be unornamented but hadn't suggested that ornamentation was criminal. But Loos' essay was not a reasoned argument for the rationality or better functionality of buildings without ornament, it was a rant, a diatribe, which ordered you to agree with him or be a criminal. He invented extraordinary facts to support his view. Here are some quotes:

---

[10] It was said that '... even the little dogs, pulling their masters along Michaelerplatz, lifted their noses in disgust.' Jackie Craven, http://architecture.about.com/od/europ1/a/goldman.htm.

The modern man who tattoos himself is either a delinquent or a degenerate. In some prisons 80% of the prisoners have tattoos. The tattooed who are not in prison are either latent criminals or degenerate aristocrats.

or

I discovered the following and communicate it to the world: the cultural evolution is equivalent to the elimination of the ornament of the usual object. I thought by this to be giving mankind something new with which to rejoice, but mankind didn't thank me.

or

Soon the streets of the cities will sparkle like white walls. Like Zion, the holy city, the capital of Heaven, then we will have succeeded.

and much more in the same vein.[11]

This essay was translated and printed numerous times in radical journals and it was a key document for the establishment of Modern Movement architecture.[12] Why this is a key document is not just because of its content, but also for its style and attitude which set the tone for Modern Movement architects (and for most architects up to the present day). Firstly, there is a hectoring, exhortatory style that brooks no argument; either you totally agree or you are a criminal. Secondly, there is the view that mankind is being given a precious gift from people who understand far better and thirdly, there is the sense of isolation from the uncomprehending mankind who 'didn't thank me'. This arrogant dictatorial attitude epitomised the behaviour of Modern Movement architects and subsequently (almost) the whole of the architectural profession.[13]

The other out-to-shocker was Marinetti, the founder and leading light of the Futurists (see page 19). He had attracted to his cause painters, sculptors, writers and musicians but, by 1913, Marinetti was often heard to say, 'By now we have all the arts with us, but no architecture.'[14] What was needed was a setting where all this wonderful futuristic art and life could take place. In May 1914, his prayers were answered in the form of 26 year old Antonio Sant'Elia (1888–1916), an avowedly avant-garde architect who was holding an exhibition with his friend Mario Chittone (1891–1957). But even better Sant'Elia had written an architectural manifesto – *The Message*. A few months later he published his *Manifesto*; here are a few excerpts:

---

[11] Corbusier was of the same mind writing 'Decoration ... is suited to simple races, peasants and savages ... The peasant loves ornament and decorates his walls'. Le Corbusier, 1927, p133.

[12] This essay is still in print and is recommended reading.

[13] It is always amusing to note the hypocrisy of the Modern Movement. Whilst Loos was ranting against the criminality of ornamentation he framed the entrance of the Goldman & Salatsch store with four marble-clad Doric columns!

[14] Tisdall, 1977, p124.

In modern life, the process of consequential stylistic development has come to a halt. Architecture is breaking away from tradition: it must start over from scratch.

Calculations on the strength of materials and the use of reinforced concrete and steel are outside the classical and traditional understanding of 'architecture'.

Modern structural materials and scientific ideas in no way lend themselves to historical styles.

The concrete, steel and glass building, bare of painting and sculpture, enriched only by the inherent beauty of its lines and modelling, will be extraordinarily brutal, ugly in its mechanical simplicity and as large as necessary.

The decorative must be abolished.

Let us call a halt to monumental, funereal, commemorative architecture. Let us blow up monuments, pavements, porticoes, stairways and sink the streets and piazzas, elevating the level of the cities.

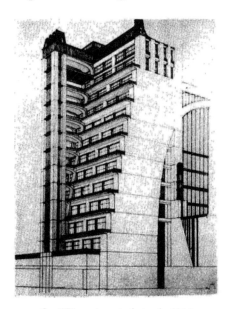

Sant'Elia gets out of step in 1914

Now there was someone to prepare drawings of the *La Città Nuova* – the New City. Unlike Garnier's carefully worked-out Industrial City, the work of Sant'Elia, still iconic in the architectural ghetto, was merely romanticised images borrowed from engineer-designed buildings. There were neither plans, nor any indication of what the interiors of the building would be like, which clearly shows that the whole idea was just a dream unconnected to any constructional reality. Whilst eulogising the straight line – 'For us the straight line will be alive and palpitating' – the buildings that Sant'Elia drew, rather than demonstrating rational rectangular functionality, are paradoxically full of geometric complexity: for example floors are not directly above one another.

In spite of the monumentality of the buildings in his New City (all of it was to be built in concrete), Sant'Elia saw architecture as something ephemeral or transitory as he thought that 'The house will last for less time than we will. Each generation must build its own city'. Which, in the case of the house was perhaps just as well, because he saw a house as an extension of the 'sensory bombardment of factory life' and of the 'flashing lights of the city' – hardly home from home.

But there was a third person who had a huge influence on preparing the ground for the coming of Modern Movement architecture. He was Hermann Muthesius (1861–1927) – a figure completely unlike either Loos or Marinetti. A Prussian civil servant, he was not out to shock or revolutionise, what he wanted was to increase the efficiency and success of Prussia. He had been a trade attaché in England between 1896 and 1903, and during this time he meticulously studied English architecture and the building industry. On his return, he wrote up his study in the form of a three-volume book, published in 1904, it was called *Das Englische Haus – The English House*.[15]

What he wanted for German architecture and design was to be 'perfect and pure utility' to be *Sachlichkeit* – a German word that cannot be directly translated but has meanings like 'objectivity', 'impartiality', 'matter-of-fact' and 'realism'. It's not difficult to see what Muthesius was aiming for. (This is what Richards, quoted at the beginning of the chapter, misguidedly thought had already happened and was to continue to happen.) In 1907, Muthesius made a speech in which he claimed that if Germans continued to make products based on outmoded designs, there would be severe economic consequences. Four months later, something called the Deutscher Werkbund – The German Production Guild – was set up to promote *Sachlichkeit* in architecture and design. As a direct result of this, two young architects Adolf Meyer (1881–1929) and Walter Gropius (1883–1969) were given the chance to design a factory for Fagus (a manufacturer of shoe lasts), which they did along *Sachlichkeit* lines.

At first glance, the Fagus factory looks all very *Sachlichkeit*, and has been called the first Modern Movement building, being the first attempt at the 'perfect glass box' – something that became a fetish for Modern Movement architects. Certainly there is none of Sant'Elia's wilful geometry, or any Loosian criminal Doric columns, or even a Behrensian neo-Greek concrete entablature. It looks as if everything is going to turn out okay after all. But what's happened at the corner of the building, there doesn't seem to be any structural support? This non-loadbearing corner was made possible by the use of a reinforced concrete structure and is the 'famous glazed corner', but this is neither logical nor rational. As Risebero points out, it is a 'distinctive modernist trick of keeping all structural columns away from the corners, as if to emphasise the non-loadbearing function of the external glass wall.'[16] A trick eh? Suddenly not so *Sachlichkeit* after all.

Now the story really begins

The photograph of the factory also shows another rather odd feature, which is the presence of five, what look like old-fashioned shop awnings, sticking out half-way up the building. They can't have been

[15] The first complete translation into English was published in 2007.

[16] Risebero, 1982, p164.

that easy to fix to the building without causing weatherproofing problems, or that easy to provide weatherproof operating mechanisms. But why are they there? Too much window of course, hence too much light and too much heat-gain, it's called a greenhouse.[17] Okay, so it's not actually *Sachlichkeit*, but what's important is that it looks *Sachlichkeit* – it came to be known as the machine aesthetic. Not much different from the New City really.

In 1914, the Werkbund held an exhibition with several buildings on display, one was a model factory based on the corner-tricked, be-awninged, Fagus factory, but the building that excited most interest was a pavilion for the Glass Industries designed by Bruno Taut (1880–1938) – unsurprisingly it had quite a lot of glass.

A brilliant combination
of glass, steel and concrete

Taut's pavilion was, according to some 'the most brilliant combination of glass and steel achieved by any architect (before) 1914.'[18] Inside this bizarre building, looking like something out of an early science-fiction film was a stepped concrete waterfall with a coloured glass ceiling above. There were also accompanying sound effects. Nothing was rectangular and it is difficult to see how it fitted in with Muthesius's plans. Perhaps he was too occupied with his ideas for industrial standardisation, which resulted in the *Deutsche Industrie-Normen* better know as the DIN standards. This resulted in a trend towards modular coordination[19] that ran, completely ineffectively as it turned out, through Modern Movement architecture.

But in 1914 another aspect of the Modern Movement appeared in the shape of sketches done by one Erich Mendelsohn (1887–1953), and were a sort of mad version of the drawings of Sant'Elia. The effectiveness of rectangular buildings had been known at least since classical Greek times – the Parthenon, Roman basilicas, country cottages, Christian churches, nineteenth century factories – but Mendelsohn thought otherwise, especially for factories where car bodies were to be made.

This was the other extreme of the 'perfect-glass-box-Fagus-factoryism-*Sachlichkeit*', perhaps it should be called *Sachlichkeit Wahnsinn*[20] – its official name was Expressionism.[21]

---

[17] Over 60 years earlier the exhibitors at the Great Exhibition of 1851, in the iconic Crystal Palace had to protect themselves from the 'greenhouse effect' by constructing ad hoc canopies of festooned draperies. These according to Kenneth Frampton were '... as much against unacceptable "objectivity" of the structure as they were against the sun.' Frampton, 1980, p35.

[18] Banham, 1960, p81.

[19] The most famous Modern Movement architect of all, Le Corbusier, became obsessed with his one semi-mystical take on modular dimensioning. See Chapter 6 for a fuller discussion.

[20] Barmy sensibleness.

[21] Expressionism is not easy to define (like most other isms) but in this context it refers to a contemporary art movement where the artist did not portray things objectively, but attempted to portray the artist's subjective emotions when confronted with the object. How this applies to buildings is anyone's guess.

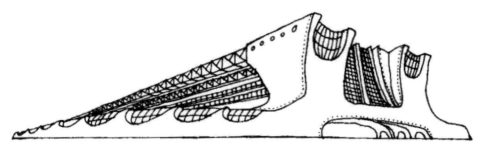

Obviously this is where they make car bodies

Apparently, this childish 'sketch' is '... commonly written off as Expressionist fantasy' but according to Reyner Banham '... this project embodies important structural ideas.'[22] What are these? Well, according to Mendelsohn, 'This sketch of a bodywork factory derives its dynamism fully from the forces in its steel construction', and that's not all, 'The row of gantries ... draws the forms together at the highest level ...' and more in the same vein. But 'Mendelsohn's definition of dynamism varied, although he seems at times to suggest it is more than an expression of internal patterns of stresses in a building ...'.[23]

Anyone who understands anything about 'the internal pattern of stresses in a building' will know that the patterns of stress vary constantly due to variations of loadings from the movement of people and machines, the effect of temperature variations, the constantly altering wind forces and from other effects. So, the idea that the factory form gave dynamic expression to the internal stresses is complete nonsense, because the stresses are varying continuously so are dynamic in that sense, but the structure has to resist these as a static object. Humans are particularly sensitive to vibrations, so buildings have to be very stiff to avoid discomfort. Furthermore, the structure has to be able to resist every variation of internal stresses so there is no 'fixed' shape that 'expresses' the pattern. The question 'what shape should a structure be?' is extremely complex to answer, and can only be attempted by those with proper knowledge – i.e. structural engineers.

And this brings up two important points about the Modern Movement. Firstly, structural elements, or the lack of them as at the Fagus factory corner, became one of the Modern Movement architects' obsessions. Secondly, the architects simply couldn't grasp the point that, by looking at a geometric shape that could be used for a structure, no information about its behaviour is obtained.[24] This desire to use engineering elements as part of the architecture resulted in a love-hate relationship with technology which had important consequences for many projects and ultimately for the profession of structural engineering – themes explored in later chapters. It was loved, as these elements clearly expressed the modernity of the architecture, and hated because the engineering proposals made by the Modern Movement architects were rarely accepted by the engineers. But that was all to come.

---

[22] Banham, 1960, p174.

[23] ibid p168.

[24] When Modern Movement architect Oscar Niemeyer (b1907) was interviewed in 1988 he demonstrated this clearly. On being asked 'Is your priority the shapes, or engineering solutions?' he answered, utterly predictably, 'If shapes are beautiful they will have a function. I wish to explore the possibilities of reinforced concrete. I like to experiment – keep reaching out until the engineers tell me to stop.' *Building Design*, 24 June 1988, p22.

So, by 1914, the Modern Movement had, so its converts thought, a new modern approach to building design which was relevant to modern life in a way that all previous approaches weren't. This approach had a number of rules, for instance:

•   Historical references, decoration and ornament in buildings were to be abolished; building design had to start from scratch.

It is entirely unclear why this small group of mostly unqualified people decided that buildings should not have historical continuity nor be decorated, after all they always had been. Were they reacting to spontaneous public demonstrations against buildings being decorated or having historical references? Of course not. Had they done a careful scientific analysis of the advantages and disadvantages of building decoration and historical references that showed that they were bad? Of course not. Perhaps they just had no talent for decorating buildings or using historical references. But anyway they were merely expressing personal preferences (like not liking waltzes or tennis) and turning it into a Modern Movement commandment, presumably written in concrete.

This, then, was the way of the Modern Movement, a small group of people turning their entirely personal preferences, which had no basis in any sort of logic, into commandments or edicts. By 1914 several edicts or commandments had already been handed down. What were they, apart from the one against decoration and history? Well they were:

•   Concrete and steel was to replace brick, timber and stone.

•   Walls should have as much glazing as possible.

•   Roofs, by implication, should be flat.

Even if these rules had no rational basis they were easy to follow, but there were more such as:

•   Materials must be used honestly.

Who would want to use materials dishonestly? Clearly no one, but what does it mean? Well nothing actually. Brickwork, according to Berlage, should not be covered with plaster as that was dishonest, so what was one supposed to do with plaster? Could plaster be honest? If so how? Could paint be used, seems unlikely. Should one be able to see the foundations of a building, wouldn't covering them up be dishonest? Well probably not... but there again. And there was:

•   Building design was to be based on rational, scientific principles.

This edict could be thought acceptable, though it might lead to an architecture that may be a little inhumane (and did according to Richards), consisting of Gropiusian blocks of glass and steel, but as Taut, Sant'Elia and Mendelsohn had already shown, functional logic – at least that used by the Modern Movement – could lead to just about any shape.

But Modern Movement architecture couldn't be based on scientific principles, as no member of the Modern Movement had any useful training in science or engineering. In fact, the inability to comply with this edict was probably the main source of many of the Modern Movement's multifarious shortcomings.

Nevertheless, these commandments, with very little alteration, formed the basis of the Modern Movement canon, and with them the Modern Movement architects were ready to conquer the world. However, the conquest had to wait a little as, also in 1914, World War I began. This finished the Futurists, as it finished many other things, including a way of life. Sant'Elia was killed in 1916[25] along with millions of others. After the war, Marinetti sided with the Italian Fascists led by Mussolini, which lost him his credibility with most European intellectuals.

But Holland had managed to keep out of the war, and it was here that the flickering flame of the Modern Movement was kept alight. In 1917, architect Jacobus Oud (1890–1973) and painter Theo van Doesberg (1883–1931), whose real name was Christian Küpper, founded an avant-garde art magazine they called *De Stijl – The Style* which led to the De Stijl movement. The founders were quickly joined by architect Gerrit Rietveld (1888–1964) and the painter Piet Mondrian (1872–1944).[26] In 1917, Marinetti sent copies of Sant'Elia's drawings and his manifesto to De Stijl. In spite of receiving Sant'Elia's ranting *Manifesto*, the group's take on city life and modern art was slightly different. Theirs, instead of an emotional overthrow of all that went before, was a cool abstraction of that with which they were now confronted – modern urban life. The most important member of the group was Mondrian who, after passing through various 'isms', had arrived at Neoplasticism[27] – with this he represented the world not as reflection of what was seen, nor as subjective emotions, but as a geometrical abstraction. This abstraction, painted as rectangles without texture or gradation of tone, was supposed to represent the new impersonal, mechanical and technical world, in which industrialisation now obliged mankind to live.

Helped by the rectangularisation of the cosmos and the influence of Berlage and Wright, the De Stijl architects arrived at what they hoped would be an impersonal architecture of plain vertical walls and flat roofs free from decorative elements. They considered that the use of reinforced concrete '... removes the personal character from a building ...' and that '... construction of a machine is analogous to the construction of a work of art.'[28]

---

[25] In 1912, Sant'Elia had entered a competition for a cemetery at Monza with a monumental, decoration-encrusted fantasy, designed during his Stile Floreale phase, which epitomised everything he was to attack. This resulted in a commission for a military cemetery at Monfalcone, of which, ironically, he was to be one of the first occupants. After World War I, the only other Futurist architect, Mario Chiattone (1891–1957), returned to his native Lugano. Here he pursued a successful career designing neo-classical buildings that had been described by the Futurists as 'that idiotic flowering of stupidity and impotence'.

[26] Mondrian, whose paintings of red, blue and yellow squares are now world famous, achieved little commercial success in his lifetime.

[27] Neoplasticism was supposed to represent the 'fact' that '... nature can be reduced to the plastic expression of definite relations' and 'The distinctive element of Neoplasticity was its desire for objectivity and ... its anti-individualistic tendency,' and it was '... inspired by the rectilinear mystical cosmology [what's that?] of Schoen-maekers ...'.

[28] Banham, 1960, p152.

What De Stijl was doing was removing the emotional excitement and romanticising of machines (a central theme of the Futurists) and replacing it with a type of cool acceptance of the machine and its inevitable link with art. This could result in building proposals that were a type of three-dimensional version of Mondrian's rectangular cosmos. Or it could go in the other direction, where the elevation of a building becomes a Mondrian painting.

 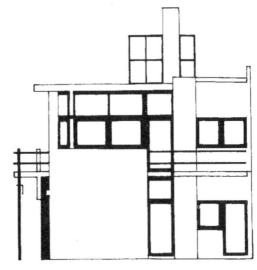

Rectangular cosmos – the 3D version   Architecture as a Mondrian mural

This work of De Stijl is close to the rectangular pre-war work of Gropius and Meyer, but now the 'perfect-glass-box', which was to continue as part of Modern Movement typology, has changed into a box, or series of boxes, that is architecture as 3D rectangular abstract art. Because it was bare and rectangular it looked, to some anyway, as though it was functional and efficient whereas it was no more than 'machine aesthetics'. This type of aesthetics, though derived from machines in a completely intellectualised manner, was purely a design style, a 'look', that had nothing whatsoever to do with what real machines actually looked like.

Whilst the flames were being fanned in Holland another Modern Movement fire was being lit in a far off and most unlikely quarter – Russia. After the almost completely unjustified declaration of war, by the Austro-Hungarian Empire on Russia's ally Serbia, Imperial Russia entered World War I. Although its armed forces were far bigger than those of the Germans, they were no match for the technical superiority of the German army. By early 1917, the mythical Russian steamroller, in fact a poorly equipped, supplied, armed, trained and led army, had been effectively defeated.

A real machine complete with its 'aesthetics'

In February 1917 the despotic Tzar was overthrown and replaced by a provisional government led by Aleksandr Kerensky (1881–1970), and in June 1917 the last offensive was launched and was a total failure. The Russian people were exhausted, thousands had died and the country was in ruins. Taking advantage of the general chaos, Vladimir Ilich Ulyanov (1870–1924), better known as Lenin, managed to overthrow the provisional government by force, in October 1917. Lenin inherited a war with Germany but he had to sue for peace. The peace agreement Lenin obtained was disastrous, then Russia was plunged into a civil war, plus numerous wars of ethnic independence, which lasted another four years.

It was against this backdrop of unbelievable chaos, violence, deprivation, confusion and suffering that the wide-ranging Constructivist movement appeared. Unlike their Western European counterparts, the radical avant-garde Constructivists were actually in a situation about which the Futurists could only dream.

Malevich leans towards Mondrian in 1915

The situation for avant-garde art in Russia before the revolution had been complicated because, as Imperial Russia was a police state, Russian avant-garde artists usually left for Western Europe and, depending where they ended up, were subjected to different influences. Kasimir Malevich (1878–1935), stayed in Russia and developed an approach to painting that was near to that of Mondrian, giving it the status of an 'ism' – he called it Suprematism.

Malevich soon managed to convert Vladimir Tatlin (1885–1953) (whose wonky tower, already shown on page 2, became the most famous Constructivist product) and Alexander Rodchenko (1891–1956). But soon Tatlin and Rodchenko broke away to either 'construct art' or make 'constructions' it is not clear, but anyway they became Constructivists. Another group became the Productivists who wanted artists to stop 'Constructing', and start 'Producing', things like chairs, ovens and buildings, and even totally barmy sports clothes... and of course manifestos:

Drop dead Constructivist cool

We do not need a dead mausoleum of art where dead works are worshipped, but a living factory of the human spirit – in the streets, in the tramways ...

or

The proletariat will create new houses, new streets, new objects of everyday life ... Art of the proletariat is not a holy shrine ...

Given the catastrophic situation it's hardly surprising that these avant-garde artists had little opportunity to build any buildings, so they could muse, which they did, often on an impossibly grand scale.

An office block 'straddles' a motorway

But as soon as Lenin had finished the chores of making a disastrous peace with the Germans, winning the civil war, crushing the aspiring independence of ethnic minorities and instituting a new police state, he had time to turn his attention to the Constructivists who were given short shrift. Lenin who liked Balzac, Courbet and Greek classical architecture, pointed out that:

I cannot value works of expressionism, futurism, cubism and other isms as the highest expression of artistic genius. I don't understand them. They give me no pleasure.[29]

Trotsky thought that Tatlin's wonky tower was rubbish, and none of the work of the Constructivists struck a chord with the general population. As there was no room for dissention or alternatives in Lenin's police state, the Constructivists were phased out, having made little or no architectural impact on Russia.

The end of the World War I also brought huge changes to the rest of Europe. New nation states were formed, women were emancipated (with a very small 'e'),[30] and science and industry advanced apace. The modern architects thought their time had come, which it hadn't. As the 1920s unrolled, the centres of modern architecture became Paris and Germany. The Futurists and Constructivists were finished as actual movements and although De Stijl continued it no longer had the same impact.

The reason that Paris became important was it was here that Charles-Édouard Jeanneret-Gris (1887–1965), a master of self-publicity, transformed himself into Le Corbusier, the greatest modern architect of the twentieth century (the life and times of Le Corbusier are critically discussed at length in Chapter 5). Meanwhile, in defeated Germany the Weimar Republic was formed and the Deutscher Werkbund continued.

Probably the most important event of the early 1920s for the Modern Movement was the setting up of the Bauhaus at Weimar in 1919, with Walter Gropius as its head.[31] In some ways the Bauhaus was a sort of Constructivism located in one place and acting as a school. But it was much more than a school as it became a centre for an alternative way

---

[29] Jencks, 1973[1], p83.

[30] Like being able to vote a bit, smoke in public and play sports in clothes that allowed some athletic movement.

[31] The full story of the Bauhaus is complex. Essential reading is *Bauhaus* by Magdalena Droste.

of life – for instance women were accepted and took part on an absolutely equal footing with men.

The Bauhaus lasted until 1933 and went through various phases, but the aim was to produce people who would be able to bring about the new world that was to be designed in a modern way – that is Modernism or, for architecture, the Modern Movement.

Like Modern Movement buildings, the main purpose of Bauhaus artefacts was to *look* modern. But Gropius was prevented from having architecture taught at the Bauhaus by the authorities, and, in 1924, the Thuringian authorities effectively closed down the Bauhaus by withholding funds.

After a lot of political manoeuvring, the Bauhaus re-opened in 1926 in Dessau, still with Gropius at the helm. What's more, he managed to get new buildings, which he had designed, built both for the school and for some of the teachers and students.

Regarded as one of the masterpieces of Modern Movement architecture, the buildings complied with the edicts: flat roofs, made of steel and concrete honestly on display, acres of glass walls and not a decorative element in sight – wonderful, or that's at least what one

Worthy buildings for a worthy cause

Bauhaus handicrafts find a home

visitor, the psychologist and art theorist Rudolph Arnheim thought. He wrote: 'It is a triumph of purity, clarity and generosity ... Every object displays its construction, no screw is concealed ... It is very tempting to see this architectural honesty as moral, too'.[32] (The locals called it 'the Aquarium'.) Gropius had even managed to include an administration block that 'straddled', if not a motorway, at least a road – why this was rational or functional is hard to understand. But this Modern Movement paradise wasn't just the buildings; all the furniture and fittings were designed and made at the Bauhaus.

The building of the Bauhaus was one of the high points of the Modern Movement in the 1920s; the other was the Second Werkbund Exhibition in Stuttgart in 1927. For this, a small housing estate was built – the Weissenhof-seidlung. Here, anybody who was anybody in the small world of the Modern Movement got to strut his stuff.

Some, perhaps by now, familiar names appear, Behrens, Taut, Gropius, Oud and

---

[32] Droste, 1993, p122.

Le Corbusier, but the name to note is that of the organiser of the exhibition, Mies van der Rohe (1886–1969). He, with Gropius and Le Corbusier, became one of the big three of modern architecture, revered to this day.

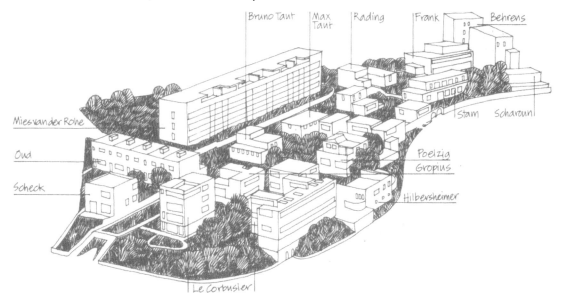

The Modern Movement gets it together

But what of the exhibition? According to Dennis Sharp[33] it was a '… spectacular success …' and a '… key event in Modern Movement history …' but '… the results suggested a uniformity of approach if not a conspicuous conformity …' and 'It did, however, to many a layman look almost the same …'. The reason it all looked the same to 'many a layman' was, because not being versed in the arcane delights of Modern Movement aesthetic nuances, the designs were seen as just a load of slightly weird, white boxes posing as housing.

Mies van der Rohe, together with the Parisian Le Corbusier, were both advocates of the perfect box. Le Corbusier, who ploughed a lonely furrow for the Modern Movement

Vive la différence

in France, was during the 1920s an architect of the white cube. In this decade he produced plans for rebuilding Paris and prototypical cities for three million people, but all he managed to get built were a few cubical houses for rich intellectuals.

His only foray into the realm of housing for 'the people' was a small estate near Bordeaux called Quartier Frugés. It was an

---

[33] Sharp, 1972, p87.

45

American journalist William Cook gets a white cube from Le Corbusier

Where the workers didn't want to live

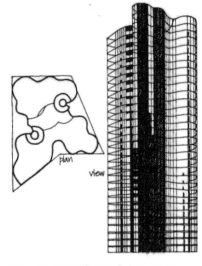
Mies stands the Crystal Palace on end

unqualified failure on all levels – economic, cultural and technical. But, with an arrogance that became de rigueur for Modern Movement architects (and eventually the whole profession), Le Corbusier thought all the failures were due to anyone or anything but him or his poor design.

Ludwig Mies van der Rohe had worked for Behrens for several years before World War I. After spending some time in Holland, where he was influenced by Berlage, he returned to Berlin to set up his own office in 1913, but, in 1914, he was conscripted into the army. On his return to Berlin he was immediately caught up in the Modern Movement. In 1919, for no apparent reason, he made a proposal for a 30-storey skyscraper. This had a rather Mendelsohnian plan and was to be clad entirely in glass.[34]

This was the last time Mies, as he's known in the architectural ghetto, had any truck with curves, after that he was a strictly perfect-box-man. The perfect boxiness of Mies was slightly different from the white cubes, though he was willing to have a shot at these. What he was after was the perfect glass box, where possible with a steel rather than a concrete structure, well, a steel structure on display anyway, that was to 'honestly express the structure'. If for some reason, as happened from time to time, the structure had to be concrete, then Mies would clag an 'honestly expressed steel structure' on the outside (to some this might seem like the d(ecoration)-word). At the Werkbund Exhibition Mies was white-boxing with the rest but, in 1929, he had his first go at a glass box.[35]

But what had happened to the car-body-factory designer Mendelsohn? He wasn't at the Werkbund party. Well, in 1920, he managed to bring one of his swirly designs to life. It was for an observatory, and was to be made of concrete

[34] A larger version, 70 storeys, was built in Chicago in 1968. It was called Lake Point Tower and was designed by ex-Mies-students John Heinrich and George Schipporeit.

[35] A copy was built in 1985 in Barcelona. It is now a pilgrimage site for design freaks.

to show that this wonderful modern material concrete could be made into just about any shape imaginable – and furthermore any shape in concrete would be honest.

But it couldn't be built out of concrete because it was impractical, too expensive, or there wasn't any concrete – opinions seem to differ. It had to be built of brickwork, with some difficulty no doubt, and smoothed over with generous helpings of a mixture of sand and cement, to look like concrete, which it didn't. Normally no one would care one way or the other if this 'dishonest' use of the despised brick was supposed to be an 'honest' use of concrete. It only matters because a central reason for much of Modern Movement architecture was an obsession with honesty, but according to Risebero '... the idea was to symbolize modern technology rather than use it'.[36] Well that's okay then, it wasn't dishonest after all.

Mies's first, of many, glass boxes

Honestly curved concrete – oh really?

Worthy of mention at this juncture is the setting up, in 1928, of C.I.A.M, which stood for Congrès Internationaux d'Architecture Moderne. This was basically the official party of Modern Movement architecture, and conferences were held on an irregular basis to check on how the gospel was spreading, honing the gospel itself – the party line – and to worship at the feet of the great leaders (Le Corbusier, Mies and Gropius). It was the first step in imposing their view of architecture, basically undecorated boxes with the occasional swirly thing, on the whole world.

As the 20s became the 30s, the super-duper jazz age began to run out of steam – or of money at least, as in 1929 the American stock market crashed sending the United States and most of Europe into a huge economic depression. This meant, for architects, that there were few buildings to design, let alone build. But worse was to come, in every way as it happened: in 1933 Adolf Hitler came to power in Germany. By 1933, in spite of what books on modern architecture promote, very little modern architecture had been built anywhere and few architects were interested in it.[37] As many areas of Germany had

---

[36] Risebero, 1979, p244.

[37] At that time most architects learned their trade by being a pupil of an older and established architect, and usually picking up on his aesthetic taste. There were few schools of architecture, and modern architecture was only taught at the Bauhaus. Everywhere else 'traditional' design was taught.

Workers get boxed-in in Berlin

socialist local authorities, an 'enlightened' few thought that building social housing using Modern Movement architects would be doing the workers a favour – usually it wasn't. For instance, the housing built for the Werkbund Exhibition was difficult to let, and for Le Corbusier's effort '... to attract reluctant tenants they made some major changes ...'.[38]

Well, the workers in Germany weren't going to suffer much more, from modern architecture that is, because like Lenin, Hitler didn't like the stuff: and what's more his right-hand man, Albert Speer, was an architect with a classical bent. The first step was to close down the Bauhaus; this happened in 1933. Architects who were Jewish, like Mendelsohn, took the hint and left but others, like Gropius and Mies, stayed on hoping they would be able to work something out with the new leaders. But they couldn't so they also left – eventually. Virtually all the German Modern Movement designers, including the architects, ended up in the United States.[39] Some stopped off in England for a bit, and a few had time, not only to spread the word but to actually build a white box or two. Naturally this was tremendously encouraging to the few in number, but emergent, English modernists.[40]

In the early thirties in the United States, Modern Movement architecture was virtually unknown as '... few buildings were designed in the United States in the International Style outside of California.'[41] American modern architecture, what there was of it, was done by Frank Lloyd Wright. But the way for the entrance of the European émigrés had been paved by architect Philip Johnson and art critic Henry-Russell Hitchcock by presenting, in 1932, an exhibition, with accompanying book, at the Museum of Modern Art called 'Modern Architecture: International Exhibition'.[42]

Actually, America already had a Modern Movement architect who had been working, fairly quietly, in California for years; he was Rudolf Schindler (1887–1953). Born in Austria he emigrated to the United States in 1914, and after working for Frank Lloyd Wright in Chicago, he moved to Los Angeles in 1920. But his white boxes had a difference; they were, in the main, built of 'honest' sticks and plaster (stucco).

But Schindler, in spite of his whiteness and boxiness and lack-of-decoration-ness, did not get invited to the 1932 Museum of Modern Art junket. This was a mainly a European

---

[38] *The Architect's Journal*, 1 June 2006, p26.

[39] Mies was invited, and went, to the United States in 1937 at the invitation of Philip Johnson, which has a certain irony as Johnson was an avid Nazi at the time.

[40] At the time even the teaching at the Architectural Association in London, which was to become a byword for radical architecture, was based on 'traditional' design – see Crinson, 1994, p105–107.

[41] Duncan, 1986, p149.

[42] The title of the book was *The International Style: Architecture Since 1922.*

California honest boxiness

affair, from which most benefited enormously, and no one more than Gropius and Mies. Gropius became the Professor of Architecture at Harvard University in 1937, and in 1938 Mies became the director of the School of Architecture at the Armour Institute in Chicago (later to become the Illinois Institute of Technology or IIT for short.)[43] From these academic power bases they could now spread the gospel of functional, steel, concrete and glass, undecorated boxes, which is what they did by word and deed – thus begun the Modern Movementisation of the world. The loser in this process was Le Corbusier, whose visit to the United States, in 1935, was, mainly due to his arrogance and insensitivity, a disaster.

So Hitler, in denying Germany the benefits of modern architecture, inadvertently gave it to the world.[44] But what is odd is that this so-called modern architecture had been defined before World War I. Glass boxiness by the Fagus factory, concrete swirliness by the car-body factory, and some wonkiness from the Constructivists, nothing much altered after that.[45]

What did alter however was that, as buildings following the edicts were built, a whole host of problems emerged. But the followers of the Modern Movement gospel were unable to grasp that the problems were with the designs, in fact with all the basic concepts. They plugged on in the mistaken belief that everything would turn out all right in the end. So far the end is not in sight.

Glassy perfection at Crown Hall

Take the glass wall for instance: even in 1911, Gropius had had to 'decorate' his glass wall with shop awnings. Now in America, Mies could indulge his penchant for glass boxes ad infinitum. One of many was the Crown Hall (revered in all books of architecture as a masterpiece) built, in 1955, to house the School of Architecture – the perfect glass box.

---

[43] See pages 236–241 (Chapter 13).

[44] As William Curtis noted '... with the dousing of the Modern Movement in Europe in the 1930s, it seemed as if the liberal generosity of America was allowing a flame to keep burning which might otherwise have gone out.' Curtis, 1983, p398.

[45] Few people have registered this rather fundamental fact, but apologist for the Modern Movement, Nikolaus Pevsner pointed out, in 1966, that 'To me what had been achieved in 1914 was the style of the century. It never occurred to me to look beyond. Here was the one and only style which fitted all aspects that mattered, aspects of economics and sociology, of materials and function'. *The Listener*, 23 December 1966, p953.

Of course when the students actually tried to study in their new building, they found they couldn't. The Venetian blinds needed constant adjustment, also it was too noisy and too public. So the students repaired to the basement, leaving the great glass box intact and unsullied by humans.[46] (And, according to architectural pundit Jonathan Glancey[47] '... the exposed structural steel beams are, in fact, a bit of a fraud: they are effectively a form of severe decorative [!] cladding over an internal structure ...'.[48])

It was only in 2006 that the British Government abandoned a scheme to build new schools as 'glass palaces', as controlling heat and cold was a 'nightmare.'[49] A decision any sensible person would have come to in 1911. And this glazing doesn't only cause problems with heat, light and sound, it has also injured probably thousands of people as they tried to break down the outmoded concepts of inside and outside.

Another Modern Movement breakthrough

And it wasn't just the glass... There were problems with almost every aspect of Modern Movement buildings, with the initial cost of building, the cost of maintaining, altering and repairing them. Frequently the building technology failed, flat roofs being a particular problem, environmental problems abounded with heat gain and loss, too much or too little light, noise and acoustic problems and more... And the joke is that few of these problems existed with 'traditional' buildings. Architect, cartoonist, and astute observer of the architectural scene Louis Hellman, writing in 1986,[50] considered that Modern Movement architecture was a

Technical Failure, a Climate Failure, a Cultural Failure and a Social Failure

in other words:

THE MODERN MOVEMENT WAS A TOTAL FAILURE

---

[46] It's amusing to note that Mies was perfecting his perfect glass boxes at the height of the cold war, when a large number of people took the possibility of an attack by nuclear weapons seriously. In the United State a huge amount of work was done to try and reduce the effects of such an attack. It was found that the safest building would be circular on plan, with a flat roof and *no windows*. Vanderbilt, 2002, p86.

[47] Glancey, 2003, p197.

[48] A glance at the construction photo shows that this is hardly likely to be the case. Mainstone, 1975, p158.

[49] *Guardian*, 8 February 2006, p12.

[50] Hellman, 1986, p162–169.

A false dawn

But no-one was listening. Charles Jencks thought that Modern Movement architecture had ended in 1972, with the demolition of the Pruitt-Igoe estate in St Louis. Unhappily he was dead wrong.

So it's clear that there is something called 'modern architecture' and it's equally clear that on the whole it doesn't work. As television critic Nancy Banks-Smith noted: 'In my experience if you have to keep the lavatory door shut by extending your left leg, it's modern architecture.'[51]

The puzzle is why this deeply flawed project did not just die a death like so many other irrelevant isms of Modernism? The answer is far from simple, and there are many aspects. It is with these aspects that the rest of this book is concerned.

---

[51] Fletcher, 2001, p417.

4. And the Old Stuff?

The architects of the Modern Movement thought that architecture, like painting, writing and other creative endeavours, had to be re-thought so that it could become 'modern', in the sense that it should be part of Modernism. For this new architecture to be modern it needed, by definition, to reject what had gone before. So conflict arose between the architects who wanted a 'new' approach, modern architects, and those who felt what had gone before had some relevance; these architects were christened, rather predictably, 'traditional' architects. This meant that architects were either 'modernists' or 'traditionalists' – there was no real middle ground. Through the first part of the twentieth century, the modernists and traditionalists battled for supremacy, mainly in the schools of architecture, with the modernists eventually coming out on top. After World War II, not only had the Axis powers been defeated but so had the traditional architects. To continue to espouse the virtues of traditional architecture was seen by the international architectural community as eccentric, if not actively reactionary.

But before rejecting something, particularly something that had held sway, in one form or another, for hundreds of years, some idea of what it was needs to be clear. Was the rejection of traditional architecture[1] like rejecting the idea of a flat earth? Were the ideas and actual buildings of traditional architecture so wrong that they obviously needed to be replaced, like flat-earth world maps? It's not that simple.

This new architecture was an intellectual architecture in the sense that it had cultural pretensions. What they thought should be replaced was the existing intellectual approach to architecture which, for the French modern architects anyway, was epitomised by the Beaux-Arts approach.[2] Beaux-Arts architecture was concerned only with 'important' buildings, mainly those commissioned by the government.

Typical 'Beaux-Arts' design

---

[1] The term 'traditional architecture' is used in this chapter for any building design before about 1914, which did not follow the dictates of the Modern Movement. As will be seen this is a blanket term for a rather complex situation.

[2] The term 'Beaux-Arts' is shorthand for the types of designs that were encouraged by the architecture department of the Paris-based École des Beaux-Arts. This approach was not unique to the Parisian school, but was the approach used in many schools of architecture throughout Europe but especially in the United States.

In the end it would turn out that modern architects wanted to reject not only the Beaux-Arts approach but also all others, while attempting to embrace a 'style' – in fact, pragmatic solutions to serious engineering challenges – produced by nineteenth-century engineers. Yet the prime aesthetic target identified by the modernists was the Beaux-Arts tradition. What, then, was the Beaux-Arts tradition? A simple answer would encompass buildings built in what is sometimes called the French Classical style – but this answer is far too simple, because before Modernism there was a far greater range of styles than this alone, and the modernists wanted to reject the lot.

In fact, what the modernists wanted to reject, and even destroy, was the Western European architectural tradition itself, because this is what the leading figures of the Modern Movement saw around them. Western European architecture derived from ancient Greece and from ancient Rome; but it came from these sources in rather different ways.

The most beautiful building ever

The architecture of ancient Greece that served as a model for much subsequent architecture was that of the temples. Best known is the Parthenon in Athens; as the statue of Venus de Milo is to sculpture and the Mona Lisa is to painting, so the Parthenon is to architecture – 'The combination of sculpture and architecture, stone technology and geometry has never been equalled'.[3] Even modern architects can find themselves overawed by it.[4]

As with all other buildings of ancient Greece, all that now remains of the Parthenon is a ruin, and what's more it is only parts of the stone structure that remain. The years have bleached and weathered these stone remains, so it is easy to imagine that the original buildings were cold and austere, dominated by large, closely spaced, fluted stone columns. But this is far from the truth. Not only were large parts of the buildings made of timber, all the floor and roof structures for instance, but the stone was often brightly painted and the interiors decorated with paintings and colourful hangings.

The Romans were greatly influenced by Greek culture and art, including Greek architecture. But, unlike the Greeks, the Romans developed a much more widespread use of the arch and the barrel vault as spanning elements for their major buildings. A barrel vault, which is really a long arch, needs supports that can resist a horizontal force, otherwise the supports will be pushed out and the arch, or vault, will collapse. This structural problem can be resolved by making the walls thick and heavy or by adding a side structure.

---

[3] Gibberd, 1997, p16..

[4] The doyen of modern architecture, Le Corbusier, kept a photo of the Parthenon pinned up over his workspace throughout his working life.

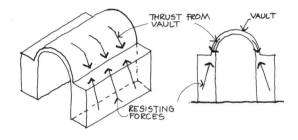

Barrel vault trying not to collapse

The Romans' culturally important structures included temples and civil buildings, but also victory columns and triumphal arches, and of course the great public arenas where violent and repulsively cruel 'games' took place. The elite also built themselves impressive villas and met in specially built baths. Both the Greeks and Romans built in an eminently sensible manner, using simple shapes as the basis for their buildings, almost invariably rectangular, except of course for theatres (semicircular) and arenas (circular or oval).

The Roman Empire in the west 'officially' ended in AD476 when the barbarian Odoacer overthrew the last emperor, but it had been in decline for a long period.[5] Why this should have been so is a complex issue on which there is no general agreement, but prominent among the reasons offered by historians are economic stagnation and the rise of Christianity.

With the end of Roman military power, the Roman way of life itself gradually came to an end. The new way of life was now dominated by the northern Germanic tribes[6] who poured into southern Europe during the fifth century. For several centuries Europe became a battleground as different ethnic groups vied for supremacy, and little in the way of important civil building took place. However, the dynamic Christianization of pagan invaders such as the Franks and Burgundians in western Europe during the sixth century began an era of church-building and the establishment of monasteries.

The first St Peter's in Rome

Churches were different in character from Greek and Roman temples,[7] as they needed to house their congregations. So it was that the Roman basilica – originally a hall for civil gatherings – emerged as the model. In AD320, after the Roman Emperor Constantine had been converted, Christianity was favoured by the Roman state. So, even before the collapse of the empire, some churches had been built. For instance, at the beginning of the fourth century, Constantine ordered a church to be built in Rome, dedicated to St Peter.

[5] The Roman Empire still existed, lingered on might be a more accurate description, in the east, becoming known as the Byzantine Empire. This ended when the Turks entered Constantinople in 1453.

[6] These tribes were collectively referred to as Barbarians mainly because they had no written language. This meant that they couldn't have constitutions, codes of law or sophisticated administrative procedures, let alone written history, philosophy or science. Nevertheless, elements of the Roman legacy remained as powerful models – for example, apart from Great Britain and Greece, virtually all of what was Roman Europe now speaks languages based on Latin.

[7] These temples were shrines to gods, so the worshippers gathered outside.

Roman baths become a church

A barrel-vaulted nave in 1125

Elsewhere, existing Roman buildings, such as the baths built by the emperor Diocletian (a great persecutor of Christians), were converted into churches.

It was only by the late 900s that there was sufficient stability in parts of Europe for large-scale building programmes to be undertaken – particularly the building of churches and cathedrals. A major influence and model was the enormously powerful monastery at Cluny, in Burgundy, founded in 940, where the main church was built and re-built several times. An idea of the second church at Cluny, consecrated in 981, can be obtained from St Madelaine at Vézelay, finished in 1125. This pattern continued over the next five centuries throughout Europe, but especially in France and England.

Because this first phase of church building was based on Roman building technology, especially the use of semi-circular vaults and arches, it was later called Romanesque. But there was a problem with barrel vaults where they crossed, because severe geometric difficulties arose at the intersection lines. The stones along these lines, the quoin voussoirs, had to be a complex almost-impossible-to-make, ten-sided shape. This problem was resolved by building stone ribs, a type of diagonal intersecting arch, along the vault intersection lines. However, this caused another problem – if the vault was semi-circular then the arches would be rather flat ellipses, not a good arch shape. So the semi-circular shape was changed to that of a pointed arch.[8]

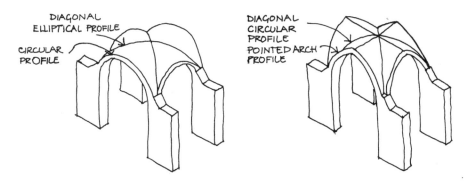

Cross-vaults with semi-circular and pointed-arch profiles

---

[8] Some people attribute this ribbed stone vaulting, along with the pointed arch and stained glass, to Abbot Suger (1081–1151), who supervised the rebuilding of the abbey church of Saint-Denis between 1137 and 1142.

As the programme of church building, and particularly the building of cathedrals, unfolded over the centuries, naves, especially of the cathedrals, were built higher and higher, while at the same time the size of the windows was gradually increased. All this was to 'glorify God' and to 'reach up to Heaven'. But as the cathedrals had to remain firmly on the ground, these aims had practical and physical ramifications.

These mainly arose from the stone vaulted ceilings. In the early barrel-vaulted buildings the vault was the roof structure, tiled on the outside for weather protection. But soon the stone vault, and the roof supports, became independent structures. The stone vaults,

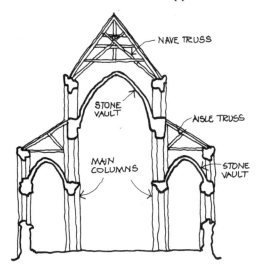

Section through a cathedral showing
separate roof and ceiling structures

Cathedral complexity reaches its apogee in 1485

that were becoming increasingly geometrically complex, spanned across the nave with a timber structure above that carried the weather-protecting tiles.

In something like 350 years, church design had gone from a plain and simple single space, based on the Roman basilica, to buildings of incredible complexity. This complexity arose not simply from the vaulting and the exterior flying buttresses that supported it; spires and towers were added, there were sculptures inside and out, and the windows had complex stone tracery infilled with brightly coloured stained glass.

But even as this church architecture of the pointed arch was reaching its apogee, a new movement was afoot. History ascribes this to one individual, Francesco Petrarca (1304–1374), better known as Petrarch. A deeply religious man, he was also a poet and scholar, particularly of the Latin language. In pursuing his Latin studies he began to discover copies of Roman literature in monastic libraries. His interest in the Romans grew, and in 1343 he wrote a treatise of three imaginary dialogues between himself and St Augustine in the presence of Truth. This was the basis of what became known as 'humanism';[9]

---

[9] This humanism should not be confused with the modern term humanism that is used today to describe a value system that does not include religious belief.

although it is not that easy to define what humanism stood for (the term was only coined in the nineteenth century). Humanists were devout Christians, but wanted a more open approach to intellectual questions than was provided for by the teachings of the church. Central was the concept of *humanitas*, which meant the development of human, rather than purely Christian, virtue in all its forms, and which included the classical world's values of compassion and mercy, but also fortitude, judgement, eloquence and even love of honour.

Furthermore, the promoters of *humanitas* weren't just thinkers; they were also men of action, educators and evangelists for their cause. Unsurprisingly, this new approach to the philosophy of life did not sit happily with the Christian view that everything was explainable as the work of God.[10] These difficulties were compounded by the enthusiasm the humanists had for classical texts, initially those by Roman authors in Latin; Greek examples were to follow after Constantinople fell to the Turks in 1453.[11] All were written in the pre-Christian era and were more concerned with earthly rather than heavenly matters.

This rediscovery of Roman and Greek culture (hence the later term Renaissance, or rebirth) had a profound effect on architectural design due, essentially, to two people, the first being Vitruvius (first century BC) and the second being Leon Battista Alberti (1404–1472).

In their search for every classic text, a copy (probably of a copy of a copy...) of a Latin text on architecture was discovered in 1414 by the Florentine humanist Poggio Bracciolini. It was called *De architectura libri decem – Ten Books on Architecture*,[12] and was written by Vitruvius, who may have been a soldier, and perhaps a military engineer and architect... This text became something of an architectural bible for the next several hundred years. The subjects of the ten books of Vitruvius were wide ranging and, using modern terminology, are:

1   Landscape architecture
2   Construction materials
3   Temples (part 1)
4   Temples (part 2)
5   Public spaces
6   Private dwellings
7   Finishes and colours
8   Water supply
9   Sundials and clocks
10 Mechanical engineering

---

[10] Extraordinarily, the English archbishop Michael Ramsey (1904–1988) saw the British 1944 Education Act (which essentially introduced free education for all) as resolving this split. He saw it as fusing 'the humanism of the Graeco-Roman world and the Biblical religion of the Jews.' Hennessy, 2006, p126.

[11] At the time few people in Western Europe knew Greek, but with the fall of the Byzantine Empire many Greek scholars fled westward.

[12] Still in print today, it is essential reading.

He wrote his book as an old man, but why is not known.[13] The original work was accompanied by a separate folio of sketches which were subsequently lost. The book concentrates, as far as buildings are concerned, on Greek rather than Roman architecture and, in Book I, states the famous dictum for building design that it should satisfy three requirements:

firmitas – it must be strong and durable
utilitas – it must be useful
venustas – it must be beautiful

Few would argue with this, but of course how strong, how useful and how beautiful are not easy to quantify! Vitruvius also claimed that nature should be used as a guide for building design. He further describes three types of Greek columns – Doric, Ionic and Corinthian – which became an obsessive interest for architects over the ensuing centuries.

The original intention of Leon Battista Alberti, a man of many talents, was to write a commentary and explanation of Vitruvius' book, but he decided instead to write a treatise of his own. This was the first 'modern' treatise on architecture, an un-illustrated 10-volume work entitled *De re aedificatoria libri decem*. Alberti's book of 1452 was written in Latin and was only available in manuscript form,[14] so the readership was extremely restricted. But Alberti was not only a theorist; he also worked as an architect. Alberti's work both as a writer and designer marked an important turning point in architectural design for a number of reasons, which were:

- It was the first book written about the practical and aesthetic aspects of architecture. Previously the information was a closely guarded secret, shared only among craftsmen in their guilds.
- It was the first time that an intellectual, from a wealthy and influential family, had acted as an architect. Previously, the work of architectural design was considered to be for lower-class artisans.
- Alberti saw architecture as a political activity and the architect as a creator of culture.
- He started the obsession with the book by Vitruvius.

Also his, and his fellow humanists, dislike of the current architecture, which they felt was uncouth, marked the beginning of the end (until the Gothic Revival that is) of what is now universally called Gothic architecture,[15] and the start of the rise of Renaissance architecture.

---

[13] Professor Morgan, latin scholar and a translator of the book, did not think that Vitruvius had any literary skill, which reinforces the idea that he was a soldier rather than a writer or politician.

[14] The first printed edition appeared only in 1485, 13 years after Alberti's death.

[15] The description Gothic was used by Renaissance writers to express their contempt, as the Goths were regarded as barbarians who had destroyed civilisation.

Alberti goes Roman in Mantua

Vitruvian man appears for the
first time but not the last

Cesariano makes it six

The first printed translation of Vitruvius was made by Giovanni Sulpicio in 1486, but it was only in 1511 that a version was published with illustrations. This version was a translation by Giovanni Giocondo, who noted that he had 'expunged his [Vitruvius'] mistakes' and added an index. With an illustrated work, it was far easier to see what Vitruvius thought was required for buildings to comply with his diktats. It was mainly about proportions, and especially the correct proportions for columns. The proportions were based on the male human body, which was seen as a perfect form. This was shown by the fact that the male body could fit into a circle – a perfect shape – with the circle centred on the navel.

It is unlikely that Vitruvius was a Christian, but his idea that men's bodies were perfectly proportioned fitted with the later Christian idea that man was perfect, as he was made in the image of God.[16] From 1486 up to the present day, new translations of Vitruvius' book have appeared with monotonous regularity, each one of course claiming to be the most accurate and faithful to the master's diktats.

Reading a translation of Vitruvius today, it is entirely unclear why this obscure Roman should have become an architectural god, or why his book should have become an architectural bible. As Bill Risebero notes, his were '... somewhat suspect and pedantic theories ...'.[17] But a god he became and, as with most religions, this allowed his followers to engage in endless disputes about what was the true message. The principal area for dispute was as to the correct proportions for the types of columns mentioned in Vitruvius' book. For instance, in 1521, Cesare Cesariano (1476–1543) published a translation with illustrations that showed no fewer than six types of stone columns.

---

[16] It is impossible to set any real store by this endlessly repeated diagram, because by drawing a circle centred on the navel, and by altering the splay of the arms and legs a large variety of human proportions can be accommodated.

[17] Risebero, 1979, p119.

How to do a Corinthian arcade

The appearance of translations of and commentaries upon Vitruvius unleashed a flood of books on the subject; following Alberti's lead, books on architecture, written by architects and non-architects alike, came thick and fast. One of most influential of these was the Vitruvius-inspired *Rules of the Five Orders of Architecture*, written by Iacomo Barozzi da Vignola (1507–1573) and published in 1562. In this book, Vignola, a practising architect, gives proportions for how the five types of column[18] should be used in different situations, such as arcades, pedestals, and entablatures. The intention was to give rules that would allow 'anyone' to be able to design, in a relatively simple way, buildings that would conform to accepted norms of beauty. His book was criticised for trying to impose a design straitjacket, but his purpose was the opposite – and Vignola himself did not feel he had to comply with his own rules.

This is really the crux of the matter for Renaissance architectural design, which in a sense became the Beaux-Arts architectural tradition. The importance of Greek and Roman architecture, and in particular their proportions, was always the inspiration. But disputes centred on whether classical architecture, and in particular Vitruvius' book, could yield definite rules, or whether such rules should serve only as a guide for individual expression. Inevitably, these two approaches tended to divide architects into two camps, traditionalists and modernists. Things came to head, or one of several heads, in seventeenth-century France, under Louis XIV, the Sun King. During his long reign – 73 years between 1643 and 1715 – France became the dominant country in Europe, not just militarily, but intellectually and artistically. The culmination of this cultural dominance was embodied in Louis' huge palace at Versailles.

It was during the reign of Louis XIV that the first school of architecture, the Royal Academy of Architecture, was founded in 1671.[19] It was established to ensure that there were architects available to design royal buildings that would be of the standard required. Its first director was François Blondel (1618–1686),[20] an experienced military engineer, who put his heart and soul into showing that from the buildings of antiquity absolute rules could be formulated that would produce harmonious and beautiful architecture. To this end he instigated, in 1674, a scheme for the meticulous measurement of ancient Roman monuments. His objective was to use these rules, when discovered, to formulate the definitive (French) classical architecture – his lectures appeared in book form between 1675

---

[18] Vignola's five orders were Etruscan, Doric, Ionic, Corinthian and Composite.

[19] This was one of a number of Royal Academies founded during the reign of Louis XIV, some of which still exist, including the Académie Française.

[20] Not to be confused with the later Jacques-François Blondel (1705–1774).

and 1683 as *Cours d'architecture –
An Architectural Course.*

French attempts to quantify
the classical tradition also gave
rise to one of the most amusing
episodes concerning a translation
of Vitruvius, when Claude Perrault (1613–1688), a prominent
mathematician and physiologist,[21]
was entrusted with a new and
definitive translation of the hal-
lowed work. This was commissioned so that graduates of the
new Royal Academy could learn
how to produce perfect architecture for the Sun King. When the
book finally appeared, in 1673,
it was the complete opposite of
what had been expected – required is perhaps more accurate
– as in it he challenged all the accepted architectural tenets, causing a scandal. Perrault concluded
that there could not be any rules
to give the correct proportions,
nor did he think the proportions
of the human body could give any
guidance for dimensioning buildings. He challenged the idea that
there was some absolute architectural beauty, and thought the idea
of making meticulous measurements of Roman antiquities to
discover rules for proportions to
be absurd.[22] What Perrault pro-

Blondel defines French classical architecture

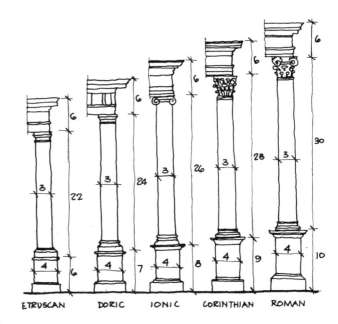

Perrault's modular column kit

posed for the five orders was a modular system which would give approximate guidance.

In fact, the battle in the seventeenth century between the traditionalists, whose aim
was to comply with the rules of classical architecture (if only they could be found), and the
modernists, for whom classical architecture was only a basis for their imaginative designs,
had already been joined in Italy. As it is easier to prescribe rules than explain imagination,
less was written by the modernists, an exception being Guarino Guarini (1624–1683) who,

---

[21] He also dabbled in architecture, being partly responsible for the colonnade at the Louvre.

[22] Thus earning himself the lifelong enmity of Blondel.

Guarini's baroque

in his treatise *Projects of Civil and Religious Architecture,* while acknowledging the importance of mathematics, also saw value in Gothic architecture and thought that 'Even though architecture depends on mathematics, it is however an art of seduction whose purpose should not be frustrated for motives linked to reason'.[23] This expressive, imaginative style of architecture is now termed the Baroque,[24] and was already being built by the likes of Francesco Borromini (1599–1667) and Gian-Lorenzo Bernini (1598–1680).

While architects in the Renaissance tradition continued to discuss for a century whether there were, or were not, exact rules for proportions, and how many types of capitals there should be, three dynamic events and processes were about to take place which would affect the way 'important' buildings were designed. These were the French Revolution, the Gothic Revival and the Industrial Revolution – all of which happened more or less at the same time, around the cusp of the late eighteenth and early nineteenth centuries.

The French Revolution of 1789 abolished the monarchy, so the French Royal Academies had to go – which they did. However, by 1816, following the defeat of Napoleon, the old academies of painting, sculpture and architecture were resurrected and combined into the École des Beaux-Arts,[25] which was to become the main target of the Modern Movement architects a century later.

What sort of designs came out of the Beaux-Arts school? Buildings were seen as standalone 'objects', and were always of 'traditional' construction, external walls constructed of stone with timber roofs and floors. The decoration or styling, if such a pejorative word can be used, was derived from Greek or Roman forms. The plans always had at least one

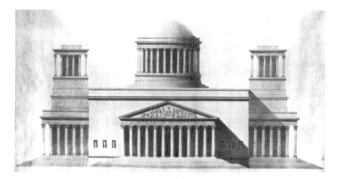
Classically based symmetrical elevation

---

[23] Evers, 2003, p130.

[24] Either derived from *barroco*, Portuguese for an irregular pearl, or *barocco*, an Italian word that meant an obstacle in logic.

[25] The history of the transformation of France's Royal Academy of Architecture to the École des Beaux-Arts is complex – for a detailed account see the chapter by Richard Chafee in Drexler, 1977.

axis of symmetry and often two or more. And this plan symmetry was always reflected in the symmetric elevations.

So what happened at the Beaux-Arts that annoyed the modern architects so much? Well, for a start, the designs produced didn't comply with any of the edicts. But what really got up their noses was that the Beaux-Arts approach harked back; in fact, harked right back to the beginnings of Western civilisation, whereas the followers of the Modern Movement were desperately, and misguidedly, trying to hark forward as fast as they could go.

Whilst the École des Beaux-Arts was promoting an architecture loosely based on classical models from Greek and Roman antiquity, another thread was about to be woven into Western European nineteenth-century architectural design: this was the Gothic Revival. The despised, by Renaissance arbiters of taste at least, Gothic architecture in fact also had its roots in Roman architecture, the earliest buildings being labelled Romanesque. However, its initial imitation of certain Roman features, such as the barrel vault, had subsequently evolved into the Gothic pointed arch, rather than following the symmetrical styles of Greek and Roman buildings (or the diktats of the yet-to-be-discovered Vitruvius).

Over the centuries some writers (these included François Blondel) had found merit in Gothic buildings, but none considered Gothic architecture to be a model of perfection and, as such, something to be imitated. But around the end of the eighteenth century there appeared architects and others who thought just that. One of the first Gothic Revival buildings, or Neo-Gothic as it's often called, was the extraordinary Fonthill Abbey, designed by James Wyatt (1746–1831) for the eccentric and enormously rich William Beckford (1760–1844). It was built on a huge scale, in a mixture of Gothic church and military styles, dominated by a central tower, 270 ft high.[26] Wyatt, who had begun his study of architecture in Rome at the age of 16, built not only in the Gothic style but was equally at home with the Palladian style, derived from Andrea Palladio (1508–1580), the Venetian architect whose elegant classical churches, villas and palaces were seen as the purest expression of High Renaissance architecture. Whereas many architects designed buildings in accordance

The architect's painting of the Gothic interior

with a belief they were seeking, and hopefully finding, some absolute beauty based on the 'correct' interpretation of historical precedents, Wyatt's eclectic approach presaged what has been called the 'battle of the styles' of the latter part of the nineteenth century.[27]

But if Wyatt was happy to build in any style the client required, including Gothic, the Gothic Revival also had its fiercely intellectual advocates, the best known being the

[26] The tower also emulated its historical counterparts in another way by partially collapsing in 1807, and completely collapsing in 1825.

[27] This term was used by apologist for the Modern Movement Reyner Banham writing '... ornamental rubbish left over from the nineteenth century's "Battle of the Styles"'. Banham, 1960, p9.

architects Eugène-Emanuel Viollet-le-Duc (1814–1879) and Augustus Pugin (1812–1852), and the critic (of almost everything) John Ruskin (1819–1900).

All three wrote influential books expounding the virtues of Gothic architecture, praising it for its truth to materials, structural rationality and constructional integrity. The brilliant Pugin, working as the assistant to the classicist Charles Barry (1795–1860), was responsible for a Gothic Revival masterpiece called the Palace of Westminster, better known today as the Houses of Parliament.

London's Gothic Revival masterpiece

As the nineteenth century wore on, architects' certainty in aesthetic matters eroded to the point that no style dominated important architecture, though historical precedents, Greek, Roman, Gothic, and others, including Egyptian and Oriental influences, were always present; and decoration became more and more over the top.

Albert's bejewelled memorial, with friends

As well as a profusion of architectural and decorative styles, nineteenth-century architecture was also influenced, rather insidiously, by the ongoing Industrial Revolution. Powered by coal and supported by iron, this revolution had begun producing the new types of buildings it required – cotton mills and train sheds for example – built in new types of materials, cast and wrought iron, and built by a new type of person: the engineer.

What the Modern Movement would come to regard as prophetic was the no-frills industrial architecture of the engineers, which, while often visually stunning, was frequently oppressive in its impact. This merely reflected the use to which the buildings were being put, and the no-frills lives of those who occupied them. While huge mill buildings may have been functional, showing the construction materials, and perhaps had some type of formal (Classical) beauty, it's hard not to see them as brutally intrusive in most townscapes.

Clearly the situation for architectural design in the nineteenth century lacked clarity, and it was not surprising that certain architects and designers reacted against the confusion with a desire for a more simplified approach, or that they should regard themselves as a progressive or reforming group. But, one could ask, in what was becoming an increasingly socially complex way of life – urban life – why would one expect only one particular aesthetic approach to architectural design? This, however, is what the Modern Movement architects wanted, and did their best to impose.

If Modern Movement architects wanted explicitly to reject the Beaux-Arts architecture of important buildings in favour of grimly functional and oppressive industrial models, they also (implicitly) rejected the architecture of unimportant buildings – vernacular architecture. Vernacular architecture concerned itself mainly with buildings that related to ordinary life – the majority of these were houses, but also included taverns, shops and workshops, along with mills, barns and other traditional farm buildings.

While the resulting buildings could have cultural significance, their prime objective was functionality (another supposed touchstone of Modern Movement architecture). The functional aspect of the building

The triumph and oppression of industrial architecture

process was to use building materials that were locally available and could be worked by local labour. These materials were limited to those derived from vegetation – timber and thatch for example – or materials that could be dug up. Dug-up material could be stone, but more commonly was earth – mud. This mud was used to make walls in various ways:[28] it could be made into bricks, sun or kiln-dried, or used in situ as mud walls or in concert with other materials, as in wattle and daub.

Over the centuries, these vernacular buildings moved into a looser category of 'traditional' buildings. These were built using vernacular-derived materials, by an increasingly wide range of local craftsmen – bricklayers, joiners, glaziers, plumbers. And some materials, or items, might not be local – some special tiles, a piece of marble and so on. And this 'new' traditional building became involved with architecture. This cross-over perhaps reached its zenith in Victorian Britain.

As the nineteenth century progressed, modified vernacular appeared by the street-load as cities began to be surrounded by ever-expanding circles of suburbs, made possible by the newly arrived public bus and rail systems,

Vernacular becomes bricks and mortar

---

[28] One of the great failures of modern building practice is to ignore the benefits of earth buildings – see Norton, 1997, for instance.

Typical terraced housing built by the street-load

Going down the pub as an architectural experience

allowing workers to commute. Most of these houses were built for the middle class or lower middle class – teachers, doctors, solicitors, clerks, shop managers, bank employees and such, and were usually speculative developments built by contractors such as Cubitt.[29] The designs came from patterns and, whilst they were basic buildings, they would sport a few architectural features drawn from Classical, Gothic or Renaissance sources.

These new-traditional-out-of-vernacular buildings were used for housing, places of entertainment, railway stations, pubs, hotels and all those buildings that were necessary for the new industrial urban life. But they were vernacular in the sense that there was no cultural agenda behind the designs – unless making a profit is counted as cultural. And, as with all profit-based activity, success is dependent on giving what the customer wants at a price she/he is willing to pay.

Almost by definition, vernacular design cannot have an intellectual aspect, as vernacular means indigenous, native or endemic.[30] It is the result of local groups 'getting into the habit' (for good reasons) of doing something in a particular way. It is not limited to buildings but affects all aspects of life including tools, clothes, boats and language, and as such is an unconscious manifestation of the way a static, and fairly isolated, group lives. The effect of the process of industrialisation was to accelerate the dynamic aspects of life thus destroying, or at least radically altering, what is often called 'the traditional way of life.'

When the vernacular is used consciously, whether intellectually or commercially, it almost inevitably loses its essential qualities. And this presents a difficult problem for those who want the vernacular tradition to continue under the radically changed social conditions.

---

[29] Thomas Cubitt (1788–1855) was among the first of many subsequent nineteenth-century London property developers.

[30] *Chambers Dictionary*, 1994, p1932.

In the nineteenth century there were many people who, whilst realising that the process of industrialisation was a genie that couldn't be put back into its bottle, wanted vernacular building traditions to continue – and amongst those were some leading intellectuals. The most prominent in Great Britain were William Morris (1834–1896) and John Ruskin. Both were middle class and wealthy, so neither had the slightest idea what real 'vernacular' living meant – therefore were able to idealise it. This idealisation was based on the fallacy that 'honest toil' was spiritually and physically rewarding.[31] This 'honest toil' was carried out by craftsmen whose (supposedly) endlessly joyous lives produced beautiful artefacts. Morris' dictum was that no one should bring anything into a home that was not both 'beautiful and useful'.[32]

The joy of honest toil

Both Morris and Ruskin spent considerable parts of their personal fortunes on various attempts to stem the tide of industrialisation; they shared a particular horror of machine-made objects, produced as they were by people forced to undertake mindless and soul-destroying toil. Both produced books and articles, and gave lectures extolling various virtues of hand crafts, and both were very concerned about architecture, Ruskin writing two books that have become classics.[33] For Ruskin 'A day never passes without our ... architects being called upon to be original and to invent a new style ... We want no new style of architecture ... The forms of architecture already known to us are good enough for us, and far better than any of us.'[34]

Morris was at once a designer and man of action, setting up enterprises to carry out his beliefs – one of these produced wallpaper that Morris designed himself, now world famous and still available. He had briefly worked as an architectural assistant, and was directly responsible for a building that appears in dozens of books about architecture – a house designed for Morris by Philip Webb (1831–1915) that became known as 'the Red House'. For many later propagandists of the Modern Movement this was the turning point; it finished off the stylistic mishmash of nineteenth-century architecture and heralded in the new, the new that was to become Modern Movement architecture.

[31] Morris and Ruskin were not alone in their idealisation of 'honest toil'. Architect Antonio Gaudí wanted to create 'a whole society based on honest labour and art'. Hensbergen, 2001, p20.

[32] Even towards the end of the twentieth century the purveyor of semiology, Roland Barthes, was bewailing the lack of wooden toys that '... were only possible in the days of the craftsman'. Carey 1992, p216.

[33] *The Stones of Venice* and *The Seven Lamps of Architecture.*

[34] From *The Seven Lamps of Architecture*, quoted by Pevsner, 1968, p18.

A polemical house in the country

But how can the Red House be described? It's obviously not a classical design nor really a Gothic one, and a bit too grand to be vernacular. Here are some comments:

... a medieval vernacular style ... the interior more forward looking. Gibberd, 1997, p106.

... part Gothic, part Georgian, part simply traditional. Andrews, 2001, p482.

... the archetype of the vernacular movement. Risebero, 1979, p229.

... [the Red House] is an exception in its day and more prophetic of the coming twentieth century than anything in the field of domestic architecture in any country for 30 years. Pevsner, 1968, p23.

It was built in a spirit contrary to the past century. Pevsner, 1960, p58.

... in general character it might be taken for a slightly unusual farmhouse: and in its time something quite revolutionary. Richards, 1940, p63.

The Red House has been talked of as a revolutionary building, but is part of the High Victorian School of Modern Gothic. Dixon, 1978, p50.

Today the Red House looks like a slightly austere typically Victorian house, but when it was built it caused a sensation. It was thought shocking that cultured artists should ape the crude buildings of the lower orders. Modern Architecture was born. Hellman, 1986, p84.

... the Red House ... in a style which except for a few minor details was close to ... William Butterfield's Gothic revival vicarages. Frampton, 1980, p43.

This collection of comments shows an almost bizarre diversity – all of them can't be right or, if they are, all this wrangling over style and labels can't mean anything (maybe it doesn't). A bit of a muddle – so why do some claim it's a forerunner for the Modern Movement? According to Pevsner, it's because of exposing the brick walls, using the plan to generate the elevations and showing some elements of construction inside. Well, the Beaux-Arts were keen that the plan dictated the elevations, it just so happened theirs were axial, while vernacular buildings frequently showed constructional elements internally, particularly floor joists and beams. But Pevsner also considered a fireplace to have a '... truly revolutionary character ... and completely functional in displaying its brick courses horizontally where the logs are laid and vertically where the smoke goes up'.[35] This may seem 'functional' to Pevsner, and it may be what Modern Movement architects think of as 'functional', but, in fact, it hardly matters in which direction the bricks are laid.

The revolutionary and functional harbinger of the Modern Movement

Indeed, it's hard to see what this house had to do with the Modern Movement, with the vernacular or with Neo-Gothic for that matter, or even how to see that it was particularly shocking to all but a super-sensitive few. Actually, the house began what is now called the Arts & Crafts Movement, probably much more influential than the Modern Movement. It was, as the house shows, based on a type of eclectic, intellectualised, perhaps romanticised is a better word, attempt at vernacular building – hardly what the Modern Movement architects were to purvey.

As stated earlier, the principal target of the Modern Movement was Beaux-Arts architecture. But not only was Beaux-Arts architecture to be proscribed, but so was every other sort of architecture, except of course that which had been produced by the engineers. In reality, this made no practical nor cultural sense, as what industrial engineering architecture was doing was showing a way forward for building types that hadn't previously existed, not for ones that already did, such as houses, churches, pubs, theatres, schools and hotels, all of which functioned perfectly well in all sorts of styles, forms and materials. Furthermore, it is obvious that a complex society, such as exists today, cannot be served, nor should be served, by architects whose vision is limited by a loathing for all 'historic' styles, and whose work is dictated by the empty canons of the Modern Movement.

---

[35] Pevsner, 1968, p23.

5. An Unhappy Marriage

Before the nineteenth century, buildings were designed by a variety of people from various backgrounds. Some called themselves architects others called themselves surveyors; some buildings were designed by military engineers or by the people who actually built them. Some were gentlemen and some started life as workmen, for instance Leon Alberti (1404–1472)[1] was an ordained priest whereas Andrea Palladio (1508–1580)[2] trained as a mason. But they all had one thing in common, the way they designed their buildings not based on scientific discoveries but on various 'rules of thumb'.

But for hundreds of years, perhaps starting with Euclid (c.300BC), attempts had been made to develop a system of purely logical thought – mathematics. Furthermore, mathematics and other methods of logical thought were applied to try and explain observed physical phenomena – this used to be called natural philosophy but is now called science.

The father of the Enlightenment

By the seventeenth and eighteenth centuries this way of providing explanations based on logic, was accepted by a substantial part of Western European intelligentsia. Because of this, this period has been labelled the Age of Reason or the Enlightenment. Some consider Isaac Newton (1643–1727) to be the father of the Enlightenment[3] by presenting the world with the theoretical explanation of the behaviour of the solar system.

Hand in hand with theoretical work, much experimental work was carried out over this period. For instance, between 1766 and 1774 the gases hydrogen, nitrogen and oxygen were discovered. And the interplay between theory and experiment gathered pace. This gave rise to sciences such as chemistry, biology and physics, all underpinned by the ancient 'science' of mathematics.

But the rise of science seemed to make little impact on building design during the Enlightenment. Perhaps the most interesting case is that of Christopher Wren (1632–1723) and his friend and colleague Robert Hooke (1635–1703). Wren, Britain's best-known architect, and Hooke were scientific prodigies as well as being ingenious and able experimenters, and both worked as architects. Wren is of course best known as the architect of

---

[1] Alberti was highly educated and his major contributions were various treatises, including ones on architecture – he is considered to be a prototype for the Renaissance 'universal man'.

[2] Palladio is regarded as the greatest architect of the sixteenth century and the Palladian style of architecture is named after him.

[3] Newton published his major work, *Principia Mathematica*, in 1687. In this he hinted at the differential calculus but only published it explicitly in 1704. By then, it had been independently discovered and published by Gottfried Leibniz in 1684; this led to a long-running and unpleasant dispute between them.

St Paul's Cathedral, but no visitor can fail to be impressed by it as an engineering achievement, particularly the dome structure.

If anyone would have been able to bring scientific knowledge to bear on the practical and theoretical aspects of structural engineering, the partnership of Wren and Hooke seemed to be the ideal candidate. But there is little evidence that the engineering of the dome and supporting structure, when examined in detail,[4] was designed on the basis of scientific understanding.

There are in fact three domes, an outer one which is hemi-spherical and made of a timber frame, an inner one which is also hemi-spherical and made of brick, and a central conical one, also of brick. The conical one, which is the load-carrying structure for the outer dome and the heavy lantern, is only visible from inside the structure.[5] The total load is then carried to a complex 'ring doughnut-like' brick transfer structure via an inclined drum, and thence to the eight supporting piers.

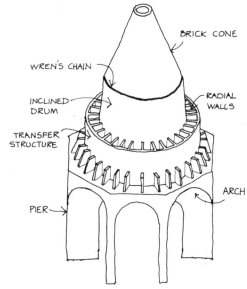

The dome structure of St Paul's Cathedral

It is clear that Wren understood that a dome would tend to 'burst' under vertical load,[6] so he put chains around the bottom of the domes, how many is not clear. There is some evidence that he tried to find diagrammatically how the vertical forces acted in the dome,[7] but there is no evidence that he tried to decide the size of the chains, or for that matter the size of anything else, by calculation or by experiment. It does not seem that Wren had a clear idea how the transfer structure shown in the diagram, the 'ring doughnut', was to act as a structure, so he filled it with all sorts of bits of iron reinforcement.[8] It took nearly another hundred years before theoretical and experimental science was applied to building projects.[9]

---

[4] Millais, 2005, p285–293 for a detailed examination of the dome and supporting structure of St Paul's.

[5] The central conical dome can be seen by the public if they choose to climb to the lantern viewing gallery – well worth the effort.

[6] This effect had been noted by many people including Leonardo da Vinci who stated that it was '... after the manner of a pomegranate or orange which splits into many parts lengthwise ...'.

[7] Heyman, 1999, p41. This book is an excellent introduction to the historical development of structural engineering.

[8] Due to the rusting of this reinforcement and consequent cracking of the brickwork, almost continuous remedial work has had to be carried out in this area. In fact, during the 1920s, the whole supporting structure was considered to be is such a bad state that the closing of the cathedral to the public was considered.

[9] It was only in 1742 that an attempt was made to do numerical calculations for an actual building. This happened when Pope Benedict XIV asked three mathematicians for a report that would explain why cracks had appeared in the dome of St Peter's.

About the same time as the rise of scientific thinking, radical technological advances were being made, mainly by a separate group of 'practical' people. They were also using logical thinking, but this time to improve or re-think ways of producing goods and transporting them. The basis of these improvements was the discovery, in 1709 by Abraham Darby, of a method of smelting iron ore, using coke (obtained from the abundantly available coal) instead of charcoal (becoming increasingly expensive due to the shortage of trees) to make cast iron. This made iron affordable for the construction of physically large objects, leading to the development of machines and, in particular, the steam engine. The new skills required for the construction of these industrial objects produced a special group of men. They called themselves engineers, or civil engineers, to distinguish themselves from army or military engineers.

These civil engineers,[10] like their military counterparts[11] not only designed the new machinery, mainly powered by steam, but were perfectly able to design any new buildings that were required due to this industrial process. They designed factory buildings, mills, engine sheds, warehouses, dock and harbour buildings, and in so doing created a new 'functional' aesthetic.

A nineteenth century warehouse

Such engineer-designed buildings used the traditional building materials of brick, timber and stone, but incorporated the newly available affordable iron where it was sensible to do so.

In the nineteenth century these civil engineers began to organise themselves into groups, which was the first step in getting professional recognition.[12] In Britain, in 1771, John Smeaton had formed the Society of Civil Engineers, still in existence as the Smeatonian Society, and in 1818 the Institution of Civil Engineers was formed. Architecture, on the other hand, was not a new profession, and, until the nineteenth century, it had not been regarded as a profession. But with engineers trying to become recognised as professional people, clearly architects weren't going to be left out so, in 1834, the Institute of British Architects was formed, and in other countries similar institutions were formed.[13] Initially there was a great deal of overlapping in the

---

[10] Much of the practical knowledge of these civil engineers, which contributed so much to the development of industrialisation, derived from the craft of the millwrights.

[11] Part of the training of military engineers was in 'Practical Architecture'. British military engineers were responsible, during the nineteenth century, for all the multifarious construction associated with the rapidly expanding British Empire.

[12] Professions were really a nineteenth century idea. Before then medical doctors, lawyers and the clergy were the only groups regarded as professional people.

[13] Sometimes these were joint institutions for engineers and architects such as the Société Suisse des Ingénieurs et des Architectes formed in Switzerland in 1837. But the tendency was to form separate societies and hence separate professions.

work of the newly regarded professions of engineer and architect, the exact duties and training not having been defined; this was to come later.

In this period of rapid change, due to the economic and social effects of the industrialisation process, there were basically four styles of building. There were two 'architectural' styles, one based on classical Greek architecture and another based on the later Gothic architecture; there was the new 'functional' architecture of the industrial buildings; and there was the 'vernacular' architecture of mainly domestic buildings. When buildings were built in the architectural styles, then the designer was likely to be an architect. These architects were often also responsible for the design of 'functional' buildings, whereas the design of 'vernacular' buildings was left to local builders.

Many notable buildings and other structures were built during the nineteenth century,[14] so is instructive to see how these two groups, engineers and architects, interacted when working together. For example the Palm House at Kew, designed by the architect Decimus Burton (1800–1881) and the 'engineer'[15] Richard Turner (1798–1881), was built in 1848. The idea of a greenhouse or glasshouse only came into being in the nineteenth century and was made possible by the new availability of glass as an affordable material.[16] These new greenhouses were built for two purposes. Some, like those at Kew, were built to house and grow exotic plants collected from foreign habitats so they could be studied and catalogued, whilst others were built by the rich on their country estates. In these were grown exotic or out-of-season fruit and vegetables, which were then used to impress guests when served at dinner.[17]

The Palm House at Kew Gardens

Richard Turner, who had constructed a number of glasshouses in his native Ireland, made the initial proposal to the Director of Kew gardens. His proposal was presented to

---

[14] The nineteenth century is often regarded as a period of poor architecture, especially when compared to the Greek, Roman, Gothic and Renaissance periods, but it was a period of extraordinary architectural richness and interest.

[15] Here the term engineer is put in inverted commas as it is not entirely clear that Richard Turner regarded himself as one. He owned an iron works and was primarily a business man but undoubtedly had considerable ability as an engineer.

[16] This was made possible by new manufacturing processes such as those developed by Robert Lucas Chance in 1832 and James Hartley in 1847.

[17] 'Each pineapple we eat cost us five pounds', Sir Charles Tennant (1823–1906) would boast to his guests. Wilson, 2003, p46.

a meeting of Commissioners which Decimus Burton had been asked to attend. Turner quickly realised that for his design to proceed, it would have to be with the approval of Burton. They worked together on several designs until the final one was approved.[18]

However the engineer was keen to decorate the structure, earning the architect's displeasure. Burton wrote to Turner telling him that all extraneous ornaments should be dispensed with. This is perhaps the opposite of what one might expect, the 'functional' engineer decorating the building, whilst the architect wanted to remove any decoration. (In the end, some decoration was added to the functional structure.)

Decoration of the Palm House

How Turner arrived at the sizes of the structural elements is unknown. No calculations exist or are known to have been made; presumably he made them the size he deemed adequate. As it turned out, he was amazingly accurate, because in the late 1980s the whole building was subjected to complete renovation, which included a structural appraisal by the engineers Posford, Pavry and Partners. No strengthening was found to be necessary. Thus the original design could be maintained in all its elegant glory.

As the new grouping of building designers, engineers and architects struggled to find roles for their new professions, they came to work together in other ways. During the nineteenth century there was a boom in building railways, starting in Great Britain. These were private enterprises, and when their lines terminated in great cities, such as London, they wanted to arrive with panache. These railway termini, most of which

An internal view of the St Pancras trainshed

still exist, would have a great train shed for the arrival of the trains and a grand hotel to accommodate the passengers. Most of these termini clearly demonstrate how these two groups saw their roles at the time, an engineer designed the shed and an architect designed the hotel; St Pancras station, the London terminus of the Midland railway, is a perfect example.

---

[18] For a detailed account of the design process see *Richard Turner and the Palm House at Kew Gardens* by Edward Diestelkamp in *Transactions of the Newcomen Society 54*, 1982, p1–26.

The shed had a world record span of 73 m (240 ft),[19] a record broken only 21 years later. The structure consisted of a series of clear-spanning trussed wrought iron arches and it was designed by William Barlow (1812–1902). Barlow was an experienced engineer and the son of Peter Barlow who was a pioneer teacher of structural engineering to military engineering students at the Woolwich Arsenal. The train shed was built between 1866 and 1868, and on 1 October that year the first train pulled out.

The design of the hotel was a completely different affair and its designer, architect George Gilbert Scott (1811–1878), had no role in the design of the train shed. He was the winner of a limited – eleven entries – architectural competition for a 150-bed hotel. His entry was a red-brick Gothic fantasy and had not 150 beds but 300. His audacity paid off. The hotel partially opened for business in 1873, being finally completed in 1876.

Whilst a state-of-the-art metal roof was built over the tracks, the structures for the roofs of the hotel are by contrast reminiscent of the heavy timber structures seen in Gothic cathedral roof spaces. Scott was responsible for various station buildings such as the booking hall; built in a style similar to that of the hotel. What role Barlow had in the engineering aspects of Scott's work is unknown.

A recent view of the hotel at St Pancras

Perhaps the most impressive structure to be built in the nineteenth century was the Eiffel Tower. With no projected use, it was to be a temporary exhibit for the 1889 Paris Exhibition, its main purpose to show the world what engineers, and in particular French engineers, could do. They could and they did. The Eiffel tower is now so well-known that it is hard to imagine what impression something so huge must have made; it was two and half times higher than anything that had been built previously.

The idea of building such a tower was not new, several proposals had been made, some possible, some impossible. And the idea was not Eiffel's but was proposed by two of his engineers – Emile Nouguier and Maurice Koechlin (1856–1946).[20] Their first scheme, prepared in 1884, shows a functional pylon, not unlike a large version of the pylons that carry electrical power lines today.

The two engineers then asked the head of Eiffel's architectural department, Stephen Sauvestre (1874–1919), to look at their proposal and to make any additions he felt necessary.

---

[19] Huge spans for the train sheds were completely unnecessary from any practical point of view, it was sheer megalomania. Small platform canopies would have served the purpose of protecting the passengers from the weather. Today, similar megalomania is seen at airport terminals, where humans wander inside unnecessarily huge and high buildings, serving only to impress.

[20] Gustave Eiffel, a remarkable man, always worked with engineers better than himself, Théophile Seyrig (1843–1923) being the best-known.

He added arches, galleries at three levels and an onion-shaped finial, these all being shown on a free-hand sketch, the style contrasting strongly with the precise style of the engineer's drawing. Luckily his sketch survived.

The tower that was built was a compromise between the two: galleries were added, the tower ended with a dome and arches, less prominent, were added at the lower level between the inclined legs. The additional arches are the most interesting, as they serve no structural purpose, but are decoration in the form of structure.

These examples of world-famous constructions show how the arrival of engineering structures of iron and their functional style, and the division of building designers into engineers and architects caused confusion in terms of decoration and interaction. Sometimes engineers wanted to decorate their structures, sometimes they asked architects to decorate them, sometimes architects built new medieval buildings next to functional ones. No rules seem to apply but what rules, if any, should?

In spite of these apparent conflicts neither the new group of engineers nor architects saw any. Architects admired

The Eiffel Tower as an engineer's pylon and the engineer's pylon with architectural additions

The salon of a successful nineteenth century engineer's house

engineer's functional buildings and structures and, vice versa, engineers liked the Classical and Gothic styles that the architects favoured. What could show more clearly what you liked than the house in which you lived?

But, even as architects and engineers were forming themselves into two professional groups, something else was happening which was to be decisive in causing a deep and fundamental split between the two professions; this was the emergence, during the nineteenth century, of mathematically-based methods for the calculation for engineering systems.[21]

Before the advent of iron and the process of industrialisation, buildings and bridges were mostly made of heavy materials like brick and stone. This meant that the weight

---

[21] In 1870 a report on the education of engineers stated that '... it is not the custom in England to consider *theoretical* knowledge as absolutely essential.' Buchanan, 1989, p169.

Small stone bridge over Bull Run

of the building, or bridge, was large compared to any weights that were put on it in use. Imagine the effect of a horse and cart crossing a stone arch bridge; the weight of the horse and cart will be so small compared to that of all the stone used in the bridge's construction that it is rather like a person carrying a brief case. The bridge, or the person, hardly notices the extra weight of the load compared to the weight that's already being carried – itself.

However, the advent of iron and industrial processes altered this dramatically. Firstly, iron is extremely strong for its weight compared to brick or stone. This means that if a load is to be carried by a piece of structure, one made of iron can be far smaller, and therefore lighter, then one made of stone or brick. And, what's more, some forms of iron – wrought iron and the more modern steel – are able to resist pulling forces (forces that cause tension) which stone and brick are unable to do. The result of this is that the use of iron for structures meant that they could be lighter and could take forms that stone and brick couldn't; beams and trusses for example.

Even as the forms of structures were changing, so were the loads. With the arrival of heavy machinery and especially the steam locomotive, the loads increased enormously.

Metal railway viaduct built in 1857

So now, instead of the horse and cart, bridges had to carry traction or railway engines, which could weigh over a hundred tons. So instead of the load being small compared to the weight of the structure, the situation was completely reversed; the weight of the load was now often far higher than the weight of the structure that was carrying it. This was quite a new situation, because with the older lightly-loaded heavier structures, if they were going to collapse they almost always did so during, or shortly after, construction. On top of which, there were hundreds of years of experience of building these heavy structures, which allowed various non-scientific 'rule of thumb' sizing methods to have evolved.

So what to do? Bridges or industrial buildings could have been built with 'guessed' structures, and then be loaded with trains or machinery; if they collapsed, then they could be re-built with stronger structures until finally they supported the loads – perhaps an acceptable procedure for a bookshelf or kitchen stool but obviously no good for a major structure. What was needed was some way of predicting that the structure would be adequate before it was built. For this to be possible two things were needed. Firstly, accurate technical information about loads and the strength of structural materials, and secondly, a general predictive procedure that can be applied to any proposed structure.

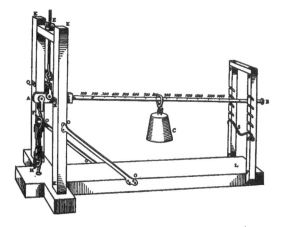

Early material testing machine

The first requirement was not too difficult. Loads, especially of machinery, can be calculated; loads for general uses are less easy but possible with a bit of common sense. And calibrated testing machines were built to stretch, bend, and crush samples of material.

The difficulty was the second requirement, but luckily people, mainly European mathematicians, had been working on this; not because they were interested in helping in the design of railway bridges or industrial buildings but as intellectual research. What they had been working on was a piece, or pieces, of mathematics that would mimic the behaviour of various structural elements, the most basic being the beam.[22] Provided that certain simplifying assumptions were made about a beam, that its material was homogeneous for instance, then an equation can be written that relates the deflection of a beam to the applied load. This equation, called the Governing Equation of the Beam, is what's known as a fourth order ordinary linear differential equation, has the form:

$$EI \frac{d^4 u}{dx^4} = p(x)$$

This equation, published at the end of the eighteenth century,[23] mimics mathematically the behaviour of a beam by relating the applied load, $p(x)$ to the deflection u. And in solving this equation not only is the deflection given, but also information about the forces in the beam. But only someone who has received special training, both in maths and engineering concepts can understand and solve this equation.[24] The maths and engi-

---

[22] Whilst most people have a clear idea of what a beam is, to derive the mathematics some simplifications are made. For these to apply, a beam should be no wider than its depth, and have a span of no less than eight times its depth.

[23] The beam equation was the result of the work of the Swiss mathematicians Leonard Euler (1707–1783), Daniel Bernoulli (1700–1782) and the French engineer Charles Coulomb (1736–1806).

[24] The solution of the beam equation is fully explained in an approachable manner in *Building Structures*, Millais, 2005, p386–396.

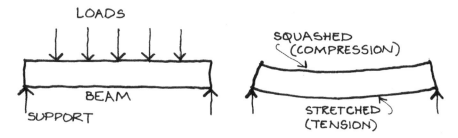

The effect of load on a simple beam

neering concepts required do not form part of any normal school curriculum so they have to be learnt as part of a university course. This means that this basic calculating tool for engineering structures is only understood by a few – the engineers.

While mathematicians continued, during the nineteenth century and up to the present day, researching to find mathematical mimics for more and more complex engineering situations, engineers gradually absorbed the simpler parts of their work.[25] As most metal structures were assembled from straight elements that functioned as beams, columns or ties, often in triangulated constructions, calculation procedures were developed for these, but towards the end of the nineteenth century a new, and much more complex, structural material appeared – reinforced concrete.

Concrete[26] had been used as a material since Roman times, and was used for foundations and the dome of the roof of the Pantheon, built in Rome in AD120. But, like stone and brick, this concrete, often called mass concrete, could only support compressive loads. For concrete to be able to support tensile loads, such as occur in beams, the concrete has to be reinforced – hence reinforced concrete.

With the now available affordable iron and later steel, rods or bars of this metal could be put into the concrete mix. When this hardened it bonded to the metal, so that the

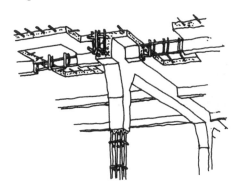

now reinforced concrete would act compositely. Provided that the metal was in the right place, that is where tension would develop, this new material could act as beams, columns or even ties. And not only that, because as concrete started as a wet mixture it could, by being poured into a mould, be made into any shape. In 1892, François Hennebique patented a whole system of reinforcing concrete with steel rods, and his system, no longer patented, is still basically being used worldwide.

The Hennebique reinforced concrete system

[25] The time lag between the mathematician's discoveries and the adoption of their work by the engineering community is usually between 50 and 100 years!

[26] Concrete has three ingredients, cement, water and a strong filler, usually stones in the form of sand and gravel. The cement reacts chemically, in an extremely complex way, with the water, hardening with time to become a strong binder for the stony filler material. The Romans used naturally occurring cement, a volcanic dust called pozzolana. A process for making artificial cement was invented in 1811 by Joseph Aspin.

In terms of making calculations for this new material, whole new problems had to be faced. Not only could shapes more complex than simple beams and columns be made, a slab for instance, but how the bars of steel interacted with the surrounding concrete had to be understood.[27] Even the mathematical models that mimicked the behaviour of structures more complex than a beam or column did not help much. So something apparently as simple as a slab needed a rather difficult equation[28] which, unlike that of the beam, could not be solved easily. For a circular slab of radius **r** the equation relating the deflection **w** to the load **q**, takes the following form:

$$\left(\frac{\partial^2}{\partial r^2} + \frac{1}{r}\frac{\partial}{\partial r} + \frac{1}{r^2}\frac{\partial^2}{\partial \theta^2}\right)^2 w = \frac{q}{D}$$

The solution of the equation for a slab, along with solutions of equations for structures of even more complex shapes, demand a far higher level of mathematics than that required for the beam equation. Even today, university engineering courses often only consider these as a special option for the more mathematically gifted.

So the picture presented by the end of the nineteenth century was radically different to that at the start. Building designers had gradually but steadily put themselves into two groups, the architects and the engineers; they created separate professional institutions; and more and more their scope of work became mutually exclusive. Engineers became increasingly interested in solving the technical problems that were becoming ever more complex whereas the architects were battling to confront the aesthetic confusion that the industrialisation process had presented. As a result the engineers were losing any aesthetic interest or control and the architects, due to the rise of mathematically-based calculations, were losing understanding of many of the technical aspects of their work.[29] Architect Martin Briggs could not have been alone when, in 1907, he lamented that '... where elaborate steelwork enters the architect's design he has to employ an engineer ... there remains only one conclusion, that a joint production of this sort cannot be a complete success ...'.[30]

Clearly, however, the architectural profession did not want to admit publicly that they had lost all technical understanding of the buildings that they were designing, so they would claim[31] that they did have one. This was not based on a grasp of the technical concepts nor of the mathematical mimics , but was based on an 'intuitive' understanding.[32]

---

[27] To try and mathematically mimic concrete is extraordinarily difficult, and this time mathematicians showed little or no interest. Therefore engineers, through a mixture of tests and mathematical modelling, had to provide themselves with satisfactory calculation procedures. Even today these have not been finalised.

[28] The slab, or plate as it is usually called in the technical literature, equation was first presented by Sophie Germain (1776–1831) in 1816. By so doing she won a prize awarded by the French Academy. Further work was needed, and this was done by CLM Navier (1785–1836) and presented in 1823. However, this work was of little interest to engineers at the time.

[29] Although aspects of structures have been dealt with here, and structures are probably the technical aspect most closely linked to architectural design, similar techniques were being applied to heating, lighting, acoustics and so on. Each technical advance in these areas left the architects understanding less from the technical point of view.

[30] This was printed in the *Architectural Review* vol. 21, 1907, p226. Many other similar statements can be found by diligent reading of the architectural press.

[31] In 2003, in a moment of unusual candour a professor of architecture, Sarah Wigglesworth, admitted that 'I am absolutely hopeless with structures. I know nothing about them at all'. Larsen, 2003, p82. She went on to describe her approach to the understanding of structural behaviour as 'totally, totally intuitive'.

[32] Proper technical understanding only comes by going through the 'hard, technical grind'. Stewart, 1975, p319.

But there is no intuitive understanding of structural behaviour any more than there is of any other technical situation. It's a bit like looking at a television set or a car engine and claiming that you understand how they work by 'intuition'. This self-deluding approach, often supported by individual engineers, mainly for commercial advantage, was to cause havoc in the second half of the twentieth century.[33]

The other problem that the industrialisation process posed for the new type of architect was that of aesthetics or style. Apart from vernacular buildings, aesthetics were based on two models, the Greek, or Classical model, and the Gothic style. Both these models were based on buildings constructed from brick, stone and timber. Now the architects had to cope with, or choose to ignore, the possibilities of metal and reinforced concrete structures and a new vernacular – the engineering functional style.[34]

Some architects were aware of these new challenges; George Gilbert Scott for instance, thought that 'modern metallic construction opens out a perfectly new field for architectural development', but then built a brick Gothic hotel next to a 'modern metallic construction' at St Pancras. Viollet-le-Duc also thought that architecture 'belongs almost to science as to art' but, like Scott's, these were empty words. Many authors, writing on architecture of this period, thought that architects simply ignored the challenge, if that's the right word, of the new situation but this is not true. Certainly some architects grasped the new materials of iron and glass with enthusiasm.

A Guimard Metro entrance

One such group were the architects that are now considered to be part of Art Nouveau. It is Nikolaus Pevsner's[35] opinion that these architects should be given the credit for the 'discovery of the aesthetic possibilities of iron and glass'.[36] Perhaps best known are the entrances to the Paris Metro designed by Hector Guimard at the very end of the nineteenth century and into the twentieth; these entrances are now as Parisian as the Eiffel Tower.

What is called Art Nouveau was not just about the use of iron and

---

[33] A couple who had appointed an architect to design a house for them discovered that they would also have to appoint a structural engineer, a quantity surveyor, a mechanical engineer, a party-wall surveyor, a services engineer, a concrete consultant, and maybe a computer and a telephone consultant, just for a family house. Bedell, 2005, p107. Most 'uninitiated' members of the public would expect their architect to deal with all these technical and design issues.

[34] For a survey of the functional engineering style in Great Britiain, see the evocative photographs of Eric de Maré in Richards, 1958.

[35] He was a world-renowned architectural writer and critic as well as being the Slade Professor of Art at Cambridge University and later the first Professor of the History of Art at Birkbeck College at London University.

[36] Pevsner, 1968, p94.

Horta's socialist iron and glass in 1899

glass in buildings, but it produced a whole variety of objects, from jewellery to pots, from furniture to wall paper. Sadly, however, it realised no designs for steam engines or cars.

Due to its exuberance, its clear image of luxury, and because it did not have an obvious social message, Art Nouveau is often written off as a slightly degenerate fin-de-siècle frippery – not to be taken seriously. But a number of architects pursued a whole career with Art Nouveau buildings, the best known being Victor Horta (1861–1947) and some, including Horta, had socialist leanings.

In the United States of America, iron was also instrumental in allowing building designers to create a new building form – the skyscraper. These came into being as it became profitable to build office accommodation higher and higher in city centres, especially New York and Chicago. What made the use of high buildings possible was the introduction of the safe passenger lift by Elisha Otis (1811–1861).[37] Initially these skyscrapers just looked like 'high houses' as Pevsner[38] put it.

Iron shows the way in 1902

---

[37] Otis, an inventive mechanical engineer, devised a system that locked the lift car to the guides if the supporting cable broke. He dramatically demonstrated his invention at the Crystal Palace in New York in 1854. He was hoisted high into the air on a platform and then had the supporting cable cut.

[38] Pevsner, 1968, p36.

Sullivan 'refraining from ornament' in 1912

Gradually the brick or stone external envelope of the iron frame was reduced to a cladding of the beams and columns of the frame. The large rectangular openings were then infilled with large windows or panels of other materials. The best known architect of these early skyscrapers was Louis Sullivan (1856–1924), credited with the over-used aphorism, or perhaps slogan would be a better word, 'form follows function' and wrote that '... we should refrain entirely from the use of ornament ...',[39] but like Scott and Violette-le-Duc, he was not as good as his word.

In the period immediately following its introduction, the use of reinforced concrete was largely left to the engineers, mostly being ignored by architects. Max Berg (1870–1947)

Perret's concrete church in 1922

and the Perret brothers were rare examples of architects who built with the new material, Auguste Perret (1874–1954)[40] even going so far as to build a church with the concrete structural elements internally visible.[41]

By the end of the nineteenth century the distinct professions of architect and engineer were firmly established in most developed countries. Separate education systems were being developed for each profession, that of an engineer becoming more and more technical, that is mathematical, and that of the architect becoming more concerned with creativity than practicality. Both professions set up educational standards to ensure members were 'adequately' trained.

Unsurprisingly the two professions, having set their priorities for membership – technical competence for engineers and creative ability for architects – attracted quite different types

---

[39] Sullivan, 1979, p187.

[40] Perret was initially a heroic figure for the young architects who were responsible for 'modern' architecture. But as he refused to toe their party line his later work was largely written out of history.

[41] Concrete that is visible is called 'fair-faced' concrete, and it is this use of concrete that has been responsible for much of the dreariness of twentieth century building. The use of a reinforced concrete allowed Perret to flood the church with coloured light in a way the builders of Gothic catherdrals could only have dreamt about.

of people. And the personalities of engineers and architects became more and more incompatible. As the great engineer Fritz Leonhardt (1909–1999) noted, 'I have tried my whole life long to fill the gap between architects and engineers; I didn't have much success doing so.'[42]

When Michael Graves was asked by his mother whether he'd like to be an engineer or an architect, he asked what an architect did. His mother explained.[43] 'I want to be an architect,' Michael exclaimed. 'But I haven't told you what an engineer does,' said his mother. 'I don't need to know,' said Michael – he became a well-known architect. And at the end of the twentieth century an English woman became an engineer and not an architect because she was '... crap at art, and better at maths, physics and geography ...'.[44]

During the first half of the twentieth century the effect of the incompatibility simmered under the surface but, with some high-profile projects in the second half, the conflict became open. Eventually, some engineers succumbed to architectural pressure – often with disastrous effects for the clients, both in capital and maintenance costs – blessing the world with a series of misshapen buildings.

A misshapen building of the late twentieth century

In the second half of the twentieth century architects became more and more obsessed with structures and their ability to conceive them. This 'ability' was based on their own erroneous assessment that they had some understanding of structural behaviour. Seizing this rather strange 'opportunity', many engineers made it their business to help architects realize their misshapen projects.[45] And now, according to Adam Poole anyway, 'The cultural tension between architects and engineers is one of the things that makes construction tick.'[46] This is usually called putting a brave face on it.

---

[42] *The Structural Engineer*, May 1987, p183.

[43] How Michael Graves' mother knew what architects and engineers did is not recorded.

[44] *New Civil Engineer*, 2 June 2005, p50.

[45] Chapter 10 shows what effect this has had on engineers and engineering.

[46] *New Civil Engineer*, 10 June 2007, p10.

6. That's a Rather Nasty Corbuncle

For architects, one name stands out as the ultimate modern architect; that of Le Corbusier. He was the embodiment of everything a modern architect should be, and many consider him, although not single-handedly, to have actually invented what is called modern architecture. He was responsible for the relentless promotion of many, if not all, of the ills that have made Modern Movement architecture such a consummate failure. But even today he remains, for architects and members of the design ghetto at least, a cult figure. In 2005, when an architectural magazine introduced an All Fools Day spoof about cloning an architectural genius, the cloning material was to be a part of Le Corbusier's toenail.

Le Corbusier, or to give him his real name, Charles-Édouard Jeanneret-Gris, was born on 6 October 1887 in La Chaux-de-Fonds, a small town in the French part of Switzerland. His mother, Marie-Charlotte-Amélie, was a music teacher, and his father, George Édouard Jeanneret-Gris, a craftsman watch-enameller. The family were neither poor nor rich but, due to the father's craftsmanship, middle-class. Édouard, as Charles-Édouard was known, had an elder brother Albert, and it was he, not Édouard, who appeared to be the gifted one – he had his mother's gift for music and did indeed become a musician.

Édouard seems to have been a quite average child with no special abilities, intellectual, athletic or artistic. However, he did have one unusual trait, which was that he never stopped drawing when he got back from school. This compulsive drawing could have been due to his pure love of it, but more likely it was an attempt to attract some maternal attention.[1]

Le Corbusier´s birthplace

---

[1] Throughout his life he would write letters to his mother 'constantly exaggerating what he had achieved so that his mother would finally love him.' *Sunday Times*, 6 July 2008, p29.

In 1902, at the age of 14, Édouard entered the local École d'Art, which wasn't an art school but had been set up to train young people in the applied arts. This was the first step for Édouard to become, like his father, a watch engraver, but he never became one for two reasons. First his eyesight[2] was simply too weak for the visually demanding work of watch engraving, and the second was the presence of Charles L'Éplattenier (1874–1946).[3]

For Édouard, and probably for many others, Charles L'Éplattenier was what's known as an inspirational teacher. He saw it his duty, not only to teach the syllabus of his course, but to expand the horizons of his pupils and encourage them to reach the maximum of whatever potential they had. Perhaps due to the fact that Édouard was physically unable to become a watch engraver, Charles L'Éplattenier conceived the idea that he should become an architect. With some persuasion Édouard and his parents agreed to this proposal.

But instead of following the usual way of becoming an architect (that is becoming a pupil of an established architect), at the age of 18, and without any previous experience whatever, he was given his first commission. This was for the design of a house for a watch manufacturer called Louis Fallet. The commission came via L'Éplattenier and clearly the 18 year old Édouard could not undertake it alone. He was helped by a competent local architect called René Chapallaz, and L'Éplattenier and others helped with the decoration. It was basically a house designed and built in accordance with the local regional style, but with the decoration enhanced, presumably under the influence and guidance of the ever present L'Éplattenier.

The Fallet House

Édouard was involved with two more regional houses built for relatives of the Fallet family. But instead of pursuing his architectural career in his home town, between 1907, the year of the completion of the Fallet house, and 1911, he went on a number of extensive visits abroad. First, carrying with him both his drawing equipment and a book by Ruskin,[4] he visited Italy. Most importantly

---

[2] In fact, he later made a feature of his bad eyesight by always wearing his trademark attention seeking glasses: a trait unsurprisingly copied by many other architects.

[3] Charles L'Éplattenier was appointed a teacher at the École d'Arts at the age of 23. By then he had already studied at the École d'Art Decorative in Budapest, the École des Arts Décoratifs, and the École Nationale des Beaux-Arts in Paris

[4] John Ruskin, who held strong opinions about almost everything, loved the 'true' Gothic architecture, only to be found in Venice, and abhorred Renaissance architecture – views with which Édouard agreed. In fact Édouard saw Venice through Ruskin's eyes.

for Édouard's future work was the huge impact made upon him by a monastery at Ema close to Florence. His journey ended with some fruitless months in Vienna.

Next he went to Paris where he managed to get a part-time job with the Perret brothers, which lasted from mid-1908 until late 1909. This experience was to have an enormous effect on Édouard, as the Perret brothers were using reinforced concrete frame structures for their buildings. He was advised by Auguste Perret to learn about mathematics and engineering. He followed this advice by taking private lessons from an engineer named Pagès, but to no avail. One of the hallmarks of his subsequent career was his consistently poor grasp of the basic technology that related to buildings.

He returned to Switzerland only to leave again in 1910 for Berlin, where again he managed to find employment, this time with Peter Behrens. This was another important experience, as Édouard was exposed to efforts being made to fuse engineering with design. This was reinforced by his contacts with the Deutscher Werkbund.[5] The Werkbund, a group of artists and industrialists, was one of many attempts to reconcile 'art' with the realities, and possibilities, of the emerging industrial society. But Germany did not suit Édouard and he returned once again to Switzerland in 1911.

Lamp designed for AEG by Behrens in 1906

In the same year he was off again, this time on his most important journey – his *Voyage d'Orient*. This took him, and his friend Auguste Klipstein, through the Balkans to Turkey, on to Greece and back through Italy. The exotic eastern Mediterranean countries were something of a relief after the grey efficiency of Germany, and had a profound effect on Édouard.

One of Corbusier's travel sketches from 1911

He enjoyed staying, for two months, in a room with white-washed walls and spent nearly three weeks in the monasteries at Mount Athos. In Athens he became spellbound with the Acropolis, visiting and drawing it every day for three weeks.[6] After Greece he went to Italy, where he studied Roman architecture, and fortified himself for his return to the cold Jura by revisiting the monastery near Florence.

---

[5] In fact, Behrens was one of the founders of the Werkbund.

[6] The idea of taking a notebook with you on your travels, to make notes and sketches seems fairly commonplace. However, what is interesting in the case of Le Corbusier is that he carefully kept all these notebooks, apparently intending them for publication. Thus the idea of his artistic archive appeared early. It is still possible to buy facsimile editions of his travel notebooks!

Back in Switzerland, Édouard was given a part-time teaching job by his mentor L'Éplattenier, and in 1912 was able to go back to being a local architect. This was due to commissions for two houses; one from M. Favre-Jacot and the other from his parents. In 1912 he set up his own architectural office, and in 1913 produced a business card. On this card he offered architectural advice on interior design, house re-design, furniture and garden design. Also, rather oddly, the words 'béton armé' (reinforced concrete) were written boldly on the card. Édouard couldn't have known much about reinforced concrete, but the card implied otherwise.

After these two houses work dried up giving Édouard time for architectural speculation. He spent considerable time on a prototype house for the 'masses' – this came to be known as the Domino, sometimes written Dom-ino, house. The main feature of this was a rudimentary reinforced concrete frame with six columns and concrete floor slabs.[7]

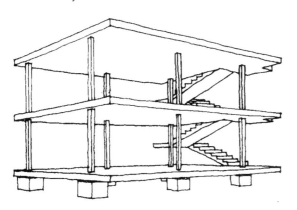

The concrete frame of the Domino house

Although nothing came of his speculative house 'design', the image of the frame became iconic for modern architects and for Édouard himself; apparently he kept a copy of it pinned to a notice board in his office, next to a photo of the Parthenon, throughout his life.[8]

But, in 1916 things looked up, or at least that's how it seemed. Édouard received a commission from Anatole Schwob to design a large, and luxurious, house. Schwob was a very prominent local businessman, owning an important watch factory; furthermore the Schwob family was a virtual dynasty in the area. He could not have wished for a better client – but Édouard, in important aspects, was to make a mess of it.

The project was a turning point in architectural terms for Édouard. Here, unlike his previous projects that had followed local custom, he introduced ideas that were the result of his travels and his work experience with Perret and Behrens. Some of these were to stay with him throughout his career.

The house was to have a structure in reinforced concrete,[9] after all Édouard was an expert. In fact, reinforced concrete was used in the area, but for factories not houses. A form of central heating was used, based on a hot air system. The roofs were flat, hardly a good idea for a building, as water tends to run downhill, so sloping roofs are always better. These were introduced to provide roof terraces, which became one of

<hr />

[7] The floor slabs were not supported by beams, and in 1915 Édouard tried to patent this idea. However, this type of slab, usually called a 'flat slab' had been patented in the USA years before and had been used by the engineer Robert Maillart as early as 1907 in Édouard's native Switzerland.

[8] Of course Édouard wasn't alone in his admiration of the Parthenon, sharing it with Adolf Hitler amongst others. Carey, 1992, p199.

[9] It is rare that a house needs a structure of reinforced concrete. For example, in Great Britain at the beginning of the twenty-first century, most houses constructed use the sensible combination of brick and timber structures.

The Schwob's Turkish villa

Édouard's trademarks. The appearance of the house was unlike anything seen before in La Chaux-de-Fonds, and it earned the local pejorative nickname 'the Turkish villa'.

The Schwobs, however, were initially pleased with their house – except for the fact that it was hugely over budget and costs were out of control. Anatole Schwob could probably afford the cost overrun but, as a successful businessman, he did not like financial irresponsibility. A bitter dispute between Schwob and Édouard ensued which almost ended in court. This was avoided, but any idea of a successful local career was ruined. Édouard decided, in 1917 at the age of 30, to leave for Paris.[10]

The essential difference between the Schwob house and the earlier projects was not the concrete frame, nor the flat roofs, nor the cost overruns, but that it was built to satisfy the architect – Édouard – rather than the client.[11]

The only contacts Édouard had in Paris were his old employer, Auguste Perret, and a boyhood friend (now an engineer) Max DuBois, and it was DuBois who got him a job – in a block-making factory in some managerial role. In the long run, however, it was Perret who was more important as he introduced him, in 1917, to Amédée Ozenfant (1886–1966).

Ozenfant, who ran a fashion shop, had connections with the Parisian intellectual avant-garde, and Édouard and Amédée hit it off from the start.

With this friendship, he could begin realizing his dream of becoming a modern artist. He started doing modern paintings,[12] but perhaps more importantly, Édouard and Amédée founded a new painting 'ism' called Purism.[13] Thus they were not only artists but intellectuals as well, an essential attribute for a modern artist.

Purist painting

---

[10] Although Paris was an intellectual centre, France was in an unwinnable position in a war with Germany, whereas Switzerland was at peace. But Édouard was Swiss not French, though he later became a French citizen.

[11] Perhaps this is not strictly true as in 1912 he designed a house for his parents, now known as the Maison Blanche. Here Édouard 'experimented' with light. As a consequence it had too much glass which made it impossibly expensive to heat in the winter. After a few years his parents gave up the struggle and left.

[12] Édouard continued painting on a regular basis throughout his life, and so could be described as an artist who designed buildings or an architect who painted.

[13] Purism was based on the earlier Cubism, with its message expounded in a book, jointly written by Jeanneret and Ozenfant in 1918, called *Après le Cubisme*. Purism had almost no followers.

To keep themselves in the avant-garde scene, the pair founded, in 1920, a magazine that they called *L'Esprit Nouveau*.[14] The Purist pair would write some articles under pseudonyms.[15] In their magazine, they would often include items about architecture, which were suitably iconoclastic. Édouard also cultivated a distinctive appearance;[16] his get-up included heavy black-framed round glasses,[17] a dark suit, a bowler hat and a bow tie – 'an extraordinary mobile object under a bowler hat' as the painter Fernand Leger described him.[18] He was to maintain this attention-seeking 'anonymous' appearance throughout his life.[19]

The carefully arranged persona in 1930 and 1960

The 1922 version of the Citrohan prototype

As well as becoming a modern artist and intellectual, Édouard was still working on his architectural prototypes, as he was yet to get any real jobs. One of these was a house type called the Citrohan, named after the Citröen car. By this time Édouard had completely embraced modern technology, and especially the assembly line mass production pioneered in America by Henry Ford. He was convinced that in the future buildings would be produced in this way.[20]

The Citrohan house, designed with his cousin Pierre Jeanneret (1896–1967), was a seminal project, so warrants some examination.[21] Unlike the Schwob house, everything was rectilinear and completely without decoration. But both had rein-

---

[14] The idea of producing a magazine as propaganda was common among modern art 'movements' – for instance, the Futurists founded *Poesia* in 1905 and *De Stijl* was founded in Holland in 1917.

[15] Édouard's pseudonym was the all-important Le Corbusier. This was based on a corruption of the name of an ancestor called Le Corbezier.

[16] His 'carefully arranged persona' as WJR Curtis described it. Curtis, 1986, p50.

[17] Already poorly sighted, in 1918 Édouard had the misfortune to lose the sight in his left eye; this meant that the 'greatest architect of the twentieth century' was unable to see in three-dimensions. The irony of this has escaped most commentators although WRJ Curtis (ibid) noted that it 'gave rise, perhaps, to some curious spatial ambiguities'.

[18] Blake, 1960[1], p13.

[19] After Corbusier's lead it, became quite common for architects, famous or aspiring, to turn themselves into a type of living trademark by adopting a slightly weird personal style. For instance the 2008 Pritzker Prize winner (see Chapter 12) Jean Nouvel (b1945) always appears dressed all in black with his head freshly shaved; when on his summer holidays he appears dressed all in white!

[20] The ideas of mass production and modern technology were to stay with him all his life. This was somewhat unfortunate as he never understood either, but it allowed him to give himself a technological veneer.

[21] Pierre Jeanneret had received formal training as an architect in Switzerland, and went to Paris, in 1920, to work for the Perret brothers.

forced concrete frames and flat roofs that were to be used as terraces. The new 'innovation' was that the living area was double height with the sleeping area on a mezzanine, with the guest/children's bedrooms rather inconveniently located on the roof. Another important point was that the house was as if part of a terrace – a slice.

There were two main sources of inspiration for this house. One was the flat-roofed, white-washed houses that impressed Édouard on his travels in the Greek islands, and the other was the Parisian Café Mauroy, much frequented by artists and intellectuals at the time. The kitchen, in this café, was at the back under a mezzanine with a double-height window to the street elevation.

Although a fundamental aim of modern architecture was to be 'functional', with the possibility of production by assembly line methods, the Citrohan house didn't meet either of these objectives. It was non-functional in a number of ways:

Flat roof: In areas with rainfall, which is where most humans live, a flat roof is never a good idea because, unlike the sensible pitched roof, it tends to leak. For a flat roof to be waterproof the whole roof has to be an impervious layer which, for a number of technical reasons, is not easy to achieve. Furthermore, if the roof leaks, the actual source can be difficult to locate, as the interior appearance of water may be a long way from its external entry point.

Double height living space: This has a number of practical drawbacks that include the fact that heating with ground level appliances, stoves or radiators for example, is inefficient as the heat rises; cleaning and redecorating walls and ceilings is difficult; the upper wall areas are inaccessible for shelving or picture hanging, and so on.

Wall size windows: Huge double height windows present their own problems; these include the heat gain in hot weather – the greenhouse effect – and heat loss in winter; the poor sound insulation of glass (meaning noise can enter, or leave, with ease); the difficulty of cleaning; and providing curtains or blinds over such a large area.

Flush external walls: The walls were white planes with no weathering around the openings or at the top. This means, in practical terms, that the wall will stain and there is a strong likelihood that leaks will occur around windows and doors.[22]

Although the windows were seen as a mass-produced product, the house itself presented no opportunities for mass production. The idea was that the house was universal, for anyone and everyone in any location. In fact, it was not a house that many people would choose as a home – it was basically a small art gallery with living accommodation.[23]

---

[22] Which is what happened when houses based on this prototype were built '... it looked wonderfully machine made – at least for the first month or so, then cracks and streaks appeared ...'. Blake, 1960[1], p67.

[23] As one commentator put it: 'it [the Citrohan house] seemed to be directed at the habits of an artist-monk ... cross-bred with the cell of a monastery'. Curtis, 1986, p54. Or another, '... the living room is waiting for the installation of an exhibition of primitive sculpture rather than chairs and tables suitable for family use.' Dunster, 1985, p35.

In 1922, Édouard's luck changed largely as a result of his relentless attempts at self-publicity. He was asked to exhibit in the Salon d'Automne. He showed a model of the Citrohan house, now 'improved' by being raised up on concrete columns, and was asked to provide an exhibit for the urban section. He asked the director what was expected, and was told that something like 'a fountain in a square would be appropriate'. Édouard replied that he would 'design a fountain with a city for 3 million people' – which is what he did.[24]

The city was to have 24 60-storey office blocks in the centre with the middle-class office workers housed in the surrounding area. The residential accommodation was to be in long blocks of 'stacks' of Citrohan houses. The workers were to be housed on the periphery in 'garden cities' together with industrial areas, which presumably would provide them with jobs. There were to be large open spaces between the buildings so the whole effect was as if they had all been placed in a giant park which he referred to as a 'lung'. The overall area of the city was four times that of Manhattan.

The 1922 fountain in a city for 3 million people

There was perhaps not much original about Édouard's megalomaniac proposal; the design of whole imaginary cities had been done many times.[25] Garden cities had also been proposed and skyscrapers already existed, though not in the same style, in New York and Chicago. And Édouard's previous mentor, Auguste Perret, had made a proposal for skyscrapers with a similar cruciform plan. But the exhibit was impressive, with a huge model on display. It had the desired effect of bringing Édouard's architectural work to the notice of the Parisian avant-garde. It also had a secondary effect, which was to become the primary goal of his life, establishing him as the architect of whole cities. Whilst the city was in a park, the plan was rigidly geometric with one main axis of symmetry and the other of 'almost' symmetry, reminiscent of plans from the École des Beaux-Arts. (This similarity is perhaps odd given that Édouard, together with the rest of the Modern Movement, regarded the work of the École des Beaux-Arts as the embodiment of everything that was wrong with architecture.)

Édouard's exhibits did the trick and he came to the notice of a number of potential clients. These were rich members of the Parisian avant-garde, often American, who wanted to show how modern they were by not only buying modern art and attending concerts of modern music, but by actually living a modern life. And for this, obviously, they had to live in a modern house, and Édouard was only too pleased to oblige.

---

[24] Tzonis, 2001, p72.

[25] Perhaps the best known imaginary city was the vast Industrial City proposed by Tony Garnier, and developed between 1899 and 1904 (see pages 32–33), and the Futurist Sant' Elia had made his proposals for a 'New City' in 1913 (see page 35).

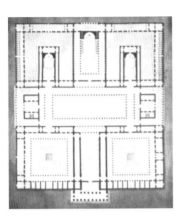

A Beaux-Arts plan

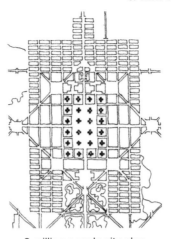

3 million people city plan

To undertake real architectural design Édouard, in 1923, went into partnership with his cousin Pierre to form Atelier 35S. And it was around this time that Édouard decided to call himself by one of the pseudonyms under which he had written – and so the architect Le Corbusier was 'born'.

This change of name was a way of becoming more than just an architect, it allowed him, with the 'Le' and no first name, to become something objective like a 'historical phenomena' or 'object type' as some writers have called it.[26] (What did you call him to his face? Le? Monsieur Le Corbusier? Édouard?) This pseudonym also, according to Jencks, allowed him to write about himself in the third person and he could use it as a protective mask or means of self-dramatisation, all part of his need for importance and fame. And as he achieved these objectives, his aficionados shortened his name to the knowing Corbu or Corb.

Architects' view of Le Corbusier according to cartoonist Hellman

This new persona was reinforced by another important event in 1923, the publication in book form of the architectural items that Édouard and Amédée had written for their magazine. The book was called *Vers une architecture* and was initially published under their joint pseudonyms Le Corbusier-Saugnier.[27] The book, hard to categorise, is now thought of as one of the most influential, widely read and least understood of all architectural writings of the twentieth century. On publication, the architectural profession showed little interest as the Modern Movement was not really relevant to them. But gradually, during the century as Modern Movement architects took control, it achieved cult status.[28]

But what was it and what did it say? Written in a declamatory style, it was basically a

---

[26] See, Curtis, 1986, p51, or Jencks, 1973[2], p55.

[27] Amédée's pseudonym Saugnier was gradually removed from the book in successive editions. In 1925 the Purists split after a disagreement on how to hang some pictures. This breaking up of friendships was one of many of Édouard's unendearing characteristics.

[28] Salingaros compares *Vers une architecture* to Hitler's book *Mein Kampf*, on the basis that both books are recipes for destruction. Salingaros, 2006, p182.

manifesto calling for a revolutionary approach to architecture. The central theme was that architects had got lost in 'styles'. 'The styles are a lie' [29] or

> If we challenge the past, we learn that 'styles' no longer exist for us, that a style belonging to our own period had come about; and there has to be a Revolution.[30]

It was engineers not architects who understood how to design for a modern age:

> The Engineer's Aesthetic, and Architecture, are two things that march together and follow one from another: the one being now at its full height the other in the unhappy state of regression.[31]

There are many more references extolling the virtues of engineers, together with photographs of cars, liners and aeroplanes. Of these, the most interesting from the point of view of Le Corbusier's work (as he now must be called), is one of the liner *Aquitania* compared with some well-known buildings.

A real living machine lurks behind the discredited past

He tries to show that 'official architecture' is out of touch with the true Classical sense and he attacks the École des Beaux-Arts. Mass production is seen as the way forward: 'We must create the mass-production spirit'[32] and on page 10 the (now repeated ad nauseam) phrase 'The house is a machine for living in' appears.

Well, if a new approach to architecture by knowledgably using modern technology would produce benefits – in terms of economy, better environment, more efficient construction, and so on – then clearly Le Corbusier's wake up call would have been welcome. But modern technology, in the hands of Le Corbusier and his followers, brought none of these benefits.

Interestingly, *Vers une architecture* already shows Le Corbusier's dishonesty, which was to become one of his hallmarks, and, for that matter, of the Modern Movement, in a

---

[29] Le Corbusier, 1927, p9.

[30] ibid, p13.

[31] ibid, p7.

[32] ibid, p12.

Le Corbusier's 'flat-roofed' grain silo

The real silo with pitched roofs

rather obscure detail. On page 29 there is photo of an example of an engineer's modern design – a grain silo – with a suitably 'modern' flat roof. But Le Corbusier had doctored the photo to suit his thesis; the real silo had (sensible) pitched roofs!

The appearance of the book enhanced Le Corbusier's reputation amongst the Parisian avant-garde, and reinforced their desire to have Atelier 35S design them suitably modern houses. The houses that were designed for them were based on variations of a 'white cube'. One of the first, in 1923, was pair of semi-detached houses, one for his brother Albert, the other for the banker and collector of avant-garde art, Raoul La Roche – the house became known as the Maison Roche.

A 1920s white cube

Others followed: for his friend Ozenfant (also 1923); for the American journalist and amateur artist William Cook (in 1926); and for Sarah and Michael Stein, the brother of avant-garde writer Gertrude (also in 1926) amongst others. Also in 1926, Le Corbusier published his *Five Points of a New Architecture* – if *Vers une architecture* was less than clear, nothing could be clearer than the *Five Points*. What were they?

1   The building had to be lifted up on columns to free the ground for circulation and other uses. These columns were called pilotis.

The French word for column is colonne whereas pilotis is the French for the poles that are used to support houses over water. By using this more picturesque word for what is no more and no less than a colonne, Le Corbusier was attempting to give a banal object an air of mystery. Eventually every modern architect, of whatever nationality, would be talking confidently about pilotis as though they were different, in some important way, from columns.

2   Internal walls should be non-loadbearing so they could be positioned without constraint – the plan libre.

This meant that all buildings had to have a reinforced concrete frame rather than the cheaper system of brick walls and timber floors. Often Le Corbusier would curve the internal walls to show that they were non-loadbearing – few people could have grasped this point let alone found it of interest.

3 External walls should be non-loadbearing, so the external enclosure was freed from any load-bearing function – the façade libre.

This is in effect what is now known as the curtain wall, which was far from a new idea, having been used in buildings since the second half of the nineteenth century. Curtain walls, if they are to be effective technically, are far more expensive than simple brick ones.

4 Windows should be in long strips – fenêtre en longeur.

This type of window is excellent if you need a wide view, as those do on the bridge of a ship. However, few people spend hours staring out of a window to no purpose. Windows in buildings, unlike those on ships, are principally to provide natural light and to give the occupants what's called outside awareness. Le Corbusier's previous mentor, Auguste Perret, fiercely criticised the strip window, claiming that a window should 'embrace the presence of an upright human being', and so should be vertical.[33]

5 Land lost underneath the building should be replaced by 'land' on the roof – the toit jardin.

This compounds the problems of the flat roof, as now the roof has to carry the extra load of soil which, if the plants are to flourish, has to be permanently damp. Oh, and getting wheelbarrows up and down several flights of stairs is not that easy.

Le Corbusier published a diagram that showed how 'light' a house became, compared to a normal one, if his five points were applied. Not one to miss a graphic trick, however

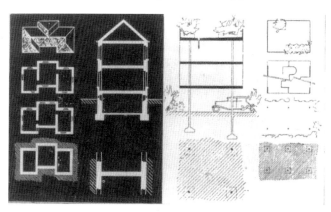

The lightness of the five-point house

crude, Le Corbusier chose to print the five-point house with a white background, whilst the normal house had a black background, making it look 'heavier'. But if the background were reversed then the five-point house would seem a little heavier.

The apogee of the cubical-white houses, les Maisons Blanches, is considered by many to have been

[33] Actually Perret was even more damning when, as a member of the committee of the Exposition des Arte Décoratifs, he vetoed the proposal to give Le Corbusier's Esprit Noveau pavilion the top prize, commenting he could see no architecture there at all. Britton, 2001. p70.

reached with the final one, the Villa Savoye of 1928. This was an example par excellence, of the five points – the perfect, cubically-white, living machine. But what was a modern life like in one of these cubical living machines? Well you had to put up with a building that malfunctioned technically, there were cracks and stains and leaks and condensation and..., and of course you'd already paid way beyond the initial budget. But some people could cope. Raoul la Roche 'enjoyed living in the villa, despite its many technical deficien-

The perfect, cubically-white, five-point living machine

cies, such as a noisy central heating system that was never resolved and an ever pending lighting solution'.[34]

But others were less enthusiastic – the Savoye family for instance. Pierre Savoye was a Parisian banker and not a member of the avant-garde. What he wanted was a weekend house in the country for his family. There is no evidence that he had any interest, one way or the other, in modern architecture – but he chose Le Corbusier to be his architect. The outcome was a disaster. The final cost of the project was far in excess of the budget, there were technical problems, as always, and the house was so uncomfortable for family life that the Savoyes hardly used it.[35] It later served as a military billet for both German and Allied soldiers, then was used as a hay barn by local farmers. In 1959, scheduled for demolition, it was 'rescued' by the then French minister of culture André Malraux – it is now a historic monument!

The lauding of the Villa Savoye, in numerous books, and by numerous Modern Movement architects, encapsulates beautifully the basic deceit of the Modern Movement. Here is a building that is supposed to be a house – a role it was never able to fulfil – later promoted endlessly as one of the high points of Modern Movement house design.[36]

In the 1920s Le Corbusier was not only occupied in supplying his friends and relations[37] with over-priced, technically flawed, uncomfortable living machines. In 1924 he

---

[34] Tzonis, 2001, p56.

[35] In fact, though to some extent obsessed by housing, Le Corbusier had no real family life. When he finally married his long-term girl friend, Yvonne Gallis, in 1930, he told her 'no children' and was quoted as saying, 'I hate children, they are the curse of society. They make noise; they are messy and should be abolished,' – a statement that might have endeared him to the Anglo-American film comedian WC Fields (whose famous quote was 'a man who hates dogs and children can't be all bad') but few others.

According to architectural critic Kenneth Frampton, Le Corbusier's buildings were published as 'Purist set-pieces, pristine, empty, luminous spaces, removed from the quotidian contamination of domesticity'. Frampton, 2001, p33.

[36] 'The Villa Savoye is an expression of pure Voltairean rationalism, precise, geometric and man-made, whose relationship with nature is carefully controlled' Riseboro, 1979, p250. Or 'the Villa Savoye could only have been built by a master'. Blake, 1960[1], p62.

[37] In 1925 Le Corbusier put his aged parents into one of his white cubes near Lake Léman.

was commissioned to design housing for the employees of Henri Frugès. Henri Frugès was the millionaire son of an industrialist, and had inherited timber and sugar businesses in France and the colonies. Although not part of the intellectual avant-garde, he was interested in modern art and architecture. He thought, naïvely as it turned out, that the quality of his employees' lives would be improved if they were to be put into some living machines. He suggested a few model dwellings but Le Corbusier, ever the cynical opportunist, persuaded him to build a whole 'Quartier' at Pessac near Bordeaux – what he called the 'cité jardin horizontale'.[38] The initial phase was to be of 53 housing units, all based on the prototypes that Le Corbusier had developed. The whole project was a complete failure at all levels – constructional, economic and cultural.

Le Corbusier had developed various innovative building techniques, such as making walls of sprayed concrete, of which he had no practical experience. Consequently the contractor had enormous difficulty in using the expensive equipment, causing delays and extra costs. And, either out of arrogance or ignorance, the correct procedures for obtaining the necessary building permissions had not been followed. Hence there were problems with planning permission and drainage connection which caused delays of several years.

By the time the initial phase was ready, (the second phase was never built) Henri Frugès had become a nervous wreck,[39] and his employees didn't want the houses; either because they didn't like them or couldn't afford them, or a combination of both. But eventually, one way or another, the houses were occupied even though the agent's brochure warned that 'The external appearance is not always pleasing at first sight,' and it became known locally as the 'Sultan's District' or the 'Moroccan Settlement'.

A visit to the Quartier Frugès today reveals an interesting indictment of Modern Movement architecture. The houses have had three different destinies. A number have been modified by their occupants to make them 'homely.' The alterations include adding pitched roofs, porches, shutters and reducing the size and shapes of the windows. Others have

Quartier Frugès in 2007

been left to the mercy of the elements, and these have become stained, cracked and rusty, presenting a dreary picture of semi-dereliction. Still others have been bought by Le Corbusier fans, in the main architects, who want to restore them to their former 'glory'. Unfortunately, due to the inherent conceptual and constructional errors, this requires an almost total rebuild.

---

[38] Again, trying to imbue a quite ordinary piece of building, a smallish housing estate, with a special name that implied that it had some special quality.

[39] He eventually went bankrupt.

Although Atelier 35S only managed during the 1920s to build a few houses, Le Cor-busier had other things on his mind – re-designing the world. His scheme for a city of 3 million inhabitants had whetted his appetite for what is known as urban design – the complete design of whole cities. In 1925, in the Pavilion de L'Esprit Nouveau,[40] he exhib-ited the Plan Voisin. This was a proposal, sponsored by the car and aircraft manufacturer Voisin, for the rebuilding of the centre of Paris, with the streets re-aligned on a rectangular grid and dominated by cruciform-shaped skyscrapers.

Le Corbusier rebuilds Paris

His master plan for Paris received what he seemed to crave – unprecedented outrage.[41] Even such an architectural supporter like WJR Curtis,[42] is heavily critical of this proposal, using phrases like '[his plans] ... have killed the urban body (and the urban spirit) ...' or, 'His simplistic diagram ... instituted grotesque clashes of scale ...' or again, 'That Le Cor-busier's urban model contained basic flaws is beyond question ...'. But blinded by his view of his own genius, Le Corbusier was unable to draw these self-evident conclusions.

Le Corbusier would often portray his work as though it was based on rational and sci-entific principles, implying that his designs had some sort of logical inevitability. He would refer to research and experiments, as though he was dispassionately working towards optimum solutions for the human condition. Nothing could be further from the truth. Le Corbusier never had even a minimal grasp of the basic laws of physics that determine the technical performance of buildings – heat transmission, load-carrying systems, sound insulation, acoustics, the effects of natural and artificial light or the technical performance

---

[40] This was an exhibition building, based on the white cube, which formed part of the Exposition des Artes Dé-coratifs. Le Corbusier made no attempt to hide his contempt for the decorative arts, so it's difficult to understand why he was permitted to have his 'own' exhibition stand. Many of the organisers were vitriolic in their hatred of his work, and his exhibit was erected in the furthest corner of the site behind an 18 ft high fence.

[41] Throughout his life, Le Corbusier would seek attention by various forms of annoying behaviour. It's hard not to link this to his childhood, where his parents always favoured his more attractive and talented brother Albert. However, the brothers always had a cordial relationship.

[42] Curtis, 1986, p65–66.

of construction materials. All this was only too obvious with his white cube buildings. But worse, he was unable to grasp the basic essential of the scientific approach – that is formulating theorems, and accepting them or rejecting them on the basis of experimental results. This was because, in the words of one historian,

> Experience rarely changed his perceptions, reality rarely challenged his myths ... In the end his idea of reality, rather than reality itself, dominated so that it could serve his polemics and rhetoric.[43]

With the Wall Street crash of 1929, there were fewer rich Americans about to indulge him, and the world economy went into recession. Luckily (for him at any rate), towards the end of the 1920s Le Corbusier was having some success with larger buildings. In 1926 he had entered, and nearly won, an international competition for a new headquarters for the ill-fated United Nations forerunner, the League of Nations.[44] Also in 1926, he was invited to enter a competition, in the Soviet Union, for the design of a new headquarters for the Central Union of Cooperatives – the Centrosoyuz. After a lengthy process, Le Corbusier was declared the winner, and after an even lengthier process, and many complications, it was built – being completed in 1936.

Here Le Corbusier applied his five points relentlessly – but the strip windows had become glazed walls. If roof gardens were intended, all the photos show them less than flourishing. Nowadays similar, and similarly dreary, buildings form a backdrop to cities worldwide. Le Corbusier had received a warm welcome in the Soviet Union where, thanks to the efforts of the avant-garde group the Constructivists, the Modern Movement had the

Making the Soviet Union even drearier

upper hand. However by the time the building was completed Stalin had moved against them, so it was condemned as an 'alien' building.

At the beginning of the 1930s Le Corbusier also got some opportunities to show the French what he could do with larger projects. One was a residential block for Swiss university students to be built in Paris. He presented his scheme, yet again based on the five principles – and again with glazed walls, with the building

---

[43] Bacon, 2001, p158.

[44] He lost the competition on a show of hands by the judges, the non-modernists winning. This caused outrage in the modernist camp and embittered Le Corbusier. One outcome was the forming, in 1928, of the modern movement pressure group, and source of propaganda, the Congrès Internationaux d'Architecture Moderne or C.I.A.M for short. Le Corbusier was to play a leading role.

balanced on a single row of wobbly pilotis. The client had technical doubts, and sent the proposal to Switzerland for a technical assessment. This assessment opined that the scheme 'was quite useless in its present form'.[45] The pilotis problem was resolved by massively increasing the size of some of them; in fact, as there was still only a single row, the massive size was required to stop the building being blown over, rather than to support the vertical loads.

The vertical slab

The resulting rather uninspiring design, of a 'vertical slab', with curtain-walled long sides and blank end walls, can be seen gracing the suburbs of towns and cities almost everywhere – but usually supported on something more sensible than massive concrete pilotis. But the blank end walls were blank because the slab was a prototype for another Corbusian scheme to conquer the world. He wanted to do this with the 'road town'[46] – a single block that was miles long. Le Corbusier prepared a scheme – Plan Obus, during the 1930s, to inflict this inhuman concept on Algiers.

Meanwhile back in the real world Le Corbusier was having yet more technical problems, which were due to his apparent inability to understand the fact that a glazed wall caused environmental problems. Maybe this criticism is not quite justified, as Le Corbusier had proposed that the glazed walls were double, with air in the space between them being heated and cooled. But such a system, even if it was technically feasible,

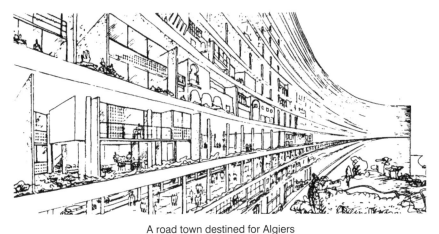

A road town destined for Algiers

---

[45] Curtis, 1986, p105.

[46] The road town had already been proposed, in 1910, by Edgar Chambless.

was untried and exorbitantly expensive and hence never used. So there were environmental problems, not only with the Pavillion Suisse and the Centrosoyuz buildings, but also with a building he designed for the Salvation Army, the Cité de Refuge in Paris, and even his own flat![47]

As for many others, the 1930s was a lean time for Atelier 35S, but Le Corbusier kept himself busy by writing, lecturing and designing unwanted and unrealised urban projects. He also designed furniture.[48] In his furniture designs he was 'helped' by the interior designer Charlotte Perriand (1903–1999), but would omit her name from the credits if possible. A number of their designs became modern furniture classics, if that's not a contradiction in terms, and are still available, at considerable cost one might add. Predictably, a chair had become 'a machine for sitting in'. One of the least useful was their chaise-longue.

A modern movement 'classic'

Whilst the machines-for-sitting-in were not particularly comfortable, the now famous chaise-longue is neither comfortable – as only one position can be maintained – nor practical, as it needs space and is difficult to mount or dismount. But, with his avowed interest in mass production (remember the exhortations in *Vers une architecture*?), it might be thought that the furniture would be easy to manufacture. Not a bit of it, it was difficult to make.

The chaise-longue had two main parts; a support frame made from oval tube (is that off-the-shelf?) and a complicated sled contraption of leather and tubing. However, this item is much loved by Modern Movement aficionados, who, in putting one in their home (or better still office), can demonstrate to the world their sophisticated modern taste.

Le Corbusier also went abroad to spread the message – that he was the greatest architect in the world – and to try and drum up work. Probably the most important visit was the one he made to the United States of America in 1935. He was invited by the Museum of Modern Art to give a lecture tour; they had also arranged a travelling exhibition of his work.

The stage for modern movement architecture had already been partially set in 1932, when critic Henry-Russell Hitchcock and architect Philip Johnson[49] had mounted an exhi-

---

[47] At the Centrosoyuz building the glazing and heating systems had to be changed. The Pavillon Suisse had to have aluminium sunshades added, which caused one critic to lament that it interrupted the purity of the original form, though they did allow the client to use the building. At the Cité de Refuge there was a long dispute with the client. In his new flat, the penthouse of a block he designed in 1933, his wife is reported to have complained that 'All this light is killing me, driving me crazy.'

[48] Like many architects, Le Corbusier thought he could design anything at all, a bit like a wine-grower being able to raise beef cattle.

[49] The incredibly rich Johnson, who wore 'Le Corbusier' glasses, had begun his architectural career designing Modern Movement buildings. In the 1930s he had spent several years, and a considerable chunk of his fortune, in trying to create an effective American Nazi party. After World War II, shrugging off his fascist past, he became a big-business architect eventually forsaking the Modern Movement mantra.

bition of European modern architecture called 'Modern Architecture: The International Style'. But the modern movement was far from being accepted by the American architectural profession in 1935. Firstly, many American architects had trained in Paris at the École des Beaux-Arts,[50] or at American schools that were 'Beaux-Arts' in their approach – and they were 'the enemy' for Le Corbusier. And secondly the influential Frank Lloyd Wright was an American. Wright, who was 20 years older than Le Corbusier, considered that he had invented modern architecture and had, in comparison to Le Corbusier, built a vast body of work. Also, he probably had an ego even bigger than that of Le Corbusier and he held the Modern Movement in utter contempt. He had expressed this in writing, and would constantly make derogatory remarks about the European modern architects in general and Le Corbusier in particular, referring to him as 'that pamphleteer'.

Whether Le Corbusier was aware of these circumstances is not clear, but on arriving in New York he was met by the press. Probably they didn't really know who this strangely dressed, almost blind, non-English speaking Frenchman was, but they asked, through an interpreter, what he thought of New York – he replied with typical attention-seeking lack of tact: 'The skyscrapers are too small'. He got his headlines but also alienated a number of people.

To cut a quite complicated story short, the visit was a failure. His lectures were well attended but delivered in French, during which he made crude crayon drawings on large sheets of brown paper. He was enthusiastically received by the more rebellious students but by rather fewer members of the architectural profession. He had many meetings with city planners, where he was able to explain to them where they'd gone wrong. He explained that Manhattan should be knocked down and rebuilt according to his grid and tower block principles. They didn't knock Manhattan down, as it turned out, and he left empty-handed. All he got was a generous helping of rejection on which to feed his bitterness.

In 1936, Le Corbusier went to Rio de Janeiro, where he had a bit more success

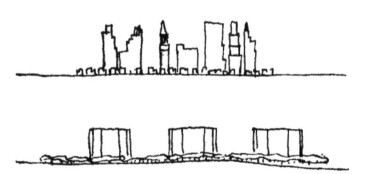

The redesign of Manhattan

acting as a consultant to admiring architects Lucio Costa (1902–1998) and Oscar Niemayer (b1907).[51] They collaborated on a design for a large and suitably impersonal block, to house the Ministry for Education – it was completed in 1943.

Returning to France there was little work and little else to do but wait for the next world war, which commenced in 1939. With the war, Le Corbusier and his cousin Pierre ended their partnership. Pierre allied himself with the Resistance who fought, clandestinely, the Nazi invaders

---

[50] Of all the foreigners who attended the École des Beaux-Arts in Paris, Americans were in the majority, with over 500 students.

[51] In the late 1950s, they got an opportunity to put into practice the lessons in urban design they'd learned from the master. They designed Brazil's brand new capital Brasilia, widely regarded as a total disaster.

whilst Le Corbusier took a less resistant course – he courted the Vichy government.[52] For a short while Le Corbusier held the position of chief of the state housing organisation in the Vichy government. While there, he proposed that a single architect be appointed to oversee all the work – it's difficult to imagine that he didn't see himself fulfilling this role. But, due to his lack of what are now known as interpersonal skills, he annoyed so many people that he was sacked. He tried to speak to Marshal Pétain in an attempt to be reinstated – no interview was granted so he went to the Pyrenees to wait out the war as best he could.

With the Liberation in 1944, the people of France were confronted with the situation that many of its citizens had fought, and died, to free France from the Nazi invader, whilst others had, with varying levels of enthusiasm, collaborated actively with the enemy. Unsurprisingly revenge was sought, and the collaborators were punished, some even being executed. As a one-time employee of the Vichy government, that is the enemy, Le Corbusier should have been accused of being a collaborator. But he avoided this by making it appear as if he had been part of the Resistance! In 1944, he became chairman of the City Planning Committee of the Architect's National Front, an organisation actually sponsored by the Resistance.

Le Corbusier, then aged 57, must have thought his time had finally come, and that he would be able to put into action his urban vision in war-damaged France. In 1945, he was invited to prepare plans for the semi-demolished city of Saint-Dié – here was his chance. As usual, inhuman tower blocks were to stalk the land, but the Popular Association of War Victims, a large and mainly left-wing local group, flatly rejected this idea – they wanted the city to be rebuilt as it had been – they wanted their homes back. Clearly these people were deluded, so instead of trying to work with them, Le Corbusier went behind their backs. He tried to pull every political string he could get hold of so that the city would be reconstructed to his satisfaction, rather than that of its inhabitants. But Le Corbusier had miscalculated; the string-pulling was to no avail. Instead of redesigning or resigning, Le Corbusier simply absented himself – catching a boat for New York and leaving his clients to their own devices.

While on the boat, Le Corbusier perfected his dimensioning system – Le Modulor. For hundreds of years, attempts had been made to find numerical relationships that, when applied to buildings, would automatically result in beauty. These attempts tended to involve the Golden Section and Fibonacci series,[53] numerical systems that for some people had almost mystical qualities – Le Corbusier was no exception. Le Corbusier also considered the metric system inhuman, which it is as its basic unit – the metre – is one 10 millionth of

---

[52] With the defeat of France, in 1940 by the German army, the French negotiated a peace which allowed the south of France to be governed by the French. In the town of Vichy a pro-Nazi puppet government was set up under the 'leadership' of the aged Marshal Pétain – this became known as the Vichy government. 'The Vichy regime ... rounded up Jews even more enthusiastically than the Nazis demanded'. Robb, 2007, p357.

[53] The Golden Section is the ratio 1 to 1.618033 +more decimal places. So a rectangle with sides 1 and 1.618033 will have 'perfect proportions'. Fibonacci numbers, named after a twelfth century Italian monk, are a sequence where the next number is the sum of the previous two, so 1, 1, 2, 3, 5, 8, 13 are Fibonacci numbers. Fibonacci numbers derived from the golden section are 1, 1.618033, 2.618033, 4.236066, and so on. Any two sequential numbers of these Fibonacci numbers are in the ratio of the Golden Section.

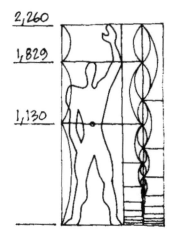

2,260

1,829

1,130

Modulor Man and his
Fibonacci numbers

the distance from the North Pole to the Equator. Before the introduction of the metric system, in 1795, measurements were related to the human being – like foot or inch (the width of a thumb hence pouce in French). On the voyage, Le Corbusier was finally able to relate the Golden Section to Fibonacci numbers and the human being – it was based on the 1.83 m (6 ft)-tall Modulor Man.

The height of Modulor man was made up by one Fibonacci sequence, called the red sequence, so 43 +70 = 113, 70 + 113 = 183. And another, the blue sequence is a Fibonacci sequence that arrives at 2.26 m, the height of Modulor Man's upstretched arm. Thus, according to Le Corbusier, if all parts of a building were dimensioned according to this scheme, every part would comply with a human version of the divine proportion. Of course one might speculate, if someone was of quite a different height to Modulor Man, a child say, would this cosmic harmony still apply? But there again Le Corbusier hated children. Le Corbusier was proud of the Modulor as an intellectual achievement,[54] publishing two books about it.

In 1946, Le Corbusier was commissioned directly by the Minister of Reconstruction to build a housing block in Marseilles. This time there would be no irritating users to bother him; his clients were French bureaucrats, none of whom would ever have to live in the building. The project was called the Unité d´Habitation, now universally known as Unité, and was to be Le Corbusier's crowning achievement. He stuck to his winning five-point formula, but now applied to a building of vastly greater size. The building was 165 m long, 24 m wide, it had 17 upper stories and was 56 m high, and was to house 1,600 people.[55]

Point one was applied, the enormous and over-sized columns, sorry pilotis, lifting the whole building off the ground. But point two, the plan libre, was less clear. Points three and four, the façade libre and the fenêtre en longeur had metamorphosed into something rather more complicated. But point five was there; there was a toit jardim. And the Citrohan house was also there, as the building, like some of those in his 1922 city for 3 million people, was a stack of them. But, to ensure the whole project was both beautiful and human, the Modulor system of measurement, or proportions, was used.

The method of building was to be innovative. First the pilotis supported table was to be built at first floor level, and then an insitu concrete open frame, a bottle rack, was to be built above.[56] Next, totally prefabricated individual flat units were to be slid into place in

---

[54] He liked to quote Albert Einstein who had told him that the system 'made the bad difficult and the good easy'. But Le Corbusier was quite happy to ignore it if it suited him, in fact, he even banned its use in Atelier 35S for some months.

[55] At the end of the war some 4 million French people were homeless, so they could be housed in about 2,500 Unités. Whether this was the intention of the French Government or Le Corbusier is not recorded.

[56] Originally the frame was to be made from steel, but post-war shortages put paid to that. How this frame was to be fire-proofed was unclear... no doubt Corbusier had another 'good' idea up his sleeve.

Unité, the concrete ocean liner

the frame. Each flat unit was to be lined with lead to provide sound insulation.[57]

One doesn't need to have much building experience to realise that, the 'sliding-in-whole-units' idea was completely impractical, especially in view of their complex shape, but it wasn't obvious to the team – of course, the idea had to be abandoned.[58] Eventually the units and their external wall were built from a number of prefabricated elements. But even with the abandonment of the whole unit approach, the project exceeded the initial budget and took five times longer to build than was planned.

The plan was not really free, as each living machine went right across the building, so it was 24 m long (not a Modulor dimension), but was only 3.66 m wide – a blue Modulor dimension (140 + 226). So it was a sort of tunnel. The double-height parts were 4.79 m high (red Modulor) whereas the single-height parts were 2.26 m high (blue Modulor). This meant that Modulor Man could touch the ceiling in the single height spaces! The single-double height units interlocked in pairs around a central, shared access corridor.

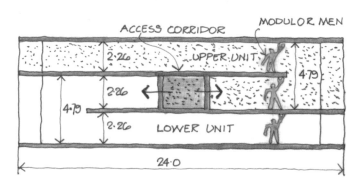

Section through the interlocked machines

The façades included balconies and brises-soleil. What are brises-soleil? After his numerous problems with sun entering south-facing windows, towards the end of the 1930s

---

[57] How sound travels between occupied spaces is one of the least understood aspects of building design. There are two types of noise, airborne noise – next door's television – and structure-borne noise – your neighbour drilling into a wall. Airborne noise transmission is reduced by thick walls and double-glazing. Structure-borne noise transmission is only reduced by having independent structures mounted on special pads – this is notoriously difficult to achieve in practice. How the, hardly cheap, lead lining was to work is unclear.

[58] In 2008 a hotel was built where the rooms, based on modified shipping containers, were 'slid' into a steel frame. This is the first time it has been tried and it remains to be seen if it is a success. *New Civil Engineer*, 13 March 2008, p11.

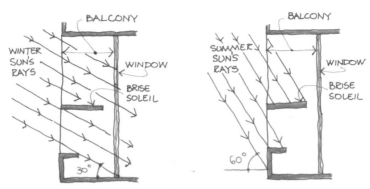

The brise-soleil in action

Le Corbusier invented the sunshade – and to show that he had, he gave it a special name – the brise-soleil – another word of Corbuspeak. At the Unité these brises-soleil were positioned 2.26 m above the balcony floor, and stopped the entry of the sun's rays when the sun was high in the sky, whilst permitting their entry when the sun was low.

But at the Unité the main elevations face east and west, so for much of the morning and afternoon the hot Mediterranean sun enters the machines – rendering the brises-soleil effectively useless. Using sun charts, all this could easily been calculated before construction. In the event, residents added good old-fashioned blinds to make up for the defects of the brises-soleil.

As well as being useless, the dirt-attracting top was inaccessible for cleaning, which was just as well as, with no protection, there was a reasonable chance you'd plunge to your death. But even if they were of limited practical use they did add 'interest' to the building's elevations, which were enhanced by having the walls of the balconies painted in a variety of colours.

So, at Unité, the façade libre became an assemblage of balcony upstands, cross-walls and brise-soleil, allowing the light to create endlessly changing, fascinating patterns. Alternatively it could be seen as a huge area of dreary bits of stained concrete dotted, incomprehensibly, with splodges of crude colour. Unlike the white cubes, now concrete was on show everywhere. Actually, Le Corbusier had invented a new type of concrete for this project; it was called béton brut – more words of Corbuspeak to be added to the international architectural vocabulary.

Of course it wasn't an invention at all,

Brise-soleil back-up

The interesting façade

107

it was just ordinary concrete poured into badly-made timber formwork.[59] As the surface of the hardened concrete follows the profile of the formwork, if badly-made formwork is used, then the resulting surface will be rough in a random way – this was what Le Corbusier wanted. And there was a toit jardin, but due to the 17-storey wheel-barrowing problem, there were only a few sad plants but loads of exciting of béton brut.

The exciting toit jardin of béton brut

To alleviate the occupants' need to leave the building to shop, there were shopping streets on levels 7 and 8. Thus, if you lived on level 16, you'd pop to the shops by walking up to 70m along a low, windowless corridor and then descend 8 or 9 levels, reversing the process with your purchases.[60] And even going into a unit, quite a tortuous route might be needed. In an 'up-going' unit you entered via the kitchen, went through the dining area, and then into the double-height living area. But, in a 'down-going' unit, you again entered via the kitchen to arrive in the dining area. But to get to the double-height living area, you had to descend the stairs, go through a service area then double back to the living area.[61]

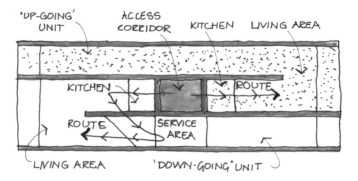

Living room routes

And not only were the routes tortuous, several spaces had no natural light at all, such as the bathrooms and some of the children's bedrooms. It's hard to imagine that building regulations would allow this, and anyway it was against Le Corbusier's own 'rules'.

---

[59] Formwork is the technical name for the moulds that are made to hold wet freshly-made concrete until it hardens.

[60] It was quite likely you would return empty-handed, as most of the shops soon closed, or never opened. This was for the simple reason that there weren't enough people living in the building to economically support the shops – that the population needed to support any economic activity is a basic commercial calculation.

[61] Few people like their guests or even friends or relations entering their home through the kitchen.

Never slow to tell people what to do, he gave orders for what one should demand of a house[62] such as:

Demand a bathroom looking south, one of the largest rooms in the house.

Demand one really large living room.

And he exhorted:

Never undress in your bedroom.

and:

Teach your children that a house is only habitable when it is full of light and air ...

With some of the children of 4 million homeless people being put to bed in small, windowless cells, buried deep in their tunnel-like flats, this could prove a little difficult.

But in 1952 the building was complete and in 1953, C.I.A.M held a party on the roof of the Unité, attended by, among scores of admirers, Walter Gropius, who ordered, 'Any architect who does not find this building beautiful had better lay down his pencil'.[63] Orders from Walter were not lightly disobeyed, and anyway the architects and architectural writers loved it, or so they wrote:

... the ultimate revelation of architectural truth. Blake, 1960[1], p120.

Time has proved the visionary quality of Le Corbusier's work .... Cantacunzino, 1966, p 90.

... is a treasure. Knobel, 1985, p48.

Many design problems solved, including those of the dwelling unit. Sharp, 1972, p192.

... impressive modelling of the façade. Gössel, 2005, p263.

... the building for which a generation of architects waited. Banham, 1962, p110.

...a breathtakingly heroic monument .... Frampton, 2001, p164.

and on and on, but just a minute, what else are they writing?

---

[62] See *The Manual of the Dwelling*, in Le Corbusier, 1927, p114–115.

[63] Blake, 1960[1], p124. Walter Gropius, better known for his teaching than his buildings, was, along with Mies van der Rohe and Le Corbusier, one of the big three of modern architecture.

just a crooked machine and a poor solution. Tzonis, 2001, p160.

... the sense of isolation which the uniqueness of the Unité must give its occupants is precisely the opposite of what was intended. Cantacunzino, 1966, p91.

... Corbusier betrayed the human contents to produce a monumental aesthetic effect. Mumford, 1963, p81.[64]

... has significant problems for a model for housing ... the corridors are depressingly dark and gloomy .... Knobel, 1985, p48.

... the tawdriness of the consequences became a byword for the failure of modern architecture. Reyner Banham quoted in Curtis, 1986, p173.

... attuned to the needs of twentieth century living in plan, section, elevation, or general spatial organization, the Unité is a farce. Blake, 1977, p33.

... in reality the Unité was expensive, uncomfortable and out of tune with the needs of the working class families it was meant for. Hellman, 1986, p147.

... the system of corridors meant leaving your unit was to enter 'enemy territory, creating insecurity and fear'. Gössel, 2005, p263.

So it was a total disaster then? What about all these apparent problems? Oh don't worry because these are just:

The usual roster of criticisms ..., according to Curtis, 1986, p174.

and anyway Charles Jencks (1973[1], p24) thinks that:

... hostile critics of the Unité can be answered because its multivalent form allows opposite interpretations and thus diffuses univalent criticism.

Home sweet home in enemy territory

So if people are unhappy about going down a dark corridor to their flat, or their child doesn't like waking up in a window-less cell, they can cheer themselves up with the thought that they live in a multivalent form. If they can't then they should live somewhere else, because the Unité was for a rather special sort of person.

---

[64] In this book Mumford devotes a whole chapter, called 'The Marseille Folly', to an attack on the Unité.

Le Corbusier finds the perfect tenants

The perfect tenant is immortalised

To make sure these special tenants knew that they were at the right building, Le Corbusier helpfully had their effigy cast into concrete at the base of the building.

Unsurprisingly, the French government decided that they wouldn't build the 2,499 more Unités they needed to house the homeless. But surprisingly, four more modified versions did get built, three in France and one in Berlin.

When the Unité was completed in 1952 Le Corbuiser had reached the usual retirement age of 65, and having crowned his brilliant career with the equally brilliant Unité, one might have thought he would rest on his laurels, and enjoy the worldwide adoration he was, at last, receiving from the international architectural community. But no, there was more to do.

In 1950, he had been asked if he would design a chapel at Ronchamp, to replace the one destroyed in the war. Le Corbusier was not religious, nor was he particularly keen on the Catholic Church, but a job's a job. The official name was the Chapel of Notre-Dame-du-Haut, but it is universally known as Ronchamp. In 1955, when Le Corbusier's design was revealed to the architectural community there was a communal gasp. What had happened? Had the master gone mad, or was he leading them to a new and previously unknown development of the Modern Movement?

From the outside the building looked as though it was from a tale of fantasy or from a film by Murnau.[65] The inside was like a grotto,[66] light filtering in through small windows glazed with coloured glass – hardly rational and functional! Even more

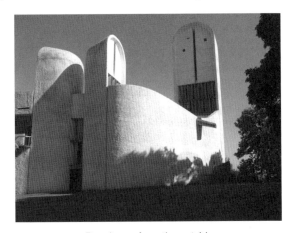

Ronchamp from the outside

[65] FW Murnau (1889–1931) was a director of expressionist silent films. To create a sense of psychological disorder, the sets would have buildings with disturbing non-rectangular geometry.

[66] Maguire, 1965, p48.

strangely the roof did not seem to be joined to the walls of the building, but somehow to hover just above them.

There were so many puzzles. For a start, what was a rationalist, logical, functional, modern architect doing designing a chapel? How could a chapel function like a machine? Was it a worshipping machine or what? And it got worse.

What had happened to all the rules that the master had set out? Where were the five points of architecture? Nothing was rectangular; the walls weren't vertical; it was all too much. Everyone was confused, so the master explained: '... a space cannot be described in words' you have to 'observe the play of the shadows, learn the game ...' as the building was in 'conformity with the horizons ... the acoustic response – acoustics in the realm of forms'. So it was all pretty clear really. Of course it wasn't: his explanations made no sense at all.

Ronchamp from the inside

So what was going on – crisis in rationality or irrationality – how could these be connected? According to Charles Jencks,[67] the orthogonal geometry was still there, it's just that 'the secondary amoebic curves had finally broken through'. Others thought that he'd gone beyond the rational to a new rationality – whatever that could mean. But all this supposes that the work of Le Corbusier was based on any rationality in the first place, which it wasn't. It's just that he implied that it was: quite a different matter.

At Ronchamp some of the construction was also of the beyond-the-rational type. For instance, the very heavy looking roof was made of two skins of concrete, 60 mm thick, held 2 m apart by a series of thin concrete webs, and was supported, only very occasionally, on small concrete posts. Some of the walls, up to 3 m thick, had an inner core of very thin concrete elements, with the outer skins constructed of sprayed concrete.[68]

As a church, Ronchamp didn't work very well. According to one writer, 'as a place for liturgy any barn would be better' and for the development of church building it was 'a blind alley'.[69] But what it did do was to allow Modern Movement architects to now pursue any whimsy, without even having to pay lip service to 'functionality' – which many of them proceeded to do with a vengeance.

In 1950, Le Corbusier finally got the chance he'd been waiting for nearly all of his professional life – to design a city. Due to the partition of India in 1947 the Indian state of the Punjab no longer had a capital, as Lahore was now in Pakistan. It was decided that a new capital was to be built at Chandigarh. The first plan was done by Albert Mayer (1897–1981), an American planner, who was keen on the garden city and liked picturesque roads and green spaces. The buildings were to be designed by Matthew Nowicki

[67] Jencks, 1973[1], p153.

[68] Perhaps to show that sprayed concrete was a good method of making walls and that he was right at Quartier Frugès, and everyone else was wrong.

[69] Maguire, 1965, p48 & 51.

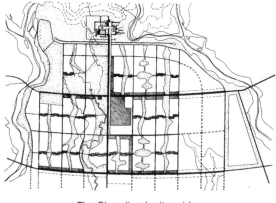

The Chandigarh city grid

(1910–1950), but he was killed in a plane crash before he could start. After a bit of to-ing and fro-ing, Le Corbusier agreed to be the architectural consultant for the city and to be the exclusive designer of the new parliament buildings. But he wasn't going miss the opportunity of designing a city, so he managed to sideline Mayer and re-plan the city on a grid.

With the buildings, Le Corbusier seemed to be battling with his 'rationality' and his 'irrationality'. Most of the buildings he designed fitted into a basic rectangular pattern, but his irrationality kept appearing as bits of weird béton brut.

Amoebic curves reappear in India

In spite of Le Corbusier filling his notebooks with sketches of Indian life and artefacts, he was unable (or more likely couldn't be bothered) to understand much about the Indian way of life. But Le Corbusier was never interested in how anyone wanted to live or work, he was only interested in how he thought they should.

The houses, for which he was not the architect just the provider of guidelines, were a total failure. Their occupants changed the bedrooms into sitting rooms, dining rooms into bedrooms, papered over windows for privacy, and cooked on the floor not the worktops. The shopping areas were planned to provide a range of shops which did not suit the Indian way of shopping, which was essentially a bargaining process which required a number of similar shops in the same area, exactly the opposite to what was provided. Parks were unused and the road system was too wide;[70] in other words the usual patterns of failure or, as Professor Tzonis

---

[70] When built that is. Now of course, with the car, they are too narrow.

sums up Chandigarh, 'Functionally, neither the city nor the buildings were a success.'[71, 72]

From early in his career with the Quartier Frugès fiasco, through almost every project up to his Indian swansong, Le Corbusier's built projects repeatedly exhibited a whole gamut of failures. Budget overruns were endemic, environmental problems normal, maintenance often problematic, and quite frequently the end users were unhappy.

Almost nothing he did was original: white cube houses had been built before; reinforced concrete construction was well established; his five points of architecture were present in the early work of Auguste Perret. His cruciform skyscrapers had already been proposed by Perret and Sullivan. Frank Lloyd Wright, amongst others, had already used concrete as a visual material, and there were abundant schemes for utopian cities.

Le Corbusier's approach to building design was dishonest and uncaring. He promoted the idea that he was pursuing research into how buildings could be functional – functioning as machines. But he did no real research, nor did he have an understanding of any type of machine technology. Nor was he interested in the user's needs or wishes. So, at Quartier Frugès the occupants altered what they could, Pierre Savoye couldn't bear his weekend house, the occupants of the Pavillion Suisse were cooked in the summer, his own wife was driven crazy with light, at the Unité some children slept in windowless cells, Ronchamp was no good as a church and the occupants of the Chandigahr houses papered over the windows.

Even today, for the international architectural community, Le Corbusier remains a reference, thus they ape his myopia. This is in spite of the fact that books which are written to explain his greatness are peppered with endless examples of the shortcomings of his buildings.[73] As Philip Johnson wrote, he was '... an objectionable man ... I would not live in any of his houses.'[74] In 1977 architectural writer Ian Nairn (1930–1983) called Le Corbusier 'The Blind Mechanic' and asked '... how many have been killed by Le Corbusier and his influence?' In a 2008 article a subtitle read: 'He is the inspiration behind a million charmless tower blocks and multi-storey car parks.'[75]

But no one, at least in the architectural community, seems to be able to draw the obvious conclusions – perhaps it would be too damaging.[76] Too damaging to admit that, like modern art, modern architecture is not intended for ordinary people. But unfortunately modern architecture, unlike modern art, can't always be avoided by ordinary people, and perhaps ironically, especially ordinary people who need social housing.

---

[71] Tzonis, 2001, p212.

[72] For a sustained and devastating critique see 'Chandigarh was planned by experts but something has gone wrong', *Smithsonian Magazine*, June 1972, p56–63.

[73] Not to mention his shortcomings as a human being as he was arrogant, dishonest, devious, vindictive, bullying, tactless, selfish, sexist, an opportunist...

[74] Bacon, 2001, p42.

[75] *Sunday Times*, 6 July 2008.

[76] With one rather surprising exception; the German-American architect Peter Blake (1920–2006), who wrote eulogising books in the early 1960s, about Le Corbusier, Mies van der Rohe and others. In 1977, he either came to, or took leave of his senses – depending on your point of view. He wrote a book called *Form Follows Fiasco: Why modern architecture hasn't worked*. In the preface, he writes 'This book is, of course, largely an indictment – of the glaring fallacies advanced by the Modern Movement, and of those who, like myself, swallowed and also promoted them whole'. The architectural community has yet to take heed.

7. Lessons for Everyone

In Australia in the 1950s, opera, grand or otherwise, did not have a big following.[1] However, symphonic music was a different matter. The popular Sydney Symphony Orchestra, directed since 1947 by the brilliant Eugene Goossens, could sell out most of their regular concerts. But they had to play in the assembly hall that was part of the Town Hall complex, an unattractive space with poor acoustics. It was Goossens' dream to have a performance space that was dedicated to symphonic music, and so the idea of what became called the Sydney Opera House was born.[2] Goossens managed to plant the idea into the head of a very different man, Joe Cahill. Unlike the urbane Goossens, Cahill came from a poor background; starting work at 15 he had educated himself at night school and, via trade unions activism, had became an experienced and effective Labour politician. By 1952, at the age of 61, he had become the Prime Minister of New South Wales. Without Cahill's immense political ability the project would never have been built but, like Goossens, he did not live to see it completed, dying in October 1959.

The dreamers Goossens and Cahill

The story of the design and construction has been told many times in books and articles from various points of view,[3] so what's the point in going over it again? Well, because most accounts, though dwelling to more or less extent on the problems, always have a bottom line of '... in spite of everything the building is wonderful/beautiful/marvellous etc...' that is to say that all the effort was worthwhile, which is a very moot point.

But Sydney Opera House was not just a project that encountered problems,[4] it was much more than that, because it became a paradigm not only for many more late twentieth

---

[1] Two of the greatest opera singers were Australian, Nellie Melba and Joan Sutherland, but both spent almost their entire singing careers in Europe and America. Joan Sutherland was later reported to have remarked that the Sydney Opera House was '... too monumental on the outside and not sufficiently functional in the inside.' Yeomans, 1968, p122.

[2] For Goossens the dream ended prematurely when, on returning to Sydney on 9 March 1957 from Europe, he was met by detectives. His baggage on examination was found to contain pornographic material. He was fined and he resigned his positions and left Australia never to return. He died in 1962 before the project was completed. A statue of him now stands in the foyer of the Sydney Opera House!

[3] They are informative like Yeomans (1968), or Murray (2004), uncritical like Mikami (2001), or just vacuous like Watson (2006).

[4] Nearly all building projects experience some problems for a variety of reasons such as changes of mind, unforeseen conditions or mistakes, but at the Sydney Opera House major mistakes were an inherent part of the competition and of the winning design.

century buildings but also because it showed how an architect could 'force' other professionals to agree to things that were against their experience. This was especially true for structural engineers. but it also showed how engineers could become renowned and successful by overcoming problems that never should have been there in the first place. But worst of all, the building became so famous during its construction process, due to the enormous problems that were encountered, that it put Sydney 'on the map' – it became what is now known as an iconic building.

To build any building three things are needed: a site, a design and the necessary resources – that is the money. To get the Sydney project going a meeting was convened by Cahill, in November 1954, to form a committee to advise on the building of 'an opera house'. From various possible sites Bennelong Point was chosen, this being a small peninsula that juts out into Sydney Harbour. As the site was so prominent, it was quickly agreed that a suitable design could only be found by holding an international architectural competition. As nobody had any idea where the money was to come from, no budget was set.

Already problems were looming due to the site, design choice procedure and the lack of budget. The choice of site was the cause of two problems: it was not really big enough, or perhaps, more accurately, not wide enough, and its prominence encouraged all concerned to think that the design should be in some way 'stunning'.[5]

Architectural competitions have a chequered history and characteristically do not produce sensible workmanlike designs. It is an opportunity for architects, especially unknown ones, to strut their stuff, make notice, show how wonderfully creative they are, and of course they do it all more or less for free.[6] To get a good result the brief for the competition and the requirements need careful thought, because clearly entrants cannot be expected to produce detailed designs, only ideas and strategies.[7] And of course, the lack of a budget meant that the project was already out of control.

The architectural competition, which attracted 233 entries, closed on 3 December 1956. Apart from a series of ancillary spaces, cloakrooms, meeting rooms and so on, the competition design had to have two halls, a large one seating between 3,000 and 3,500 people, and a smaller one for 1,200 people. So far so good but the large hall was given the following uses, in order of priority:

1   Symphony concerts including organ music and soloists
2   Large-scale opera
3   Ballet and dance
4   Choral music
5   Pageants and mass meetings

---

[5] Actually a building already existed on Bennelong Point, it was a disused tram depot in the style of a military fort. Perhaps previous generations had thought the site so amazing that a tram depot had to have this disguise.

[6] Open architectural competitions mean any qualified architect can enter, whether they have any experience in designing the type of building required or not. This is a bit like asking an aeronautical engineer to design a railway bridge or a brain surgeon to undertake a liver transplant; obviously the aeronautical engineer and the brain surgeon have the basic skills for railway bridge design and liver transplants but not the experience.

[7] As Peter Murray notes 'the competition system ... runs the risk of selecting a scheme that the client does not really want, an architect who can design but cannot build and a building that does not work.' Murray, 2004, p xvii. Wise words rarely heeded.

Uses were also given for the smaller hall. The brief asked for 'a sound basic scheme', and warned that 'extravagance cannot be entertained'. But it was the presence of the first two items on the list that caused the absolutely fundamental mistake, as any experienced architect should have noticed. Why was this such mistake? To see why, some understanding of the staging of opera and symphonic music is required.

All buildings for the presentation of live performances can simplistically be thought of as having three parts:

A   Public entrance – could be just a door and a box office up to grand foyers, restaurants, bars...

B   Audience space – where the public sit or stand to witness the spectacle.

C   Performer's space – this includes the actual performing area plus ancillary spaces, changing rooms, warm-up areas...

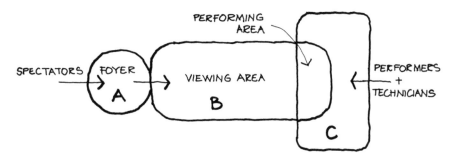

Schema for live performances

This conceptual schema applies equally to a football stadium as it does to a theatre, but of course the details of parts A, B and C are very different in each instance – and this is the point. For grand opera and symphony concerts parts B and C are very different, in fact, virtually incompatible if the highest standards are required for each type of presentation. To understand why, the requirements for spaces B and C need to be briefly considered.

Symphony concerts first: here the public come primarily to listen rather than to watch; after all the visual aspect is nearly always the same: a more-or-less standard orchestra wearing the same formal clothes sit on chairs playing their instruments whilst reading music; the only visual 'entertainment' is the behaviour of the conductor. After the audience is seated, the musicians file onto the stage from each side to take their places, followed by the dramatic entrance of the conductor. The orchestra is placed on a low platform in basically the same space as the audience. The audience want to hear the music perfectly and it is far less important for them to have a good view of the players.

Grand opera is very different, this is an acted drama where the actors do not speak their lines but sing them to musical accompaniment. Therefore the audience need to see and hear the singers and hear, but not see, the orchestra – this requires a large and sloping orchestra pit partially under the stage. The singers as well as singing are also actors, with make-up, costumes and stage movement. The performance area is a stage which can be closed from public view by curtains.

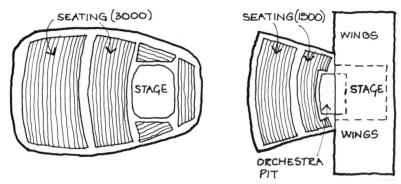

Plans of a concert hall (L) and an opera house (R)

On the stage are not only the singers but also props, that may be huge, and the back of the stage is closed off with a painted backdrop. In between acts, the singers and the stage change their appearances via costume and set changes. Not only does the stage need extensive wing space for singers waiting to come on, but also to store large props that have to be wheeled on and off. Furthermore, the huge backcloths, and sometimes other props, are changed by hoisting them vertically into a huge storage space above the stage called a flytower.[8]

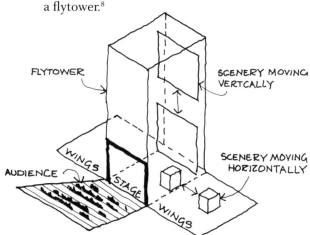

The scenery changing system for grand opera

It is easily seen that the parts B and C needed for opera and symphonic concerts are radically different, but there is one further incompatibility and that is the different acoustics needed. As a technical subject acoustics is complex, in fact like structures, often giving rise to horrendously difficult mathematics, apart from which the quality of the sound in a performance space is, rather like wine, for connoisseurs. But there is a basic measurement that needs to be right. It is measured in seconds and is called the reverberation time. This is the time required for a 'standard sound' to 'die away'. The basic considerations that affect this are the volume of the space and how absorbent the surfaces are.

A space with hard surfaces, like concrete or plaster, will sound echoey, whereas a space with heavy cloth wall hangings and an 'acoustic' ceiling will sound deadened.[9] Symphonic music, mainly written in the nineteenth century, is heavily dependent for its sound on a huge string section. This means that the sounds tend to be prolonged and thus need to

---

[8] Because of the need for a flytower, theatres and opera houses often have the overall shape of a boot.

[9] It is because of the reverberation time being wrong that in some restaurants, for instance, it is so noisy that you can't hear yourself speak.

dwell in the air for the best effect, whereas the words of operatic arias are shorter and have to die away sooner, or the words run together, becoming unintelligible.[10] It has been found that a concert hall needs a reverberation time of about 2 seconds whereas an opera house needs one closer to 1¼ seconds. Not a big difference one might think, but in practice it's very hard to vary the time for a particular space whilst maintaining its sound quality.

This opera/symphonic music incompatibility would have been a major problem with any design and it is amazing that no one pulled the plug at the time;[11] it was eventually resolved in a brutal fashion as will be seen. However with the design that was chosen there was an abundance of other problems. But first the competition itself, or rather the judges; there were five, all architects, by far the best known being Eero Saarinen (1910–1961), who was, according to much hearsay evidence, the strongest supporter of the design that was chosen as the winner. To understand the significance of Saarinen's presence some knowledge is needed of his work and how concrete shell roofs behave.

Concrete shell roofs are made from a very thin curved piece of concrete; typically a shell roof 3 inches thick can span up to 80 ft. Pioneered in the 1920s, if used properly this type of roof could be very economical.[12] To understand the most important aspect of shell behaviour one only has to blow up a party balloon and observe its, usually more-or-less spherical, shape, then fill the balloon with water and look again – the shape will be quite different. This is because the thin balloon material can only resist tension forces, so the balloon takes up the most comfortable shape for the different loads of air pressure or water pressure. Unlike a piece of modelling clay, which can take almost any shape, the balloon cannot be inflated into a desired shape – it will only take up the comfortable one. Similarly, for a concrete shell roof to be effective or economical, it has to be given a comfortable shape for its loads which, ideally, for concrete, keeps the whole shell in compression.

At the time of the competition, most of the concrete shell roofs that had been built were for industrial use and were not widely known in architectural circles. However, in the early 1950s, this changed due to the work of an amazing man called Félix Candela (1910–1997). Having trained as an architect in Spain in the 1930s he went to Mexico as a political refugee. First interested in

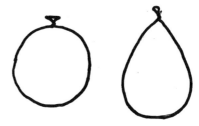

Balloon under air pressure (L) and water pressure (R)

---

[10] A string section, with continuous bowing, can produce a single sound for as long as the musicians can be bothered to bow, whereas a singer, even with the prodigious capacity of one trained for opera, can only hold a note for so long.

[11] One of the acoustic consultants for the project was Professor Cremer from Berlin, who described it 'as a mistake in the original programme ...' this was '... after six years work' and unsurprisingly '... was a major blow ...'. Murray, 2004, p120–121. It is unbelievable that no one had the courage to stop the project at an early stage before this basic error was sorted out.

[12] These roofs were pioneered by the brilliant German engineers Franz Dischinger (1887–1953) and Ulrich Finsterwalder (1897–1987). Their work, both theoretical and practical, enabled their construction company Dywidag, to build more than 32 million sq. ft of these roofs between 1925 and 1967, all built as economical solutions.

shell roofs as a student,[13] by the 1950s he was able to form a construction company which allowed him to start fulfilling his dream of being a shell builder, which he became par excellence. His shells, whilst still obeying the need to be economical solutions, were quite different in appearance from those previously built, and soon came to the notice of the architectural press.

Although an architect by training, Candela had taught himself a lot about the mathematics that mimic shell roof behaviour so, in building his shells, he combined a theoretical knowledge with practical experience; in other words he worked as an engineer. But the Candela shells caused huge problems for both architects and engineers.

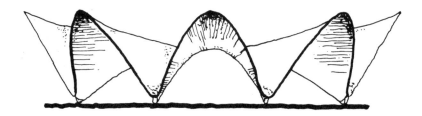

A shell roof for a restaurant by Félix Candela

Architects looking at the shells, without understanding their physical behaviour, thought a shell could be any old shape they wished to draw. For engineers the problem was quite different – few of them could understand the mathematical aspects let alone apply them.[14] However, some architects, Saarinen amongst them, conceived shell roofs that made little engineering sense, but were able to 'persuade' an engineer to make their ill-conceived creations buildable. This invariably meant that the initial architectural creation had to be substantially modified, becoming expensive and difficult to construct in the process. Saarinen's contribution to this silly state of affairs was the roof for the Kresge auditorium at Harvard University. It had a fundamental flaw in understanding.

To see what the problem was, one has to grasp the not very difficult fact that shells, like balloons, do not like sharp interruptions to their shape, loads or means of support. So having filled your party balloon with air or water, no-one should be surprised if when it is placed on a sharpish object, it bursts. But this is conceptually what Saarinen and others wanted to do! So the engineers had to introduce radical modifications to the shells where they came to a point. This destroyed the basic concept.

The fact that roofs like that of the Kresge Auditorium were constructed allows, with hindsight, two very different conclusions. The first is 'that was rather silly so we'd better not try that again', and the second is 'there you are, I told you it could be done'. Unless the

---

[13] By a strange coincidence, Candela was about to leave Spain to work in Germany for the shell pioneers Dischinger and Finsterwalder when the Spanish Civil War broke out, changing his life, as it did for countless others, irrevocably.

[14] The predictive mathematics for shell roofs are horrendously difficult and are only accessible to the few who are gifted and specially trained. This means most engineers were neither equipped intellectually nor by training to design these structures.

Saarinen's shell gets the point

second outcome shows some real benefits[15] the first conclusion is the obvious one. What the second conclusion really means is that it is possible to find, or persuade, an engineer to agree to make the engineering misconception a reality, a bit like getting an engineer to make a square-wheeled bike rideable.

Now for the winning entry of the competition: various stories have circulated about what happened during the secret ruminations of the judging panel, but all revolve around the importance of Saarinen's support for the entry that won. The winner, announced with some drama by Cahill on 29 January 1957, was Jørn Utzon (1918–2008), a 38 year old architect from Denmark. His winning design showed a project covered by a number of huge free-form concrete shell roofs. There was a sort of communal gasp as well as quite a lot of criticism. The gasp, mostly from engineers, was due to the apparent impossibility of designing or constructing the roof shells. How right they were!

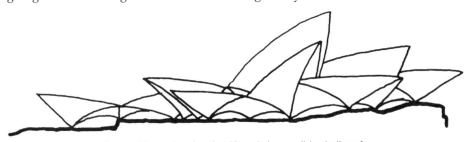

Competition entry showing Utzon's impossible shell roof

The criticism was partially aesthetic ('it looked like a group of copulating terrapins' was one view) and partly moral, in that the sensational forms have no purpose other than demonstrating the audacity of the designer,[16] and partly due to the fact that the winning entry should have been disqualified on various grounds: these included the absence of the required drawings, the lack of the seating accommodation in the main hall, and the fact that the site boundaries had been violated. The lack of seating accommodation was to prove the undoing of the architect if not the project.

But these objections were taken lightly, far too lightly, and there wasn't any real hard-nosed technical assessment of the winning design. It appears that the judging panel were unwilling or unable to do this and nothing more was done about it. It was all to go forward on the basis of 'there you are, I told you it could be done' – hardly a mature or responsible

---

[15] Tangible benefits include saving time and money in design and construction but don't include allowing the architect to parade his ill-conceived structure in the architectural press.

[16] The opinion of the famous architectural historian and critic Lewis Mumford. Mumford, 1963, p159.

A student cartoon of copulating terrapins

attitude when the winning entry presented so many obvious technical difficulties, which were:

1   No one knew how to design or construct the roof structure.
2   There was not adequate space for 3,000 seats in the main hall.[17]
3   There was no solution for the symphony concert/grand opera conundrum.
4   The wing spaces for the main stage were woefully inadequate.
5   Much of the project, especially the roofs, was of free-form geometrical shapes which would be exceedingly costly to build.

A local firm of quantity surveyors attempted to price the Utzon entry. For the shells they took the advice of the 'shell expert' Saarinen, who was able to assure them that the shells would be about 3 inches thick at the crown and 'say' 12 inches thick at the base.[18] The cost estimate arrived at was A£3.6 million; this made it, completely unbelievably, the cheapest entry! Perhaps as it was going to be so cheap all the other obvious problems would come out in the wash. And who was this Danish architect Jørn Utzon? Not much research would have been needed to discover that:

1   He did not run a large architectural practice.
2   By 38 all he had designed were a few small scale housing schemes.
3   He had never run a large project from start to finish.
4   He had no experience in designing concert halls or opera houses.
5   He had no experience of concrete shell roof construction.

And even worse:

6   He had taken no engineering advice about either the shell roof or the acoustic problems or the stage machinery.

But almost from the outset he had an important ally, an engineer called Ove Arup (1895–1988) who became a key figure, perhaps the key figure, in what turned out to be a total fiasco. At the time of the competition Arup headed a quite well-known, middle-sized

---

[17] This was the minimum number required by the Sydney Symphony Orchestra to make their concerts financially viable.

[18] Perhaps inspired by Utzon's shells, Saarinen conceived a shell roof for the TWA terminal in New York. As with the Opera House, engineering reality changed the built project rather dramatically prompting the eminent Italian-American engineer Mario Salvadori (1907–1997) to remark 'How much better they would have been if the architects involved had understood better shell analysis.'

consulting engineering practice in London. Having British citizenship by an accident of birth, he had been brought up in Denmark, being educated in both Denmark and Germany. He returned to Britain as a young engineer, to work for a Danish firm – but he was to all intents and purposes Danish.

Arup did not conform to the average idea of a technically-based engineer, he had studied philosophy at university before engineering, he had a love of classical music – playing music himself – and he believed passionately in total design. Within his engineering practice he had encouraged the creation, to the chagrin of various architects, of a group that combined architectural and engineering design.[19] Furthermore, his senior partner Ronald Jenkins (1907–1975) was one of the leading concrete shell engineers; a man of brilliant intellect as well as unswerving practicality. He, and his talented team, had already designed and built a number of technically outstanding shell roofs.[20] As soon as Utzon won the competition, Arup wrote to him congratulating him and offering his services as an engineer. His motive was Danish nationalism, '... here was a Danish architect about to undertake a large commission on the other side of the world: surely he needed Danish help' as Arup's biographer put it.[21]

The Danish duo, Utzon and Arup,

So now the square-wheeled bike had to be made rideable. The next stage was the production of what became known as the Red Book, which supposedly worked up the scheme in some detail; it was basically an exercise in salesmanship with little practical detail. With respect to the enormous shell roofs, all that was noted was that they were 'quite a problem' and that 'extensive model tests will be required'.[22] The Red Book also listed all the experts who would act as consultants for structures, acoustics, stage machinery and electrical and mechanical services; apart from Arup, who was a Dane in London, all were Danish. It is hard to see what sense this makes for a project to be built on the other side of the world with its own conditions and practices, but like so much about Sydney Opera House everything seemed to be approached with naïve optimism, never worthwhile for expensive capital projects.[23]

Let's look at the stage layout of the main hall and see why it was no good. Because of the

---

[19] This practice within a practice was originally called the Building Group and is now called Arup Associates.

[20] Ronald Jenkins, who was responsible for developing much of the most difficult shell mathematics, has largely been written out of engineering history.

[21] Jones, 2006, p175.

[22] Yeomans, 1968, p51. This is engineer-speak to say 'we don't know how to do it'.

[23] In this context the famous law of Murphy 'If it can go wrong it will' is ever present.

limited width of Bennelong Point, almost all the entries had shown the two halls back to back. This meant the public entered one end or the other and the stage areas were shared. Utzon showed the two halls side by side. This had the advantage that there was only one public entrance, which could have foyer areas with views of Sydney harbour. But it had the enormous disadvantage that even by over-stepping the site boundaries, and thus being theoretically disqualified from the competition, the stage facilities were woefully inadequate. It appears that this did not occur to anyone at the time, not even the theatre consultants, or if it did it came under the heading of 'a challenge to be overcome'.

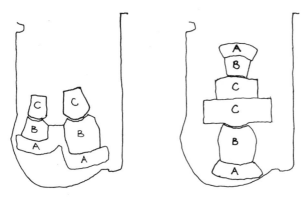

Utzon's side by side layout and the back to back layout

This challenge was overcome by a change of theatre consultant who, with Utzon, devised a complicated never-seen-before scheme, where all the things that previously would occupy the now nearly non-existent wing space would be stored below the stage level. When the scheme was presented it was very publicly rubbished by a number of opera directors, who pointed out that the time needed for scene changes would be unacceptably long. However, these criticisms were ignored, and the stage equipment was designed, fabricated and delivered on time by an efficient Austrian firm, Waagner Biro. Unfortunately, nothing else was on time so the stage machinery was immediately put into store in an air-conditioned warehouse where it remained for years before being finally scrapped.

Cahill knew that for the project to go ahead years could not be spent just designing it. His voters wanted assurance and some results. He achieved this by playing two old political tricks.[24] First of all he announced that the project would only cost A£3.5 million, which 'everyone' knew was artificially low, and secondly he wanted building to commence even if there was no design. This is what happened, resulting, unsurprisingly, in more problems.

Meanwhile Arup's firm was struggling with the square-wheeled bike. The shell shapes drawn by Utzon had no chance of being able to work as serious structures because firstly they had 'fold' lines along the crowns, meaning a smooth flow of forces would be interrupted at the 'kink', and secondly the shells, rather like the troublesome roof of the Kresge auditorium, met the ground at points. If this wasn't bad enough, the shells had no defined mathematical geometry, meaning that applying mathematical theory was impossible,[25]

[24] The practice of setting artificially low budgets for public projects and then starting them prematurely was used on numerous occasions by the 'builder of New York' Robert Moses. See *The Power Broker* by Robert A Caro (1975).

[25] Although at the time, complex mathematical shell theory had been developed, it could only be practically applied to a limited range of geometric shapes such as cylinders or what are known as hyperbolic paraboloids. The fact that a shell shape had a mathematically defined geometry did not automatically mean the shell equations could be solved for that shape.

and the various individual shells were not stable – in other words there was nothing stopping them from just falling over like a row of dominoes.

Before briefly describing the saga of the design and construction of the roof, it is worth asking how Utzon came to decide the project needed such a barmy roof. In the copious written matter about the Sydney Opera House, the roof form is frequently referred to as billowing sails, thus making a reference to the yachts in the harbour, or perhaps the boats Utzon loved sailing, or the famous racing yachts his father had designed.[26] There is no written evidence that Utzon had thought along these banal lines, but he was very aware of how prominent the building would be, with views from all sides including from above. He definitely wanted to avoid the usual boot-shaped theatrical building. The unbuildable shells at least hid the flytowers, if that was what was needed.

The structural engineers set to work on what was to prove a more than mammoth task, of trying to 'solve' the problems created by Utzon's design. What were the first tasks?

1   To approximate, as closely as possible, Utzon's free geometry with a mathematically defined one.
2   To find a structural system – as it was obvious the roofs could not be concrete shells.
3   To find a way of stopping the 'shells' from collapsing like a row of dominos.

The initial solutions to these difficulties was to base the geometry on an elliptic paraboloid,[27] and to make the roof structure from twin concrete skins, one 4 ft above the other, that were held apart by an internal two-way structure. These individual roof structures would be stopped from collapsing like a row of dominos, by linking them together – these linking structures were called louvre walls. In the end, none of these ideas were used. But that's jumping ahead, and anyway even this 'solution' did not provide any easy answers.

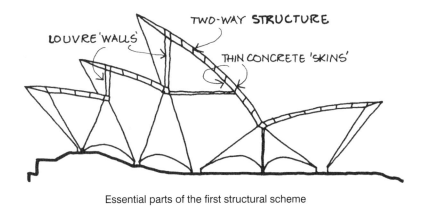

Essential parts of the first structural scheme

---

[26] Utzon's father was a renowned naval architect and had several successful racing designs to his name.

[27] This technical name is for a surface that if cut horizontally is an ellipse and if cut vertically is a parabola, rather like one half of a rather smooth rugby ball.

Although the existence of a mathematical shape meant that the position in space of every, or any, point of the structure could be calculated, without the aid of today's desktop computers or even electronic calculators, this was painstakingly laborious. The fact that the double shell structure would probably 'work' did not mean that available predictive calculation procedures could be readily applied.[28] And lastly, joining the shell via the louvre walls complicated the structural system and violated Utzon's 'vision'.

The Ove Arup brains, Møllman and Jenkins

One has to question why the engineers chose such a structure. Was it because that's what they thought Utzon wanted? Was it hoped that this would give him the same effect as the thin concrete shells that he couldn't have? What they knew was that the outside of the roof was to be covered with off-white tiles (which were to cause their own problems). The inside of the roof was to be, according to a conversation between Utzon and an assistant, 'smooth like the inside of an eggshell'.[29] But as much of the inside of the roof was hidden from view by various ceilings, it's hard to see why what it looked like was so important. All that was required was a structure that would support the various ceilings and provide some sort of backing for the roof tiles; most sensibly this would have been a steel structure which would be amenable to available calculation procedures. But the engineers laboured on with their complicated double shell structure.

Meanwhile, Utzon was busying himself with trying to solve the symphonic music/opera house conundrum. He had no acoustical expertise and was being given conflicting advice by his various expert consultants, and furthermore he couldn't even get the required number of seats into his design for the main hall! Time passed without really tangible results from either the engineers or the architect. And they were working more or less independently.

The engineers had started work on the mathematically defined scheme in January 1958. Their work involved engineers in hundreds of manhours of calculations.[30] It included sending engineers to Southampton University where, for nine months, they worked on model tests and pioneering efforts to use a mainframe computer. Even with all this effort the model tests were showing worrying divergences from calculated values. By June 1961 a feasible roof scheme had been achieved but Utzon then decided he didn't like it; he felt that the 'hidden' structure was not 'honest',[31] whereas in fact the top and bottom

---

[28] It is usual, and of course sensible, to propose structures that can be calculated by available procedures, unless there are overwhelming reasons for not doing so.

[29] Mikami, 2001, p58.

[30] The London office of Ove Arup worked in total for about 300,000 hours on the project – equivalent to about 170 man-years.

[31] On 12 July 1965 Utzon wrote a letter to the Minister of Public Works which included the following: 'After a long period, I succeeded in convincing the Engineers that the first scheme was absolutely hopeless, and that together we had not been able to achieve a(n) honest structure ...'. Jones, 2006, p222.

concrete skins were of limited structural value with the disadvantage of adding unnecessary weight.

Ronald Jenkins, undoubtedly one of the greatest structural engineers of the twentieth century, decided to leave the project and his team, tired and psychologically 'down' with the rejection of their work, was disbanded.[32] Another crisis – what to do? One needs to remember that by now four and a half years had elapsed since the announcement of the winner of the competition, and one has to ask what had happened to the competition requirements for a 'sound basic scheme' and that 'extravagance cannot be entertained'. They had been and were continuously ignored.

Arup now put the 37 year old Jack Zunz in charge of the project. It was decided to see if the 'dishonest' scheme could be modified to make it... what? Perhaps something more honest? This scheme was re-configured so that the roof structure, instead of being linked by the louvre walls, would become three independent structures. However, the basic concept of an internal structure, now changed to a steel spaceframe, with top and bottom concrete skins was maintained.

At the same time bets were hedged by developing a new concrete solution. This was to turn each shell into the form of a concrete pointed arch made from a series of ribs that fanned out.[33] To avoid the massive amounts of supporting scaffolding and shuttering that would be needed to support the wet concrete, it was decided to make these arches from precast concrete.[34] In August 1961, Utzon was presented with the two structural schemes. He rejected the modified Jenkin's scheme as it was still 'dishonest'.

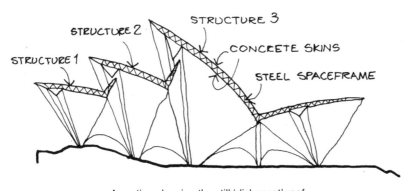

A section showing the still 'dishonest' roof

It was pointed out to Utzon that the ribbed scheme would probably be more expensive and take longer to build than the 'dishonest' scheme, but that's the one he wanted, and he stated, 'I don't care what it costs, I don't care what scandal it causes, I don't care how long it takes, but that's what I want'.[35] Hardly a responsible attitude towards any client let

---

[32] Hugo Møllman was so incensed that he left Arup's and returned to Denmark.

[33] It's amusing to note that a ribbed underside was exactly what Utzon did not want, well initially.

[34] The term 'precast concrete' refers to a technique where pieces of concrete are made away from their final placement. They are then joined together to make the whole structure. Joining the pieces together is often easier said than done.

[35] Murray, 2004, p31.

alone a public one.[36] Furthermore, the revised cost estimate in September of that year was now standing at A£9.3 million, over two and half times the original one, and, what's more, work had been proceeding on site for over two and a half years.

As these radical changes were being made to the roof structure and to the engineering design team, another radical change to the roof was looming. It had always been Utzon's intention to cover the roof with tiles; clearly, no existing tile would do, so he persuaded a Swedish tile manufacture to undertake tests until they produced one he could accept. Laying these tiles on huge double-curved roofs, where the actual curvature was constantly changing, was never going to be easy.

In October 1961, it was realised that if all the individual roof shapes could be made from the same sphere, then many geometric difficulties would be reduced; so that was what was decided. Because of this the roof changed shape and the overall heights increased, the highest point soaring to 180 ft above the concourse level and now being higher than necessary to hide the flytower. The roof was back on track, or perhaps finally on track. By late 1963, the engineers had designed the new structure and prepared all the construction drawings. The cost estimate had risen once again to nearly A£15 million, over four times the original. By now, the dreamers Goossens and Cahill were both dead.

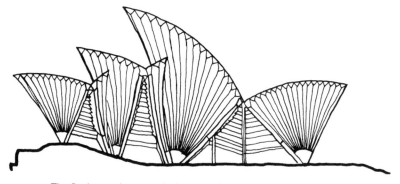

The final, massive, massively expensive, but at least honest roof

Now the roof construction was plain sailing. Not quite; there was the small matter of the supporting structures, columns and foundations – these had already been built to support the lighter double shell structure – now they weren't strong enough to support the massive arch structure.[37] To make them bigger was not easy or cheap but it had to be done: more expense, more delay.

And Utzon had still not come up with a solution to the now ongoing nightmare of the symphony concert/grand opera problem. Try as he might, he just couldn't get the seats in, and trying to provide the conflicting acoustic and staging requirements just introduced

---

[36] At one point Utzon stated that '... the acoustics didn't matter, and the number of seats didn't matter, provided the audiences were overcome by the beauty.'

[37] It is normal to design structures 'top down', but with the insistence that construction should commence before the roof had been finalised, the engineers had to size the supporting structures on their conservative best guess, that is to try and cater for any reasonable eventuality. As it happened they weren't conservative enough, never imagining that the final roof design would be so massively heavy.

more and more complications. For concerts, the opera orchestra pit would be shut by a moving floor allowing more seats; there were also to be seats behind the orchestra. The main hall would have a specially shaped acoustic ceiling but what shape would work for both symphonies and operas? No one knew.

So far, all the construction drawings had been supplied by the engineers; these were in two packages called Stage 1 and Stage 2. But the third package called Stage 3, that was to show all the internal work, was to be supplied by Utzon, and this he couldn't do because of his insoluble problems – but he kept assuring everyone that it was nearly ready, without actually showing work in progress. Nearly three more years had passed, the roof was under construction and work on the tiling system had begun.[38]

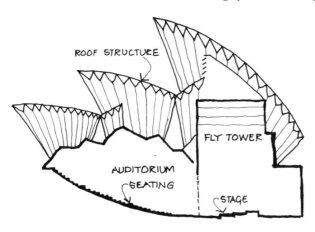

Utzon shows how the major hall should be

By now, it was 1965, the political landscape had changed, and the Labour Party had been replaced, on 1 May, by the Liberal Country Party. The new minister for Public Works was the tough, no-nonsense Davis Hughes (1910–2003), and he needed to get the Sydney Opera House finished with as little extra cost as possible – by July 1965 the estimate stood at A£24.7 million, seven times the original cost. And he needed Utzon's Stage 3 drawings to allow an accurate cost estimate to be made, but Utzon wouldn't produce them. Things were getting out of control; at a meeting in February 1966, the Australian Broadcasting Corporation's acoustic engineer pointed out that:

1   There were not enough seats in the Main Hall for concerts by the Sydney Symphony Orchestra to be financially viable.
2   The volume was too small to achieve the required reverberation time.
3   The rehearsal room was too small.
4   It was unclear how the penetration of harbour noises – it was right beside a ferry terminal – would be prevented.

By that time Utzon was in dispute about a claim for some extra fees that Hughes was unwilling to authorise. At a meeting between Utzon and Hughes, in February 1966, Utzon threatened to resign because Hughes was unable to say the disputed fees would be paid; Hughes considered it an inappropriate response and the meeting ended with Utzon

---

[38] Needless to say the roof tiling presented massive problems. The tiles were fixed to large concrete chevron-shaped panels in a factory. In spite of the spherical 'simplification', there were many different panel types (some weighing 4 tons). These were all to be fixed to bolts that were already in the roof structure, but they were all in the wrong place... Later, after some of the tiles began to fall off, in 1998–1999 many of the tiles were replaced.

walking out. That afternoon Hughes received a letter from Utzon saying due to the non-payment of the fees '… this forces me to leave the job.'[39] Subsequent events are somewhat confused. Hughes considered it a letter of resignation, whereas Utzon later claimed that it was not his intention to resign. Maybe Utzon thought Hughes would ask him back whereas after a bit of to-ing and fro-ing he accepted Utzon's 'resignation'.

There was a huge fuss, with street demonstrations demanding Utzon's reinstatement as well as worldwide outrage from the international architectural community, but by then, for a variety of detailed reasons, Utzon was not strongly supported by anyone on the project. No other consultant offered to resign in protest.[40] And in spite of some half-hearted attempts, Utzon did not return to the project, leaving Australia in April 1966, never to return. Hughes was vilified in the press as an ignorant philistine who had forced the resignation of an architectural genius.[41]

The man who undid Utzon   The man who sorted it out

But the project had to continue, so a new team was assembled under the leadership of the Australian architect Peter Hall; he was 34 at the time. He accepted the role with understandable trepidation and phoned Utzon. Utzon told him he would only return when Hall's team had failed and he would remove anything they had designed.

No doubt Hall and his team thought that their task would 'merely' be getting Utzon's stage 3 drawings up to scratch and ensure it was all built as drawn. It's hard to imagine their surprise when, on going to get the drawings from Utzon's Australian office, they found the cupboard was effectively bare. Most of whatever drawings there had been, and no one outside Utzon's employ had ever seen them, were missing.[42] Hall and his team only inherited 131 drawings, none of which could be used for any construction.[43] Yet another grand crisis, now what to do?

---

[39] Yeomans, 1968, p148.

[40] This caused a massive rift between Utzon and one of his strongest supporters Ove Arup, whose firm had in truth carried out the bulk of the design work as well as carrying far more responsibility than normal. On 11 May 1966 Utzon wrote to Arup and included in his letter were phrases like: 'I see no point in meeting or talking to you', and 'How can a consulting structural engineer dare to encroach on the architect's work in such a fantastic damaging way?' Jones, 2006, p232. Arup and Utzon met once again, in 1978, but the rift was never healed.

[41] It seems quite valid to take a cynical view of Utzon's 'forced' resignation. It is obvious he could not design out the problems of the main hall, which is why he never produced the drawings, preliminary or otherwise. In being 'forced' to resign he was actually in a win-win situation. If things subsequently went well then of course it was his design, if they went badly well of course they should have kept him… Michael Lewis (if anyone could be said to have 'built' the Sydney Opera House it was Lewis) 'had no doubt that Utzon orchestrated his resignation. Lacking any resolution of his difficulties …'. Jones, 2006, p225.

[42] In fact the missing drawings were stored in Utzon's old office. Murray, 2004, p119.

[43] Yet another unbelievable thing about this project was that the architect worked for, and received fees during, ten years and hardly produced a construction drawing, nor handed over all the information on his resignation.

It was decided, better late than never, to review the whole project before proceeding, so that was Hall's first task. Amongst a litany of omissions were:

- no accurate seating layout
- no stormwater drains
- no design of the huge glass walls
- no proper provision for any sort of cabling

and on and on.

First of all Hall, with others, went on a major fact-finding mission to see old and new concert halls and opera houses. Then they worked on their report, innocuously called *Review of Programme*, which was presented in December 1966. It was a shattering condemnation of virtually all that had gone before.

The whole accommodation was to be revised, but the major recommendation was that the main hall was to be for concerts only – at last someone had seen the light. This meant that the stage machinery, that had been in air-conditioned storage for years, was to be scrapped and the 'ugly' flytower was no longer needed, nor was the orchestra pit. After numerous protests, both for the return of Utzon and for keeping

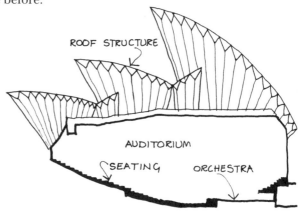

The final design for the concert hall

grand opera in the major hall,[44] the Government of New South Wales, on 21 March 1967, accepted the new proposals – but no completion date was set! By September 1967 the cost estimate was A£42.5 million, over twelve times the original estimate.

It was never going to be easy for Hall; his team was not one as such as they had never worked together before, so clearly this was going to cause problems, which it did. As well as trying to redefine the accommodation he also had another pressing problem – the glass walls. These were huge windows of a complex shape that closed the end of the shells. Until these were completed the building would be open to the elements and no work on the interior could begin. Utzon had already been in conflict with Arup engineers over this for several years without any progress being made; unfortunately under Hall, things actually got worse. In fact relations between the engineers and the architectural 'glass wall team' got so bad that Arup considered resigning, writing in a draft resignation letter that 'The Opera House has become a millstone around our neck'.[45]

---

[44] With the new arrangement opera, but not grand opera could be staged in the minor hall. However, according to music critic Norman Lebrecht, '... it is a very poor opera house.' Personal communication.

[45] Murray, 2004, p131. As it turned out, the Opera House, rather than a millstone, became a sort of golden goose for Ove Arup & Partners – 'Sydney Opera House is undoubtedly the one that stamped Ove Arup & Partners name as one of the best engineering consultants in the world.' *Building*, May 1995, p32.

One of the glass 'walls'

The glass walls were completed in 1971 and the project itself was finally opened by Queen Elizabeth II on 20 October 1973. It was over 16 years since the winner of the competition was announced and the final bill was A£51 million, an amazing fourteen times the original estimate.[46]

This project illustrates a number of important points about the behaviour of an architect, the architect/engineer relationship, and client behaviour. But first a general point should be made which is, as Alan Holgate pointed out, that:

The reader may think that the Sydney Opera House is a very atypical example to illustrate the wider problems of design and Utzon is an atypical architect. On the contrary, while the engineering problems, the personality clashes and the political manoeuvring were certainly on a grand scale, they are quite similar in nature to those which occur on many projects.[47]

The behaviour of the architect, Jørn Utzon, followed the pattern laid down for modern architects by Le Corbusier. This was that the realisation of the artistic creation of the architect was far more important than anything else, certainly more important than to meet the client's needs within an agreed budget and programme. Utzon made this clear with his comment that 'I don't care what it costs, I don't care what scandal it causes, I don't care how long it takes, but that's what I want'. He also followed Corbusier's pattern by assuming he understood technology, especially structures, when he clearly didn't, even when this was obvious. This was the case with the roof. However, this did not prevent him from playing a dominant role in decisions about the final structure, basing his interventions on the empty rhetoric of 'structural honesty'. He also felt that he had to design everything[48] and would produce free-hand sketches for others to 'work-up'.[49] Again like Corbusier, he was an excellent self-publicist and encouraged the view that his decisions were not to be questioned as, by implication, they were in the presence of genius. Perhaps the comparison with Corbusier could even be extended to his adopted role of a Corbusian 'tragic persona'.[50]

---

[46] In 1989, only 16 years later, a (A)£30 million repair programme had to be launched.

[47] Holgate, 1986, p23.

[48] Shortly after Utzon returned to Denmark in 1966, furniture that he had designed for the Sydney Opera House appeared in the shops.

[49] This method of working from sketches, usually done in very soft (6B) pencil, is a form of laziness, because the sketch obscures all the real problems which only appear when the hard work of trying to produce accurate detail drawings is carried out. Usually these are presented to the architectural genius who then scribbles all over them with the 6B pencil. In fact Utzon used to carry with him a special holder for a thick 6B lead.

[50] Corbusier had cast himself in this role due to his persistent attempts to impose his ideas on an unwilling world.

One could feel some sympathy for the client if it had not been so inept; remember that the client had the backing of a technical Public Works Department. However, not only did it present the architect with an impossible brief, but neither the architect nor the technical client spotted the deliberate mistake – in the case of the client, for nearly ten years, and in the case of the architect never. Also it is hard to understand how a public client could allow a project to go completely out of financial control[51] and have to wait 16 years to have the project handed over. The basic reason seems to have been that, until the appearance of Davis Hughes, the client saw itself as the unquestioning handmaiden of architectural genius.

The case of the engineer Ove Arup was perhaps more ambivalent. It seems clear that he personally thought that Utzon was as near an architectural genius as one could get, and as such he should do everything within his power to help or, as he rather poetically put it, 'You may say ... you should have brought Utzon down to earth. I could answer: not while there was a chance of him pulling us up to heaven!'[52] But of course behind this poetry he had teams of technically excellent engineers trying to get everything to work on Earth.

However, the basic lesson that the Sydney Opera House taught the architectural community was that if you were tenacious enough, or perhaps audacious enough, you could get just about anything you wanted built. It was a lesson quickly learned, with numerous similar fiascos taking place worldwide up to the present day. The secondary lesson was that, even if you didn't understand technology, you could find engineers who would bend over further than backwards to help you. Engineers also learnt that this bent-over-further-than-backwards position could bring its own rewards.

The architectural press almost universally praised the Sydney Opera House, 'What is clearer and at the same time more poetical than the Sydney shells'[53] being a typical comment. However, Charles Jencks considered that 'the appropriateness of the shell vaults could be questioned ...'.[54] Engineers rarely voice their opinions about such matters, normally restricting themselves to technical subjects, but a few have commented adversely, saying for instance 'the Sydney Opera House is a perfect example of a glaring discrepancy between the static concept and the architectural expression'.[55] This didn't stop the Institution of Structural Engineers awarding Ove Arup & Partners a special gold medal for their efforts.

What the public in general think is hard to judge, but the people of Sydney are pleased with their architectural equivalent of an elephant dancing ballet. Especially as it is thought to have put their city on the map, a highly questionable, but often imitated reason, for spending vast sums on inappropriate buildings.

Ove Arup received a Gold Medal from the Royal Institute of British Architects and a knighthood, and continued to be involved with his endlessly expanding firm until his death at the age of 92. But for Jørn Utzon life was not so straightforward. He remained one

---

[51] The financing of the Sydney Opera House was a complicated affair, much of the finance coming from a special state lottery, so that in a sense it could be argued that it paid for itself.

[52] *The Structural Engineer*, October 1969, p421.

[53] C Norberg-Schultz & Y Futagawa in *Global Architecture Nº 54*, March 1980, p58.

[54] Jencks, 1973[1], p66–67.

[55] Walther, 1993, p219.

Sydney gets put on the map

Utzon puts the boot in

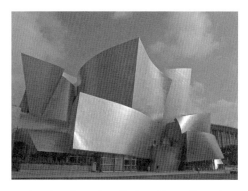

Los Angeles gets a 'Sydney Opera House'

of the most famous architects of the second half of the twentieth century and continued working, but few large projects came his way. One, due to another competition win, was for a theatre in Zurich. This time everything was rectangular, and the flytower was featured prominently, but it remained unbuilt. In 1978 Utzon was awarded the Royal Institute of British Architects' Gold Medal and in 2003, at the age of 84, he received the highest architectural award possible – the Pritzker Prize.

As an epilogue to this fiasco, at least two further concert halls were built which followed the Sydney Opera House scenario: that is they were weirdly shaped, setting everyone endless technical problems and causing spiralling costs and enormous delays. Frank Gehry designed the Walt Disney Concert Hall in Los Angeles[56] and Rem Koolhaas designed the Casa da Música in Oporto.[57]

---

[56] The outside of the building was of polished metal. This caused problems as it both heated up the building and reflected heat to surrounding buildings. Two years after it was finished the shine had to be 'taken off' the metal cladding.

[57] This building, which opened years late and more than five times over budget, also had a host of odd features. For instance, some of the stairs were not easy to use, as the handrails were made from glass plates that were neither easy to see nor to grasp. Another odd feature was that the strangely shaped main door had to be kept in the open position for access. If the weather was cold and/or windy, the door had to be kept shut, thus making the public's main entrance unusable.

All Utzon was doing was carrying on the Corbusian 'tradition' that epitomised the Modern Movement architect's approach – overbudget, non-functional and technically flawed. But clients, particularly public sector ones, haven't learned or can't learn the lesson that Sydney Opera House should teach – but perhaps they are finally beginning to.

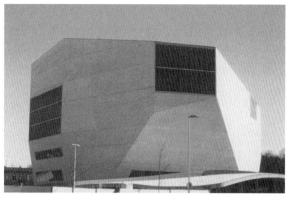

and Oporto also gets a 'Sydney Opera House'

It was thought that a down-at-heel southern English seaside town, Margate, could be regenerated by giving it an iconic building. This time it was not a concert hall but an art gallery that was to put Margate on the map. It seemed as if yet another mini Sydney Opera House saga was to unfold – all the ingredients were there. First of all an architectural competition was held, and in October 2001 the winning design, by Snøhetta and Spence, was unveiled. As the gallery was sited in the sea, it would not only have to resist storm force winds but storm force waves as well.

Another competition entry in troubled waters

Between 2001 and 2006 the client, the Kent County Council, managed to spend £6 million on the development of a design that was supposed to cost about £18 million to build. During that time, although the architect was maintained, the consultant engineer was changed three times, and the cost escalated to a predicted £48 millions. The structure, originally conceived as timber-faced concrete was changed to structural steel. In the final design this was to be clad, to produce the submarine conning tower shape, with one-and-a-half inch thick steel plate!

With the endless cost escalations, re-designs and doubt about further costs, the client sensibly, but rather belatedly, stopped the project before any construction had begun. So perhaps the lesson is finally being learned, but in this instance at a cost of six million quid![58]

---

[58] *New Civil Engineer*, 23 February 2006, p16–17.

8. Bucky and the Comic Book Heroes

Richard Buckminster Fuller (1895–1983), better known in the architectural ghetto as Bucky,[1] was perhaps as influential, for the Modern Movement, as Le Corbusier. This is rather strange as he was neither an architect nor a member of the Modern Movement. Actually, he had scant respect for architects in general, and the Modern Movement in particular, claiming in 1932 that '... the International Mode [he is referring to the Modern Movement] must perish, being eclectic rather than scientific, science being the life blood of function'.[2] By 1967, he still had little time for architects, claiming 'Architecture is voodoo. The architects don't initiate anything ...' but going on to say, significantly as it turned out, 'I think the younger architects may be changing, I think they understand what I'm saying.'[3]

At the time of writing, Buckminster Fuller is largely ignored by the architectural community, his name rarely if ever appearing in the architectural press, and few if any books about him currently grace the shelves of bookshops' architectural sections.[4] But from the late 1950s to the end of his life he was, as the familiar use of 'Bucky' indicates, one of the most famous names in the architectural firmament. He toured the world subjecting architects, but particularly architectural students, to lectures that would often last for four or five hours, sometimes even longer.

Towards the end of his 1960 seminal book,[5] Reyner Banham hints that maybe Buckminster Fuller was the way forward for modern architecture. For Colin Davies, he was the 'father of High-tech [architecture]'.[6] But who was he and what did he do? And what, for that matter, was High-tech architecture? And, more to the point, how was, if it was, High-tech architecture different from that already produced by the Modern Movement?

Although seeing himself as someone quite different from Le Corbusier, there are extraordinary parallels between the two, both in their lives, and their outlooks, achievements and influence.

Bucky preaching to the converted

[1] An even better known 'Bucky' was Bucky Barnes, comic superman Capitan America's sidekick.

[2] Bacon, 2001, p24 (originally in 'Universal Architecture' in *T-Square*, 2 February1932).

[3] Pawley, 1990, p147 (originally in *New York Times*, 23 April 1967).

[4] Though they groan under the weight of books about those he influenced.

[5] Banham, 1960, p325–326.

[6] Davies, 1988, p16.

For Richard Buckminster Fuller failure came early and often. He was born with poor eyesight and different length legs, only attaining an adult height of 5 ft 2 in. Following a childhood during which he was unpopular, badly behaved and bullied at school, he managed to follow the family tradition by being admitted to Harvard; however, he broke with tradition by failing to graduate after being expelled – twice!

Somehow, in spite his poor eyesight, different length legs and a height of 5 ft 2 in; he became an officer in the United States Navy between 1917 and 1919. In 1917, he married Anne Hewlett, one of the ten daughters of the architect James Monroe Hewlett.[7] After a large number of deadend jobs, in 1923 he went into business with his father-in-law, as president and chief salesman of a company that produced the Stockade Building System. In 1927, Hewlett sold his controlling interest to the Celotex Corporation, with whom Fuller quickly came into conflict, which resulted in him being sacked. It was one of many final straws.

In 1922 Fuller had suffered an appalling tragedy when his young daughter, already disabled by polio, died in his arms. This, together with his ignominious departure from the block company triggered a nervous breakdown – for one year he remained completely silent – a year of madness. It was in this year, during which he read, wrote and drew incessantly, that he re-thought the whole world and 'Bucky' was born. The seeds for his re-thought world were two: firstly, as he partly blamed the death of his daughter on the unsanitary living conditions that prevailed at the time, he felt there should be quite a different approach to housing. And secondly, due to his difficulties in selling the compressed wood-cement blocks, he thought that architects and the whole of the construction industry were hopelessly technically backward.

At the end of the year, he produced a document which he called '4D'. He gave it this title because he claimed to have been thinking in four dimensions during the year.[8] This document, really a manifesto, was published in 1928 as a hand-bound edition of 200 copies, which were sent to friends, relatives and prominent people none of whom understood it, prompting letters of the form 'Dear Mr Fuller, I am sorry to say I could not make head nor tail of your book.'[9] The book was full of mad Futurist type schemes, such as a 100-storey office block hung from the spokes of a wheel.

In 1929, the word most associated with Bucky – Dymaxion – was coined, but not by Fuller, from DYNamic-MAXimum-tensION. This was the first of many 'bucky-words', other examples being: world-around, sunsight, sunclipse and synergetics. He was also fond of other little-used words like geodesic and tensegrity. All of which meant that his already hard-to-understand prose became incomprehensible, as the following extract illustrates:[10]

---

[7] Hewlett had studied architecture at the École des Beaux Arts in Paris, and became the Vice President of the American Institute of Architects.

[8] What Fuller meant by 4D seems obscure. According to Kirby Urner, 'Fuller used 4D to refer to the 4 rays from a central hub that omnisymmetrically define an expanding volume (e.g. the four lines from the center of a tetrahedron to its four vertices). The Cartesian system consists of 6 rays from the origin defining an expanding cube. The expanding tetrahedron uses/defines volume more economically Bucky claimed.' Got that?

[9] Pawley, 1990, p41.

[10] Meller, 1979, p13.

Had I perceptivity at that time equal in magnitude to the scale of my intuitive prospecting of forward events, this case history's era might have been more accurately identified as that which terminated Sir Isaac Newton's normally 'At Rest' and myriadly isolated hybrid world cultures ... opened Einstein's normally 'dynamic' omni-integrating world culture to which change has come to seem essential and popularly acceptable.

Bucky became obsessed with weight, especially the weight of buildings, comparing them to the weight of airships, which were quite the rage in 1928. He thought that an airship could form the basis for a skyscraper. As airships and skyscrapers have nothing in common with each other than perhaps overall size, it's hard to understand why anyone would see a connection, but Bucky did.

Later in life, Bucky would unnerve architects and others by asking them, 'How much does your building weigh?' Unsurprisingly, few knew, which enhanced his reputation as a superior thinker. Of course, the reason few knew was that, unless you needed to carry your building around, what a building weighs is of little consequence to anything but the foundations. But a few people do know!

Like Le Corbusier, Bucky's work spawned an industry. There have been tens of thousands of words spoken and written about his ideas, thousands of them by Bucky himself. But when it comes down to it, his specific contribution was to circular houses, domes and a bizarre car. Two of these were illustrated in his manifesto; the 4D house and the 4D car, which came to be known as the Dymaxion house and the Dymaxion car. An examination of these two projects clearly illustrates Bucky's many shortcomings. First the car.

Bucky's car didn't look anything like cars of the time, or since, come to that. The original idea was that the car would have inflatable wings, but by 1932 this weird idea was dropped, and the 4D auto-airplane had become the 4D transport. Fired by his vision, and presumably using the selling skills honed on the compressed wood-cement blocks, Bucky persuaded a stockbroker who'd survived the 1929 crash, Phillip

Ready for Bucky's question

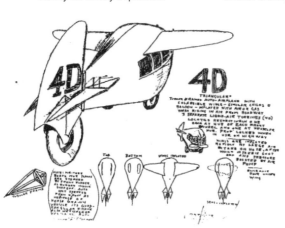

Is it a car? Is it a plane? No it's a 4D auto-airplane

Pearson, to invest money in his car design. Pearson was convinced that a design breakthrough for a car would help America out of its economic depression. By 1933, when the prototypes were to be built, the 'car' design had changed again. It was bigger and now had a single rear-mounted engine driving the front wheels instead of the twin engines of the 1932 version.

Bit more, but not very, car-like

Working with Starling Burgess, a successful racing yacht designer and builder, and taking advantage of the huge pool of skilled and work-hungry men, Bucky saw the first car built in only 4 months. Un-

The three-wheeled yacht

veiled on 12 July 1933, it was a superb example of hand-built craftsmanship, the body having been constructed like a racing yacht's hull. This, apparently, was the type of product that Bucky thought would save the world. Bucky, one of whose mottos was 'doing more with less',[11] 'calculated' that his car would be super-efficient in terms of performance. To describe the process of 'doing more with less', he coined the term 'ephemeralization'; another buckyword.

Bucky had learnt skills to work in wood and metal, but he had no training as an engineer, and it seems Burgess's technical skills were confined to yachts. Anyway, basic design flaws were built in. The car's engine was at the rear but driving the front wheels, a rather odd layout and not copied by any other design: but this wasn't the real problem. As the front wheels were the ones driving the car this meant it was difficult to be able to steer with them as well.[12] This problem was overcome by making the rear wheel steerable, but this made the car virtually undrivable. As the car gathered speed, it revealed its aeroplane antecedence, and the rear wheel tended to lift, tranferring most of the load to the front wheels thus reducing steering control at speeds over 50 mph. Another case of design arrogance and ignorance, as all flight manuals clearly identified this problem for taxiing aircraft. And it got worse. On corners, due to various design faults, the steering characteristics changed continually, something any competent automobile engineer would have foreseen. And then it got even worse. Two months after completion of the prototype it crashed, killing the driver, near the main gates of the 1933 Chicago World Exposition. This effectively ended the project.

In spite of his contempt for the Modern Movement architects, with the Dymaxion car Bucky was behaving in exactly the same way. Blinded by his view of his unique brilliance, and convinced he understood technology when he didn't, he produced a totally flawed design.

---

[11] Whether this was knowingly, and ironically, supposed to be a play on the famous dictum of Mies – less is more – is not reported.

[12] The problem of using the wheels of a car to both to steer and to drive had only been solved at that time by Citroen, but by using a very expensive and patented engineering component.

When this became obvious, rather than admitting his mistakes, he continued to make exaggerated claims for the performance of a project that was an obvious failure.[13]

The story of the Dymaxion house stretched over a much longer time period, but was also a total failure. Buildings in the 4D manifesto were hung from masts, why is unclear, as although a few buildings have been designed like this it has few technical advantages.[14] The 4D house was no different, being hexagonal in plan and hung from a central mast.

Although peddling strict scientific logic, Bucky could often be quite obscure about details and developments of his 'inventions', and the 4D house was no different. In 1928, he filed a patent application for a metal rectangular house with a pyramid roof and a central services core. By 1929, drawings show a metal house still with a central core but now with a hexagonal plan and the whole thing suspended above the ground from a central mast. Bucky, who is perhaps best described as handyman-cum-mechanic, had none of the aesthetic hang-ups of the Modern Movement, but was following their functionality edict a lot more faithfully than they were. His concept for the 4D Dymaxion house was probably the nearest anyone got to a house as a 'machine for living'. But in spite of his efforts, his house did not progress further than a model during the 1930s and it was only after World War II that Bucky was able to get back to his house.[15]

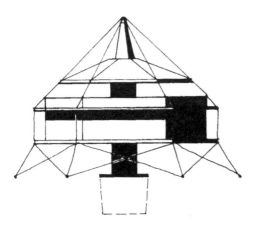

How the house looked in 1929

The first, last and only full-size 4D Dymaxion Wichita house

The aeroplane was a vital part of the technology of World War II, and the capacity of the American aero industry was hugely expanded. With the ending of the war, Bucky saw the possibility of using what would be over-capacity to manufacture his Dymaxion house, provided he designed it along the same lines as an aeroplane, and this is what he did. From 1944, he worked alongside the Beech Aircraft Corporation in Wichita, to develop the house using

---

[13] Subsequently, Bucky made wild claims about the car, including one that he had broken the lap record of a race track whilst at the wheel. Current information on the internet states the car could reach 120 mph and there is no mention of its design flaws – all part of the Bucky myth.

[14] This is because with a masted building all the loads first have to be carried to the top of the building/mast and then down to the foundations, whereas in a normal buildings the load path just goes directly down.

[15] During World War II, Bucky developed a temporary shelter unit called the Dymaxion Deployment Unit. Based on a mass-produced, circular, steel grain bin it was arguably the only successful design Bucky ever produced, which puts him one ahead of Le Corbusier.

aeroplane technology. The prototype was erected in 1945.

The whole house was made from aircraft-style components, duraluminium beams, aluminium sandwich panels and Perspex™ windows. All the components, none of which weighed more than 5 kg, could fit into a reusable steel tube for easy transport. Full of revolutionary features, it could be assembled in a day by a team of six. And, even more amazingly, carpeted, tiled and furnished, its projected cost was half that of an equivalent normal house. The publicity campaign based on the prototype resulted in orders for a staggering 37,000 units. It seemed all sorts of housing barriers had been broken. Here, totally unlike anything the Modern Movement had produced, was a house truly designed for mass production. But it was not to be.

A company had been set up to manufacture the housing units but Bucky was never able to give the go ahead for production, always finding more design issues to be resolved. Gradually his financial partners despaired and gave up, and the whole project collapsed. Now an icon in the architectural ghetto, no one has ever lived in a Dymaxion Wichita house.

Having comprehensively snatched defeat from the jaws of victory, in opposition to the hackneyed phrase, Bucky would probably find it hard to believe that his greatest achievement, which was to propel him to super gurudom, was yet to come, and it came almost by stealth. This happened when, in 1948, he was asked by friend Josef Albers (1888–1976)[16] to teach a class at the architectural summer school at the off-the-wall Black Mountain College.

It was at this point that Bucky entered the architectural ghetto that he had previously held in such contempt, and gave the Modern Movement a new impetus. It was also at this point that Bucky allegedly came up with his most important invention – the geodesic dome. Actually the geodesic dome had already been invented in 1922, in Germany, by Walter Bauersfeld (1879–1959), as a roof for his planetarium.[17]

So what's a geodesic dome? The word 'geodesic' comes from 'geodesy', which is the term given to surveying the Earth as a sphere, as opposed to making local surveys which treat the Earth as flat. Thus 'geodetic' or 'geodesic' was an adjective, whose meaning was extended to mean any curved surface. A geodesic line, or geodesics for short, came to mean the shortest line between two points on a curved surface. On a sphere these geodesics are lines that have the diameter of the sphere itself.

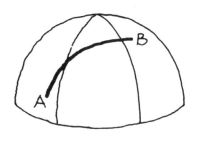

Getting from A to B geodesically

What role could these geodesics play in architecture, or structural engineering for that matter? A moot point for most, but the Holy Grail for the enlightened few, Bucky and his followers – shades of Le Corbusier! But actually what Bucky did, and amazingly managed to patent, was to provide a method of geometrically dividing up the surface of a sphere. He did this by using an icosahedron which has

---

[16] Albers had been a student and teacher at the Bauhaus, and, with the coming to power of Hitler, had been part of the exodus of modernists from Germany, emigrating to the United States in 1933, where he joined the Black Mountain College. After a somewhat tortured history the college finally closed in 1956.

[17] When covered with concrete, the structure became the first thin shell concrete structure in history. What is even more remarkable about the dome is that it was almost incidental to a spectacular scientific and technical accomplishment – the invention of the planetarium projector.

20 faces of equilateral triangles. If an icosahedron is put inside a sphere with the nodes touching the surface, and the faces are then 'pushed' out to the surface, the sphere is divided into regular curved regions. The lines bounding the regions are part of great circles – geodesics. Each face of an icosahedron can be subdivided with more equilateral triangles which generate more geodesic lines; the number of these subdivisions is called the frequency.[18]

 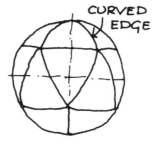 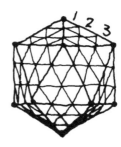

The 20-sided icosahedron   Icosahedron on a sphere   Icosahedron with divided faces

At his first summer school, Bucky got his students to build a 50 ft diameter geodesic dome constructed from old Venetian blind slats. It collapsed, making him a laughing stock with his 'supine dome' as it was nicknamed. This also shows what a poor engineer Bucky was, because a few simple calculations and tests would have shown if the slats were strong enough. However, Bucky bounced back, being put in charge of the 1949 summer school, presumably for his entertainment value.

Bucky contemplating his future as a dome guru

Unusually for him, this time Bucky managed to get the hackneyed phrase the right way round and did snatch victory from the jaws of defeat. He went on to become an inspiration to a 'new' generation of Modern Movement architects, who were children of World War II, and who were to become the comic book heroes. They were inspired directly by his teaching; he had christened the planet 'Spaceship Earth' – but also with his insistence on the value of advanced technology, especially that which was used in the aircraft industry. What happened was a repeat of the earlier Corbusian approach, in that neither Bucky nor his new followers had a substantial understanding of this new technology, they just liked the look of it.

---

[18] Fuller's patent application, filed in 1951, showed a dome based on an icosahedron divided with a frequency of 16.

Like Le Corbusier's 'innovative' buildings, buildings that were made from geodesic domes were not all that they were cracked up to be, but this only really became clear in the 1970s. Stewart Brand, writing in 1994: 'As a major propagandist for Fuller domes ... I can report with mixed chagrin and glee that they were a massive total failure. Count the ways ... Domes leaked, always. The angles between the facets could never be sealed successfully ...'.[19] But plenty were built, and many abandoned.

Even so, the new technology was becoming very exciting visually, especially with the arrival of the space race in the 1950s. At the end of World War II the erstwhile-allies-now-enemies, the USA and the USSR, vied with each other to secure the services of the Nazi military technical experts. A coup for the USA was the 'enticement' of the Nazi rocket supremo Werner von Braun (1912–1977) to develop a space programme for the USA.[20]

In the post-war period, the technical advances such as jet planes, long range rockets, atomic bombs, had created new horizons which gave the public a newfound appetite for science fiction. Von Braun realised how this could be used to enthuse the United States for real science fiction. In the early 1950s, he wrote a number of illustrated articles for *Collier's* magazine about the possibility of space flight, which boosted their circulation to four million. But with 15 million TV sets already in existence, he suggested to Walt Disney that they produce a TV programme about space travel. The programme, called *Man in Space*, was broadcast on 9 March 1955, and was watched by an astonishing 42 million people. President Eisenhower asked for a copy that could be shown to Pentagon officials. On 29 July 1955, Eisenhower announced that the USA would launch an unmanned satellite.

In the 1950s Britain was still under the impression that it was a world power, one of the 'Big Three'.[21] Undoubtedly Britain had technical know-how, but it didn't have the necessary wherewithal to bring all its grandiose plans to fruition. The country managed to build an atomic bomb of its own and also had its own rocket programme... and its own astronaut – his name was Dan Dare, but he was a character in a comic.

But not just any old comic; this was a

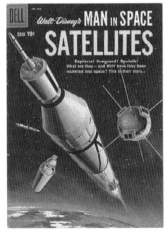

From magazine to TV to infinity and beyond

[19] Brand, 1994, p59.

[20] Before the allied capture of the V2 rocket complex, von Braun engineered the surrender of 500 of his top rocket scientists, along with plans and test vehicles, to the Americans. As part of a military operation called Project Paperclip, he and his rocket team were scooped up from defeated Germany and sent to America where they were installed at Fort Bliss, Texas. For fifteen years after World War II, von Braun worked with the U.S. Army in the development of ballistic missiles.

[21] This, in spite of Roosevelt and Stalin sidelining Churchill at the 1945 Yalta conference, which was held to shape the post-war world.

Britain's space programme in the 1950s

totally new type of comic for boys, the *Eagle*.[22] In this comic Dan Dare endlessly battled relentlessly with his foes from Venus, the Treens. They were led by an archetypal 'little green man', the evil Mekon. The strip, replete with brilliantly drawn seductive images of space 'technology' has now become a cult.

In the 1950s, British schools of architecture were in the throes of a revolution. After all sorts of manoeuvring, the 'traditionalists' had been more or less ousted and the Modern Movement was the order of the day. But instead of producing the required perfect boxes, some students felt they could go beyond the 'modern' architecture of the 1920s, and create something even more modern than the official Modern architecture. This would encompass aircraft technology and space flight, and a new and

A comical view of Archigram

totally different world. The first comic book heroes had arrived – they were called Archigram. And some of this group of mainly British, but some American, architects did actually produce comic strips of their own. But members of Archigram (who had mostly been born in the 1930s),[23] like Sant'Elia some half a century earlier, also made drawings of cities. But not any old cities, these cities walked or floated, or were in enormous towers, or had interchangeable parts that could be plugged in and unplugged at will.

The comparison with the New City of the Futurists is inescapable, this time without the poetry of Mari-

---

[22] In 2008, the Science Museum in London held an exhibition called *Dan Dare and the Birth of Hi-tech Britain*.

[23] Peter Cook (b1936), Dennis Crompton (b1935), David Greene (b1937), Warren Chalk (1927–1988), Michael Webb (b1937) and Ron Heron (1930–1991).

netti but with updated imagery. Archigram was hugely influential in the architectural ghetto at the time and still appears regularly in books on modern architecture. For example: '… the importance of Archigram should not be underestimated. They represented a profound and genuine reassessment of the Modern Movement …'.[24] But the members of Archigram built nothing of note – well virtually nothing at all – just producing a series of exciting or silly (depending on your point of view) pseudo-techno images. However, their influence was pervasive, as all of them spent most of their careers as teachers of architecture, and were thus able to spread the word.

But for all its excitement Archigram was really déjà vu, just going round the tired circle of producing drawings that looked technical, but without demonstrating the technology they were promoting was clearly understood. For architectural cartoonist Louis Hellman, 'It was the Modern Movement's last fling'. But it wasn't, as another group of comic book heroes decided to be really heroic and try and build the stuff, which they did, with unsurprisingly predictable difficulties.

In 1963, two British architects, Norman Foster (b1935) and Richard Rogers (b1933) set up an architectural practice that they called Team 4. They had just come back from the United States, where they had been doing post-graduate work at Yale University, and now they wanted to produce a new architecture that reflected what they saw as the new technological reality of the world. After some initial small-scale success, boxy buildings using, where possible, 'state-of-the-art' technology, they went their separate ways: Foster forming his practice in 1967 and Rogers, with Renzo Piano in 1970.

It took some years before Foster and Rogers were able to win projects that enabled them to show what they could really do, and what they did propelled both of them to global architectural stardom. Rogers only had to wait four years, whereas Foster had to wait a bit longer.

Rogers got his big chance by winning with Renzo Piano, in 1971, a competition for a new 1 million sq. ft cultural centre to be built in Paris, initially called the Beaubourg Centre, it was renamed the Centre Culturel d'Art Georges Pompidou or the Pompidou Centre for short. The Rogers-Piano winning entry was Archigram suffused with Victorian seaside-pier engineering.

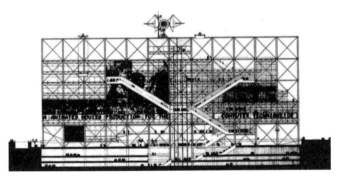

The proposed project had external escalators inside glass tubes and floors that spanned a massive 160 ft that could also move up and down. The steel frame dominated the building being protected from fire by having cooling water circu-

The multi-storey Archigrammical cultural fun palace

---

lating inside the structure.[25] Also all the services were to be left exposed, with huge ducts running up outside the building. All features worthy of an Archigrammical fantasy – but as the fantasy had won the competition it now had to be turned into reality. This resulted in many ways in a scenario similar to that of the Sydney Opera House already described, though amazingly it kept within budget and on programme. Even though the architects had sought engineering advice, the advice they got did not inhibit these features. But reality has a sobering effect, so some features had to go: no moving-up-and-down floors: no water circulating in the horizontal structure as fire protection: extra fireproof panels added to the elevations, reducing the 'transparency'. And, as the structure had not been conceived by hard-nosed Victorian pier engineers, that also had to be radically altered. For instance the outer columns became rods, while much more bracing had to be added. But after a suitably epic struggle, caught for posterity in dramatic photographs, the building opened some six years later.

The result was stunning: stunningly wonderful, stunningly awful, stunningly exciting, stunningly... well, certainly stunning.[26] And Richard Rogers was on his way.

Actually the reality tended to be rather less than stunning, because by letting it all hang out there were dozens of building details the architects couldn't

The epic battle to turn fantasy into reality

The stunningly stunning Pompidou centre

High-tech architecture after extensive renovation

---

[25] If steel is heated above about 550°C it loses most of its strength. As this, and higher, temperatures are often reached in fires in buildings; steel structures have to be protected. Traditionally this was done by encasing the steel in concrete. But under pressure from architects, who wanted the steel structure to be visible, to be 'expressed', engineers looked for other ways to provide this protection. From this a whole new discipline emerged called fire engineering.

[26] Unsurprisingly the building was not without its problems. Apparently '... dirt accumulated in unreachable corners corroding the exuberant technological display' and much worse '... the endless, indeterminate space and the highly colourful exterior elements made exhibitions of art – its chief mission – difficult ...'. Ghirardo, 1996, p82 & 86.

Foster learning Dymaxion

get round to resolve. Many of these details were left out in all weathers rather than being kept in dedicated spaces within the building, so they suffered.[27]

This new 'high-tech' version of the Modern Movement followed exactly the same path, in being neither cheap nor easy to build, nor introducing any worthwhile new technology, often expensive to run and maintain and needing periodic expensive refits. And, one might add, not setting any worthwhile precedent for cultural centres, fun or otherwise.

And whilst Norman Foster was waiting for his big chance, he found time to meet the 'Father of High-tech', the now 76-year-old guru, Bucky.

Foster's big chance came in 1979 when he was included on a list of seven to submit proposals to build the new Hong Kong headquarters for the Hongkong & Shanghai Bank. Against all odds, as his firm was by far the least experienced, he won but with some client reservations, 'The benefit of his brilliance ... could be outweighed by the lack of practicality of his designs', as client representative Roy Munden put it.

The building was to have 47 storeys, quite a tall building but nothing out of the ordinary unless you wanted it to be – and Foster certainly did. For tall buildings an important, and in many ways defining, part of the design is the choice of structure to resist the effect of the wind trying to blow the building over. There are a number of choices, but usually a stiff concrete 'mast' is built up through the building.[28] The mast, or masts, is often one or more concrete boxes that houses the stairs, the lifts and other accommodation like cloakrooms and store rooms. But Foster didn't want that. He wanted a steel structure that could

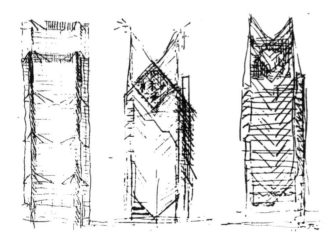

The architect attempts to stop the building collapsing

be seen – honestly expressed – that would make an important contribution to how the building looked. To this end, he did endless sketches of how this all-important structure might be/look.

The final configuration of the main structure was a complex assembly of double columns made in the form of ladders joined by a series of trusses in the shape of coathangers. Foster, whose favourite expression was the Bucky-inspired

---

[27] After being open little more than 20 years, the Pompidou Centre '... shut most of its galleries for two years ... for extensive renovation'. *The Independent*, November 1996.

[28] For more information on structures for tall buildings see Millais, 2005, p242–243, 249–250.

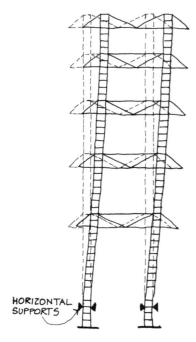

HORIZONTAL SUPPORTS

The ladders sway in the breeze

'Achieve more with less', had ended up with a structural arrangement that was far from efficient in terms of structural material. The principal span of the floor-carrying structure was a huge, Archigrammical 109 ft, though central suspension rods from the coat hangers cut this in half. As with the huge Pompidou floor span, one has to ask why a bank building, headquarters or otherwise, needs such a superhuman dimension. But the main problem for the structure was that, when the wind blew, the ladders all swayed sideways.

Late in the design process it was decided to remove the first rung, above ground level, of the ladder columns. This presented the engineers with a problem, whose solution cost the client quite a lot, as it happened. The problem was not to make it strong enough but to make it stiff enough. Stiff enough is an easy concept to understand but not so easy to quantify. A structure can be made stiffer in two ways: by altering the geometry or by making bits of the structure thicker. As the geometry was fixed, the engineers had to get the required stiffness by making the steel plates that were used to build the ladder unusually thick for building construction. This caused massive cost problems, from an initial budget for the steelwork of £53 million, the final cost rose to £119 million. This was almost the original predicted cost for the whole building shell, and more than any building had previously cost in Hong Kong.[29]

As with the Pompidou Centre, the 'honestly-expressed' steelwork had to be protected against the effects of fire. As this time no water was to cool it, it all had to be clad in fire protective material, and this had to be protected from the weather, as much of the steelwork was outside instead of inside the building. And, of course, it had to be beautifully high-tech.

The cladding was to be made of aluminium,[30] and because the building was so high-tech, instead of low-tech loose-fit it had to be made with an unprecedented accuracy of ±3 mm – 'The designers wanted it to appear as delicately tuned as a Swiss watch'.[31] For the cladding manufacturer, who was in the American Midwest, this was impossible to achieve using their usual methods. After trying various methods a special state-of-the-art, computer controlled German cutting machine was obtained which could cut metal to an accuracy of one fortieth of a millimetre – 0.001 inches. Furthermore, to obtain a durable finish, each piece of cladding had to go through a nine-stage process, ending up by being

---

[29] For the whole story of the removal of the first rung of the ladder columns, and its dramatic consequences see Williams, 1989, p137, 145, 151, 153 & 185–195, .

[30] Putting aluminium next to steel in a potentially damp environment, which is on the outside of a building, is courting disaster. This is because the presence of moisture causes electrolytic action which results in the rapid corrosion of the aluminium.

[31] Williams, 1989, p156.

baked at 260°C. Oh, and then it had to be sent to Hong Kong and fixed in mid-air to the ladders and coathangers. For each floor height of the ladder, which is from one rung to the next, the cladding required 34 shop assemblies that had to be erected in a sequence of 18 steps – all quite simple really. Needless to say, this was not the end of the problems, of course there were difficulties with the glazing... and the...[32]

By 1982 – it wasn't completed until 1985 – the building had become world-famous for much the same reason the Sydney Opera House had some 20 years earlier. Articles were written with such headlines as 'How not to build a masterpiece' and 'The sky-high costs of

High cost high-tech in Hong Kong

building sky-high', or again 'Soaring cost of Hong Kong bank eclipses down-to-earth obstacles.'[33] A damning independent engineering report was leaked to the press, and there were problems between the architects and a group that was to actually use the building.

But in spite of all this, the building got built, including its Archigrammatical features like glass floors, rooftop cranes and helipads, modules and exposed escalators. Both inside and out it looked the part for spaceship earth.

Of course, the real life Dan Dare architects Norman Foster and Richard Rogers couldn't design these projects alone. They needed teams of like-minded assistants. Among the Foster teams was someone who thought that all buildings should be designed as though they were aircraft or space ships. He was called Jan Kaplicky (1937–2009), who founded a firm called Future Systems.[34] He set his stall out fairly clearly in a long article called 'Skin'.[35] The article opens with the following statement:

Monocoque and semi-monocoque structures used for airframe, car bodies and yacht hulls have reached a level of great sophistication and reliability. This article discusses their development and how the available technology could be put to good use in the field of building.

So what does monocoque mean? The word derives from 'mono', which means single, and 'coque' which is French for shell; the alternative term 'stressed skin' is perhaps more

---

[32] The whole complicated story is grippingly told by Stephanie Williams in *Hongkong Bank* (1989).

[33] ibid, p203.

[34] Norman Foster had more than a passing interest in aircraft; he has a pilot's licence that allows him to fly jet aircraft as well as a glider pilot's licence and a helicopter pilot's licence. When he did his programme for a BBC television series on *Building Sights*, in 1994, he chose a Boeing 747 jumbo jet.

[35] *The Architecture Review*, July 1983, p54–59.

descriptive. The idea came from the aircraft industry when metal aeroplanes started to be built in the 1920s and 30s. Previously, the structure of a plane was a framework of timber or aluminium with a fabric covering – all the main loads on the plane being carried by the frame. When the fabric covering was substituted by thin metal sheeting it was realised that, if the sheeting was fixed sufficiently strongly to the metal framework, then this sheeting could contribute to the overall strength of the structure of the plane. In other words, the sheeting – the 'skin' – carried some of the loads, so was 'stressed'.

This way of building aircraft was not immediately universally accepted by aircraft designers because its advantages – maybe lighter and stiffer aircraft – did not necessarily outweigh its disadvantages – more difficult to calculate, more difficult to build (especially where heavy items, such as the engines, had to be attached to the structure), and more difficult to repair. The weight issue, though important, has to work on the all-up weight. That is taking account of the frame and its covering, engines, fuel, equipment and payload. So the expensive saving of 20% on frame weight may only contribute to an overall saving of 3% on the all-up weight.[36]

An interesting story comes from the World War II, which illustrates why stressed skin can be a disadvantage. At the beginning of the war the Royal Air Force was dependent for fighter strength on two aircraft. These were the legendary Supermarine Spitfire and the equally legendary Hawker Hurricane. The Spitfire was super-modern with the whole aircraft built using monocoque construction, whereas the Hurricane stuck to the older method, that of a frame and fabric, for the fuselage anyway. Both aircraft had the same all-weight of 6,600 lbs. But whilst the Spitfire was a better gun-platform, the Hurricane was the more effective fighter because it *wasn't* monocoque. Why? Because battle damage was easily repaired for the Hurricane, giving 63% serviceability, whereas for the more-difficult-to-repair Spitfire it was only 37%, little over half as effective. And this is for aircraft, not buildings!

But for Kaplicky it's monocoque or nothing, and in his article (manifesto is perhaps a better word) he's absolutely fed up with engineers who don't share his view:

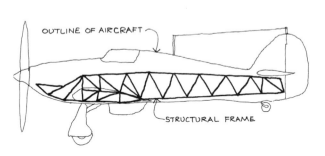

The more effective,
framed-rather-than-monocoqued Hurricane

As we struggle in the 1980s to persuade a recalcitrant engineer that the interesting bit of structure we have designed for our house is possible to build and can be calculated, we may be forgiven for muttering that the technology of this business is steeped in the Middle Ages.[37]

[36] A more familiar example of this is bicycle weight. It is possible to buy very expensive carbon fibre frames which weigh perhaps half that of a steel one – a saving of 50%. But when the wheels, brakes and especially the person is added, the overall saving in weight is negligible, unless you're trying to break a world record.

[37] *Architecture Review*, July 1983, p55.

Or again

> One of the problems in designing innovative structures is the reluctance of many structural engineers to get involved ...[38]

and he concludes that

> ... it just means we have to get a different type of engineer involved in the design process.[39]

He goes on to claim that the load on the wing of an aircraft is '... equivalent to the total lift which is evenly distributed over the entire wing area'[40]– wrong. It is true that the load on the wings is equal to the total weight of the aircraft (if it wasn't the plane would fall out of the sky) but it's quite wrong to think it's evenly distributed – far from it, it has a complex distribution. Across the wing it is anything but even, and neither is it along the wing.[41] Using this incorrect concept, he then states that for a Boeing 747 jet the 28 m cantilever wings would be loaded by 7 kN/m^2.[42] 'If we gave our structural engineer this figure and told him we wanted a 28 m floor, we might be amused by his reaction', he sneers. Hopefully, his structural engineer would point out that the loading wasn't evenly spread over the wing, that deflections of a wing could be an order of magnitude greater that that for a floor, and that an aircraft wing cost thousands of times more than a floor. And it might be added; if Kaplicky couldn't find the sort of engineers he wanted, why didn't he just do it himself? (Probably because of the reasons given in Chapter 5.)

Anyway, none of this stopped Kaplicky and his aides from monocoquing away for years on end. They produced endless schemes, solicited or otherwise, that show aircraft wings contorted into various shapes, so that they may able to be used as buildings.

But then, in the late 1990s, Kaplicky found an engineer who was a 'different sort' and a client who was prepared to wing it, well monocoque it actually – it was called the Lords Media Centre, but really it is just the press box. This time the users got inside the wing, which then hovered above the ground on two legs.

Even though a 'new type of engineer' had been found there was no 'new type of contractor' in sight. In fact '... British contractors ran a mile ...'.[43] In the end, the wing, which was to be made of aluminium, was fabricated in two halves by a racing yacht builder and delivered to site where the two halves were welded together. Hardly easy or cheap, so, of course, the project ran over budget and programme – 'The complex construction and the extended installation period almost doubled the cost ...'.[44] Because the wing was a

---

[38] ibid, p58.

[39] ibid, p58.

[40] ibid, p57.

[41] See for instance Stinton, 1983, Figs 3.14 and 4.3.

[42] kN is short for kiloNewton, i.e. 1,000 Newtons. A Newton is a weird unit used by engineers and physicists: 1 kN is about 225 lbs, and 1 kN/m^2 is more or less 21 lbs/sq. ft.

[43] Lyall, 2003, p99.

[44] *Architectural Record*, January 2000, p30.

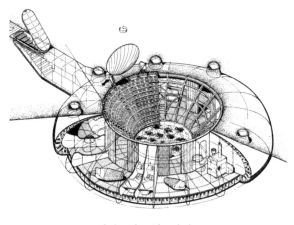

A doughnut in a hole

one-piece structure it could have no joints. As aluminium has a high rate of thermal expansion, to control the effects of temperature variation the wing had to be white. For all this effort the actual skin, the expensive double-curved, welded together aluminium only contributed 20% of the building's strength, was hardly worth the bother. But the bother was worth it because it was the world's first monocoque building – well done everyone.

Presumably, with all this super aircraft high technology the press corps are over the moon with their monocoque press box. Well not quite. Says one user:

> We do get very, very, hot if it's sunny ... they tried putting some kind of film on the inside this summer, but it didn't improve it, just made it rather difficult to look out. The nozzles for air conditioning are situated on your desk. When the air conditioning is on high [presumably every time it's sunny] it nearly blows things off the table. But they say they can't do anything about that.[45]

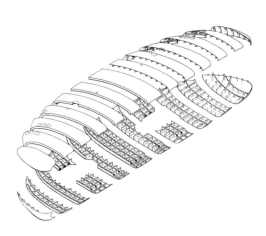

The press box wing

So we're back again to the great hero of the Modern Movement, Le Corbusier: projects late, over budget, irresolvable environmental problems and inappropriate so-called innovative technology that leads absolutely nowhere in terms of advancing useful building technology. As Louis Hellman noted 'High tech is unashamedly a style but its colours and forms celebrate the Modern Movement ... [it] tends to be very expensive, wasteful of energy ...'.[46] Or perhaps even more

---

[45] *Guardian*, 8 February 2006, p12.

[46] Hellman, 1986, p195.

damning was the eminent, and eminently sensible, engineer Frank Newby (1926–2001) when he said: 'I don't think high-tech has made any contribution to the development of structures at all ... architects just started using structure as decoration.'[47]

And even in the twenty-first century it still goes on, this odd idea that somehow space technology, inspired by films and comics, has some relevance to where people want to live or work. As though they were frustrated astronauts or fighter pilots, all imagining they are Buck Rogers, whereas most people just want comfortable, affordable buildings and not have the papers always blowing off their desks by the high-tech air-conditioning nozzles or perhaps something even worse...

A skin is stressed for the very first time

Something even worse?

---

[47] *Blueprint*, March 1989, p36.

9. Architecture of Mass Destruction

In a celebrated speech given by Prince Charles, the heir to the British throne, at the Mansion House to the Corporation of London Planning and Communication Committee's Annual Dinner, he said, 'You have, ladies and gentlemen, to give this much to the Luftwaffe: when it knocked down our buildings, it didn't replace them with anything more offensive than rubble', implying that the architectural profession had done more damage to Great Britain since World War II than the Luftwaffe had during it. Reading the whole speech, it seems that the point of the remark made about the Luftwaffe was that rubble compared favourably to the buildings that had been erected in the spaces that were left, when the rubble had been cleared away.

But architects have not only 'taken advantage' of destruction by other means; war, fire, floods, earthquakes and volcanic eruptions; they (and others) have actually actively destroyed cities on both large and small scales. They have done this in a number of ways and these need to be examined, but the principal weapon of architectural mass destruction are the buildings designed by those who adhere to the false creed of the Modern Movement. Such buildings are deliberately alien, as an edict of the false creed was that Modern Movement buildings are to have no reference to anything that went before – so by definition they have to stick out like a sore thumb. This weapon can be used singly, by placing such a building in a totally inappropriate environment, or en masse in various ways. But firstly, how does the destruction take place, if not due to natural causes?

What is being talked about here is not the replacement of individual or perhaps groups of buildings, which takes place continuously in most towns and cities, but the destruction of large areas of a city in one single act. This only became possible with the physical power provided by the industrial revolution, and it started in Paris.

Napoleon III (1808–1873), after being elected president of the French 2nd Republic in 1848, carried out a coup d'état in 1852, declaring himself emperor. He ruled, dictatorially, until 1870, when his convoluted foreign policy led to his capture and defeat in the Franco-Prussian War. When he came to power, Paris was still a medieval city, with few wide roads and no adequate drainage or water supply systems. In the cholera outbreak of 1832 nearly 20,000 of Paris's 650,000 inhabitants died. What Napoleon III wanted to do was 'to take the initiative to do everything useful for the prosperity and the greatness of France ...' and this included substantially rebuilding Paris – to turn Paris into a modern city. In charge of this project was the prefect of the Seine department – career civil servant the Baron Haussmann (1809–1891). Through a massive programme of public works he transformed Paris from a medieval city to what is often called Haussman's Paris, the city of boulevards. It is often claimed that the main reason for the remodelling was, via the boulevards, to facilitate troop movements in case there was a repetition of the 1848 uprising.[1] But the remodelling was really to modernise Paris and bring economic benefits.

The indefatigable Haussmann created new systems of drainage and water supply, thus enormously improving public health and, of course, he created many new streets and the famous boulevards, but there was much more. He also created parks, new bridges, fountains and public buildings including the Paris Opéra, the École des Beaux-Arts and the huge market Les Halles, as well as enlarging the Louvre. He also cleared ancient buildings from the Île de la Cité, replacing them with administrative buildings. His projects required the demolition of some 20,000 houses and affected nearly 60% of Paris's existing buildings, but he also built 85 miles of boulevards.

Armed with a law that allowed the Parisian executive to compulsorily purchase any properties needed to carry out their schemes, large areas were bought and demolished. This was the first time that a city was remodelled by destroying what was already there and functioning, after its own fashion, rather then extending a city onto virgin land. And the owners of the property were, on the whole, fairly compensated. Of course, the non-owners, the poor, were simply thrown out on their ears with no compensation whatsoever. Furthermore, much of the work was financed by people buying city bonds, which again gave people profit. Along the new boulevards, plots were for sale for development. Haussmann's scheme laid down design guidelines for these buildings in terms of height and roof profiles that had to be at 45 degrees. The floors of adjacent buildings had to line up and there were typical features that buildings were expected to have, such as continuous balconies at the fifth floor level. Typically, these buildings would have five or six floors of flats or offices above street-level shops and cafés.

Buildings on the Haussmann scale

---

[1] In spite of all the remodelling to benefit troop manoeuvres, it took a lot longer for the authorities to put down the uprising of 1870 than that of 1848.

The scale of Haussmann's destruction was greater than that caused by the subsequent events of 1870–71[2] – 'the Prefect [Haussmann] demolished more of the city than the Germans, the Versaillais [French government forces] and the Communards combined.'[3] And the massive scope of Haussmann's work inspired many others who wanted to re-order existing cities, including of course Le Corbusier. He wanted to re-place Haussmann's Paris of

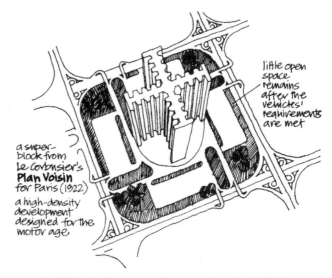

little open space remains after the vehicles' requirements are met

a super-block from Le Corbusier's **Plan Voisin** for Paris (1922) a high-density development designed for the motor age

Le Corbusier's weapon of mass destruction for Paris

suffocating city blocks with regularly spaced cruciform skyscrapers, the Voisin plan.[4] But, unlike Haussmann, Le Corbusier had no power to do this. Le Corbusier's plan was divided into three zones: work, living and circulation: but Haussmann's plan was also considered to be zoned, with the separation of circulation, living and leisure.

But whilst Le Corbusier did not have the power to re-Haussmannise Paris, across the Atlantic, starting in the 1930s, there was someone who did have the power to Haussmannise New York; his name was Robert Moses (1888–1981).[5]

In 1924, Moses was appointed the head of the New York and Long Island State park commissions. In 1933 he was appointed head of the New York City Parks Department and head of the Triborough Bridge and Tunnel Authority. He held all these positions until 1968, when he was sidelined, at the age of 80, by Nelson Rockefeller, then Governor of New York State.

Moses set out on his career as an idealist who somehow hoped to remove corruption from politics, which, for him, would represent progress. How long he maintained this idealist stance is unclear, but he transformed himself into a type of megalomaniac. Without a dictatorial Napoleon III to support him, he had to get support for his projects from

The modest Mr Moses

---

[2] At the end of 1870 the Prussian Army laid siege to Paris for five months. The citizens of Paris then rose up to form the Paris Commune which was eventually, and bloodily, suppressed by French forces.

[3] Robb, 1997, p469.

[4] See page 99 (Chapter 6).

[5] *The Power Broker* (1975), by Robert Caro, is essential reading for the understanding of modern cities.

elected officials – politicians. He had various techniques to manipulate the politicians he worked with, but the basic method was to present a project at an unrealistically low budget (compare with the Sydney Opera House). When the politicians announced the project with maximum publicity, they had to, for re-election purposes, see it through. And when Moses got the money, he delivered.

One of his earliest projects, the Jones Beach State Park on Long Island, clearly illustrates how he worked. His ideas were grandiose; he would develop a one mile long stretch of beach, backed with a car park for 10,000 cars. This was in 1926, and there wasn't a car park in the world for 10,000 cars. He wanted all the buildings to be of brick and stone, and he was far from being a supporter of Modern Movement architecture, even if he'd heard of it. He wanted the architecture '... to encourage people to have fun. It must be light and airy, gay and pleasant. There must be a thousand little touches to make people feel happy.'[6] According to one of the design team, Moses was '... more responsible for the design of Jones Beach than any other architect or engineer or all of us put together.'[7]

One of the thousand little touches

Moses had asked for $1million but had only been allocated $150,000 to build two changing room buildings and a water tower; he knew this was nowhere near enough for his plans, so he used all the money to build the foundations for one of the buildings he wanted. Then he invited the elected senators to view the work: there was nothing to see, as the sand had blown over the foundations. The senators were apoplectic; $150,000 of public money had been spent, on their authorisation, on apparently nothing. They demanded that the Governor fire Moses, but then they realised the position they were in: Moses was the only person who could turn the situation around, which he did – so Moses won. And in 1929 they were all proudly sitting in line when the beach was opened. There simply was no leisure beach like it in the whole world.

However, Jones Beach was just a small part of his plans for parks on Long Island. Perhaps more importantly, these were to be connected by dual carriage roads that were called parkways: important because Moses' real obsession was with roads on a scale hitherto unseen – 'cities are for traffic' was one of his mottos. As Moses never learned to drive, always being driven, his overwhelming desire to see massive provision for the car is not easy to understand. But, he saw cities much as Le Corbusier did, that is towers and parks linked by highways. It wasn't until he obtained power in New York City, in 1933, that he could bring the highway to the city. In New York, his highways were to have a brutal effect on residents, often poor and powerless.

In Paris, the poor displaced by Haussmann's schemes had to fend for themselves, but in Moses' New York the poor displaced by his schemes sometimes got a bit luckier – they were

[6] ibid, p222.

[7] ibid, p223.

The Cross-Bronx Expressway guts the city

The projects – mass destruction housing

put into public housing. Of course, though not officially, Moses effectively ran New York's public housing.[8] And where the poor, if they were lucky, ended up were 'the projects' as they came to be known. Bleak blocks, following perhaps unconsciously, Modern Movement designs, un-integrated into the rest of the city – in other words the prototype ghettos: '... walled towns destroying existing social values in the neighbourhoods and precluding the development of new and healthy neighbourhood characteristics', according to housing expert Eugene Klaber.[9]

So here were being built residential zones similar to those proposed by Le Corbusier. But basically Moses changed New York as he saw fit, and was probably responsible for more construction than any man who's ever lived. According to one of his bitterest critics, Lewis Mumford (1895–1990), 'In the twentieth century, the influence of Robert Moses on the cities of America was greater than that of any other person.'[10] And for 'cities of America' could be written 'cities of the world after World War II'.

The Futurists would have regarded him as a hero, throwing huge bridges across rivers, demolishing city blocks that stood in the way of his schemes, driving himself and all his staff relentlessly, but it's unlikely he'd have had much time for them. He did not tend to have high opinions of others considering for instance Walter Gropius, the 'inventor' of the perfect glass box, to be seeking to 'change the American system by advocating a philosophy that didn't belong here.'[11] His opinion of America's greatest living architect, Frank Lloyd Wright was equally dismissive. No opinion of Le Corbusier was recorded.

---

[8] Official policy was that '... tenants will not be evicted from the site of public improvement unless and until quarters equivalent to those occupied are available'. Moses officially toed this line but according to Caro, 1975, p968 et seq., the reality was rather different, with the poor, and especially black and Hispanic poor, often being badly treated.

[9] Stern, 1995, p68.

[10] Caro, 1975, p12.

[11] ibid, p471.

Obviously, it's almost impossible to imagine what would have happened without Moses, both to New York and cities in general, but it was his emphasis on the private car, and his antipathy towards public transport – 'By building highways Moses flooded the city with cars. By systematically starving the subways and the suburban commuter railroads, he swelled that flood to city destroying dimensions'[12] – that seemed to dominate his vision of a city.

The reason that the work of Moses is important in the context of Modern Movement architecture is not because he was part of it, he wasn't, but because his remodelling of New York was entirely in line with the thinking of the Modern Movement. Zoned cities, the residents in high rises, over-provision for the car[13] and the city interlaced with neighbourhood-destroying urban motorways; the Modern Movement dream come true, just a nightmare for the recipients.

And it was Moses' image of a city that captivated a new and up-and-coming profession: that of city planner.[14] This new breed wanted to do away with the old messy cities and rebuild them with city motorways, and industrial zones and areas of mass housing, but they just didn't have the power, that is until a lot of cities worldwide did need rebuilding, having been bombed flat in World War II. At the beginning of the war, the Germans had the upper hand, and were thus able to cause widespread damage to many European cities, but especially to British cities, as Britain remained unconquered. As the tide turned, British and American bombers carried out massive bombing raids on German cities.[15] It was during these raids that it was discovered that whole cities could be turned into a firestorm if the bombing pattern was correct. So research was carried out in a remote part of the American state of Utah to perfect this. It was called the Dugway Proving Ground, and here replica German and Japanese domestic buildings were constructed to perfect firestorm techniques. They were helped in this by Modern Movement architect Erich Mendelsohn prompting Tom Vanderbilt to muse 'One wonders, too, if Mendelsohn as a modernist might have seen in the destruction of these densely compacted vernacular houses an opening for the building site of a better tomorrow'.[16]

Due to the pattern of warfare in World War II in Europe, the main destruction of cities took place in Germany and Britain, but towns and cities were destroyed elsewhere.

---

[12] ibid, p19.

[13] Modern Movement hero Le Corbusier always had any building he managed to complete professionally photographed, often with a car in the foreground. Decades later, Quinlan Terry, an architect who has rejected the Modern Movement mantra lock, stock and barrel for designs based on previous models, was upbraided by ghetto writer Deyan Sudjic, for his '… lonely crusade against … motor cars …'. Sudjic, 1992, p66.

[14] Town planning was a newish profession that arose in the 1920s (the Royal Town Planning Institute was founded in 1914) on the back of utopian ideas of how towns and cities *should* be. The town planners' approach was basically that of Le Corbusier/Tony Garnier/Robert Moses for city centres, and the Ebenezer Howard approach, the garden city (basically slightly picturesque leafy suburbs), for the outskirts and 'new' towns.

[15] And American bombers caused the total devastation of Japanese cities. After several days and nights of bombing, two thirds of Tokyo was destroyed, 700,000 buildings being left as complete ruins. The reason that Hiroshima and Nagasaki were chosen for the first, and so far only, use of atomic bombs was that these were two of the few cites of any size still undamaged by US bombing.

[16] Vanderbilt, 2002, p72–73

The market in the new Royan

Some, like the historic centre of Warsaw,[17] were rebuilt as replicas whereas others, like Royan, felt the full force of the Modern Movement.

In Britain the story was rather different as the destruction continued long after the war! This was because in 1947, when Britain was in the grip of a post-war economic crisis,[18] the Town and Country Planning Act was passed. This had been framed, during the war, by a team led by Modern Movement architect William Holford,[19] and it gave the planning departments of towns and cities sweeping new powers for 'The Redevelopment of Central Areas'. These became better known as Comprehensive Development Areas, or CDAs, to those in the know. In these areas, the planners using their draconian compulsory purchase powers, often demolished huge areas that were left over from the work of the Luftwaffe. It is telling that city architects, who presumably had wind of, if they were

Dreariness sets in

not active participants in, the framing of the new act, were 'planning' the future as the bombs fell. For instance '... Coventry city architect, DE Gibson, found time to point out to a friend, indicating this devastated area or that, the site of a new town hall, a new school, a new shopping centre.'[20] This left Coventry with a city centre that is a byword for urban dreariness.[21]

---

[17] After the heroic, but ill-fated, Warsaw uprising of 1944, the German forces razed the historic centre of Warsaw to the ground whilst the Red Army looked on.

[18] It is somewhat ironic that, for a whole raft of complex reasons, the defeated Germany, well the Western part anyway, eventually emerged from World War II stronger than Britain, who'd been part of the winning Allied team. Of course it was the United States who emerged the strongest, followed by – irony of ironies – the totally defeated Japan as the second strongest.

[19] Holford had been appointed, bizarrely it may seem as he was only 28 at the time, a professor of town planning at Liverpool University. The school of architecture at Liverpool was one of the first to embrace the Modern Movement creed.

[20] McAllister, 1941, p12.

[21] Before the war, according to AN Wilson, the centre of Coventry was '... a charming old town' but he goes to say that after the war the new cathedral (in the centre of town) was surrounded '... by the predictable hideousness of a postwar town'. Wilson, 2003, p413–414.
In a 2001 listener's poll, the BBC found that 17% of those who responded wanted Coventry's city centre demolished.

Rebuilding was put into the hands of a new generation of architects who felt the time had come to give the people of Britain the benefit of Modern Movement architecture. But, due to the economic straits in which Britain found itself, this all took some time, more or less until the end of the 1960s.

Gradually, with a general despair amongst the public at what the architectural profession was producing, and what was being destroyed in the name of (architectural) progress,[22] the voices of preservation began to be heard. This was not because there was a new nationwide interest in architectural history and heritage, but mainly because many people feared that, as architectural historian Vincent Scully put it: '... whenever we see a building being demolished, we automatically expect it will be replaced by something worse'.[23]

But whilst many city dwellers, and for that matter recipients of social housing, got architecture based on the Modern Movement diktats, whether they wanted it or not, another group did want it. This group was called big business. The idea of building a large, and eye-catching, building as headquarters for your company was not new. In the macho world of corporate image size does matter, so often these, what now have become known as 'signature buildings', are big – which usually means a skyscraper. How tall can or should a building be? And how tall does a building have to be to become a 'skyscraper'?

No interesting answers are forthcoming, but the reason that buildings got tall in Chicago and New York, starting in the 1880s, was simple – to make money – 'A building must pay or there will be no investor ready with the money to meet its cost', said Barr Ferree at the 1893 convention of the American Institute of Architects. However, as it became profitable to build higher and higher buildings, each city imposed limitations. In Chicago it was a limit on the volume, whereas in New York the buildings had to be set back from the street as they got higher. As a result the Chicago buildings were lower, but covered the

whole site with the same floor plan making them stumpy, whereas the New York buildings were 'wedding cakes'.

The American skyscraper architects of the 1920s and 1930s had, like most of their European counterparts, little interest in the Modern Movement. The architecture of these building could loosely be described as stretched French Beaux-Arts. The structures were

Stumpy in Chicago and wedding-cakey in New York

[22] The turning point, if indeed there was one, was perhaps the demolition of the Euston Arch in 1962.

[23] Sudjic, 1992, p168.

a steel frame, with concrete cast around the steel to make it fire-proof. The external cladding was of stone, with individual windows on a regular pattern. A bit more would be spent on the lower levels, with various forms of classically inspired details, and the top would often end in a flourish. Apart from luxurious entrances, the floors were usually fitted out by whoever was renting the space.

Even though stone can weather gracefully, even beautifully, it is hard to see much merit in these buildings if you're not the developer. For the passer-by, having to walk along the wind-funnelled, darkened stone canyons, they were only of interest to out-of-town 'rubbernecks'. For the standard user, neither the arrival – a wait in the lobby for the lift and then that especially unpleasant experience, the lift ride pressed too close to your fellow travellers in an embarrassed silence – nor the work space – impersonal floors tiered one on top of another – could have been particularly rewarding – so pretty much a Modern Movement experience, but not an exterior Modern Movement style. But that was about to change dramatically, and all due to Phyllis Lambert (b1927). The daughter of the president of spirit distillers Joseph Seagram & Sons, Samuel Bronfman, she persuaded her father that an architect of 'international repute' should the designer of their new headquarters in New York, so she was allowed to select one. She did; he was called Mies van der Rohe, the perfect-glass-boxman himself. And his design for the Seagram Building became for office skyscrapers what the Unité became for blocks of flats.

The biggest perfect-glass-box
the world had ever seen

The Seagram Building broke the mould. It was not wedding-cakey nor was it stone clad – with Mies? Heaven forbid, it was clad in glass of course, from top to toe. And none of those tarty entrances or roof-level flourishes either. Yes, it was the biggest perfect glass box in the world, well, at the time anyway. The architectural ghetto was beside itself and stayed beside itself:

By almost any standards the building was a superlative success. Blake, 1960[2], p104.

...it is one of the postwar masterpieces of world architecture. Sharp, 1972, p223.

There may be a few buildings in New York as beautiful ... there are surely no postwar skyscrapers as truly exquisite. Goldberger, 1979, p160.

... contrasting with the stone-clad skyscrapers of New York ... simple elegance and technical excellence .... Risebero, 1979, p277.

... a glamorous new precedent for the skyscraper. Sudjic, 1992, p85.

... a new breed of skyscraper ... an uncluttered tower of great elegance. Gibberd, 1997, p156.

Unlike commentary on the Unité, there are few architectural dissenting voices, because whilst people can identify with living problems, *working* in featureless floors is thought to be perfectly acceptable.

Naturally, the building was the most expensive office block ever built, and, due to the floor height glazing, blinds had to be installed. The glazing was of tinted glass which produces a depressive effect on the occupants, and the blinds, due to architectural order, were made so only three positions were possible – up, down and halfway. As few people feel comfortable working next to floor height glass when perched several hundred feet above the ground, visual walls were created by pushing anything to hand, filing cabinets or potted plants against the windows, to reduce panicky feelings.

The building was designed in obsessive detail, to ensure it was functional, which is what made it so expensive. And, as usual, the structure had to be expressed. As Mies put it, 'My idea, or better my direction in which I go is toward clear structure and construction – this applies not to any one problem but to all architectural problems.'[24] The real structure, steel beams and columns, safe in their fire-proof concrete casings, wasn't much to look at, so the whole building had vertical, specially manufactured, I-beams, made of the very expensive bronze, used as window mullions. These were fixed on the outside so that everyone could see that the building had an honest steel frame, well inside it, not that many people could have cared a jot. This is yet another example, on a massive – and massively influential – scale of decorative dishonesty posing as constructional honesty. And what's more, these dishonest-honest 'columns' didn't reach the ground; a touch of irony perhaps?

But amongst all this praise for the technical perfection of everything to do with the Seagram Building one critic, Charles Jencks, found a flaw. He discovered that at one point things that should have lined up didn't, so according to him:

In this case, the even rhythm of the window bay is broken by the remaining half-bay, a result which would not matter in a richer architecture or one based on a botched aesthetic, but which is a near disaster in an architecture claiming consideration in the classical tradition of perfection.[25]

---

[24] Stern, 1995, p344.

[25] Jencks, 1973[1], p102.

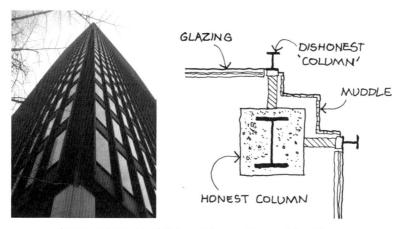

GLAZING
DISHONEST 'COLUMN'
MUDDLE
HONEST COLUMN

An expensive touch of dishonest irony, with a muddle at the corner

And then there was the previously unheard-of plaza. This, by breaking the usual rule of wedding cakeyness, actually changed the rules. In 1961, the step-back rules that produced the wedding cakes was changed to FAR, which stood for Floor Area Ratio. So now a building could have a total floor area that was the site area multiplied by a factor, usually about 12. But, if you presented the public with a plaza, then the ratio could be higher and so more profitable for the developer. So plazas with huge glass and steel boxes became the in thing. But did these plazas actually provide places where one could see the city animated? Not usually, as they were bare and inhospitable – 'it soon became clear that some of these new plazas were far from the civilised, urbane spaces enthusiasts had promised'[26]

Desperate stragglers animate the city

– and they were plagued with unpleasant gusts of wind caused by the presence of the tower[27] – 'populated by desperate stragglers buffeted by vortices ...'.[28]

There is often a sad pond or two (the Seagram Building plaza had two), sorry 'water features', which, partly due to the local wind conditions, tend to fill with rubbish which then bobs uninvitingly until the plaza cleaners turn up. Oh, and if there are fountains the wind causes the users to be sprayed once in a while. But, apart from these carping criticisms, such features do offer a human touch...

And if one got bored with the animation and rubbish in the Seagram plaza, the building

---

[26] Sudjic, 1992, p86

[27] As a huge building presents a large obstruction to natural wind flow, the wind has to flow around the building, and this causes disturbed wind patterns with locally much higher wind speeds. At ground level this is experienced by passers-by.

[28] Blake, 1977, p78.

The plaza giving a human touch

Mies rubbernecked in New York

could always be rubbernecked.[29]

Gradually, as the worldwide business community was won over to Modern Movement architecture, now usually called the International Style, every city needed a clutch of glassy, steely towers sprouting out of desolate windswept plazas, and profitability saw that a lot of cities got them, and are still getting them![30]

But if the presence of huge towers in a city has the effect of mass destruction on city life as imagined by many people,[31] provided the density of these towering architectural weapons is reduced, then only local damage ensues. But there is one experience of modern life that takes place in buildings and landscapes that are virtually nothing but mass destruction, in various senses. These places are called airports.[32] Air travel, existing as an exciting experience for the very rich before World War II, only became important for large numbers of people after the war.

It has been noted that the airport is a paradigm for the modern city,[33] and it certainly matches up to what the Futurists saw as a modern life – people constantly on the move,

---

[29] In 2006 the Seagram Building became a 'landmark'. Sudjic notes, without intended irony that 'All that it takes for an eyesore to become a piece of priceless heritage, it seems, is the elapsing of time'. Sudjic, 1992, p170.

[30] One of the worst affected cities will be London, because 'Ken Livingston [the then Mayor] is allowing a forest of giant towers to dwarf and destroy the intimate landscape of London', says Simon Jenkins, *Guardian*, 28 September 2007.

[31] Generalities like this can't really be substantiated, but it's hard to imagine citizens of Amsterdam, Florence or Prague, or even the Haussmannised Paris, wanting to visit Houston or similar cities for the architectural experience, whereas vice versa provides an important income for the cities mentioned.

[32] 'It can hardly be a coincidence that no language on earth has ever produced the expression "as pretty as an airport". Airports are ugly. Some are very ugly. Some attain a degree of ugliness that can only be the results of a special effort ... and architects have on the whole tried to reflect this in their designs.' These are the opening lines of D Adams' 1988 novel *The Long Dark Teatime of the Soul*.

According to Steve Richards, 'Andrew Marr wrote recently that the two ugliest words in the English language were "Heathrow Airport". He speaks for many.' *The Independent*, 7 June 2007, p31.

And from a 2001 BBC poll, 'Nothing could disguise voters' loathing for Heathrow Airport, however, with more than 25% voting it their most-hated building.'

[33] 'All Heathrow lacks to qualify as a conventional town is a housing area: if you discount hotels. The transience of the airport embodies contemporary urbanism in a real, as well as a metaphorical sense.' Sudjic, 1992, p145.

technology at the forefront, open round the clock seven days a week, the buildings constantly being altered or rebuilt. Naturally, the Futurist dream did not inspire the creation of airports; most of it derives from the functional needs of operating passenger and cargo planes and the insatiable need for people to travel about.

On the other hand, the major expansion of airports was after World War II, by which time architects who adhered to the Modern Movement creed were in almost total ascendance. On top of which it had been embraced, for commercial use at least, by the business community. So it was unlikely that any airport building with architectural pretensions would be designed by a non-Modern Movement architect. Although airports were covered with buildings scattered, to a casual eye, almost randomly, most of those with these pretensions were for buildings where the public would be – the passenger terminal. Some of these took quite odd forms.

Some of these attention-seeking buildings subsequently caused trouble due to their perceived architectural merit. As the airports continually evolved, often these buildings became redundant but ironically had to be kept because they were such brilliant examples of modern architecture – thus compromising progress![34]

An oddly-shaped passenger terminal from the 1960s

At this point, it is worth asking how do airports affect people in general, and what role, if any, do Modern Movement architects have? Airports affect the public in two ways, firstly their presence in the local environment and secondly as users. The first effect, their presence in the area, seems to be entirely negative as no-one, given any choice, wants to live near one or even be near one. Houses with easy access to airports do not command premium prices, nor do those on noisy flight paths. So the siting of new airports, which are 'needed' for the ever increasing volume of traffic, is always problematic due to the 'nimby' effect.[35] Whilst it is obvious that Modern Movement architects have no responsibility for the modern airport sited near important cities, as has been seen, airports and aeroplanes are deeply embedded in the 'philosophy' of Modern Movement architecture and architects.

---

[34] For instance the owners of Kennedy Airport wanted to demolish the TWA terminal building designed by Eero Saarinen, but were foiled by modern architecture preservationists. *New York Times*, 4 April 2001.

[35] 'Nimby' stands for 'Not In My Back Yard'.

No longer des-res

But if the siting of airports is decided by government planners, the passenger terminal is a different matter: they are always in the hands of architects, more interested in the operators needs (their clients) and making an architectural 'statement' than creating an appropriate environment for the travelling public. At a human level, the idea of air travel was[36] for many people an exciting prospect, not an ordinary event in their lives. Usually it is to go on holiday to a faraway place, a pleasant prospect, so many air travellers are in a good mood. They need to be, because the reality, looked at coldly, is rather different. The public encounters the terminal in three roles: as traveller, as someone saying goodbye, and as someone saying hello.[37] The fact there are only these three interlinked groups shows how sterile the human animation of these terminals is. No one pops into a terminal for a coffee, to meet friends, take a stroll or buy a paper or magazine; nor do tourists actually visit airports for pleasure and interest.

The idea of the terminal operator is to get rid of the people as quickly as possible – throughput – whilst at the same time extracting as much money from them as possible – merchandising opportunities. The people from the three groups also want to reduce the time spent there to a minimum. Arrive and get on or off a plane as quickly as possible and likewise the goodbye and hello groups. But it is not usually that quick for a variety of physical and bureaucratic reasons. There is the check-in, the security check, the passport check, waiting in the departure lounge staring at screens to see where and when your plane will leave, getting to the departure gate, waiting at the departure gate, boarding the aircraft, leaving the aircraft, more passport checks, the baggage retrieval, the custom checks...

Are any of these experiences pleasant, interesting or rewarding? Not for most people, who only bear them due to what air travel brings them – going where you want to be or going home. And what do architects have to do with any of this? Well, they are responsible for much of the physical environment in which these irritating occurrences take place. But who can talk of the architecture of any baggage reclaim hall or the waiting area at a departure gate?

---

[36] 'Was' is used rather than 'is' as nowadays the fear of terrorist action, on top of the worry of a crash (which is almost always fatal for all the passengers), takes quite a bit of pleasure out of the experience for many people.

[37] There is also the vast staff needed to keep the whole show running. Unlike other forms of travel, air travel needs armies of staff to handle baggage, make security checks, do passenger check-ins, check passports and customs non-compliance, to control emergencies (police, firefighters, doctors and nurses), drive buses to car parks, to man the dozens of food and retail outlets and to clean and maintain the whole place. Then there are technical staff, not only aircrew but air traffic controllers, aircraft maintenance and emergency repair crews, refuelling staff and staff monitoring the tarmac, and probably many more... However, their 'architectural' needs are usually of little interest...

So what environments do the architects provide for the users of these terminals? Do they provide pleasant areas through which to stroll to the departure gate, so that the stressed passenger[38] gets some ambiental relief as though strolling through a monastery cloister, a formal garden? No way, they have to pass through aluminium, pastel-shaded plastic and horribly carpeted or tiled corridors, often windowless and seemingly endless and directionless – just follow the signs. Or the check-in area? Here people often have to wait for longish periods: are there seats? No, you have to wait in a shambolic queue with people with trolleys and cases, shuffling forward to be processed.

It is often in this area where it is possible to see the architect playing at being a structural engineer, because these areas are fitted into vast oversized halls with some complicated roof structure on display high above. Sometimes these vast halls have huge glazed walls so that panoramic views of the visual mess that make up most airports, can be had. What can usually be seen is a complex and unplanned collections of sheds and various other ugly buildings, with equipment, pipes and parked vehicles; nothing worth a panoramic view – in fact the opposite.

An airport that is fun with lots of light and a high degree of clarity.

Architect Richard Rogers' vision of his new building for Madrid airport was 'An airport that is fun, with lots of light, great views and a high degree of clarity.'[39] This seemingly positive statement raises all the usual questions. How can an airport be fun? Excuse me, but no-one goes to an airport to have fun do they? And 'lots of light'? The usual Modern

[38] 'According to an experiment ... conducted by the neurophysiologist David Lewis, the stress that passengers endure when traveling through Heathrow is higher than that of a Formula 1 driver during a race ...'. Roger Collis writing in the *International Herald Tribune*, 23 August 2007.

[39] *The Architect's Journal*, 27 April 2006, p28.

Movement hang-up that everyone wants to think they're outside when they're inside. And how does 'lots of light' enter? Through yet another glazed wall of course, giving 'great views' of what? Oh yes – and a high degree of clarity. Sounds excellent, but what a Modern Movement architect means by clarity is quite different to the clarity the average air traveller needs. As there is, as yet, no standard design for airport terminals, this means that the user is dependent on signage rather than the language of the building to indicate where to go, which means, especially for users who do not speak the language (or those who can't see well or read) that there is no clarity.[40] But the efforts of the architects have done nothing to stop, and have probably helped, airports being '… part of a soggy, lowest-common-denominator world culture.'[41]

Big brother architects blend in

The Modern Movement wrecks a traquil scene

But it isn't only with massive skyscrapers or airport terminal buildings that Modern Movement architects wreak destruction on towns and cities. This can be done by scale and/or form. For instance, when a group of Modern Movement architects[42] chose to site their new office building, sorry studios, near a small square surrounded with vernacular buildings, the result looms over the square with all the charm and friendliness of a secret police headquarters. Or a wonky box can be lobbed into a tranquil canal side setting like a visual hand grenade.

It would be completely wrong to lay all the ills of modern cities at the door of the Modern Movement architects. After all they didn't invent the car, the aeroplane, the skyscraper or, in fact, anything of note. But they did enthusiastically take up all the things that have made much about modern cities environmentally less than pleasant.[43] All their efforts at 'cities of the future',

---

[40] In 2006, the Madrid terminal was so much fun that it was awarded the prestigious Stirling Prize.

[41] Marchant, 2003, p97.

[42] This group included 'prize-winning' architects Alvaro Siza Vieira and Eduardo Souto Moura.

[43] It was reported in the *New Civil Engineer*, 18 April 2002, that a survey showed that 80% of people dislike their urban environment.

from Tony Garnier to Le Corbusier to Archigram, showed buildings, roads and spaces that ignored the overworked cliché – the human scale. So for instance, where the market place determines the price of domestic property, people with money do not want to live next to motorway interchanges and airport accesses but in leafy Georgian squares, conceived before the advent of the modern traffic, or even Haussmann's boulevards. And, in the countryside, they choose houses in villages attuned to the horse rather than to the motor car.

As usual Louis Hellman has the last word (or picture, one should say)...

Modern Movement reality

10. The Supine Engineer Appears

As has been seen, by the end of the nineteenth century, building designers came from two different professions – the architects and the engineers.[1] During the early part of the twentieth century this had little impact. Architects were principally engaged in designing culturally important buildings whose architecture did not depend on engineering systems, heating or electrical supply for example, but especially structural systems. This meant that architects, using traditional guidance and rules of thumb, could design their buildings without needing to consult an engineer.[2]

During this period engineers were also designing buildings – factories, hangars, warehouses, workshops and other industrial buildings of no cultural consequence – unpretentious buildings – creating an 'industrial' vernacular. They were also responsible for large structures that had an aesthetic impact on the landscape – bridges, towers, jetties and many others of visual importance. They designed these without, on the whole, any 'cultural' advice from architects.[3] The engineers had sufficient confidence in their aesthetic ability or, as quite often happened, had no particular interest as to what their designs looked like so long as they worked and were economic.[4] As the engineers were capable of calculating the sizes of steel and reinforced concrete structures they had no inhibitions about using them. This meant that during the early part of the twentieth century most of the steel and reinforced concrete that was used for structures was used 'industrially' rather than 'culturally'. As the engineers gained confidence in their ability to predict the behaviour of structures by calculation, they designed and constructed more and more ambitious projects.

Even when a huge bridge was to be built over a large stretch of water in relatively unspoilt countryside, the engineer worked without an architect. This is what happened when Benjamin Baker (1840–1907) designed, at the end of the nineteenth century, his enormous railway bridge that crossed the mouth of the river Forth, now known worldwide as the Forth Bridge. It was assumed by everyone, including the engineer, that the aesthetic design of the bridge, which would have an enormous visual impact, was safe in his hands.

At the time of the construction of the Forth Bridge and well into the next century,

---

[1] Towards the end of the nineteenth century a new structural material, reinforced concrete, had been developed and its use was increasing. Like structural iron, this new structural material also needed to be calculated, requiring the special knowledge of the engineers.

[2] Where engineering elements were needed like floor beams or electrical equipment, although an engineering knowledge was needed to size them, they had little, or no effect, on the architectural concept or design.

[3] Occasionally architects were involved in engineering projects – Tower Bridge over the River Thames being an example.

[4] This is of course, a very moot point. However, whilst some individual engineers had an innate aesthetic sensibility, the aesthetics of their designs was not an overt concern. Two photographers, Bernd and Hilla Becher, have built an entire career on taking technically perfect photos of engineers' 'unaesthetic' designs.

The Forth Bridge

A concrete structure as architecture

Engineer Robert Maillart's cheapest design wins in 1930

architects, whilst admiring the work of engineers, did not think that their aesthetics – the engineering aesthetic – had any relevance for their work. Their designs continued to be based on the ideas of load-bearing masonry walls and traditional timber floors and roofs.

Likewise engineers did not venture in the world of architectural design, though still designing buildings, they tended to restrict their designs to buildings of utilitarian use, like airship hangars. In 1921, engineer Eugène Freyssinet (1879–1962) designed two enormous hangars at Orly. Taking the form of huge parabolic arches spanning 86 m they were made of thin, arched, corrugated concrete slabs.

Throughout the first part of the twentieth century engineers designed a whole range of new structural forms using the 'new' structural materials of steel and reinforced concrete. They could do this because they had, or were able to develop, methods of calculation that could justify their designs. Their concerns were always with economy of construction and functionality of use. Whilst some did consider aesthetics, this was not their prime goal.

The engineers could create these new forms because the new materials had different characteristics from those of the traditional materials. But a few engineers did cross the line and were able to fulfil the role of both engineer and architect – the engineer-architect.

Early examples of the work of such engineer-architects were the pioneering high rise buildings that were built in the United States, particularly in Chicago and New York, in the latter part of the nineteenth century. Although architectural histories give prominence to Louis Sullivan for these developments, the real pioneers were William le Baron Jenney

An engineer-designed building of 1892

Engineer's modern architecture

(1832–1907) and John W Root (1850–1891).[5] Both men had received training in engineering but were to work as architects during their professional careers.

Few others managed to combine the role of engineer with that of architect for the design of buildings, but there were some. In France, Auguste Perret who had received, but not completed, architectural training, was a pioneer in the use of reinforced concrete in buildings. He used concrete structures not only as beams, columns and slabs but was able, where he deemed it sensible and necessary, to create structural forms only possible in concrete.[6] In the twentieth century in England an engineer, Owen Williams (1890–1969), became an architect in 1929 with his appointment to design a hotel in London.

As breaking with the past was an essential part of Modern Movement architecture, it was predicable that modern architects would be interested in, and excited by, the new forms the engineers were developing. Their work started to appear in architectural magazines and books and, by the 1950s, the names of engineers like Robert Maillart, Eduardo Torroja and Pier Luigi Nervi, had entered the lexicon of modern architecture.

A hangar by Nervi

[5] With Daniel Burnham, John Root founded one of the most famous firms in American architectural history.

[6] As he did with a roof supported by concrete arches for a clothing factory near Paris in 1919.

Architectural writers praised these engineers, for instance Jonathan Glancey writing in 2003 says of Nervi, 'He ranks with Freyssinet and Maillart as an engineer who was also an artist, a designer who could turn logical calculations into a form of poetry realised in modern materials'.[7] It is clear what the architectural community thought of these engineers who were also outstanding designers, but how did these engineers relate to architects? Owen Williams, the engineer-turned-architect, had scant respect for the architectural profession and on one occasion opined that 'I do not believe an architect as an architect can collaborate with an engineer as an engineer'.[8] Architectural critic and historian Sigfried Giedion wrote of Maillart that 'He never encountered an architect who fully knew how to integrate his genius.'[9] Another engineer, Riccardo Morandi, writing in 1962 about architects and engineers, in the foreword to a book on his work, stated that they were '... condemned to work together in an atmosphere of mutual incomprehension ...'.[10] It seems these independent and successful engineers were less than enthusiastic about working collaboratively with architects.

Not a penguin's home from home

But there was one engineer who was dying to collaborate with architects, especially architects who espoused the Modern Movement architecture – his name was Ove Arup.[11] His chance came in the early thirties when the Russian architect Berthold Lubetkin (1901–1990) arrived in England and set up an architectural practice called Tecton. Lubetkin was a committed Modern Movement architect, but one of his early commissions did not seem to be that promising, it was for a new enclosure at London Zoo for penguins.[12] However, working with Arup, he managed to make it an iconic modern architectural design. The centrepiece of the design was two interlocked, and visually unsupported, spiral ramps.

Many have seen the Lubetkin/Arup collaboration as an example of the perfect partnership and the way forward for the previously rather separate occupations of engineer and architect. An article in an engineering journal, written in 1989,[13] claimed that a 'full integration of plan and structure ... is achieved only by a close collaboration architect and engineer...'. But was this collaboration so good? In 1989, Lubetkin wrote letters to

[7] Glancey, 2003, p336.

[8] Cottam, 1986, p163.

[9] Giedion, 1941, p475.

[10] Boaga, 1965, p9.

[11] This is of course the Ove Arup who played such a pivotal role in the design and construction of the Sydney Opera House, already described in Chapter 7.

[12] Like so many of the Modern Movement projects the Penguin Pool, as it became known, was quite unsuitable for its users – the penguins. It's now no longer used as an enclosure for penguins.

[13] See 'An architect/engineer collaboration', *The Structural Engineer*, May 1989, p198.

the architectural press[14] claiming that it was he and not Arup who had had the good engineering ideas. Arup dismissed this as ridiculous as he thought that Lubetkin had a poor understanding of the behaviour of reinforced concrete structures. Arup also claimed, in 1983, that 'A wall like the one at Highpoint would have been cheaper to build with bricks, but he [Lubetkin] claimed it was functional and economic. It wasn't functional at all: it had to be "Modern". Functionalism really became a farce.'[15] So it seems that the relationship between engineers and architects was back to square one, except that this happened in the 1980s, some 50 years after the events. And in the meantime a lot had happened to 'the relationship'.

And another name appeared that must be added to the engineers who produced new forms from new materials; that of Félix Candela (1910–1997). However, unlike Williams, Maillart, Torroja and Nervi, Candela was not an engineer by training but an architect!

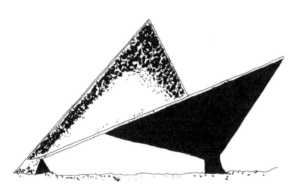

One of the shells that stunned the architectural world

Cable roofs become 'architecture' in 1967

After some difficult years, in 1950 he managed to set up, with Fernando Fernandez, a design and construction company for shell roofs; it was called Cubiertas and claimed to be a specialist in industrial architecture. At last he could indulge his passion for concrete shell roofs, something that had interested him since his student days.

Candela's company built a large number of concrete shell roofs in Mexico in the 1950s and 60s. These soon came to the notice of the architectural press and seductive photos of his work were published worldwide. For architects there was an important difference between their 'engineer-heroes' and Candela; he was an architect, he was one of them. And if he could do it, well so could they. Wrong – they couldn't. Candela had followed an architectural course, but in building his shells he was an engineer. He understood mathematically difficult shell theory, he was able to do numerical calculations, and he understood how the forces acted in the structures. He was also a builder, so he had enormous practical experience. No other architect, and very few engineers, had his experience or ability to design and build shell roofs.

---

[14] See for instance *The Architect's Journal*, 22 March 1989, *Blueprint*, April 1989 and *The Structural Engineer*, October 1989.

[15] Jones, 2006, p59.

A dominating geodesic dome

During the 1950s and 60s two other new and 'exciting' structural forms were added to the structural mélange – this time initiated by non-engineers; these were cable roof structures from architect Frei Otto (b1925), and geodesic structures by the inventor Richard Buckminster Fuller.

Neither cable roofs nor geodesic domes passed the cheapest solution test that the engineer-heroes always applied to their projects.[16] But, by now, all sorts of weird and wonderful structures, mainly for roofs, were appearing. These were invariably conceived by architects. Perhaps the weirdest from this period was the Phillips Pavilion built for the 1958 Brussels World Fair.

This bizarre building was designed by the 'great master of modern architecture' Le Corbusier.[17] It was conceived without any regard as to how it was to be built, what material was to be used or how it could perform as a structure. The project was rescued from fiasco by a Dutch engineer Hoyte Duyster, who managed to construct it from cables and precast concrete units. Before any construction could start, expensive and complicated laboratory load tests had to be carried out at Delft University.

The Phillips Pavilion was just one of many architect-inspired major pieces of structure that appeared during this period that made no engineering sense. The ill-conceived roof of the Sydney Opera House has already been described, and the inappropriate form of the roof to Kresge Auditorium has also been mentioned.

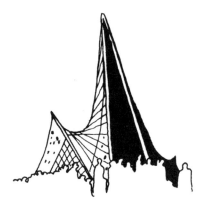

Structures get seriously weird

Perhaps sensing what was happening, some engineers went public with attempts to explain the logic of engineering, or how in fact engineers conceived and designed.[18] But they were swimming against the tide; the age of the engineer-heroes was over. So faced with this new situation, when major engineering works were being misconceived by non-engineers, what approach were engineers to take?

---

[16] To date cable roofs are not built to save money and neither were Buckminster Fuller's geodesic structures. However, in other hands, some geodesic structures are now offered as economic alternatives.

[17] The major architectural design was carried out by long-term associate Iannis Xenakis (1922–2001). Le Corbusier was enraged when the client, the electrical giant Phillips, included Xenakis' name on some promotional material. He got his revenge by changing all the locks on his office whilst Xenakis was on holiday, thus denying Xenakis access on his return. Matossian, 1985, p116–121 and Frampton 2001, p214.

[18] See for example 'Stresses and Strains' by Ronald Jenkins, *Architectural Design*, January 1957 or 'Architectural Misconceptions of Engineering' by Alan Harris, *RIBA Journal*, February 1961.

There were basically three, which were:

- Simply refuse to have anything to do with such misconceptions.

No doubt many engineers individually and/or collectively took this line, but there could be detrimental commercial side effects.

- Modify the misconception to ensure that essential engineering principles were obeyed.

This approach was often taken, but tended to involve the engineer in difficult work both technically and diplomatically. The engineer had to persuade the architect to make modifications. These were needed so that engineering principles, which the architect hardly ever understood, were obeyed. The engineer was also often involved in technical complexities that would have been avoided had a properly engineered concept been used.

- Welcome the misconception as a brilliant piece of design and as an opportunity to overcome technical challenges.

This third approach turned out to be the one followed by more and more engineers who worked with architects – in other words the supine engineer appears. In Chapter 7 it was shown how the engineers tried to cope with Utzon's every engineering whim, but they should have known what they were in for from the first stage of the job. This included a concourse which was 162 ft wide. Underneath was a vehicle circulation area, with drop-off points for visitors arriving by car or bus.

This is an interesting case[19] as it shows how far engineers were prepared to stray from an engineering approach to please an architect. The architectural scheme showed columns supporting the concourse slab, which meant the maximum span would be 60 ft, within the range, just, of 'normal' concrete structures.

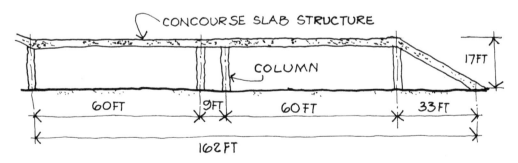

The architect's 'sensible' columns

---

[19] It is interesting because, unusually, the engineers wrote a fairly frank account of the process in *The Arup Journal*, October 1973, p22–27.

But at their first meeting, the architect asked the engineers if it was possible to omit the columns. The answer apparently was '… it was possible but it would cost a lot of money'.[20] This is the nub of the question of course, and this is where the engineer's supineness may or may not appear. What are her/his responsibilities? As the engineers go on to say, the columns '… did not hinder the traffic' but the architect had explained '… his concept demanded that the architecture should be expressed through the structure'. So off they all went trying, presumably, to have a preliminary shot at getting to heaven. But one might, and should, ask the question that if the architect wants 'architecture to be expressed through structure', then she/he ought understand structural behaviour and produce architecture that works structurally. But with a supine engineer in tow this tiresome chore can be avoided.

The engineers set to work and considered that '… the most economical answer would … be a series of box-section or I-beams …', but that this '… would obviously not have met the architect's request …'[21] – of course not, not nearly complicated enough. Eventually a suitably complex shape for the beams, that would be used to make a ribbed structure, was agreed upon. At mid-span the cross-section was T-shaped, which changed continuously until it became U-shaped at the supports. To achieve this smooth transition from the five underside surfaces of the T-shape to the three of the U-shape, four continuously twisting surfaces were needed.

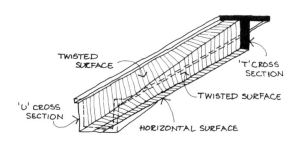

A suitably complex beam shape is found

Although this tortured structure was eventually designed and built, it is instructive to list some comments made by the engineers in their description of the design process:

This aspiration to have the structure 'truthfully displayed', to achieve 'structural honesty' … has nothing to do with choosing the most efficient structure.

… and made it impossible to justify on economic grounds.

… it would be very difficult and expensive.

… confirmed that the architect's ideas would be difficult to realise …

It was difficult to argue that this could not be done, although it posed tremendous problems …

[20] ibid, p22.

[21] ibid, p23.

The engineer's view was that ... [this] would be too high a price to pay for something which after all would not be missed by anybody. However, the architect was insistent and the engineers were bracing themselves ...

... the shape was not ideally suited to prestressing.[22]

This series of quotations shows how far the engineers were prepared to stray from the approach that had been used by the engineer-heroes. That was to conceive, design and build engineering systems that were sensible from the functional point of view, were buildable and gave value for money. Here is seen all those principles being ignored to achieve what the architect, who either didn't understand or didn't care about the engineering principles, wanted. The result was a drab – as it was made of fair-faced concrete – space, requiring copious artificial light, where all one did was to get in or out of a car or taxi![23]

The drab final result

But this supine approach gradually became the aim of engineers, especially structural engineers, who chose to work on projects that were designed by architects. In 1971, an engineer called Edmund Happold[24] outlined the new rationale in a paper entitled 'A servant of good architecture'.[25] In this article Happold tries to point out that, although an engineer should be true to the principles of engineering, these should be sublimated, not to the architect, but to good architecture. His article implies that all members of the design team will be making contributions to this higher ideal, but as the quotations given above show, this is basically idealistic tosh. What the architect wants, the architect gets. And what the architect also wants is to be surrounded by a design team who, as the quotations also show, is dedicated to overcoming all and any technical obstacles that 'good' architecture puts in its way.

Since Happold's pioneering paper, countless articles have appeared in the architectural and engineering press about the importance of engineering to architecture and how

---

[22] This is a technique where advantageous stresses are introduced into a structure before it is loaded. See Millais, 2005, p111–114.

[23] As a coda to this mini-saga it is amusing to note what Brian Murray, an architect, ex-editor of the *RIBA Journal* and founder of the design magazine *Blueprint*, says in his book about this structure. That is 'At the ends of a beam, the most effective section is a T shape, in the centre it is a U'. Murray, 2004, p25 & 27. Anyone who has even a basic understanding of structural behaviour of concrete knows this is not the case, and nicely illustrates the problem engineers are up against when trying to put engineering sense into non-engineered systems. Anyway the structure is a frame not a beam.

[24] Happold, who was also responsible for the engineering scheme of the Pompidou Centre (see pages 145–146), went on to found a very successful engineering consultancy called Buro Happold. He died in 1996.

[25] *The Structural Engineer*, July 1971, p315–319.

engineers and architects, if they were the right kind of engineer (i.e. supine), could work together successfully.[26] A typical article was entitled 'Helping Architects Achieve Their Dreams'.[27] This article profiles the approach of two young, at the time, engineers who '... do anything for the architects we like working with ...' and '... like to be involved in the creative process.' In 1991, mathematician and structural engineer Mario Salvadori (1907–1997) stated that 'I have had the good fortune to serve architects in the structural developments of their dreams',[28] and in 2005 Leslie Robertson, on being awarded a gold medal by the Institution of Structural Engineers, ended his address, in which he described various buildings on which he had worked, with 'We remain ever grateful for the opportunity to work with these creative designers and with the talented and high-tech architects who work with them.'[29]

These engineers could be even more successful if they could come up with new, exciting and innovative ideas of their own, and even better if they could do crummy, architectural-type sketches of them.

Whilst a minority of the engineering community were embracing supineness, two quite different happenings, in the 1980s, helped their 'cause'. The first came from computers. Mathematical equations that mimicked the macro-

Crummy sketch of an exciting engineering idea

scopic behaviour of many physical phenomena[30] had been derived in the nineteenth century, but took the form of differential equations. Teams of mathematicians and computer scientists got to work to write programs that could 'solve' the previously hardly-soluble differential equations of mathematical physics. This was done by dividing up the geometry of the physical object into small elements – finite elements. Then these finite elements are 'joined' together, in the computer, by hundreds (or thousands or millions) of simultaneous equations, which the computer solves. The solution of these equations provides the predictive results that the engineers needed. With more and more powerful computers, programs with user-friendly graphic interfaces are possible.

Nowadays the output from these programs, instead of being reams of numerical

---

[26] The engineers involved in all this supine collaboration were frequently structural engineers for two reasons. Firstly, the Modern Movement was very enthusiastic about structures being part of architecture, and secondly structural form is important in many cases for the form of the building. A further reason is that architects often feel that they have some understanding of structural behaviour, which is almost invariably not the case, so they can have fruitful discussions with structural engineers. This rarely, if ever, happens with other technical aspects of building design like heating, lighting, acoustics or air-conditioning because few, if any, architects pretend to understand them. So if a structural engineer states that a column should be such and such a size, the architect will often opine it's too fat, but when the engineer for the air-conditioning proposes a size for a duct it is invariably accepted.

[27] *New Civil Engineers Consultants File*, April 1988, p18.

[28] Gans, 1991, p xiii.

[29] *The Structural Engineer*, 15 March 2005, p27.

[30] The deflection of elastic structures, the flow of air around objects, the flow of liquids, and the propagation of sound in a space are typical examples.

values, can be presented in coloured graphics; so, for example, the level of stresses in a structure can be shown as different colours on three-dimensional diagrams. Engineers had been given a type of electronic magic wand. These programs could even determine what happens to the skull of *Baryonyx* when it bites (or bit, as it's been extinct for millions of years).

This availability of all-singing, all-dancing computer programs has had an enormous, and some consider dire, effect on the analytical function of engineers. Now, instead of having to carefully consider how any system works, backed up by informed preliminary calculations, it can all be crammed into the computer and, after the touch of several buttons, the technical wallpaper

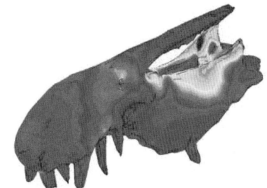

Baryonyx bites posthumously

output can be scanned for hot spots. It has also called into question the value of teaching engineers difficult mathematical theory which, due to the computer, they'll probably never use. But according to David Brohn '... quite soon no young engineer will have the slightest idea how to draw a qualitative bending moment diagram ... a reliable test for the understanding of structural behaviour',[31] clearly a worrying and unsatisfactory situation. In effect what has happened is that now any engineer can 'analyse' engineering systems that would have defeated the most brilliant engineer-hero. Furthermore, this can be done without needing a deep understanding of either the behaviour of the system being analysed by the computer, or understanding the theory the computer is applying.

Obviously a recipe for disaster, but it means that engineers, particularly structural engineers, no longer need to understand engineering behaviour properly, being safe in the knowledge that their computer can analyse 'anything'. So they can agree to, or even better, enthuse over any non-engineered concept they are presented with.

The second happening was the arrival of a cat amongst the engineering pigeons – the cat was called Santiago Calatrava (b1951). He was an architect and he was an engineer, and he produced wacky structures, photos and drawings of which always found their way into the global architectural press.

Wacky Calatrava wows the architects whacks the engineers

---

[31] *The Structural Engineer*, 6 April 2004, p18.

Now the situation with the talented engineer Candela was neatly reversed; architects could show the Calatrava engineering to 'their' engineers and say look what this engineer does![32] Game, set and match. Engineers who still adhered to the principles of the engineer-heroes, found these principles were no longer valued, at least if they wanted to work at the architectural 'cutting-edge'. If the client was prepared to pay, and the client certainly did have to be prepared for this, the engineer's role was no longer to propose sensible and cost-effective systems, but to enthuse over schemes, however barmy, and revel in meeting the 'challenges' they provided. This new approach is reported endlessly in books and articles. Nowadays, this is how one is seen to be a 'good' engineer; this is how the engineer wins prizes and can even be made an honorary member of the architectural profession.

So how does one these engineers go about her work.[33] Amongst the gushing prose about how engineer Jane Wernick worked with architect Sarah Wigglesworth is embedded the following bits of dialogue:

Sarah 'It started in a very organic way. That was when it was really out of control ...'

Jane '... you were thinking about something like a hut ...'

Sarah 'We worked in very much a hands-on way we sat doodling away in a very equal way ...'[34]

Jane '... we worked together very intensely ...'

Sarah 'I am absolutely useless with structures ... my approach is totally, totally intuitive. I am useless with numbers ...'

Jane 'I think an intuitive approach is absolutely fine ... we know how a table works ...'

Sarah '... Both Jane and I are not shy about doodling and I think that is an imperative ... I find working with engineers best if they can draw beautifully ...'

The engineer's beautiful doodles

And what was the upshot of all this intensive, intuitive work and beautiful doodling? Photographs of the finished project show something that looks as if it was bought in a garden centre, and assembled from instructions that had been written as a practical joke.

But it isn't just for bizarre bits of garden ornament that engineers are willing to go along with architectural misconceptions.

---

[32] Predictably architectural writers have compared Calatrava to their engineer-heroes – '...in a direct line... Maillart and Freyssinet to Nervi and Candela.' Molinari, 2000, p10. Of course this comparison is ridiculous, as the engineer-heroes' work was sensible and value for money whereas Calatrava's work is never built for these reasons.

[33] *Case Study 1*, Larsen, 2003.

[34] To doodle – to scrawl or scribble meaninglessly. *Chambers Dictionary*, 1993.

The doodle that wasn't a doddle to build

A 1000 ft shard of glass held
up by troublesome trees

Construction was scheduled to start on the tallest building in Europe in 2009. It is to be 310 m (just over a 1000 ft) high and is known as the 'Shard of Glass'. When the Eiffel tower was built, not quite as tall as the Shard of Glass will be, it was engineers who devised the structural system, but here it is different: 'The architect wanted columns in the building to work like the branches of a tree.'[35] If this was a sensible idea to support the tallest building in Europe then clearly it should be used. But was this 'idea' based on a deep understanding of how the structure, based on the branches of a tree, would work?[36] Apparently not as the engineer notes that '... the tree analogy has proven troublesome.'[37]

Holding up the tallest building in Europe with a structural idea that proves troublesome hardly makes much sense, but sense is no longer the only criterion. But of course the engineers would never think of insisting that something more sensible than '... branches of a tree' should be used because, for them, 'The shape is beautiful for the type of structure we wanted to design'.[38] So they *did* want something troublesome to design after all. Oh, and the 'Mechanical and electrical engineers had to work hard to make sure the building is economic to run.'[39]

A prime example of this new breed of 'creative' engineers is Cecil Balmond (b1943). Apparently he was '... becoming concerned that spaces within most buildings were restrictive and empty, defined by regular grids and planar walls', so 'He began to look for inspiration in Greek mathematics and chaos theory to step outside the conventional Cartesian logic.'[40] Working with architect Rem Koolhaas over a period of years, they produced a series of unbuilt projects.

---

[35] *New Civil Engineer*, 21 September 2006, p18.

[36] The architect for this building is Renzo Piano, who shot to fame with Richard Rogers with the structurally crippled Pompidou Centre (see pages 145–146).

[37] *New Civil Engineer*, 21 September 2006, p19.

[38] ibid.

[39] ibid.

[40] *Building Design*, 29 April 2005, p20.

Cecil caught stepping outside Cartesian logic

The Casa da Música stripped bare

Eventually some did get built, one of which was the Casa da Música in Oporto. The whole building is enclosed by an irregular, concrete polyhedron, earning it the local nicknames of 'The Meteorite' or 'The UFO'. With the cover stripped away, it is possible to see just how far Koolhaas and Balmond have stepped outside Cartesian logic, or maybe any logic at all.

Of course, logic could not be stepped outside for the engineering analysis, so the all-singing and all-dancing computers programs were used again. None of this meant the client got his project on time or within budget – the client had to spend over seven times the initial budget and wait several years for it to be completed.

This new approach to engineering has become endemic. Garry Palmer, the youngest ever director of consulting engineers Faber Maunsell, sees his role as '… chasing prestigious architectural projects … steering the firm into new, exciting realms'[41] apparently. 'The closer to impossible the project the more he wants to tackle it,' because he wants to '… work with a certain kind of architect – one that had … pushed the boundaries of what is possible.' This would hardly be music to the ears of the engineer-heroes because, as the President of the Institution of Civil Engineers in 1894 Alex Peterson noted in his presidential address 'It is quite easy to build an expensive structure, but it is an engineer's duty to build an effec-

---

[41] *New Civil Engineer*, 16 March 2006, p38.

tive structure for the least possible cost.'[42] Engineers were still doing this up to the 1960s, that is until they started to be involved in 'architectural' engineering. Even in 1989 one engineer, Anthony Flint, was trying to get engineering back to its 'heroic' principles noting that 'Innovation and gimmicky structures are seldom elegant'.[43] Or in 1997 '... the fashion equating greater complexity with high engineering excellence prevails and lacks justification.'[44]

These supine engineers are victims of the Modern Movement, having been fooled by its false tenets.[45] Now, like Modern Movement architects, their main interest is to do projects for their own satisfaction and self-aggrandisement, rather than acting in their client's, let alone society's, best interest. And it is all accepted with little or no criticism in the technical press. When the scheme for the now iconic Crystal Palace was presented to the engineering community, 150 years ago, it was heavily and relentlessly criticised in print. When the extravagant engineering design of the Sydney Opera House was presented to engineers, hardly a dissenting voice was heard. It would undoubtedly be better if the supine engineers would heed the words of the pioneering environmentalist EF Schumacher, when he said:[46]

Any intelligent fool can make things bigger, more complex and more violent.

---

[42] *New Civil Engineer*, 13 October 1988, p18.

[43] *Building Design Supplement*, June 1989, p7.

[44] *The Structural Engineer*, 18 February 1997, p66.

[45] It should be pointed out that the majority of engineers work sensibly, its only those at what they think of as 'the cutting edge' behave in the way described here. Sadly this lunatic fringe is often praised in the engineering press by ignorant 'technical' journalists.

[46] In an advertisement by ITDG (now Intermediate Technology) for *Practical Answers to Poverty*.

11. Bridges Become Silly

People have constructed bridges since time immemorial. These crossed rivers and streams, or, in mountainous regions, gorges. The natural materials available were stone, wood and ropes made from vegetation. The most basic form was a slab of stone or trunks of trees placed over a stream and acting as a simple beam.

With the development of the arch and the coming of 'civilisation' more elaborate stone bridges could be built. From the ancient world the best known bridge builders were the Romans, who, as well as building timber bridges also built numerous stone arch bridges, a few of which still stand.

Almost all the bridges that were built before the coming of industrialisation and still stand, are basically copies of the arched stone bridges of the Romans. But there are a few exceptions, one being the Mathematical Bridge in Cambridge. A timber bridge, it was originally built in 1749 by James Essex the Younger (1722–1784) to the design of William Etheridge (1709–1776). It has subsequently been rebuilt to the same design in 1866 and 1905.

A stone slab bridge

A Roman bridge still stands

The Mathematical Bridge

As a neat metaphor, the pre-industrial age could be seen to be crossing to the industrial age by using a bridge – the Iron Bridge. This bridge, built in 1779 in Shropshire in England, was the first substantial structure built of iron, and the iron was smelted using coke rather than charcoal: thus physically (as well as metaphorically) ushering in the Industrial Revolution.

The Iron Bridge was built, in the way that the individual pieces are joined, as though it was made of timber. But, as the process of industrialisation accelerated, designs of bridges made of iron proliferated. But to appreciate bridges as something more than a visual object, a basic understanding of how bridges work structurally is needed, in particular how beams work. What a bridge does is to *transfer* the weight of anything on the bridge, as well as the weight of the bridge itself, to the points of support.

The Industrial Revolution heralded by the Iron Bridge

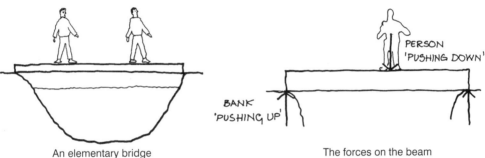

An elementary bridge   The forces on the beam

The bridge stops the people from falling into the water by supporting their weight where they are standing, then transferring their weight to the banks which, unlike the water, can support them. There are two sets of forces applied to the beam. The weight of the people and the bridge itself – the load – causes forces that are pushing down on the beam. Where the beam is supported – on the banks of the stream – there have to be forces pushing upwards: these forces are called reactions. All the pushing-down forces – the loads – have to be equal to all the pushing-up forces – the reactions – so that the beam is in vertical equilibrium. (It is usual to show these forces as arrows.)

If a simple experiment is done with a piece of flexible material it can be seen that, if supported at its ends and loaded in the middle (or elsewhere for that matter), it bends. This bending effect causes the top of the beam to squash and the bottom to stretch, with the squashing and stretching being greatest at the centre and almost absent near the supports.

As the top is being squashed this means that there must be horizontal compressive forces in the beam, and as the bottom is being stretched there must be horizontal tensile forces. So the 'bending effect' causes horizontal forces inside the beam which are compressive at the top, varying continuously until they become tensile at the bottom. As these forces are horizontal they can't contribute to vertical equilibrium.[1]

---

[1] These horizontal forces are required for moment equilibrium, see Millais, 2005, p27 et seq.

187

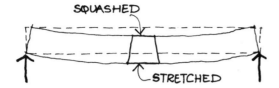

The 'bending effect' on a beam supported at each end

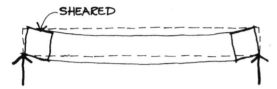

The 'shearing effect' on a beam supported at each end

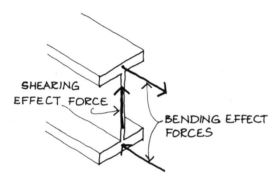

The bending and shear effect forces in an I beam

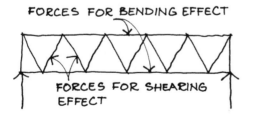

The force systems in a truss

Vertical equilibrium is maintained by a system of vertical, or nearly vertical, forces in the beam. Because these cause the beam to lozenge or shear, this is called the shearing effect. Unlike the bending effect, which is at a maximum in the centre, the shearing effect is at a maximum near the ends at the supports.

In a solid beam it is not obvious which part of the beam resists the bending effect and which part the shearing effect. However, if a beam has the cross-sectional shape of the letter I,[2] then it is far easier to see which part of the beam is resisting the two effects – the top and bottom flanges resist the bending effect by two horizontal forces, and the web resists the shearing effect by vertical forces.

Rather surprisingly, armed with these basic concepts of the structural behaviour of a loaded beam, it is possible to understand how other shapes used as spanning structures work. The trick is to find out where the horizontal forces, caused by the bending effect, and the vertical, or nearly vertical, forces, caused by the shearing effect, act in the other shapes. The structural forms commonly used for bridges, apart from beams, are: trusses, arches and suspension cables. So all that's needed is to identify which parts of the structure cater for the bending effect and which part for the shearing effect. For a truss this is relatively straightforward.

This system is very much like the ones in the I-beam, the bending

[2] Beams with the cross-sectional shape of the capital letter I are commonplace in buildings and other structures. A keen observer should be able to spot these in towns or cities.

effect is resisted by forces in the top and bottom booms, and the shearing effect is resisted by nearly vertical forces in the diagonal elements.

To see how arches and suspended cables resist the bending effect and the shear effect is not so straightforward, but as an arch is just an upside down cable or vice versa, once one is understood the other follows directly. Consider an arch. These are usually continuously curved and are also in compression, so at first sight they seem to have nothing in common with beams or trusses. But the most important thing to understand is that whenever a structure spans the bending effect and the shearing effect have to be present in one form or another. The trick is to find the form.[3] What is needed are horizontal compressive and tensile forces for the bending effect and vertical, or nearly vertical, forces for the shearing effect. In an arch, that is always in compression, this hardly seems likely.

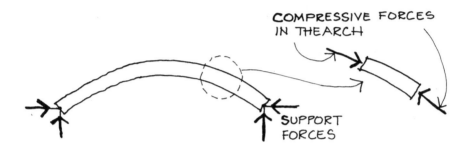

Compressive forces in an arch

To find the horizontal compression force, needed for the bending effect, and the vertical force needed for the shearing effect, the inclined compression force can be thought of as having two parts, components in technical language. One is horizontal, for the bending effect, and one is vertical for the shearing effect.

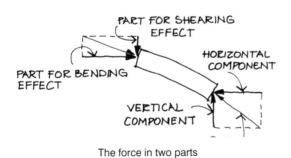

The force in two parts

But, as has been seen, the horizontal forces that resist the bending effect come in pairs, spaced a vertical distance apart. One is compressive, here given by the horizontal part of the inclined force in the arch, but where is the horizontal tensile force? The diagram that showed the arch has vertical arrows at the supports to indicate the vertical reaction, but there are also horizontal arrows indicating horizontal reactions, and these provide the clue. If an arch is to stand there must a force that stops the arch spreading. This force can be provided either by heavy abutments or by a tie member.

So that's where the 'missing' horizontal tension force, needed for the bending effect, is to be found; either in a tie member, or 'hidden' in the abutments. If the arch is inverted

---

[3] Learning this trick is not *that* straightforward; see for instance Chapter 7, Millais, 1997, 2005.

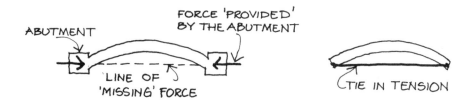

Holding up an arch

to form a suspension bridge then the 'missing' horizontal force is the one in compression. Again this could be provided by a compression member, but more usually it is provided by abutments as shown in the diagram. Usually the huge abutments needed to resist the horizontal reactions are hidden beneath the ground. Here the horizontal force is provided by a cable running from the top of the tower to the hidden abutment.

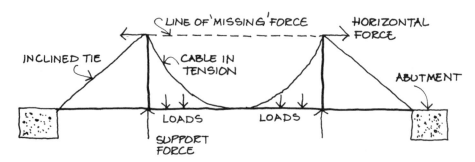

Forces in a suspension bridge

Since the beginning of the industrial period, engineers attempted to design bridges that worked well structurally, were economic to build and maintain, and were durable. This resulted in a variety of bridges, mainly built from steel or concrete. Some bridges were single spans whereas other had multiple spans. Even though some bridges could look a bit complicated, for most bridge engineers the watchword was simplicity, simplicity in form.[4]

Simple truss bridge

Simple arch bridge

---

[4] For the reader who wants to know more about bridges the must-have book is *Bridges* written by the outstanding engineer Fritz Leonhardt (1909–1999). Again, no specialist knowledge is needed.

Simple multi-span beam bridge

Gertie galloping in 1940

Gertie's disastrous last gallop

From a simplistic point of view, all the bridges shown are sensible in that they work well structurally and do not make more of an impact on the landscape that is absolutely necessary.[5] So is that all that makes a bridge sensible, minimum impact and a straightforward structural form? Well, provided the resulting bridge fulfils its function that's certainly one approach. But bridges designed along these lines haven't always fulfilled their function as quite a number have collapsed.

This can happen when engineers 'push things to the limit' which can effectively mean past the limit. This occurred with a suspension bridge built in America in 1940 – it was called the Tacoma Narrows Bridge. Immediately after it opened the bridge started to demonstrate quite alarming behaviour. Under certain wind conditions it would twist rhythmically, earning it the name 'Galloping Gertie'.

After four months of intermittent galloping, Gertie collapsed. It is one of the most famous bridge failures of all time, mainly because its galloping behaviour, and its subsequent collapse, was captured on film and it's shown, at some point, to every civil engineering student.[6] Its collapse was due to a very complex type of aerodynamic behaviour. Under certain conditions the wind caused eddy currents which had a similar effect to someone pushing a swing harder and harder. But not usually mentioned was that its deck was much, much more slender than any suspension bridge built before. Perhaps it was

---

[5] It is assumed that these bridges are also sensible from the technical and economic point of view.

[6] It is easy to access excerpts from this film on the internet.

a bit silly to design the slenderest suspension bridge ever as though it was just another design, which, as it turned out, it wasn't.[7]

As bridges have a clearly understood function – carrying the loads to the supports – this should not be compromised by basic design features that reduce their structural efficiency. But, at the same time, bridges almost invariably have a strong visual presence, so aesthetics have an important role. Here, the question is whose aesthetics are to be accommodated? Look at this bridge built in America.

An aesthetically pleasing bridge?

In trying to come to some aesthetic view, the knowledge of the structural behaviour of bridges, outlined earlier, does give one criterion.[8] Here, from the point of view of appropriate structural form, there is some visual confusion as to whether it's a beam with a decorative arch, or a slender arch carrying a heavy beam. Fritz Leonhardt (1909–1999), the doyen of bridge design, makes this point, 'A conceptually peculiar structure ... The combination of a strong beam and a thin arch is not convincing'.[9] Here is another bridge that is trying hard to be 'different'.

Trying too hard to be different?

In 1978, this pair of bridges was given an award for being beautiful but Professor Leonhardt doesn't like them either: 'These bridges are innovative as far as shape is concerned, but their aesthetic shape leaves much to be desired ...'.[10] But what Leonhardt doesn't mention is the curvy bits at the end of the

---

[7] In 1941 a report was produced by three eminent engineers called *The failure of the Tacoma Narrows Bridge*. In this report various comparisons are made with other American long span suspension bridges that had been already constructed. Every comparison shows that the Tacoma Narrows Bridge was more slender and flexible by far than any other bridge. For instance the deflection under maximum load was three and half times more than the next most flexible bridge, and the angle of twist under anti-symmetric load was more than four times greater than the next most flexible.

[8] The question of aesthetics for public objects is endlessly debatable, with never a clear conclusion. So aesthetic opinion based on technical understanding is but one with perhaps no more importance than any other...

[9] Leonhardt, 1984, p248.

[10] ibid, p256.

sloping struts. These serve no real structural purpose; they're there to win a 'beautiful bridge' award. While decorating a structure with non-functional elements is one thing, to start shaping the structure for aesthetic rather than functional ends is quite another.[11]

Once words like 'innovative' and 'award' appear, the slippery slope to structural silliness beckons, which is one (unacceptable) thing for buildings but is another (totally unacceptable) thing for bridges. But, in the 1980s, bridges started, for attention-seeking reasons rather than any other, to become silly. This was mainly due to two engineers who were also architects – Santiago Calatrava (b1951) and Marc Mimram (b1955). According to Molinari, 'The bridge for Calatrava, is meant to be interpreted as a monumental presence, a signal that constructs a new relationship with its environs,'[12] and Calatrava himself thinks that

In my view, the construction of a bridge requires a particular kind of architectural sensitivity from an engineer, especially when imagining its form, which can be conceived as an important point of reference, a note of interest in a landscape otherwise devoid of any distinctive character.[13]

Devoid of any 'distinctive character' until Calatrava's bridge arrives that is. His first effort was an arch with a road threaded through.

Calatrava's first attempt

But as a foretaste of what was to come, this fairly standard bridge form was replete with wacky details. Things 'lent over a bit', bits were tapered for no reason, and nothing quite 'lined up'. More like 'a peculiar kind of architectural sensitivity' than a 'particular' one.

In 1987, Calatrava was asked by the Junta de Andalucía to design a bridge over the

---

[11] The reader may like to look back to page 76, to see the curvy bits added by an architect to the engineer's Eiffel tower.

[12] Molinari, 2000, p158.

[13] ibid.

A peculiar kind of architectural sensitivity

Guadalquivir River in Seville. The selection of Calatrava '... emphasised the Junta's commitment to signature architecture of public works.'[14] This was asking for trouble and trouble duly arrived.[15] It was to be part of Expo '92. This time '... when imagining its form' Calatrava was determined that his bridge would be '... an important point of reference.' The result was perhaps one of the silliest bridges ever built.

Perhaps the silliest bridge ever built

This is a sort of very lopsided suspension bridge (when the cables support the deck directly, instead of the deck hanging from the cable, it is called a cable-stayed bridge). But instead of the anchor block for the cables being at ground level, this time it is a enormous sloping concrete mast! This made it very expensive and difficult to build – no surprises there. It also meant the client got one for the price of two.

Marc Mimram ploughed a similar, if less extreme, furrow, but was also capable of strange leaps of 'imagination' for the form of a bridge. In one case he partially reverted to prehistoric times by innovatively using the trunk of a tree.[16]

Back to basics

[14] Pollalis, 1999, p2.

[15] Actually there were to be two bridges of the same design but '... the complexities of the design and the projections for increased costs caused MOPU [the client] to drop the design for the second bridge ... decided to adopt a conventional design instead ...'. ibid, p16.

[16] Actually this bridge was hardly prehistoric as the walkway cantilevered off the trunk, which meant the trunk had to be restrained from twisting by using a lot of bolts and bits of metal.

Up to this time architects had taken little active interest in the design of bridges, though their appetite had been whetted by architect Max Bill's book on Maillart,[17] which gave him the status of engineer-hero. But with the endless publication of Calatrava's work in the architectural press, plus his own effective self-publicity, architects started to lose their inhibitions. During the 1990s architects acted as equal or even the lead designers of bridges, but only for footbridges: bigger bridges were left to the engineers.

But why footbridges? Because the loading on footbridges is relatively light, and because footbridges are rarely, if ever, a crucial transport link perhaps they aren't that serious compared to say, the Golden Gate or the Humber suspension bridges.

A bit too big for architects

Bridges like the Golden Gate cost a lot of money, so the choice of structural form and all the details have to pass stringent cost checks.[18] But this doesn't mean, as Leonhardt points out continually, these value-for-money bridges are totally 'non-aesthetic'. For a suspension bridge, for example, the cable and hangers are pretty much determined by the loading and span, but there are choices for the deck construction and especially for the visually dominating towers.

On the other hand, footbridges don't usually cost a lot of money, so maybe some quirkiness could be afforded: so why not ask some architects to supply it? Before looking at the results of the active roles of architects it is interesting to see what Phillip Morton Shand (1888–1960), an architect himself, had to say about architects and bridges: '... there is hardly a single one [architect] living, however eminent, who could design an ordinary steel or concrete bridge ... he was quite ready to "collaborate" with an engineer ... Since he no longer commands the technical knowledge or experience to co-operate in the design, his "collaboration" is confined to non-essentials'.[19] This was written in 1932. Now, more than 70 years later it is different. Whilst architects still do not command the (necessary) 'technical knowledge or experience' they are now concerned with the 'essentials', that is the basic concept. So, starting in the 1990s, what happened? What happened is that a large number of designs for minor bridges emerged that were geometrically complex, which meant they were often expensive, difficult to design and difficult to build. Examples of these bridges are shown on the next page.

A visit to the web site of almost any trendy engineer will throw up similar masterpieces. If a slightly closer look is taken, all the predictable difficulties emerge. Take, for example, a linking footbridge that spans a dual carriage road, a common enough

---

[17] *Robert Maillart: Bridges and Constructions* (1949).

[18] Which makes it all the more surprising that Calatrava was allowed to build quite a large bridge in Seville, that didn't pass stringent value-for-money tests.

[19] *Architectural Review*, November 1932, p169.

Award-winning bridge goes round the twist

A sculptor unrolls a brilliant idea

situation, but this one is designed by an architect... Rather than going from A to B as directly as possible, this bridge snakes across the road and is set to become a landmark, and that's not all; this bridge has '... pushed structural analysis to its limits' as it's '... difficult to analyse,' and so 'Without LUSAS[20] it would have been impossible for us to be sure of the stresses and forces in the helical members.'[21] In fact, this bridge is just a straightforward truss, but what makes it completely un-straightforward is that everything is a bit curvy. This makes it difficult to draw, difficult to do the required calculations and very difficult to build. And for what? To make it a 'landmark' of course, oh, and it's great to walk along.

Crossing a road the pretty way

The only one of its kind

But another bridge was not quite so straightforward, because it had to open, not exactly the first time a bridge had to do this, but none had ever done it this way... Winner of a limited competition, it was to carry pedestrians and cyclists across a river. The basic form was conceptually, but not visually, like Calatrava's bridge at Seville. The deck that carries the pedestrians and cyclists curves across the river, and is supported by a series of cables. These cables are held up by an arch which is tilted backwards, like the mast at Seville, to balance the deck loads.

---

[20] LUSAS is a comprehensive all-singing, all-dancing computer program used for complex structural analysis.

[21] *New Civil Engineer*, 4 December 2003, p28.

When a ship has to pass by, the whole bridge rotates about its supports (by using hydraulic rams), to a position where the curved deck forms an arch in the sky. The supporting arch just tilts back a bit more. Quite brilliant, but hold on: what are those things in the river under the bridge? Oh, those are ship protection fenders. Are they far apart? No, just 30 m. But the bridge spans 100 m, couldn't it just span 30 m and open, like Tower Bridge, when a ship passes... maybe, but how landmarkey would that be?

Everyone's very pleased with the bridge: Gateshead, where it is, has been put on the map, attracting people from all over the world, the engineers found it was a '... fascinating challenge,'[22] and it was given loads of awards by everyone – so in this case it's been a huge success. But like all these 'design-driven' bridges, rather than the purely functional ones, one has to ask:

- Why does Gateshead have to be put on the map? Where was it before?
- Should people be encouraged to cross the world to see an eccentric bridge?
- Why do engineers need such pointlessly fascinating challenges?
- Why should such a strange object be given awards?

The answer to all these questions is because bridges are now designed in the architectural ghetto, where attention-seeking designs are the top priority.

With all this effort in designing bridges the like of which hadn't been seen before, it seemed likely that someone, like the designers of the never-been-so-slender-before Tacoma Bridge, would come a cropper. And they did. It happened to the designers of a bridge that spans the Thames; it is now universally known as the 'Wobbly Bridge'.

The design was by a team of architects (Norman Foster & Partners), engineers (Ove Arup & Partners) and a sculptor (Antony Caro), and it was placed first out of 200 entries for a competition held in 1996. It was for a new footbridge to cross the Thames from the old Bankside power station, now remodelled as a gallery for modern art and renamed Tate Modern, on the south side, to St Peter's Hill that leads to St Paul's Cathedral, on the north side. Spanning between these famous locations, it was to be the first new crossing of the Thames in London for 100 years, and was to be built to celebrate the millennium. Naturally the proposed bridge generated quite a lot of interest. What the architect, the engineer and the sculptor designed was a suspension bridge, but not an ordinary suspension bridge, but one where the 'dip' of the cables was six times shallower than any ordinary one. And these 'shallowest-ever' cables not only went up and down, but also in and out.

A bridge designed by an architect,
an engineer and a sculptor

---

[22] *The Structural Engineer*, 6 February 2005, p35.

The architectural ghetto were ecstatic, the first new bridge across the Thames in London, and it was designed by an architect – ghetto spokesperson Dejan Sudjic thought that the bridge had 'muscles that rippled under the skin like a racehorse'.[23] It opened on Saturday, 10 June 2000, two months late and £2.2 million over budget. On the opening day it is estimated that 90,000 people crossed the bridge, with up to 2,000 people being on the bridge at any one time. And as the people walked across the bridge it started to sway, either amusing or alarming depending on one's disposition. This was not supposed to happen. Attempts were made to limit the number of people on the bridge, causing queues and defeating the purpose of the bridge, which was, after all, to provide an easily accessible link between the north and south banks of the Thames. On the following Monday the bridge was closed until further notice. There wasn't enough egg for all the faces that needed it. As, in the public's eye, the bridge had been designed by the architect Norman Foster, the press made a beeline for his door.

There's no eggs on Norman

Foster tried to distance himself from the fiasco telling the press that 'This is an engineering issue.'[24] Meanwhile the engineers were desperately trying to find out what had gone wrong. The bridge, oddly-shaped as it was, had been thoroughly and competently analysed and designed, and the design had been checked by independent experts. What had happened, it transpired, was that the mass of people walking across the bridge had produced a completely unexpected dynamic load – it is called synchronous lateral excitation.

When people walk, they take about two steps a second, and a normal group of people crossing a bridge will be walking at fairly randomly varying speeds. But as the bridge 'fills up', people are forced to walk with the crowd, so everyone's speed is the same; only about one and half steps are taken each second. When a person walks, each step causes a vertical force. But each step also causes a lateral force (of about 4% of their body weight). This lateral force is applied in alternate directions at half the rate of walking, so for two steps per second each force is applied once a second.

As the people all started to walk with the same step rate, but not in unison, the frequency of the steps started to coincide with the rate with which the bridge wanted to sway sideways. As the bridge started to sway in time to the walking, more and more people 'got in step', and this made the swaying worse. To understand this, four concepts need to be grasped; these are natural frequency, exciting force, self-exciting force and damping.

All these can be related to the common example of a child on a swing. If the swing

---

[23] *The Observer Review*, 11 June 2000, p7.

[24] See the front page of the *Evening Standard*, 12 June 2000.

(with the child) is pulled up and then let go, the child will swing freely at a steady rate. This rate is called the natural frequency, because it's natural to the system and only depends on the weight of the child and the length of the supporting chain. If someone starts to push the swing to keep it going this is an exciting force. A child learns to keep the swing going by causing a self-exciting force. Finally, if the swing were

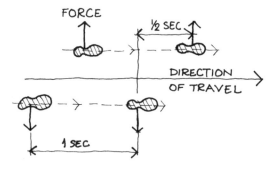

Normal walking forces

to be supported by rigid bars, and if at the rotation point there was a lot of rust or the bars were clamped rather tightly, this could make it hard to swing. This resistance to swinging is called the damping.[25]

Swinging as a dynamic system

Each engineering system that can vibrate will do so at its own natural frequency, and if there is an exciting force present of the same frequency and there is negligible damping, the system will resonate. So, for the swing, if the person doing the pushing does it in time with the natural frequency, the child will swing higher and higher. In theory, a system will resonate with bigger and bigger movements.

What happened with the Tacoma Bridge was that eddies caused by the wind, set up exciting forces that coincided with a natural frequency of the bridge, and the bridge had virtually no damping. In the end, the movements got so great that parts of the bridge broke leading to total collapse. With the Wobbly Bridge the situation was similar but not so catastrophic. The people walking in unison started to 'swing' the bridge, a self-exciting force. There was little damping, so the swaying became alarming but the people were 'unable' to destroy the bridge.

So what to do? As can be seen from the child swinging, the swing will not swing if the exciting force does not coincide with the natural frequency or there is a lot of damping. There was no way to alter the exciting force, short of controlling access to the bridge.

---

[25] Damping is basically anything that inhibits the continued vibration of a dynamic system. This is usually done by some sort of friction or hydraulic system though there are others. For the swing the rusty or clamped support causes friction between the moving parts. Other forms could be the child dragging its feet along the ground or hydraulic dampers, like car shock absorbers (which are themselves dampers), being operated by a link system to the rotating parts.

The bridge gets braced and damped

And there was no way to alter the natural frequency of the bridge short of more or less rebuilding it. So the answer had to be damping. Although, as the swing example shows, the concepts are not that complicated, to make accurate calculations can be fiendishly difficult. But these were made and it was decided to install a system of dampers below the deck. These were joined to new horizontal cruciform steel bracing members, and additional vertical damping was added near the piers. This was done, costing £5 million, and the now non-wobbly bridge re-opened on 22 February 2002. And it hasn't wobbled since.

Unsurprisingly, the Wobbly Bridge affair caused consternation in the engineering ghetto, with resentment that the architect got all the kudos until there was a problem, and then the engineers were brought into the limelight to be publicly castigated. It was all so unfair. But the engineering ghetto were to find it even more unfair when a huge bridge, called the Millau Viaduct, was built in France.

Whatever may be thought about the environmental issues surrounding the building of this enormous viaduct, as a feat of engineering it is stunning. With seven spans, it crosses the Tarn Valley with some of its piers being taller than the Eiffel tower. So, shouldn't engineers be collectively proud of what a member of their profession can do? Well they may be, but for most people, including the popular press, the bridge was designed by architect Norman Foster.

The eminent engineer Michel Virlogeux (b1946) explained how it all came about in lengthy interview given in February 2005.[26] He was head of the bridge department of the state transport agency SETRA, and he was responsible for the design of a new bridge that would cross the River Tarn. He decided the road should descend into the valley, and then cross with a 700 m long viaduct. But a colleague asked 'Why do we have to go down? Why don't we go straight across?'[27] To Virlogeux it was clear this radical idea was the solution.

The engineer or architect designed viaduct

After some months of work, a seven-span, cable-stayed viaduct was the favoured design. Virlogeux thought that the design would just go ahead without any interference – he was wrong. The head of SETRA was an engineer, but he was

[26] *New Civil Engineer*, 10 February 2006, p18–20.

[27] ibid, p19.

replaced by a politician. Virlogeux had produced a drawing that showed the bridge with the Eiffel tower next to, and smaller than, the highest piers. After the drawing was published in the papers 'everyone' wanted to be involved in this amazing project. Lobbies were formed of contractors, design engineers and architects, vying with each other to get in on the act. The new director realised that the department's bridge – Virlogeux's bridge – would not get accepted, so he organised a type of competition – there was a huge response. Seven architects, including Foster, and eight engineers were shortlisted to answer three questions:

- What do you think of the seven SETRA proposals?
- How would you improve on them?
- Have you other solutions?

In the end Virlogeux's original, seven-span, cable-stayed, straight-across-the-valley design won; but then Virlogeux was dealt a severe personal blow. The SETRA director declared that the department's engineers would no longer work on it, and the project would go ahead with an external engineer-architect team. What was Virlogeux to do? After 20 years with SETRA he left and teamed up with Foster to form *the* engineer-architect team that brought the project to fruition.

So what came out of this marriage of convenience? Did Foster design the bridge? 'The bridge hasn't been designed by Foster, that's very clear. I'm the designer'[28] said Virlogeux, and in fact, 'Responsibility for design was written out of Foster's contract.'[29] Virlogeux claims to be '... unruffled by the widespread misapprehension that UK architect Foster designed the leggy multi-span cable stay wonder.' But he 'admits he has been overshadowed by a man who played second fiddle throughout the whole design and construction process.'[30] So what did Foster do if he didn't design the bridge? Well, he made the columns 'rise apparently straight from the ground' and he made the deck 'flow seamlessly into the hillside at either end' and he influenced the shape of the piers and was instrumental in the removal of 'unnecessary' intermediate columns in the first and last spans. Yet, according to Vilogeux, 'He could not have made the Millau Viaduct the triumph it is without Foster.'[31]

An article based on an interview with Foster appeared in a subsequent edition of the same magazine.[32] The article states, contrary to Virlogeux's definitive statement, that Foster's '... winning design has been transformed into eight soaring spans of concrete and steel'. The article continues with 'His overall concept for the bridge ...' and 'Foster maintains it is critical to follow a project from start to completion.' and 'You have an interest in every stage – not simply "we are the designers"'.[33] If the Foster + Partners website is visited, the first image that appears is one of the Millau Viaduct (Well, it did on 30 July 2008).

---

[28] ibid, p20.

[29] ibid.

[30] ibid, p18.

[31] ibid, p19.

[32] *New Civil Engineer*, 16/20 December 2004, p16–17.

[33] ibid, for all quotations.

And if one follows the web site to the Millau viaduct, the following text appears:

> Bridges are often considered to belong to the realm of the engineer rather than that of the architect. But the architecture of infrastructure has a powerful impact on the environment and the Millau Viaduct, designed in close collaboration with structural engineers, illustrates how the architect can play an integral role in the design of bridges. It follows the Millennium Bridge over the River Thames, in expressing a fascination with the relationships between function, technology and aesthetics in a graceful structural form.

There is nothing about Michel Virlogeux designing the bridge, or for that matter even contributing to the design. At the end of the text his name is mentioned last in a list of 'consultants'.

So the matter of who designed the Millau Viaduct seems unresolved; the popular press attributes it to Foster. The fact that the public thought that an architect had designed one of the world's major bridges made members of the engineering ghetto more than unhappy. The letter pages and opinion columns of the technical press seethed with pent-up rage and frustration. No engineer thought that architects had made any contribution to bridge design in general: 'It's bonkers to put architects in the lead for bridges ...'[34] and so on, but jealousy of architects' self-promotional skills also emerged: 'We have much to learn about self-promotion from our architect friends' was an editorial comment.[35]

By 2008, the Royal Institute of British Architects was so convinced that architects were better at designing bridges than engineers, that it held a competition, for a bridge, that was only open to architect-led teams. This prompted one engineer to remark, taking

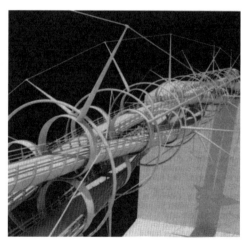

A cracker of a design or a design that is crackers?

some historical liberties, that it '... would be like Newton asking Shakespeare to front his scientific manuscripts ...' which could lead to the public thinking that '... Shakespeare was responsible for the Three Laws of Motion.'[36]

But when engineers decide to give themselves a chance at self-promotion they show just how inept they are. In 2006, to celebrate the bicentenary of the birth of the great nineteenth century engineer Isambard Brunel (1806–1859), the *New Civil Engineer* and the University of Bristol held a competition. It was for a design for

---

[34] *New Civil Engineer*, 13/20 April 2006, p8.

[35] ibid, p13.

[36] *New Civil Engineer*, 12 June 2008, p9.

a bridge that would span across the Clifton Gorge, as does Brunel's famous suspension bridge. A staggering 600 entries were received, and an item was published about them with the ambiguous headline 'Clifton crackers revealed'.[37]

But worse was to come, the design chosen as the winner had been designed by an architect!

The winning design that wouldn't stand up

So end of story really, it turns out that architects can design bridges and can win bridge competitions set by engineers. But hold on, the judges have some comments about the winning design they chose. They said '... it was likely that the arches would have to be modified with the addition of extra structural members to make it work'[38] (!) and not only that, 'There was also some concern over precisely how this bridge could be practically constructed.'[39] Clearly the engineers are in a state of total confusion, they set what purports to be a serious competition for a bridge design, then chose as the winner a design (by an architect) that wouldn't stand up and couldn't be built. So not much hope from that quarter.

It seems that for the foreseeable future the public will pay for overcomplicated, overpriced landmark bridges designed by architects, with bridge engineers acting as supinely as do their colleagues who are concerned with buildings. Perhaps at some point simple, elegant, unassuming bridges will come back into fashion but don't hold your breath.

In 2007 under the headline 'Top bridge designers unite to bring design back down to earth'[40] it was reported that the world's top bridge designers are to write guidelines to stop clients picking 'iconic' i.e. silly designs! In 2008, the Royal Institute of British Architects decided they wanted engineers to join their bridge competition judging panels, um makes sense, as they '...can't do it alone,' and to '... ensure the winning design is structurally sound'[41] – finally...

---

[37] *New Civil Engineer*, 25 May 2006, p18.

[38] *New Civil Engineer*, 13 July 2006, p16.

[39] ibid.

[40] *New Civil Engineer*, 28 June 2007, p9.

[41] *New Civil Engineer*, 31 January 2008, p6.

12. Fooling Yourself All the Time

Before World War II, very few buildings that followed the diktats of the Modern Movement were built. Most architects, and the buildings they designed, followed what could be called traditional design, though that description is really over-general. During the 1930s a few architects who were followers, or considered themselves part of, the Modern Movement managed to get teaching posts in schools of architecture where, presumably, they were tolerated by the 'proper' architects. But gradually some got into positions of power in schools, which they immediately used to increase the number of Modern Movement architects in teaching positions and, at the same time, remove those who were unsympathetic.

By 1960, in Great Britain, and in much of the rest of the world, schools of architecture were dominated by Modern Movement teachers and the Modern Movement diktats were the only ones taught. Thanks to this and other manoeuvring, the design guidelines that were to be used, and were used, for the massive reconstruction that was required due to the extensive war damage, were founded in the Modern Movement.

It didn't take long for the general public, after their initial enthusiasm in actually having somewhere to live and work, to realise that Modern Movement architecture was not for them. However over the ensuing years their desires were largely ignored by the architectural profession. Soon pejorative comments about Modern Movement architecture began to appear in the non-architectural press – architects could not have been unaware of the unpopularity of their designs, but they chose to ignore it and soldier on with their Modern Movement vision.

But if your endeavours are constantly sneered at and openly criticised and if you choose to ignore these views, then your self-esteem needs to be bolstered in some way. What Modern Movement architects did was to invent various strategies to convince themselves, if not others, that what they were producing was of value, and that they were, in fact, talented and often great architects. Their strategies were:[1]

1   To produce initial creative sketches that showed how, in a moment of inspiration, the architect had understood the whole design.

2   To make sure that glamorous photos were taken of any finished project that, devoid of people, could be published in selective and fawning architectural magazines. And could eventually, with a bit of luck, form the basis of an architectural monograph.

---

[1] No one can be surprised that a pioneer, if not the originator, of most of these strategies, was the 'master of modern architecture' Le Corbusier.

3   To create endless prizes for projects; the judges were invariably other architects, so that many architects were able to design 'prize-winning' projects.

4   To coin, and endlessly repeat, catch-phrases that were supposed to encapsulate essential truths about (modern) architecture.

5   To develop an arcane, if not to say incomprehensible, 'theory' which showed that their designs had an intellectual basis.

These strategies are worth examining one by one.

The idea of the 'creative sketch' is to show that the architect has been able to completely understand the task in hand – design a theatre, a house, a swimming pool, whatever – in all its complexity and, in a lightning sketch, demonstrate the solution. The sketch is not drawn accurately or in any detail, usually the architect uses a suitable designery tool – a very soft pencil, a stick of charcoal or perhaps a thick felt tip. It is sufficiently vaguely (badly) drawn to make sure there are many options left open, and it is almost invariably a sketch of the building as an object – a sculpture.

The master shows architects how to draw

The result of an inspirational lunch

When Le Corbusier visited the United States in 1935 he gave a series of lectures[2] which were illustrated by drawing a series of what can only be described as badly-drawn, childish sketches. For his followers, at that time a minority, it clearly demonstrated how a great architect put across his ideas.

Sometimes, if the architect is famous enough, these sketches can be done over a meal with the client. In front of the awe-struck client, the architect will, as the client outlines his requirements, take a designery pen from his pocket, immediately show the client how it should be. Very occasionally an architectural genius is caught in the act of creation.

Perhaps the most surprising thing about these creative sketches is that they are kept. But not only are they kept as evidence of the master's genius, they also form an essential part of the archive of any project.

---

[2] These were given in French – see Chapter 13.

Caught in the act of creation

Whereas, for those outside the architectural ghetto at least, the creative sketches seem badly drawn and of consistent poor quality, the architectural photograph is at the other extreme: it's taken with meticulous care and has to be of flawless technical quality. For this a special type of photographer is required – the architectural photographer. The architectural photographer can be likened to the fashion photographer – both creating fantasy out of everyday objects; in the case of the fashion photographer out of clothes and people, and in the case of the architectural photographer out of buildings. But the architectural photographer does not photograph a building 'as found'. First of all evidence of human habitation must be removed,[3] then the photographer and/or the assistant starts with the preliminary work. This includes carrying out any cleaning,[4] removing unsightly objects, and then positioning such props as are necessary. Next the lighting has to be perfect, done by using special photo lights and/or getting the natural lighting 'just right', which can of course mean waiting hours, or longer.

Again, the pioneer here was Le Corbusier. Each time he actually had one of his designs built he would employ a professional photographer to take pictures of his creation: '... Le Corbusier was one of the first architects of the twentieth century to set such store by the precise photographic record of his finished work.'[5] His buildings were not photographed as though they were being used by human beings but as 'Purist set-pieces, empty, luminous space, removed from the quotidian contaminations of domesticity and the depredations of time ...'.[6]

Since Le Corbusier the 'tradition' of the architectural photograph as empty set-pieces has gone from strength to strength, and every time an architect has one of his/her designs built, the photographing ritual inevitably takes place. This ritual takes place inside the building...

No contamination of domesticity

The fruit of a 1985 ritual

---

[3] Ideally architectural photos are taken after the building is complete but before it has been sullied by non-architectural human hands.

[4] The photographer usually arrives with enough cleaning material to get him a contract as an office cleaner.

[5] Frampton, 2001, p33.

[6] ibid.

...and outside the building. Here, if possible, the building is photographed as a timeless object, again set apart from daily life – no people, no parked cars, no nothing – just a beautiful object that just so happens to be a building.

A building as a beautiful object

Or part of the building may be photographed to form an abstract composition.

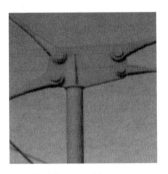

Building, architecture
or abstract art?

Of course it's not the choice of the photographer to take photos that show buildings as single objects, abstract images or spaces desperately devoid of humanity, it's the choice of their clients, the architects, because this is how they see their buildings, as artistic objects untainted by the occupation and usage by ordinary people. All the occupants do, thanks to their total incomprehension of architecture, is just bugger up the spaces, not only with their presence but their insistence on producing mess and clutter; by sticking up postcards, or photos of their ghastly relatives, or similar architectural crimes.

Some think that how a building will look in 'the photographs' partly drives architectural design. According to Stewart Brand,[7] 'Tales were told of ambitious architects specifically designing their buildings to photograph well ...'. Ove Arup who was one half, with Berthold Lubetkin, of the 'architectural-engineer dreamteam' of the 1930s,[8] wrote retrospectively (in 1979) of Lubetkin that 'He just cared for the pictures in the architectural magazines.'[9] Architect Frank Duffy talked about 'the curse of architectural photography, which is all about the wonderfully composed shot, the absolutely lifeless picture ...'.[10]

But success in the Modern Movement dominated architectural ghetto is measured by the appearance of these sterile, stylised photographs of an architect's work in architectural magazines and books. The ultimate accolade is a whole book, a monograph, devoted to a

---

[7] Brand, 1994, p55.

[8] See pages 174–175 (Chapter 10).

[9] Jones, 2006, p60.

[10] Brand, 1994, p55.

single architect with her/his name appearing proudly on the cover for all (of the architectural ghetto) to see. Most of the content of these monographs is graphic, with a major part usually being photos. So, no photos, no chance of success, let alone architectural stardom.

But this graphic material, sketches and photos are even more important if an architect is to win an award. Stewart Brand again '... the award system is based on photographs ... Just purely visual photographs taken before people start using the building.'[11] Like other attention-seeking groups,[12] the architectural ghetto is awash with awards. These awards start at local level and reach up to national and international levels. They are for projects and also for architects themselves – a type of lifetime achievement awards. These awards are sponsored by a variety of organisations, usually professional architectural bodies; they are also sponsored by manufacturers of building components as well as individual foundations. It is enlightening to look at who and what wins awards. With so many awards on offer, only two are briefly examined. They are: the Pritzker Prize and the RIBA Stirling Prize. These prizes are awarded annually, the first for lifetime achievement and the second for a project.

The Pritzker prize is funded by the Pritzker family, whose fortune is based on the ownership of the international chain of Hyatt hotels. The prize was inaugurated in 1979 and is according to their web site[13] 'architecture's most prestigious award' or even more pompously as 'the Nobel of architecture.' Amongst the 30 recipients of the award from 1979 to 2008, were Norman Foster in 1999 at the age of 64 and Jørn Utzon in 2003 at the advanced age of 85. The award is presented at a grandiose ceremony in a famous location (in 2000, for instance, it was presented at The Jerusalem Archaeological Park) and is attended by the great and good of the architectural ghetto.

As the prize has only been going since 1979, all the recipients are members of the Modern Movement-inspired 'establishment' and the list contains the usual suspects. In 2004 it was given to Zaha Hadid (b1950), the only woman to receive the prize by that date. Hadid is an architect whose work is 'deconstructivist'. This is a term derived from the arcane philosophising of Jacques Derrida (1930–2004) and gave intellectual respectability to her advanced wonky boxes.

In an article about Hadid written by Joseph Giovannini, he notes that 'she entered an exploratory realm where she developed forms that are distorted and warped in the throes of Einsteinian space.'[14] She may well have entered a realm where forms are 'distorted and warped', and it seems most likely she has, but Einsteinian space has absolutely nothing to do with it.[15] Like Archigram, Hadid's reputation is mainly as a 'paper architect' but since 1994 an increasing number of her warped and distorted projects have been built. The building illustrated, the Phaeno Science Center, was also shortlisted for another prize, the Stirling Prize. For this the judges opined that 'There is something almost Joycean in the

---

[11] ibid.

[12] There are now twice as many cinema awards – around 9,000 – as there are feature films produced each year according to the *Observer*.

[13] www.pritzkerprize.com/164/pritzker2005/mediakit/mediakit.htm#abriefhistory.

[14] See page 36 of http://www.pritzkerprize.com/143/mono2004/Hadid.pdf.

[15] Buildings exist in a local, three-dimensional Eucildean (i.e flat) space whereas Einsteinian space is neither flat nor three-dimensional. Furthermore space and time are combined into the concept of spacetime, a very different matter.

More gawky than pretty

babble of collaged constructional languages.'[16] The same source claimed that the building was '... more gawky than pretty'. All of which goes to show that you can equally win the architectural equivalent of the Nobel prize with relatively few built projects, and the built few can definitely come within the oddly-conceived category.[17]

The RIBA Stirling Prize was set up in 1996 to commemorate the British architect James Stirling (1926–1992). He was, during his lifetime, Britain's major architectural star, winning the RIBA Gold Medal in 1980 and the Pritzker Prize in 1981. His early work was fairly 'perfect-boxy' but he soon went a bit wonky, which didn't help the building's owners or users.[18]

Stirling goes a bit wonky

Towards the end of his career he committed the unforgivable sin for a Modern Movement architect: he started to decorate his buildings, using garish colours – pink, mauve, acid green. Even worse, he began to introduce historical references. This confused everyone, so that when he died his reputation rather went with him. In spite of this, in 1996 the prize was inaugurated, to be awarded to a building designed by a member of the RIBA and built anywhere in the European Union. The results in many ways were predictable: in fact, exactly what would be expected to win architectural prizes. For instance, in 1999 the prize went to the only monocoque building that had ever been built, the Media Centre at Lord's cricket ground,[19] and in 2002 the prize was won by the only-one-of-its-kind bridge

---

[16] See RIBA Report No 7082.

[17] While the distorted buildings of Hadid evoke, in some people anyway, Einstein, Derrida and Joyce, it can be difficult to see if the Modern Movement is alive and well. Apparently it is because 'Agreeing with Zenghelis and Koolhaas that modernism had not been given its fair theoretical due, Hadid joined the cause, producing designs inspired by the Russian Suprematist painter, Kazemir Malevich, twentieth century Western abstraction, and social utopianism.' That's a relief. (See 'Zaha Hadid' by Elyse Weingarten in *EGO*, January 2005.)

[18] In the late 1960s Stirling designed a housing scheme for Runcorn. The scheme was so problematic that is was demolished in the 1990s! See also page 259.

[19] See pages 152–153 (Chapter 8).

at Gateshead.[20] But in 2005 the jury topped even these strange choices; they chose the Scottish Parliament Building.

The building was controversial from the outset, with questions being raised as to whether a new building was needed. But Donald Dewar (1937–2000), who was the First Minister for Scotland, was adamant that a new building was needed and so, of course, an international architectural competition was held. Obviouly, no architectural competition can be

The fragmented, non-orthogonal, non-hierarchical, dynamic composition

won with a straightforward, sensible, easy-to-build design, and the winning project by Enric Miralles (1955–2000) was certainly none of these. Inspired in part by tethered upturned fishing boats, the building was a geometric nightmare or, as architect Clare Wright put it, '[it was] a fragmented, non-orthogonal, non-hierarchical dynamic composition'.[21] In other words, a geometric nightmare.

Inside, over the debating chamber, 'The complexity of the roof structure is particularly dizzying.'[22] But for the engineer 'The stability of the structure was extremely complex due to the discontinuities in levels and interaction of all the elements requiring extensive three-dimensional analysis,'[23] because 'This structure is entirely sculptured and its geometry required unique nodes and bracing systems.'[24]

When buildings have this level of complexity, in terms of geometry, structural behaviour, or building construction, problems are inevitable.

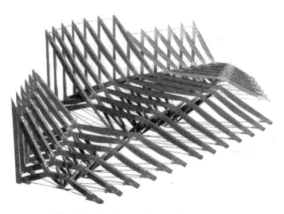

The dizzyingly complex roof structure

This is because the conceptual designers, the architects, are simply unable to foresee, at the drawing stage, all the problems the complexity brings. On the Scottish Parliament Building this happened with a vengeance.

The architects alone produced 20,000 drawings because there was no repetition. But even with this they issued around 18,000 architect's instructions for alterations

[20] See pages 196–197 (Chapter 11).

[21] *RIBA Journal*, October 2004, p36–37.

[22] *Building Design*, 15 October 2004, p14.

[23] *The Structural Engineer*, 7 March 2006, p31.

[24] ibid.

during construction. It's not hard to imagine what knock-on effect this had for all those involved. The programme extended, and the costs escalated, rounding out at about nearly half a billion, yes billion, pounds.

What did 'ordinary' people think of the building for what comedian Billy Connolly called a 'pretendy wee parliament'? One correspondent wrote, 'If there were an award for the ugliest carbuncle then the new Scottish Parliament would win hands down.'[25] A local art magazine, a publication that one would have thought would support such an artistic creation, had several highly critical articles that included such comments as 'The debating chamber is a cacophony of triangular beams ...' and 'How, I wonder can anyone think in it' and 'It is strangely old-fashioned and anti-social'.[26]

Unsurprisingly there were teething and unforeseen maintenance problems.[27] But there was worse to come when a timber member, weighing 100 kg, of the cacophony of triangular beams, broke free of its moorings and dangled threateningly over the debating politicians. The chamber was cleared... Predictably, and quite rightly, this prompted concern about the whole complicated roof structure. It transpired that the connection that failed had been incorrectly made, but due to the complexity of the roof it was not abundantly clear for what load the connection should have been designed.[28]

But of course the architectural ghetto is unable to seriously recognise it for what it is: an enormously overpriced, overcomplicated, difficult-to-use, expensive-to-maintain, inappropriate building. No it's not, because, for one architectural commentator: 'This is an organic, non-hierarchical building and in this respect reflects the most important changes to society in the twentieth and twenty-first centuries, the growth of the democratic ideal' and in light of the cost and programme overruns 'It would be a shame if these aspects detracted from the importance of this building or affected the approach to architectural values in others to come.'[29] For another this is '... a work of uncommon poetry, optimism and courage', but '... one would struggle to find a precedent for it in the history of modernism.'[30]

For the judges of the Stirling Prize 'The Scottish Parliament Building is a remarkable architectural statement which has an enormous impact ... on the users who repeatedly move through a series of extraordinary spaces and their changing effects' and 'The proof of the extraordinary architectural ambition and design vision is to be seen in every aspect and detail of the finished building.' And they thought that 'the architect has formulated the philosophy of the role of the Parliament and reflected it in his architectural interpretation.'[31]

---

[25] *New Civil Engineer*, 4 November 2004, p9.

[26] *Artwork*, Issue 128, 2004.

[27] For instance due to the complexity of the building it takes two weeks to clean the windows . *Artwork*, Issue 137, 2006.

[28] See for instance *New Civil Engineer*, 16 March, p5; 23 March p6–7; 6 April 2006, p6. As a temporary measure timber elements were strengthened with unsightly tensioned webbing straps, until a permanent solution was found.

[29] *RIBA Journal*, October 2004, p36–37.

[30] *Building Design*, 15 October 2004, p14.

[31] See http://uk.archiseek.com/scotland/news/2005/000177.html

What this short survey of award-winning architects and buildings shows is that they are won on what is construed as 'architectural merit' alone. Any other criteria such as value for money, user satisfaction or ease of maintenance are completely ignored. Once, on a jury, architect Herb McLaughlin suggested that they call the clients of the shortlisted projects to '... see how they feel about the buildings, because I don't want to give an award to a building that doesn't work.'[32] Needless to say his suggestion was ignored because the awards for architects are given by architects, and are only concerned with what the architectural ghetto perceives as important, which is architecture that conforms (however far-fetchedly) to the commandments of the Modern Movement. This is because, as Bernard Rudofsky (1905–1988), an architect himself, pointed out in 1964, '... most of them [architects] are concerned with problems of business and prestige.'[33] Architectural awards exist solely to give architects prestige within the ghetto and to allow them to tout for business as 'award-winning architects' – go to any architect's website to see this in action.

As all the awards go to architects that have come from the Modern Movement persuasion what it is that they have in common? How is it expressed? As there is no coherent theory other than a random set of diktats, a number of slogans are used as shorthand to sum up their position. Contrary to all evidence, there is still a belief that what is being produced is based on some sort of inevitable logic, something scientific. Two words constantly appear to reinforce this idea and these words are honesty and functionality. They appear in various guises but they are always used to promote the idea that effective and efficient buildings are being designed.

Perhaps the basic phrase, or slogan, is 'form follows function'. Normally attributed to architect Louis Sullivan,[34] who said '... the drifting clouds, over all the coursing sun, form ever follows function, and this is the law,'[35] it was, in fact, first used by the sculptor Horatio Greenough (1805–1852) entitling a book *Form and Function: Remarks on Art*.

In many cases, both in nature and in human artefacts, form does indeed follow function; for instance a bird's egg. Nature 'knows' as humans do, that a sphere encloses the maximum volume for the minimum surface area, so many eggs have this shape, but not those of birds, whose eggs are ovoids. Why? Well maybe because this shape allows them to fit together better in a clutch, but for birds that only make vestigial nests, it stops eggs rolling away; as spheres roll in any direction but ovoids in circles. In buildings perhaps the most obvious example is the pitched roof. The function of the roof is to shed rainwater and it has been known since time immemorial that the form of the pitched roof is ideal – except for Modern Movement architects that is, who favour the form that doesn't follow function, the flat roof.

But for whole buildings it is not easy to see how this dictum can make any sense, particularly as Modern Movement buildings come in all manner of arbitrary shapes. What is more surprising is when buildings are shaped after things that seem to have no

---

[32] Brand, 1994, p55.

[33] Rudofsky, 1964, p4.

[34] 'Louis Sullivan's empty jingle' as Reyner Banham called it. Banham, 1960, p320.

[35] Fletcher, 2001, p383.

connection to buildings whatever. As ever, Le Corbusier seems to have been the pioneer in this, with his continuous references to the ocean liner. According to Kenneth Frampton '... two heterotopic[36] paradigms were to prevail throughout Le Corbusier's career ... the transatlantic liner ...'[37] – Le Corbusier made numerous drawings where ocean liners were juxtaposed with buildings,[38] in particular the Unité is seen as a land-based liner and the aft superstructure of the Aquitania looks suspiciously like the Villa Savoye.[39]

In January 2005, award-winning (the Stirling prize twice!) architects Wilkinson Eyre won a competition for a major building in Liverpool. The architect's website claims 'The team has therefore created an architecture that will express the development's varied functions as a series of visually unified forms ...',[40] so form does follow function after all. Well apparently not quite, because according to Wilkinson 'Some people are horrified and some amused by the inspiration for our Liverpool project ... which is my mobile phone – a Motorola V600.' This was because the phone has a '... mould-formed plastic aesthetic ... This is relevant to our Liverpool project, where the form has been generated by the U-shaped 10,000-seat arena ...'.[41] With such irrefutable form-following-function logic, another award must be in the bag.

The Aquitania sails away with the Villa Savoye

The inspirational phone

While, for buildings at any rate, it seems that it is not easy to get form to follow function, then at least it seems reasonable to expect that 'less is more'. Usually attributed to the perfect-boxman Mies.[42] When applied to Modern Movement architecture some people have made it into a joke – 'less is a bore' or 'less is less' or 'less is a snore', or more tellingly, and especially if Mies was involved, 'less is more expensive'. Buckminster Fuller turned it round to 'more with less'. But 'less is more' does sounds as if it ought to mean something – but what?

---

[36] Heterotopic: In the wrong place, in an abnormal place, misplaced. From the Greek roots 'hetero' meaning 'other' + 'topos' meaning 'place' = other place.

[37] Frampton, 2001, p176.

[38] For instance, Tzonis, 2001, p158 & 161.

[39] See page 1(Introduction) and page 97 (chapter 6).

[40] See http://www.wilkinsoneyre.com/main.htm (accessed in October 2008).

[41] *Building Design*, 4 February, 2005.

[42] It actually comes from a poem by the un-Modernist Robert Browning, who, in his 1855 poem *Andrea del Sarto*, wrote the line, 'Well, less is more, Lucrezia: I am judged'

Less is more...?

What do Modern Movement architects think this means? They never say explicitly as this would break the spell, but as it is so closely associated with Mies it is normally applied to the 'perfect-glass-box' strain of architecture. This basically means monochrome, sterile, inhuman boxes – windows without frames, cills or worst of all curtains;[43] cupboard doors without handles; spaces as though they had been drawn with a few straight lines from a perfect pen. Less – that is as little as possible – is more – pure, or something like that. A famous example is the Glass House by the at-the-time Mies acolyte Phillip Johnson. The hard-line 'less is more' tendency is now known as minimalism.

Related to the fundamental 'less is more' is 'God is in the details', also often attributed to Mies,[44] this aphorism is far clearer as it demands that if your architectural creation is to be 'divine', then great (perhaps obsessive is a better word) care has to be taken with the details of your architectural project. What is usually meant here by 'details' is how different constructional parts of the project meet visually. For example, how a wall meets the floor, or how a window is inserted into a wall. All these connections and junctions have to be carefully considered with the aim of producing, if possible, a state of 'less is moreness'. The 'God is in the details' credo gives rise directly to the better known 'the Devil is in the details'. Ironically, for buildings, the attempts by Modern Movement architects to put God into the details often means that the Devil arrives. This happens for two reasons.

Firstly, architects rarely have the capacity to put God into all the details that are needed; hence, during construction, many Godless details are 'discovered'. Naturally extra expense and delays mount up before God is persuaded to intervene. The second reason is that the Godly details do not follow 'normal' building practice, so extra confusion has to be clarified by the architect explaining exactly how the details are to be physically achieved.[45]

Closely related to these slogans was Le Corbusier's concept of a house. For him a house was not a home, somewhere to be safe and comfortable, somewhere that somehow

---

[43] When Mies was less-is-moring with two apartment blocks in Chicago, initially the tenants were forbidden to have any curtains or blinds to shade the all-glass walls. After a revolt by the occupants, uniform metallic blinds were grudgingly permitted. Needless to say Mies himself passed up the offer to live in one of the apartments, choosing instead to continue living in a spacious, traditional, luxury apartment a few blocks away.

[44] It appeared in 'On restraint in design', *NY Herald Tribune*, 28 June 1959, but actually the saying is generally attributed to Gustave Flaubert (1821–1880), who is often quoted as saying, *'Le bon Dieu est dans le detail'*.

[45] Before buildings were designed by Modern Movement architects, it was quite usual for the architect to only supply the contractor with plans and elevations of a building. This was because the builder and the architect were in accord as to how all the details, based on established craftsmanship, would be made; so few, if any, 'detail' drawings were needed.

reflected the personality of the owner or occupier. No: for him, and for the rest of the Modern Movement, 'The house is a machine for living in.'[46] Although now hackneyed by over use, it still represents part of the mind-set of the architectural ghetto. If a house is just a machine then all other buidings must be de-humanised, made machine-like, and hence, by association, functional. Which clearly means they cannot be decorated in any way.

For Modern Movement architecture decoration is absolutely out of the question because, as Adolf Loos pointed out, 'ornament is a crime';[47] this slogan, unlike the others mentioned, rarely if ever appears in print. But this statement is considered an essential truth. Yet ornament is used frequently in Modern Movement architecture, but in the guise of functionality. This has already been pointed out in a number of cases, the pioneer being Mies. He would decorate his buildings with what looked like structural elements, to indicate that beneath the surface there was in fact a structure. At least his decoration was harmless, if often very expensive.[48]

Structure as decoration in other hands was extremely harmful. The shell roofs of the Sydney Opera House were, for the architect Jørn Utzon, a form of decoration. The idea of building decorative roof structures caught on in a big way, and dozens of projects were subsequently decorated with ill-conceived weirdly shaped roofs, setting engineers the 'fascinating challenges' they came to crave. Not only were structures used as decoration but so were building services, all those pipes and ducts through which run water, gas and hot air, for instance. These are usually hidden from view for a variety of good reasons, but with the high tech version of the Modern Movement these suddenly came into view. And not only inside the buildings, but also on the outside!

Underpinning all these 'truthful' slogans is one implied word – honesty. Few people would disagree that this word represents a wonderful concept that is unambiguously a good thing. It also allows Modern Movement architecture to take the moral high ground, because materials (they will say) are used honestly and structures are honestly expressed. In 1988, the then architectural correspondent of the *Guardian* newspaper, Martin Pawley (1938–2008), wrote a whole column with the title 'The future of architecture hangs upon the concept of honesty.'[49] On and on he goes '... commissions executed with the ruthless structural honesty of Lloyd's are so rare that they are invariably honoured by other architects', and 'The reason why structural honesty is admired dates back to the beginning of the Modern Movement', and 'Without truth

Functional decoration or decorated functionality?

---

[46] Le Corbusier, 1927, p10.

[47] See pages 33–34 (Chapter 3).

[48] See page 164 (Chapter 9).

[49] *Arts Guardian*, 11 January 1988, p10.

to materials architects cease to be designers ...' and he ends, 'Without the dedication ... to the principle of truth to structure and truth to materials ... architecture will cease to be an independent art and we shall all lose.' Arrant nonsense, of course.

One of the reasons that the Sydney Opera House was such a fiasco was not only because of the technical problems caused by Utzon's decorative shells, but because when he saw the engineer's solution he rejected it as not being 'honest'.[50] This is really a bit rich when one thinks of why Utzon wanted to cover his buildings with decorative shells in the first place. The reason was to *hide* the flytower over the stage and thus disguise the resulting boot-shaped building.[51] What's honest about that? With this type of honesty one can't help but be reminded of a line from the film *Chinatown*. When the 'hero', a private detective called Giddes (played by Jack Nicholson), is asked of the policeman Escabal, 'Is he honest?' he famously replies, 'As far as it goes...'.

And why this constant and endless harping on about 'structure'? Because 'Architecture is only made possible through structure ... a building's form will always be wholly reliant on its structure', writes professor of architecture Kurt Ackermann.[52] Architectural literature is littered with such statements as though an oft-told lie indeed comes true. The main reason that architects go banging on about 'structures' is because they don't understand their behaviour; if they did they would not see them as separate entities that have to be truthfully expressed, but merely as part of the overall building concept. This goes right back to the basic division of architecture and engineering that is discussed in Chapter 5.

It is not difficult to conclude that these slogans, which are supposed to contain essential truths about Modern Movement architecture, are spurious to say the least. So it is hardly surprising the resulting designs are so inappropriate. But what is surprising is that the engineer who was in many ways responsible for engineers 'wanting to make architects' dreams come true', Ove Arup, was by 1983, prepared to say things like 'architects don't mind cheating' and 'Functionalism really became a farce' and 'There is a lot of humbug in architects'.[53] But the mantra that apparently particularly irritated him most was the 'expression of structure' and he claimed that '... it remains the duty of the engineer to point out that the beautiful structure is rarely the same as the economical structure'.[54] On the other hand, these comments are hard to square with his behaviour during the design of the Sydney Opera House, and that of engineers from his practice on projects like the Hongkong & Shanghai Bank and the Pompidou Centre amongst many others.

To give Modern Movement architecture intellectual clout there is a theoretical side. This usually produces writing that is little different from *Ulysses* by James Joyce. For instance:

---

[50] See footnote 32 on page 126 (Chapter 7).

[51] See the diagram on page 129 (Chapter 7).

[52] Ackermann, 1991, p177.

[53] Jones, 2006, p59 & 60.

[54] ibid, p165.

At the same time, the History Building stretched the brick and glass syntax of Selwyn and Leicester until the crystalline form of the glass began to overwhelm the controlling armature of the brick ... the coupled elevator stair tower ... an articulation of access reminiscent of Kahn's 'servant' element ...[55]

Or this quote describing an architect's design process:

The method I have followed divides into four stages. First there is the search for fragments of today's society ... An illogical, alienating image ensues ... In the fourth and final stage the design method is put to the test ... The function is 'distorted' to fit the space.[56]

And an award-winning architect talking about how his office works:

In OMA, the process of formal synthesis is closer to morphogenetic processes than to the classical precepts of hylomorphism. Morphogenesis as an approach to form in its fluid state, rather than in its eternal or ideal state ...[57]

Where does this smug intellectual style, incomprehensible to those not willing to play the game, come from? Philosophy of course, and there is nothing more intellectual than that. But theoretical writing about architecture uses a very narrow part of this huge subject, and is mainly drawn from a recent tendency called Postmodernism and its offshoot Deconstructivism.

The seminal 'theoretical' work on Modern Movement architecture is *Theory & Design in the First Machine Age* by Reyner Banham, but it appears noticeably short on anything that could be called philosophy, or anything that could be called theory come to that.[58] Words like philosophy, modernism, design or theory do not appear in the index, nor is there any reference to philosophers – but there is to relativity! On page 112, for instance there is a long quote from Boccioni's *Technical Manifesto of Futurist Sculpture*:

We must begin from the central nucleus of an object as it strives for realisation, in order to discover the new laws, that is, the new forms, that relate it invisibly but mathematically to the plastic infinity within, and visible infinity without.

and much more in this obscure vein. Banham comments assuredly:

The drawing discussed above is, of course, a more or less programmatic demonstra-

---

[55] Frampton, 1980, p268.

[56] http://www.archiprix.nl/e/2002/ontwerpmeth.html (October 2008).

[57] Quote by Rem Koolhass in *El croquis 53/79 OMA/Rem Koolhaas 1987-1998.* In fact the design process worked so well that when they designed an concert hall in Oporto, it opened years late and was five times over the initial budget. See pages 134–135 (Chapter 7) and page 184 (Chapter 10).

[58] As N Salingaros notes, '... a voluminous body of writings has been mistaken for "architectural theory" even though it is nothing of the sort.' Salingaros, 2004, p159.

tion of the field theory of aesthetic space, a space which exists as a field of force or influence radiating from the geometric centre of the objects which give rise to it, and is a remarkable poetic achievement born, presumably, of Bergson and Einstein.

This is meaningless twaddle laced with terms borrowed from mathematical physics – field theory for instance.[59]

An important figure was Ferdinand de Saussure (1857–1913). Saussure, the father of linguistics, analysed language and in particular tried to look beneath the 'surface', the surface of language. By the 1950s some literary critics were using the linguistic approach to understand literature.[60] This was done by trying to analyse the text without reference to the author's intention; this approach became known as Literary Theory or Critical Theory.[61] It is interesting to note the use of the word 'theory' which has pseudo-scientific connotations.

This 'close reading' of the text showed that definitive meaning could not be given to a literary piece, and this gave rise to what is known as Postmodernism: 'Denial of the practical possibility of objectivity is held to be the postmodern position, and a hostility towards claims advanced on the basis of objectivity its defining feature'.[62] It was called Postmodernism because it came 'after' Modernism, though it is highly debatable if Modernism was or is dead.

Hard on the heels of Postmodernism came its offshoot Deconstructivism. This is usually linked to Jacques Derrida (1930–2005) who would say things like 'Deconstruction is not an enclosure in nothingness, but an openness to the other.'[63] Yes well...[64] Deconstruction pursued the idea of looking beneath the surface of anything to find hidden or subversive meanings:

> Thus, viewed in this way, 'the term "deconstruction" refers in the first instance to the way in which the "accidental" features of a text can be seen as betraying, subverting, its purportedly "essential" message'. (The word accidental is usually interpreted here in the sense of incidental.)[65]

---

[59] The insertion of words borrowed from mathematical physics is commonplace in 'theoretical' writings about architecture, and only serve to demonstrate the writers' total ignorance of any concept used in mathematical physics. Cf footnote 15, p208.

[60] This approach to literary criticism was directly influenced by the Russian Formalists. This group, that based their criticism on Saussurre, existed from 1915 to 1929.

[61] The work produced by the Frankfurt School was also called Critical Theory, which can give rise to even more confusion.

[62] As Postmoderism is notortiously difficult to define, this statement could be disputed.

[63] 'Jacques Derrida' in *Dialogues with Contemporary Continental Thinkers*, tr. and ed. by Richard Kearney, Manchester University Press, 1984, p124.

[64] According the John Carey, Derrida managed 'to evolve a language that is impenetrable to most native English speakers', and probably native speakers of an other language come to that. Carey, 1992, p215.

[65] Rorty, Richard in *The Cambridge History of Literary Criticism: From Formalism to Poststructuralism*, vol. 8, ed. by Raman Selden, Cambridge University Press, 1995.

Venturi's Mum shakes the architectural establishment

What on earth have any of these arcane ponderings got to do with architecture one might ask? Rather a lot actually, or, in some cases, too much. The publication of a book by Robert Venturi in 1966,[66] and his design for his mother's house at about the same time, had an enormous impact. In the book, the hegemony of the Modern Movement slogans was challenged and his mother's house thumbed its nose at Modern Movement orthodoxy. It had sloping roofs, windows set in walls and what look suspiciously like decorative elements. Not only that, there was no attempt to muddy the difference between 'inside' and 'outside', and it seemed pretty clear where the entrance was. All concepts that were anathema to the Modern Movement crowd. To an outsider the house looks little more than slightly off-beat, but Venturi 'arrived, through a sophisticated thought process, at deliberately banal designs.'[67]

In 1972, Venturi compounded his heresy by publishing a book that lauded the raw energy of the 'architecture' of America's gambling mecca Las Vegas.[68] With this some floodgates opened, and previously staid, fully paid-up members of the Modern Movement establishment embraced kitsch. This divided the architectural ghetto as several big name Modern Movement architects crossed the Rubicon, Michael Graves and James

Stirling for instance, but the biggest name was the ageing perfect-glass-boxman Phillip Johnson. In 1982 he completed a skyscraper in New York, the AT&T building, that contradicted the perfect-glass-box Seagram Building. It had windows punched into walls but, even more outrageous, it ended with a flourish with its eye-catching, Chippendale-style, broken-front roof pediment.[69]

Why has this got anything to do with philosophy or architectural theory? In 1977, in the magazine *Architectural Design*, the term 'post-modern' was introduced to the architectural ghetto by that inveterate categoriser of architecture Charles Jencks.

Johnson gets ahead once again

---

[66] It was called *Complexity and Contradiction in Architecture.*

[67] Risebero, 1982, p243.

[68] Co-authored with Denise Scott-Brown and Steve Izenour, it was called *Learning from Las Vegas.*

[69] Perhaps Johnson's betrayal is not that surpising as one of his best-known sayings was that 'We architects are all whores.'

Amongst his categories was the Metaphorical, which included such Modern Movement masterpieces as Le Corbusier's Ronchamp, Utzon's Sydney Opera House and Saarinen's TWA Terminal. Venturi fitted into another category, that of Historicist-Regionalist-Pluralist, whereas the ex-Mies-acolyte Johnson was assigned to the category Quasi post-modern. So that sorted everything out then. Well not quite, because Postmodernism's side-kick Deconstructivism had yet to make an appearance, but it did in 1986.

In the August edition of the *Architectural Review*, EM Farrelly claimed that 'Postmodernism is dead', detecting that a 'New Spirit had come into architecture.' This 'new spirit' was based on a load of old stuff like Constructivism, Dada and Surrealism mixed with the fashionable Pop, Punk and New Wave. In 1988 New York's Museum of Modern Art held an exhibition called Deconstructivist Architecture, organised by none other than the all-things-to-all-men Phillip Johnson. First up for deconstruction was Coop Himmelb(l)au (1968) whose '... projects are driven by critical theory, poetic transubstantiation of technology and the complex usage or programs that they house'.

Driven by critical theory

This application of critical theory allowed buildings to be designed that made Mendelsohn's swirliness look positively staid. And because the deconstructed architects could find supine engineers who owned computers with all-singing, all-dancing programs, and gullible clients, it is assumed, deconstructed buildings began to stalk the land. And what's more the buildings could be justified by theory! As deconstructed Daniel Libeskind explains:

> As Paul Valery pointed out the world is permanently threatened by two dangers: order and disorder. This project develops the realm of the in between, the interest, the realm of democratic openness, plurality and potential.....The Museum is therefore a catalyst for focussing energies, both entrepreneurial and spiritual, and moulding them into a creative expression.[70]

---

[70] see http://www.daniel-libeskind.com/projects/show-all/imperial-war-museum-north/ (November 2008). Apparently 'words spin out of him [Libeskind], many of them with little apparent meaning.' *Guardian*, 16 October 2006, p20.

Post-modern architects rejected Modernism by using decoration, and thus had opprobrium heaped on them by the keepers of the Modern Movement Holy Grail. But the Deconstructed architects avoided this because they had, for all their blatant swirliness, kept faith; they had said no to decoration. This is nonsense as, like Utzon, they were just using bent geometry as decoration and dressing it up in spurious philosophical clothes.[71]

Even some architects weren't best pleased with all this theory. In 2001, Robert Campbell wrote an article in which he christened 'theoretical' architectural writing Archispeak,[72] and gave numerous examples such as: 'Adornian referent, fractured embodiment, graphic, transubstantiality, semiotic traceable referents ...'. He concludes that 'Archispeak makes people think they are smarter than they are (when they write it) or stupider than they are (when they can't understand it). Either way, Archispeak is doing harm.' Well, if Archispeak is doing harm, then what harm is being done when it is turned in actual buildings? Presumably the non-functionality of the functional Modern Movement buildings is being replaced by the non-functionality of the dysfunctional Deconstructed ones.[73]

Functionality deconstructed

So the architectural ghetto members are able to fool themselves all of the time. The architectural masterpiece starts as a scribble – 'Herzog & De Meuron sketched the façade and roof as a random scribble'[74] – which, in a moment of creative genius, captures the essence of the design. The scribble is then, often with huge difficulty and at great expense (Sydney Opera House et al) turned into a giant sculpture which can be used, more or less, as a building. Before the sculpture has been sullied by this mundane requirement, specialist photographers capture its beauty. The photographs are then used to enter the

---

[71] For a clinical dissection of the spuriousness of Deconstructivist architecture, *Anti-architecture and Deconstruction* by Nikos Salingaros is essential reading.

[72] *Architectural Record*, October 2001, p79–80. The December issue printed numerous letters of support.

[73] One of Libeskind's buildings, a museum extension in Denver, was so deconstructed that it made some vistors feel nauseated and dizzy – see *Time*, 18 December 2006.

[74] *New Civil Engineer*, 23 November 2006, p23.

architectural sculpture into beauty competitions, which are so numerous that some sort of award is almost bound to be forthcoming.

The judges of the competitions, almost invariably other architectural sculptors, test the entries against the rules of entry, that is against the slogans of the Modern Movement, before the awards are made. When the creation has been suitably garlanded it will appear in the architectural pink press – the magazines. Here, just to maintain the myth that what is on show is more than just a superficial compliance with the slogans, a theorist will offer an analysis of the work. And everyone is pleased with themselves, unless of course they are not a member of the architectural ghetto.

If a sufficient body of slogan-complying, theoretically-analysed work is produced then the additional acolade of a monograph can be sought. And eventually, with a large slice of 'luck', all these scribbles and photographs and awards and theoretical explanations could result in the ultimate honour – the gold medal: and entrance into the hall of fame is assured.

In the case of Herzog & De Meuron's 'scribble', it was turned into, with considerable difficulty, the main stadium for the 2008 Beijing Olympic Games. Nicknamed 'the Bird's Nest', the stadium, whose structure consumed an unbelievable 45,000 tons of mangled steelwork (nearly half a ton for each spectator), has been described as a gigantic pile of grey spaghetti – hardly appetising.

45,000 tons of grey spaghetti

One can't help wishing that there was an architectural equivalent of the Golden Raspberries (awarded to the worst films, film stars and film makers).

13. Learning How to Get it Wrong

Art, architecture and structure all rolled into one

Generations of Modern Movement architects haven't just appeared, they have been through a process of architectural education – they have been taught to be Modern Movement architects. And this process was, as Modernism was itself, a reaction and rejection to what went before. But what went before was, by the time Modernism came along, far from clear cut.

Whichever way it is looked at, architecture is about building. So, one would have thought that the training of architects would, or should be, closely linked to the actual building process. Before there was any definition of architecture there was building, and this building was originally done by many, if not all, of the members of the social group. It was done in the way that was traditional to that group.

But with coming of civilization, there was a division of labour, so some people became specialised in building trades, and buildings were decorated by sculptors, painters and people who created intricate mosaics and other forms of decoration. Sometimes, as in the case of caryatids,[1] the roles of sculptors and builders became blurred, and practical and aesthetic functions were combined.

The buildings of ancient Greece and the Roman Empire were central to the development of European architecture, but little is known about how 'architects' were trained or exactly what function they fulfilled. With the collapse of the Roman Empire much, but not all, of the Roman's building skills were lost. However, they were gradually re-learnt so that between the tenth to thirteenth centuries, a huge programme of church building,

A medieval 'architect', far right, holds a drawing instrument?

---

[1] According to a disputed account by Vitruvius, caryatids were a symbolic punishment of the Greek state of Caryae. Because they sided with the Persians, the Greeks took the town and killed all the men. The women were taken into slavery and were forced to keep wearing the flowing clothes that showed they were married. Their statues were used in buildings, to remind people of their sins.

but more especially cathedral building, could take place throughout much of Europe.

The designers of these cathedrals were master masons and carpenters, who belonged to craft guilds that were shrouded in secrecy, so whatever training they received, it remained inside the group. But it seems they must have done some form of drawing as an 'architect', in a contemporary illustration, is depicted holding a geometric instrument.

But in the fifteenth century there was to be a radical change due to the discovery, by the humanists, of a Roman text about building and architecture: the *Ten Books on Architecture* by Vitruvius.[2] The first chapter is called 'The Education of the Architect'. And Vitruvius actually has quite a lot to say[3] – here are a few quotations:

> ... he must have a knowledge of drawing so that he can readily make sketches to show the appearance of the work he proposes.

> As for philosophy, it makes an architect high-minded and not self-assuming, but rather renders him courteous, just, and honest without avariciousness.

> Consequently, since the study is so vast in extent ... I think that men have no right to profess themselves architects hastily, without having climbed from boyhood the steps of theses studies ...

> ... how can an architect, who has to be skilful in many arts accomplish these feats – in itself a great marvel ...

This book directly inspired Leon Battista Alberti, and he instigated the idea that architecture could be an intellectual rather than a practical endeavour. Absolutely central to this new approach was the idea of learning to be an architect by making drawings of buildings, rather than being involved in the physical process of building; as Vitruvius' exhorted 'Let him be educated, skilful with the pencil, instructed in geometry ...' . Although Alberti was one of the first to explain how to draw in perspective, he was in favour of drawing plans and elevations for buildings done in such a way that made them useful for construction. He wanted drawings made for architecture '... on the basis of controlled measurements.'[4] But rather oddly he did no such drawings nor did his contemporaries; these only came about 100 years later. A drawing of a plan of his church for St Sebastian, done by an assistant, exists but clearly is of little use for construction.

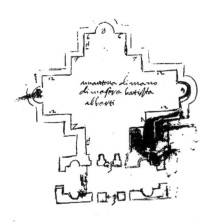

No use for construction

---

[2] See page 57 (Chapter 4).

[3] In the English translation by Morris Hicky Morgan (Dover Books) it runs to nearly nine pages.

[4] Tavares, 2004[1], p93.

However, once this new approach was established, those who conceived buildings could come from two extremes. At one extreme was the unlettered master craftsman who was skilled in the physical use of materials and could conceive and build buildings without a set of drawings. His aim was to complete a project to the satisfaction of the client whilst at the same time making a profit.

At the other extreme was the architect as 'Renaissance Man'– an intellectual aesthete, whose architectural concepts were entirely cerebral. He had no training or expertise in the practice of building. His architecture was carried out using drawings which showed how his intellectual construct would appear. The Renaissance-Man-architect's aim was to produce a building of artistic merit, if not a work of art. The building was to equal the beauty of those of Antiquity, and this would be accomplished by correctly following their example and the edicts of Vitruvius.

In 1671, the 'intellectual' approach officially got the upper hand with the setting up of the first school of architecture. This was the Royal Academy of Architecture (Académie Royale d'Architecture), which was part of the Royal Academies that were established to ensure that France would be the world's cultural leader and thus bringing glory to France and its king Louis XIV.[5]

In England the Royal Society, a learned scientific body, was established in 1660 under the restored monarch Charles II. No equivalent of the French Royal Academies would exist in England until 1768 with the founding of the Royal Academy. A founder and first president of the Royal Society was Britain's best-known architect, Christopher Wren (1632–1723) designer of one of Britain's most famous buildings, St Paul's Cathedral. Wren had no training either as an architect or as any sort of craftsman; he was a mathematician and scientist.

Done with no architectural training

In 1669, Wren was appointed Surveyor General and was in charge of the Royal Works. This was an integrated unit of designers, draughtsmen, clerks and craftsmen, and in Wren's time someone could be 'trained' as an architect by moving through the Royal Works. Wren's approach to architecture was based more on empirical building construction than any 'theory'.[6]

From the eighteenth century, architects in Britain were also trained by being pupils of established architects, a system that lasted until after

---

[5] The powerful finance minister Jean-Baptiste Colbert (1619–1683) saw the setting up of the Architectural Academy as a way of attacking the medieval guilds that still controlled architectural design.

[6] In 1665–6 Wren went on a long visit to France to discuss science and see architecture. On his return he brought back a huge number of books, including many on architecture.

World War II. But some attention was paid to architectural teaching at the Royal Academy whose first president was William Chambers (1723–1796). He had trained as an architect in Paris under J-F Blondel, however the Academy's educational role was mainly for artists.

In 1789, Europe was shaken by the French Revolution, and with the removal of the King all the French Royal Academies were closed down, though all re-emerged in the early nineteenth century relatively unchanged. The Royal Academy of Architecture became the architectural school of the École des Beaux-Arts, which basically carried on the tradition of J-F Blondel, producing architectural designs based on the classical 'rules', but modified by 'reason'.

Students at the École were split into three groups. Those trying to gain entry were called the *aspirants*. The entrance exams were in mathematics, descriptive geometry, history, drawing and architectural design. The *aspirants* were allowed to use the library and attend lectures. There was no limit to the number of times the exams could be sat. On average, two years of study were needed to pass these exams.

Having passed the exam, the student entered the second class and was entitled to call himself an *élève de l'École des Beaux-Arts*. No fees were charged, and anyone between the ages of 15 and 30 could enter. To pass to the first class, the student had to accumulate points – *valeurs* – which were gained from competitions – *concours*. These were either quick designs that took 12 hours, or major designs – *projets rendus* – for which two months were allowed. Students could enter as many competitions as they wished. The judging was done in camera by professors. Students could stay in the second class until they were 30 years old.

Successful students would pass to the first class, where they had to enter more complex competitions, some of which had medals or money as prizes. There was no particular end to the first class, because the aim of every first class student was to win the annual *Grand Prix de Rome*.[7] The competition took place over six months in three stages, with a complex judging process. The student who won the prize was sent to Rome, where he was supported for four or five years of study, much of which was to study the ancient monuments.[8] On his return, he was made *Architecte du Gouvernement*, a prestigious job for life. If he had higher aspirations, like becoming a professor at the École, the progression was more difficult as there were only eight professors, and they had tenure for life.

From today's standpoint, the architectural department of the École des Beaux-Arts was run in what seems to be a casual way, and very different from the way today's schools of architecture are run. Firstly, there was no design tuition; this was given in any number of private *ateliers*, which were run as businesses by anyone who wished to do so. They could be practising architects, 'academic' architects or someone who wasn't an architect at all. Secondly, there was no final qualification; it was enough for someone to label themselves as an *ancien élève de l'École des Beaux-Arts* to be able to pursue a successful architectural career.

---

[7] Actually the competition was open to any French citizen between the ages of 15 and 30, but it was virtually unknown that anyone but a first class student would win it.

[8] A student could enter the competition as many times as he wished and it was often won on the fifth or sixth attempt, or in the case of one Edmond Paulin, on his eight attempt!

The study building on the École 'campus'

Beaux-Arts architecture goes up in the world

In the nineteenth century students from many countries studied architecture in Paris at the École des Beaux-Arts, and on returning influenced architecture and architectural education in their own countries. Of the foreign students, over 500 were American. The first was Richard Morris Hunt (1827–1895); he studied painting and sculpture as well as architecture, and became a founder member of the American Institute of Architects. Once back home, he designed many famous buildings, including a Beaux-Arts skyscraper in 1873. Called the Tribune Building, it was one of the first buildings to have elevators; it was demolished in 1966.

By the nineteenth century there were schools of architecture in many countries, at which core subjects such as geometry, construction, and drafting techniques were taught. On aesthetic matters they followed the model of the École, which purveyed a perfected version of classic Greco-Roman architecture.

However, at the beginning of the nineteenth century, the hegemony of an architecture based on Greek and Roman models was challenged by the revival of the Gothic.[9] This was the architectural manifestation of the Romantic Movement. Its most important advocates were Eugène Viollet-le-Duc (1814–1879) and Augustus Pugin (1812–1852).

In studying medieval structures, Viollet-le-Duc became convinced that their (as he saw it) rational structural systems should be the basis of a new nineteenth-century architecture. Between 1854 and 1868 he published his massive, ten-volume *Dictionnaire Raisonné de l'architecture Française du XIe au XVIe siècles* (*Systematic Dictionary of French architecture from the XIth to the XVIth centuries*),[10] and between 1863 and 1872 he published the two-volume *Entretiens sur l'architecture* (*Discourses on architecture*).

Pugin, too, was an enthusiast for medieval architecture, but, unlike that of Viollet-le-

---

[9] See pages 63–64 (Chapter 4).

[10] Frank Lloyd Wright thought '[Viollet-le-Duc's]' *Raisonée* was the only sensible book on architecture in the world. I later obtained copies for my sons. This book alone enabled us to keep our faith in architecture in spite of architects.'

Duc, who was an anti-cleric, his enthusiasm was driven by a fervent Catholicism. At the age of 24 Pugin published *Contrasts*, in which he compares a 'holistic' medieval (Catholic) town and its nineteenth-century successor, ravaged by industry and Classicism.

A medieval Heaven   versus   A classical/industrial Hell

The nineteenth century also saw the rise of professional engineers and architects, so the question arose as to who was sufficiently qualified? Initially it was those doing the job, but gradually the idea arose that some evidence of proper training should be required; this, inevitably, fuelled endless disputes. One of these came about in Britain towards the end of the century, when some architects wanted 'qualified' architects to be registered. This led to a dispute between 'professional architects' and 'art-architects'. Furthermore, the 'art-architects' were divided into those who thought 'art' was academic aesthetics and those who thought 'art' was linked to 'craft'.

The concentration on the craft of building and the valuing of vernacular architecture was another thread of Romanticism and led to the Arts and Crafts skein of architecture, as it became known. It was everything that the Beaux-Arts was not. Its plans were rarely symmetrical; the 'orders' never appeared nor did any other classical device; materials and crafts were local rather than 'classical'; drawing was not an end in itself but a means of communication. In other words the Arts and Crafts movement attempted to 'design' the 'undesignable' – the vernacular[11] – the architecture of the builder. For a short period, the teaching of architecture in Britain followed this approach.[12] However, its hegemony, at least as an approach to teaching architecture, was short-lived, and soon after the turn of the twentieth century the Beaux-Arts tradition regained control.[13]

While the Arts and Crafts movement was attempting to 'carry on with tradition' and the Beaux-Arts were trying to create 'up-to-date Antiquity', there was another group being taught architecture, a group that became the engineers. Here again France led the way with the setting up, in 1795, of the Central School for Public Works (École Centrale des Travaux Publics),[14] which one year later became the famed École Polytechnique.[15]

[11] See pages 65–67 (Chapter 4).

[12] For instance it dominated the Liverpool University School of Architecture, the Architectural Association, the Birmingham School of Art, the Glasgow School of Art and the Edinburgh School of Applied Art.

[13] Here only Britain is being referred to; in France it was always in control, as it was in the United States.

[14] In the eighteenth century there was already technical education being given at schools for military engineers and in 1747 the Royal School for Roads and Bridges (École Royale des Ponts et Chausées) was established.

[15] The École Polytechnique remains the most prestigious French college; entry is by competition ensuring that its students are the best of the best.

In 1829, the École Centrale des Arts et Manufactures was established in Paris specifically to train *ingenieurs civils*. The students were taught practical scientific technology and were expected to produce project designs, so that 'The graduate of the École Centrale was thus ready to make a blueprint for "a guard-house, a railroad station, a hospital, a school, just as well lay out the plan of a road, a canal, a port, a viaduct, or a tunnel".'[16]

In Britain, it was only in 1835 that engineering courses were established,[17] but in 1812 a school for military engineers had been established in Chatham. In 1825, its founder Lt. Col. CW Pasley was ordered (!) to teach an architectural course. His notes appeared as a textbook called *Outline of a course of practical architecture.* His book is mainly a handbook on brickwork construction, but engineers of the British army were responsible for the design and construction of many of the buildings in the British Empire. They were also responsible for civil buildings as well.[18]

By the end of the nineteenth century the separation of engineers and architects was complete.[19] The Beaux-Arts architectural education held sway in France, the United States and other countries whereas in Britain the Arts and Crafts movement dominated architectural education. But this was to change. Interest in craft work in the architectural schools was declining and in 1904 CH Reilly (1874–1948), a converted classicist, was appointed professor of architecture at Liverpool University, where he remained until 1934.

A professor of classical architecture

So, at the beginning of the twentieth century architectural education, at least in France, Great Britain and the United States could be summarised as follows:

1 Architecture was taught academically, with designs based on classical models.
2 Great emphasis was placed on superb draughtsmanship.
3 There was no direct link to building crafts.
4 The profession of architect was divorced from that of the engineer.
5 The skills that engineers were being taught, particularly that of mathematical modelling, did not form a serious part of the curriculum.
6 There was no engagement with any social issues.

And it stayed that way up to and partly beyond World War II. Looking back at this 'Beaux-Arts' architectural education it's possible to see that it was fundamentally flawed. It ignored the defining characteristic of contemporary society, namely the process of industrialisation, including its theoretical and social aspects. Its social dimension was concentrated on the manifestations of entrenched power – the church and money.

[16] Weiss, 1982, p150.

[17] These were courses on 'engineering and the application of mechanical philosophy to the arts' at University College, London. In 1840, a similar course at King's College added architecture to the syllabus.

[18] For instance the famous Albert Hall in London, was designed by the military engineer Capt. Francis Fowke (1823–1865). Finished after his death by Lt. Col HYD Scott. Dixon, 1978, p173.

[19] See Chapter 5.

It was the irrelevance of this approach to architecture and architectural education that allowed, or even encouraged, the emergence of the superficially more relevant Modern Movement approach, with consequent disastrous results. After World War I, whilst the Beaux-Arts architectural education continued in France, Great Britain, the United States and many other countries, in Germany something very different was about to happen. It was called the Bauhaus.[20]

Its founder and first director was the pioneer of the perfect-glass-box strain of Modern Movement architecture, the Sachlichkeit Walter Gropius. He explained (or pronounced) that 'The approach to any kind of design – a chair, a building, a whole town or a regional plan – should be essentially identical'.[21] This sums up the problem in a nutshell, because it's patently obvious that to design something properly requires an understanding of the project: thus designing a machine gun requires a quite different area of knowledge from that required for designing a railway tunnel or an apartment block. What Gropius was talking about was visual design, what today is called styling, which is superficial in the true sense of the word. And this was what was taught at the Bauhaus – superficiality. In spite of this basic flaw, it is difficult to underestimate the importance of the Bauhaus on the design ghetto in general, and the training of its members in particular, as 'The way our environment looks, the appearance of everything from housing estates to newspapers, is partly the result of ... the Bauhaus, which also left an indelible mark on art education throughout the world'.[22] The key word here being the 'appearance' of everything.

The Bauhaus lasted barely 14 years, from 1919 to 1933, and its architectural department was not established until 1927. So architecture was taught for only the last six years of the school's life. In January 1928, the founder Gropius suddenly resigned. The new director was an architect, Hannes Meyer (1889–1954), who had arrived only nine months before to lead the architecture course (the students told Gropius that Meyer's appointment would be a catastrophe). Meyer, who held uncompromising left-wing views, 'fervently believed that it was the architect's job to improve society by designing functional buildings that would improve the lot of the common man'.[23]

So what happened at the Bauhaus that made it so influential? The Bauhaus' existence can be divided roughly into two periods, the 'metaphysical' period between 1919 to 1927, and the 'functional' period that lasted from 1927 to its closure in 1933.

The metaphysical approach was put in place by the mystical Johannes Itten (1888–1967) who was a follower of an Eastern philosophy called Mazdaznan.[24] He conceived and taught the *Vorkurs* (the Preliminary Course) which became 'the backbone of

---

[20] Literal translation from the German is 'building house'. See pages 44–45 (Chapter 3).

[21] *Encyclopaedia Britannica,* Vol. 13, fifteenth edition, 1993, p896.

[22] Whitford, 1984, the back cover.

[23] Whitford, 1984, p180.

[24] In 1917 the American novelist and social critic Upton Sinclair (1878–1968), published an attack on religions called *The Profits of Religion.* Mazdaznan appears in part six which is entitled 'Church of the Quacks'. In this section, it is revealed that the leader of Mazdaznan in the United States, Dr. Otoman Prince of Adusht Ha'nish prophet of the Sun God, Prince of Peace, Manthra Magi of Temple El Katman, Kalantar of Zoroastrian Breathing and Envoy of Mazdaznan living, Viceroy-Elect and International Head of Master-Thot, was jailed for six months for fraud.

The Bauhaus' resident mystic

Bauhaus education.'[25] So what happened on the *Vorkurs*? Superficially it could be seen as a type of playgroup for young adults: 'Play becomes party – party becomes work – work becomes play' was an Itten saying. Students were confronted with a variety of materials, and were encouraged to learn to 'understand' them by physical contact and by making 'things' from them. Importantly these 'things' had to be free from usefulness or previous arts or crafts.

Some have seen a sinister side to Itten's *Vorkurs*. The key aim of this course was to wipe the students' minds 'clean', as Itten envisaged his students '... returning to a child-like state, from which they would develop their innate abilities'.[26] According to Whitford, 'Its critics have seen the *Vorkurs* as a kind of brain-washing in which everything students had previously learned was drummed out of them and they were receptive to new ideas and methods'.[27] Having been re-programmed, the students then became 'apprentices' and were sent to learn crafts in workshops.

In 1923 the *Vorkurs* was taken over by Josef Albers and László Moholy-Nagy (1895–1946). They removed the mystic elements but, according to architectural historian Joseph Rykwert (b1926), it was '... more of a play therapy'.[28] Moholy-Nagy dressed in a red boiler suit and wore metal-rimmed glasses, he was influenced by Dada and the Constructivists. The idea of their *Vorkurs* was still learning by playing around with unlikely objects and materials to make a 'thing'.

Although supposedly central to the Bauhaus, the role of crafts and craftsmanship was never very clear. Were the apprentices to become craftspeople? If so, they could do it

A Vorkurs 'thing' from 1920

A Moholy-Nagy-inspired 'thing'

---

[25] Droste, 1993, p25.

[26] Itten himself thought that 'Every new student arrives encumbered with a mass of accumulated information which he must abandon before he can achieve perception and knowledge that are really his own'. Banham, 1960, p278.

[27] Whitford, 1984, p55.

[28] Crinson, 1994, p94.

Hand-crafted industrial Bauhaus object from 1924

in the time-honoured way by serving apprenticeships, but this isn't what happened. Students didn't stay long enough in any of the workshops to become real craftspeople. (To become a proper craftsperson, five to seven years, or some 10,000 hours, is the usual period.) After Moholy-Nagy became influential, they hand-crafted what looked like industrial, machine-made objects.

In 1926, Gropius set out the objectives of the Bauhaus workshops in a document entitled 'Principles of Bauhaus Production'. Apparently, the 'Bauhaus workshops are essentially laboratories in which prototypes suitable for mass-production and typical of our time are carefully developed and constantly improved.'[29] As usual with the Modern Movement, virtually all the statements about, and attempts to connect with technology, were pure fantasy. For instance, the following quotations from *Industrial Design* by John Heskett clearly show the true picture:

... the experience gained in them [the workshops] bore little relation to industrial practice – page 102.

... in terms of Bauhaus prototypes actually put into production, the results are quantitatively insignificant – page 102.

... notable German designer ... Wilhelm Wagenfeld, a former Bauhaus pupil and teacher who came to reject the ideas of that institution as theoretical and self-centred – page 112.

But this had already been noted in 1938 by Eugene Schoen who thought that 'Plainly the industrial designer per se should be discouraged and design in industry by the creators of the objects themselves should be encouraged ...'.[30]

With the appointment of Hannes Meyer as director in 1927, things changed. Meyer's approach to the teaching of architecture was laudable: for him buildings made 'living' possible by catering for the 'biological, intellectual, spiritual and physical' needs of the users. Exactly, at last someone had a handle on the problem. Architectural theory (*Baulehre*) was taught over two years and the syllabus covered heating, structures, ventilation, building design (!), day-lighting, town-planning and so on. Much of the teaching was done by engineers. And then there was a building department (*Bauabteilung*) where systematic approaches and working in 'co-operative cells' for large projects was 'taught'.

Not only that, students worked on real projects that had been awarded to Meyer. For this they were put into the 'co-operative cells' which acted as 'vertical work gangs',

---

[29] Heskett, 1980, p101.

[30] Duncan, 1986, p270.

Blocks being scientifically harmonised with next door

layering juniors, seniors, experts and novices. This arrangement was because Meyer considered 'the "architect" is dead.'[31] His idea was that buildings would be designed by 'creative teams' which would include all and any necessary specialists. All very sensible, so it seems a shame that one of the few buildings Meyer and his students designed, the Trades Union school residential block in Bernau, had five blocks of similar appearance, when one block had a different function: 'Meyer claimed [it] was the result of scientific analysis ...but for design reasons [!] [the fifth block] was harmonised with the buildings next door.'[32]

To be fair, Meyer really had little time to establish his ideas or his architectural course, because as he couldn't or wouldn't rein in the actions of the Communists in the school, he was forced to resign in 1930. Mies van der Rohe was appointed the director and, as Whitford puts it, 'The last, depressing years of the Bauhaus had begun.'[33]

Under Mies effectively nearly everything changed. He was by then highly-regarded in some avant-garde circles, and had a practice in Berlin, so he became a part-time director. All political activities were banned, though, under Mies, the first organised Nazis appeared amongst the students! The importance of the workshops was reduced, and the Bauhaus became primarily a school of architecture. In the teaching of architecture, theory was separated from practice, and theory dominated everything. Mies was indifferent to social issues and whereas Meyer spoke of *Bauen* (building), for Mies it was *Baukunst* (building art), as for him architecture was art. Apparently Meyer's pupils '... filled every last centimetre of their exercise sheets with calculations and diagrams and thus "legitimised" their designs,' whereas '... sheets surviving from Mies' seminars are empty; extremely delicate designs often "swim" on outsize pieces of white paper ...'.[34] Mies himself taught only the final year students, who found it advantageous to produce designs that mimicked those of their master.

In the meantime, even with Mies' new authoritarian apolitical

His master's pencil

---

[31] Droste, 1993. p192.

[32] Droste, 1993, p195.

[33] Whitford, 1984, p191.

[34] For both quotations see Droste, 1993, p214.

approach, the closure of the Bauhaus was a foregone conclusion. The Nazis were in the ascendant, and in spite of Mies' efforts, the school couldn't shake off its Commie past; besides which the Bauhaus buildings had flat roofs. According to the Nazi's twisted ideology the problem wasn't because these usually leaked, but because 'the flat roof did not belong to Northern climes but had manifestly come from subtropical regions. It was therefore oriental and Jewish.'[35]

One Bauhaüsler finds his metier

Early in the morning of 11 April 1933 the police arrived in trucks, closed the Bauhaus, and took away anyone who did not have satisfactory papers. And that might have been it – the end of just another vaguely idealistic, socialist, avantgarde, communal artistic experiment. But it wasn't. The reason it wasn't was because a significant number of Bauhaüslers, as members of the Bauhaus were called, went, in the 1930s, to the United States. But some stayed, including Fritz Ertl (b1908),[36] who had studied architecture at the Bauhaus between 1928 and 1931. He became the chief architect of the Auschwitz concentration camp,

But as 'we all know' the Bauhaus didn't disappear to become a footnote to cultural history: it became iconic. Mies' architectural school set the pattern for Modern Movement schools of architecture that came to dominate the world of architectural education. How did this happen? The action now shifts to the other side of the Atlantic, to the United States.

American architectural education had been dominated by the Beaux-Arts tradition. But it was hardly surprising, given the rapid advances in science, technology and in other areas, that some younger aspiring architects began to question its relevance. Did making accurate drawings of plaster casts of Greek sculpture and exquisite drawings of correctly proportioned Doric, Ionic and Corinthian columns really train a person to produce appropriate architecture for the twentieth century? It seemed unlikely, so a number of American architectural teachers and students started to look elsewhere for inspiration, and their gaze alighted on the European Modern Movement, whose pseudo-functional boxes were appearing in radical magazines.

In avant-garde circles, Le Corbusier's seminal work *Vers une architecture*[37] was already known in the 1920s and, in 1927, Jane Heap (1887–1964)[38] organised an exhibition called

[35] Whitford, 1984, p195.

[36] He was tried, and acquitted, of war crimes in 1972.

[37] See pages 93–95 (Chapter 6).

[38] Jane Heap was the co-editor of the influential modernist literary magazine *Little Review.* She spent most of her life devoted to the Greek-Armenian mystic philosopher and cult leader GI Gurdjieff. By a strange coincidence, he was also the life-long spiritual mentor of Frank Lloyd Wright's third wife, the Serbian-Montenegrian dancer, Olga Ivanovna Milanov Hinzenberg. It was she who turned Wright into a cult. It is interesting to note all the cultism and mysticism that accompanied the rational and functional Modern Movement.

'Machine Age Exposition' in New York. This exhibition, of over 400 items, was heavily influenced by Le Corbusier, and its objective was to promote modern art to be a reflection of American technological achievements, says Mardges Bacon, 'The significance of Jane Heap's innovative exhibition should not be underestimated.'[39]

Four years later, the Architectural League of New York held an exhibition that included work of some architects that had modernist leanings, but rejected the work of other (younger) more hard-line modernists. Philip Johnson (who was soon to become the director of the Department of Architecture at the fledgling Museum of Modern Art) organised a rival exhibition of the rejected work. To 'promote' the show, Johnson hired a sandwich-board man to parade up and down in front of the League's offices with a message that said 'See really modern architecture rejected by the league.' The League was furious and tried to have the man arrested; the newspapers featured it and modern architecture was brought to the general public's notice for the first time. Johnson followed this up with more promotional exhibitions such as 'Modern Architecture: International Exhibition' in 1932,[40] and the 'Machine Art' exhibition staged in 1934. In 1935, Le Corbusier finally arrived in the United States and spent several months touring schools of architecture to strut his stuff (in French, which made it incomprehensible to most of his listeners).

Instrumental in organising Corb's American jolly, was Joseph Hudnut (1886–1968) at the time Dean of Columbia's school of architecture but now forgotten. Hudnut can be seen as a pivotal figure (perhaps a 'Frankenstein' figure would be more apt)[41] in 'saving' Modern Movement architecture from quite possible oblivion, and bringing it to the world.[42] Hudnut had studied architecture between 1906 and 1917, following a Beaux-Arts curriculum; he won prizes, and in the early 1920s he designed a number of pleasant, smallish buildings in what he considered the appropriate style for the location.

Hudnut finds an appropriate style in 1923

It's quite probable that Hudnut would have quietly followed a career designing such buildings if he had not, in 1917, met Werner Hegemann (1881–1936). A city planner, the erudite Hegemann, taught Hudnut that city planning was 'the basis of architecture' and clearly made Hudnut think much more deeply and widely about architecture. Probably, Hegemann was, in some way, responsible for Hudnut's conversion to Modernism. However, it wasn't a 'flash of the blinding light of truth' type of conversion, but one that took place over almost ten years. Oddly, Hegemann himself was a sharp critic of the Modern Movement gang.[43]

---

[39] Bacon, 2001, p21.

[40] See page 48 (Chapter 3).

[41] Frankenstein, in Mary Shelly's book, wasn't a monster but the person who created one.

[42] See Pearlman, 1997, p455–456.

[43] ibid.

In 1926 Hudnut was appointed professor of architectural history at the then-still-Beaux-Arts Columbia University. The incumbent director expected Hudnut to take over the directorship when he went, and in 1933 this is what happened. But what happened next was not what was expected. Hudnut had given up architecture itself in 1926, being unhappy, one must assume that he couldn't use his knowledge of architectural history to produce buildings that would square with the way Hegemann had made him think about architecture. This prompted Hudnut to do something very strange; he decided to abandon the whole of the Beaux-Arts curriculum and create America's first school of modern architecture; and perhaps even more strangely, he thought that he'd be better at the job if he never designed a 'modern' building himself. And he never did![44]

But although Hudnut brought the work of Corbusier, Gropius, Mies and the rest to the attention of his students, he didn't really know what 'modern' architecture should be. He was a follower of John Dewey (1859–1952) who taught that 'the quest for certainty' should be rejected. This meant that Hudnut could never offer his students '...any definite way to translate his ideas on architecture and planning into formal terms or design preferences' as Jill Pearlman puts it.[45]

In 1935 Hudnut was head-hunted to be dean at Harvard University. Shortly after his arrival he managed to amalgamate the previously quite separate schools of architecture, landscape architecture and city planning into the Harvard Graduate School of Design or GSD. He also removed books on history from the library, had the classical plaster casts destroyed, and redesigned the faculty brochure using 'modern' graphics.

In 1936, Jean-Jacques Haffner, the Beaux-Arts professor of architecture, left. Here Hudnut, and his supportive President, chemist James Conant, saw an opportunity to bring to

The Frankensteinian, tweedy, modernist professor

the school a big name modernist architect. Three big names were considered – Jacobus Oud,[46] Gropius and Mies – and they were secretly sounded out. Oud wasn't interested but both Mies and Gropius were, but when Mies found out he wasn't the only candidate being considered he withdrew, leaving Gropius to come first out of one.

Gropius arrived at GSD in 1937; what then happened basically determined how architecture would be taught up to the present day. Gropius wanted to create (in spite of various protests to the contrary) a GSD Bauhaus. He wanted the students to go through the brain-washing process of the *Vorkurs* and he wanted it to be run by Albers,

---

[44] 'Ironically when he retired (1953) ... Hudnut left the city for ... his first modern house'. Pearlman, 2000, p231.

[45] Pearlman, 1997, p463.

[46] Oud was from de Stijl and had been invited to contribute a perfect white box to the Weissenhof-seidlung in 1927 (see page 45, Chapter 3). He later severely blotted his Modern Movement copybook when, in 1941, he designed a new headquarters for Royal Dutch Shell in The Hague. It had, horror of horrors, decoration. Taverne, 1996.

who had run it in Germany. Then he wanted students to design projects as though he was designing them.

Students hanging on to every word

Unlike Hudnut, Gropius was quite definite that he knew what modern architecture was; after all he had invented it, in 1914,[47] well the perfect-glass-box variety anyhow. With absolute confidence in his views and his charismatic personality, many students '... hung on Gropius' every word' and was, according to Hudnut, a 'religious leader'.

Almost from the outset Hudnut realised that he had made a dreadful mistake, though he never expressed it as such.[48,49] In the initial period the two worked in reasonable harmony, but Gropius was just feeling his way as he knew what he really wanted – a new Bauhaus. This was the beginning of a battle that was to last until both left the GSD, Gropius in 1952 as a hero, and Hudnut in 1953 as a nonentity.

So what was it they disagreed about? Actually more or less everything. Gropius wanted a GSD Bauhaus, Hudnut didn't. Gropius wanted the creative play-therapy of the *Vorkurs*, Hudnut didn't think creative teaching should be separated from technical teaching. Gropius did not want architectural history to be taught, Hudnut thought it had a role. Gropius was convinced that 'the intellectual groundwork of a new architecture is already established' whereas Hudnut felt that modern architecture was 'in the process of formation' and that it had still not achieved a '"genuine" modern form'. And worse still, Hudnut began to have grave doubts about the designs that the students were producing; that they did not have sufficient '... sympathy for the human' as he wrote in 1943[50] and that modern housing had '... no soul whatever'.[51]

But Hudnut was always going to be the loser. Gropius was a hero of 'modern' architecture, leading light of the revolutionary C.I.A.M,[52] a designer of iconic buildings, the director of the legendary Bauhaus, charismatic and definite and a brilliant self-publicist.[53] Hudnut wasn't really any of these things, one colleague describing him as '... the last, least modern individual you could find'; so he lost out; and so did architectural education many would say.

It should be said that Hudnut's wasn't a completely lone voice; Gropius was also

[47] See pages 36–37 (Chapter 3).

[48] Perhaps he was aware of the problem earlier, as he would sarcastically refer to Le Corbusier as 'the great man'. Bacon, 2001, p95.

[49] It's not that unusual for the actions of a secondary figure to have monumental consequences, as the role of career politician Fritz von Papen (1879–1969) in the rise to power of Hitler shows.

[50] In the *Architectural Record*, January 1943, quoted by Pearlman, 2000, p220.

[51] ibid, quoted by Pearlman, 2000, p222.

[52] See page 47 (Chapter 3).

[53] And he had an old Bauhaus buddy at his side, the almost equally legendary Marcel Breuer.

criticised by one of his own – his friend Martin Wagner (1885–1957), a modernist city planner appointed to the GSD in 1938 at Gropius' request. In 1940, Wagner claimed that Gropius had betrayed his principles by no longer confronting contemporary social and artistic issues, and that there was no essential difference between his formalism and that of the despised École des Beaux-Arts. And, just as at the École, the Harvard GSD students simply copied their teachers' work. Wagner was right, of course: unsurprisingly, the thanks he got for it was to be written out of history.

In fact, Gropius was doing exactly that of which Wagner had accused him, creating his own École (perhaps *Gropiustichebauenkunstschule* – Gropiusan School of Building Art) would be a better description) that existed solely to enforce his own design rules. What's more, he wanted his design philosophy to spread throughout the world, and as he was a smart operator he knew how to do it. He used several techniques. He made some of his students, acolytes really, into teachers,[54] so his word would continue whilst he was on his lecture tours captivating audiences with his message at schools, clubs and societies throughout the United States. By 1952, there were over 100 of his graduates strategically embedded as teachers in universities across the country. After the war, Gropius became an 'inveterate proselytiser for his version of architectural education'[55] and, by the 1960s, nearly every architectural school in the whole world was running an introductory *Vorkurs* indoctrination course.[56]

It is interesting to note the quasi-religious terms used to describe Gropius and his work. For instance, Pearlman writes 'he used his ... personality to spread his creed', and that he was an '... effective propagandist for his beliefs'; for AL Huxtable he was 'a prophet whose time had come'. When he left the GSD, the *Harvard Magazine* claimed he was almost 'a spiritual leader', while for the students he was the 'master mould into which they poured their talents'. Clearly, if what Gropius had been teaching was cold functional logic and reason, the alleged foundation of Modern Movement architecture, then none of these terms would have been applied, but, of course, what he was really teaching was *die Gropiustichebauenkunst*.

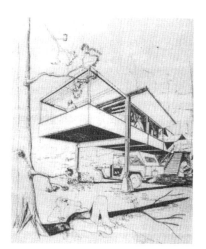
Talent moulded in 1947

In the event, Gropius wasn't to change the face of architectural education single-handedly; he had, if not exactly an ally, then someone in Chicago who was like-minded: it was the perfect-glass-boxman Mies. In 1938, Mies became director of architecture of what is now the Illinois Institute of Technology,

---

[54] As it takes years to become even a proficient professional architect it is clearly ridiculous to imagine that someone can go straight from being an architectural student to someone teaching architecture. But Gropius was teaching not architecture but machine-aesthetic styling.

[55] Crinson, 1994, p114.

[56] It could 'change a student's entire approach to creativity and, indeed to life' (as indeed was supposed to do), quoted by Pearlman, 1997, p230.

or IIT. This time he was not subjected to any demeaning selection process, but was lured there by money; even better, he was to have a completely free hand and also get to design the new campus – an offer which, under the circumstances[57] he couldn't refuse.

Mies, who couldn't speak English, arrived with Bauhäuslers Ludwig Hilberseimer (1885–1967), who also couldn't speak English and Walter Peterhans (1897–1960) who could.[58] Until they learnt English, Mies and Hilbs, as Hilberseimer was known to the students, had all their utterances translated by John Rodgers, who'd worked for Mies in Germany. Looked at coldly, it is rather difficult to see why Mies had the profile to become professor of architecture and the dean of the faculty; he was over 50 and had only built a handful of modestly sized buildings; his teaching experience was limited to three years as a part-timer; and he couldn't even speak the language! However, he got the job and by 1960, the at-the-time-admirer-of-Mies, Peter Blake, could write, 'In the architectural schools of the United States, Europe and the Far East, Mies today reigns supreme.'[59] How did this happen? What did Mies teach?

As at the Bauhaus, how Mies really taught was by example, the implicit idea being, 'I'm a genius so if you do as I do some of my genius just may rub off', or, as Blake put it, 'Mies has provided a vocabulary; most use it to write prose; only a few can write poetry'.[60] What Mies was trying to do, like the Beaux-Arts architects before him, was to discover a universal beauty that would apply to all and any building; the central idea was that mankind needed not special but universal solutions; 'I am, in fact, completely opposed to the idea that a specific building should have an individual character,' as Mies put it[61] – in other words, the endless quest for the perfect steel-and-glass box.

To teach this Mies acted like a Zen master. A visit to him in 1940 was described by occasional student Herman Lackner (1912–1998): '... the master was like Buddha ... the divine worshipers gathered around him. He didn't talk much ...'.[62] The few things he did say were gnomic utterances such as 'education must lead us ... from chance and arbitrariness to clarity and intellectual order',[63] or '... every decision leads to a special kind or order',[64] or 'Form is not the goal, but the result of our work. There is no form itself.'[65]

To go with these enigmatic pearls, Mies, similarly to Corb, affected a 'persona'. Mies, a large and heavy man who, due to arthritis, had difficulty in walking, always appeared in hand-made dark suits, white shirt and dark tie, always with a white handkerchief in

[57] In 1936 Mies, who had no moral qualms about working for the Nazis, was under the impression that he would be put in charge of the rebuilding of Berlin's civic centre – a civic centre that would befit the projected thousand year life of the Third Reich. Due to an administrative cock-up the job went to Albert Speer; and due to another cock-up the Third Reich only lasted 12 years.

[58] Moholy-Nagy was already there. He had arrived in Chicago in 1937 to carry on the good work by setting up the New Bauhaus. This eventually became the Institute of Design.

[59] Blake, 1960[2], p112.

[60] ibid.

[61] Stern, 1995, p344.

[62] Interviewed by Betty Blum in 1983, for the Art Institute of Chicago.

[63] Blake, 1960[2], p 113.

[64] Blake, 1960[2], p73.

[65] Lambert, 2001, p43.

The Buddha meditates on a cigar

his breast pocket, always smoking a large cigar. His lifestyle also fed an image. He lived alone, in a large apartment virtually devoid of furniture – just a few black leather sofas and chairs; the white walls hung with his collection of Paul Klee paintings. His main pleasures were reading German philosophy, contemplating his Klee paintings, and thinking.

According to Mies, 'The function of education is to lead us from irresponsible opinion to truly responsible judgement ... a way of doing should be the essence architectural education', and 'It is my opinion that everything should be guided by reason ... everything leads to reason ... the student should attack everything by reason.'[66] Seems reasonable; every building project is just subjected to reason and everything else will come out in the wash. But it didn't, because professional training was to lead to '... clear and unequivocal spiritual orientation' as what was needed was a '... sufficient insight into spiritual relationships.'[67] It's not easy to know which should come first, the spiritual orientation or the attack of everything by reason. Well, there were people on hand to help the students, apart from Mies himself, because Mies wanted four professors. He wanted them to be a city planner, an abstract artist, a painter and a sculptor – but no architects!

The students got taught; to draw, to study form and rhythm, along with advanced visual training, basic construction and advanced problems involving the expression of structure (!). To understand structures, the students made models. For a whole list of reasons,[68] this is pointless; all the student learns is how to make models of structures.

What Mies wanted, ostensibly anyway, was to teach his students about 'space' and 'construction' and especially 'structures'. Leading by example, how did he do? One of his most famous projects was the Farnsworth House, and what did the client say? She thought that it was far too expensive, terribly impractical, and cost a lot to maintain.[69] Oh well, you can't win 'em all. Perhaps things would be better when he

A pointless exercise

---

[66] Carter, 1974, p159.

[67] Lambert, 2001, p181.

[68] Little can be learnt from a model of a structure unless it is carefully built of structural materials with known technical characteristics, and then it has to be carefully loaded and the results obtained from accurate instrumentation, otherwise it's just playgroup stuff.

[69] Actually the client, Edith Farnsworth, had entirely missed the point. As Peter Blake points out, as 'the Farnsworth House was meant to be ... a clear and somewhat abstract expression of an architectural idea' (so it wasn't a house, then, or even a universal solution). Blake, 1960[2], p88.

designed the building for the school of architecture itself at IIT – the Crown Hall.[70] It was to be, according to Mies, 'one big room ... a calm, open space'.[71] It was one room and it was big all right (220 ft by 120 ft), and it was certainly an open space; but calm? Not really. One couldn't see out, due to the translucent glass at the lower level; on the other hand, the clear glass at the top made it too bright, so the blinds had to be constantly adjusted. But this 'calm, open space' was still no good, as it was too noisy, so the architectural students decamped elsewhere: the 'universal solution' had apparently failed again.

God takes a rain check at IIT

The roof structure of the hall was supported by four massive, solid steel beams, spaced 44 ft apart, positioned above the roof. None of these structural choices 'were guided by reason', in fact the opposite.[72] And, in the case of at least one of his buildings on the ITT campus, God was not getting a look-in.[73] It's difficult to see why the students, or anyone else for that matter, kept faith – but they did.

What was, or is there to learn from Mies? Whatever it was, or is, it's not easy as '... there is no larger obstacle in learning from Mies than the opacity of his own mind. His enigmatic posture ... a Trappist's discipline'.[74] But it's not really that difficult as 'What [Mies] actually did was to invent a style that looked "rational" — repetitive, austere, mathematical, cold — but was no more the product of objective scientific method than any other architecture.'[75]

MY BUILDING – RUINED!

The universal solution comes a cropper once again

Quite so.

But off all the disciples went, spiritually orientated and guided by reason, heading into the Miesian-Gropusian sunset and they were all happy. Actually what architectural education, and subsequently the profession, did was to head off down another blind alley from which they have yet to return. In the 1970s a huge estate was built in the north of Berlin – it is dreary, ugly and without 'soul' – fittingly it was called Gropiusstadt. Luckily for Mies, all he got was Mies-van-der-Rohe Strasse in his home town of Aachen.

---

[70] See page 49 (Chapter 3)

[71] Lambert, 2001, p448.

[72] The worst place for a steel structure is outside the building as it causes problems for the weather-proofing and for the maintenance of the structure. In this case it also meant that the top parts of the beams were difficult to stabilise structurally.

[73] A famous Mies 'saying' was 'God is in the details' – see page 214 (Chapter 12).

[74] Trigueiros, 2000, p7.

[75] Hellman, 1986, p109.

A fitting memorial

Old dogma bad

New dogma good

So the old dogma, the Beaux-Arts, was roundly defeated by the new dogma, the Modern Movement. It was certainly defeated in Boston anyway, when the extension to the public library, designed by Miesian disciple Philip Johnson, showed the Beaux-Arts original up for what it was – not a universal solution.

So did anyone object to this revolution in architectural education? Not many, but a few did. Peter Blake for instance thought that '... most teachers of architecture now ... never learned how to build. Their lessons are paper lessons, their theories, paper theories.'[76] And Peter Buchanan, at the time joint editor of the prestigious *Architectural Review*, also had a few quibbles. He wrote an article with the title 'What is wrong with architectural education?'[77] adding 'almost everything'. This article is really an exposé of the sham of architectural education, and should really be quoted in full; here are just a few excerpts:

> ... architectural education is based upon ... [the] role model ... of the architect ... [as a] designer aspiring to genius

> ... the architectural studio often resembles a kindergarten of uninhibited free expression.

> ... [architectural education] led much student design far from the disciplines of architecture into the realms of bad art.[78]

> '... working details ... is just another shallow graphic exercise ...

---

[76] Blake, 1977, p66.

[77] *Architectural Review*, July 1989, p24–26.

[78] Prize-winning Modern Movement architect Siza Vieira apparently couldn't decide whether to become an architect or a sculptor. *Público*, 14 January 2007, p55.

the engineer becomes a nursemaid, looking after the architect and getting his play-things built.[79]

[the students suffer from] ... the inadequacies and inexperience of many teachers – a considerable number of whom, especially the more influential ones, have built very little if anything at all.[80]

... theory tends to be used as a refuge of obfuscation, esotericism ... in which teachers carve a safe haven in which to hide their inexperience and lack of real commitment to architecture and the welfare of mankind.[81]

And did anything change after this devastating exposé? Did the staff of whole schools resign in shame? Of course not, they just carried on as before, following the course set out for them by those great architectural educators Gropius and Mies.

Yehuda Safran, a writer and architectural critic, who apparently has never built anything, is also the design tutor of Studio 6 Advanced Architecture Studio at the prestigious Columbia University. Safran guides the students with: 'Sometimes, in order to see and to understand a thing, we need to create a distance. Sometimes a significant image from distant places or ages is called upon to give perspective: the pueblos of New Mexico, the arenas of Arles and Lucca, the Etruscan town, the villages of the Dogon. The town, if it is like any piece of physiology at all, it is more like a dream than anything else.'[82] The students are able to draw up projects on this basis which makes sense to them, if few others.

Today, anyone who wants to become an architect has to go to a 'school of architecture'. After several years, about six or seven usually, and having jumped through all the necessary hoops, they are supposed to emerge equipped to become an architect. Probably the least-equipped person to design a building, or in fact have anything to do with buildings at all, is someone who's been through this process.

One person who had followed a course of architectural education described it as being initiated into, and being trained as a priest for, an arcane and draconian religion. This training causes severe mental strain on its participants, which results in what psychologists refer to as cognitive dissonance (stress arising from trying to entertain

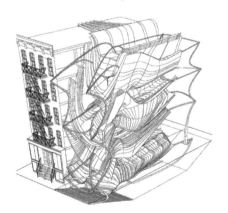

The student makes sense

---

[79] See Chapter 10: The Supine Engineer Appears.

[80] Peter Cook, founder member of Archigram (see pages 144–145), and trendy professor of architecture, has built virtually nothing. At the age of nearly 70 he designed the Kunsthaus; it is a blue, amorphous blobby thing, '... the locals ... love their friendly alien', says Cook; we bet. *Building Design*, 10 December 2004.

[81] 'The architectural deans [of Harvard and Columbia] (Mr Silvetti and Mr Tschumi) were appointed to their exalted positions because of "gems of pretentious illiteracy" not because of their built work ... and these men would invite younger versions of themselves to fill faculty positions'. *Architectural Record*, December 2001, letter on p17.

[82] See http://www.arch.columbia.edu/gsap/10448 (accessed in January 2007).

two conflicting points of view).[83] This is because what is taught (inculcated is more accurate) is clearly at odds with their previous experience, and indeed the views of everyone they know who has not received their indoctrination. Thus, if their beliefs are questioned by a non-believer, their eyes take on a glazed look – rather than explain their point of view coherently and logically, they will mutter things like 'you just don't understand'. Most take refuge in the design ghetto, which is peopled by fellow unquestioning believers.

However, evidence of their dissonance appears constantly. A typical example is a book called *Architecture Source Book: A visual guide to buildings around the world* written by architect Vernon Gibberd in 1997. On page 122 he describes Le Corbusier and Mies van der Rohe as 'the two great masters of the [modern] movement'. Here we see the indoctrination process at work, because no one who has been through the process can think of Le Corbusier and Mies van der Rohe as anything but great masters.[84, 85] Yet on page 121 we read that 'In the first place ordinary people didn't like the International Modern very much, and with familiarity seemed to like it less and less' – this is the architect in a 'truthful' phase. Continuing in the 'truthful' phase, Gibberd writes on page 149 that 'Le Corbusier had something to answer for', while 'His [Mies van der Rohe's] influence is in many of the tawdry-looking schools and factory units ...' and, also on page 149, '... Le Corbusier neglected the social side-effects of his doctrinal authoritarianism ... [while] Mies was building flats with even greater arrogance ...'.

The indoctrination of the students is carried out in different ways, the central, and most important, method being the 'crit'. Crit is short for critique or criticism, and is used to test, on a regular basis, the faith of the noviciate. The students are normally split into groups for each year; these groups are often called units. Each unit has one or two design tutors whose role it is to guide their flock along the road of righteousness. This is done by setting the students tasks to test their fervour.

These tests are called 'design projects' or 'scheme designs'. The design tutors produce a document, often called a programme, which outlines the test. These may be small tests, 'design a fountain for a poet' for instance, or they may be big, 'design a group of houses in a bucolic setting for a group of faith-healers'. What the student has to do is to produce work that firstly shows imagination, secondly it has to comply with the basic articles of faith and thirdly, and this is important, that it follows the design tutor's interpretation of the religion. On a given date the students are examined publicly on their faith. They have to exhibit what they have produced; this is usually in the form of drawings, but could be models, videos or any other form.[86]

The students are then tested by a form of inquisition. This is a panel of people, suitably qualified in the faith, who arrange themselves in a seated line in front of the noviciate. More or less anyone else can watch the fun, other students, tutors or just someone passing by. First

---

[83] Cognitive dissonance is a psychological state that describes the uncomfortable feeling that is caused when one's beliefs are at variance with what one 'knows' to be true.

[84] Walter Gropius and Alvar Aalto are the other two 'great masters'. The fifth 'great master' was Frank Lloyd Wright, but he also appeared to be something of a heretic, which could cause the novitiates extra mental problems.

[85] One can check this point personally by, on meeting an architect, innocently asking him (or her), 'What do you think of Le Corbusier?' 'He was a genius', you will usually be assured.

[86] At one school of architecture a student showed his faith by *dancing* his project.

of all the supplicant professes his faith using whatever props he has to reinforce his piety. The inquisitors then go to work testing and probing the faith of the victim, traps are set, and it commonly ends in public humiliation. Furthermore, the inquisitors can use the occasion to demonstrate their deep and spiritual knowledge of the religion. Sometimes the actual spiritual advisor of the victim is put in an awkward position as bile and vituperation rains down on one who's supposed to be in his spiritual care. In these cases, the design tutor almost invariably sides with the inquisitors to attack those he is supposed to guide. To side with the victim would be to support a heresy which would court disaster for the tutor's position.[87]

Interestingly, the extent to which architectural students have been indoctrinated was empirically tested in 1987.[88] Architectural students and other students were shown photos of unfamiliar people and buildings and were asked to rate their attractiveness. The correlation of all student's ratings for the attractiveness of people was very high, but not for the buildings. Amongst the non-architectural students the most disliked building was the architectural students' second favourite building. Other tests have shown[89] that, as architectural students progressed through their course, their aesthetic taste for buildings, compared to that of other students, diverged more.

All of which goes to show that architectural education works wonderfully if it is to produce graduates who know little about how to build a building, little about the basic technology that applies to buildings, nothing about designing buildings that non-architects like, and an awful lot about how to produce stylish graphics to please their design tutors – who often know very little about buildings, having built little or nothing themselves.[90] In other words, the students are taught to produce 'paper' architecture[91] by, in the main, 'paper' architects. This 'paper' architecture has to comply with the cultural rules of the Modern Movement, and has no connection with what 'most people' would consider practical reality.

This divergence between what architects want and what everyone else wants has also caused problems on the home front. Alain Sarfaiti's architectural endeavours ended his marriage (see page 3), and Le Corbusier's design for their new home drove his wife crazy.[92] Writing in 1972 Ivan Chermayeff noted that as '... acceptance of contemporary architecture does not exist' designing such houses '... loses friends, if not wives and husbands ...'.[93] When prize-winning architect Will Alsop was asked, in an interview in 2007, why he didn't live in a house of his own design, his answered: 'I rather like my wife. If I built my own house, she'd leave me. So I feel very comfortable not doing that, though of course I often have daydreams about it.'[94]

---

[87] Design tutors are often in a precarious position themselves. They are hired by the year and are usually young architects trying to get noticed in the hot house atmosphere of schools of architecture; but one false move could mean they're out.

[88] Halpern, 1995, p161–162.

[89] Halpern, 1995, p162.

[90] In advising students how to choose a design tutor Ellis Woodman (*Building Design*, 16 September 2005, p13) recommends that the student should '... go for the tutor whose presentation includes the most buildings.'

[91] See pages 8–10 (Chapter 3).

[92] See footnote 47 on page 102.

[93] Chermayeff, 1972, p14.

[94] *The Observer*, 8 April 2007.

14. Not Putting Up With It

In major cities, buildings like the Pompidou Centre in Paris or the Tate Modern in London are often held up as examples of how modern architecture 'works' as each building attracts thousands of visitors. But do people flock there because they are aficionados of modern architecture and/or modern art?[1] Well clearly some are, but for the majority it is a 'grand day out'. Casual observation of either of these sites is that the modern art on display is given fairly short shrift, and the most popular exhibit is the gallery shop full of logoed tee shirts, umbrellas and other tourist tat, perhaps a postcard for a friend – mostly 'I was there' merchandise. Then it's off to the 'tea rooms', where overpriced cakes and buns are on offer often washed down with mouth-burning tea or coffee served in dreary polystyrene beakers. So why do people bother? For various reasons, but mainly because both are places to go to, and, having made it to the tea-room, visitors find that both buildings provide outstanding views of the city. At Pompidou there is the added fairground excitement of the ride up and down the external escalators. As Deyan Sudjic put it '... attracting countless thousands of visitors who never have any intention of looking at the art ...'.[2]

The fairground ride to the tea rooms

So do these high attendance figures for icons of modern architecture indicate that's what the general public really like?[3] There's scant evidence that this is the case. In the early 1940s, proselytiser for 'modern' architecture JM Richards, wrote '... in all but a few cases even the best modern architecture has at present only a limited amount of positive appeal to our eyes.'[4] Blimey, even the proselytiser doesn't like it much and he's hardly alone. Some 50 years later the *Financial Times* printed this:[5]

---

[1] In a 2004 survey, Tate Modern was placed fourth in a list of Britain's ten worst buildings.

[2] Sudjic, 1992, p135.

[3] While the Pompidou Centre is certainly an icon of 'modern' architecture Tate Modern's modern-architectural iconic status is less certain. The building is a huge threatening brick box, built to house giant turbines, boilers and their ancillary equipment. Outside, the brick elevations were designed by the very un-modern architect Sir Giles Gilbert Scott (1880–1960). Previously known as Bankside power station, it was scheduled for demolition until the Tate took it on. It was revamped, more shop-fitting than vamping in actuality, by architects Jacques Herzog and Pierre de Meuron.

[4] Richards, 1940, p13.

[5] *Financial Times*, 17/18 January 2004, Weekend section, pW2.

The 20th century saw the rise and fall of modernist rationalism in many activities. Nowhere was the change more visible, or the results more disastrous, than in architecture

Distinguished architectural historian Joseph Rykwert (b1926) thinks that 'Most modern buildings hate people',[6] and without much doubt, vice versa in the majority of cases. For the members of the architectural ghetto, the general public are basically the enemy, or the 'baying masses' as ghetto spokesman Damian Arnold christened them.[7] Diane Ghirardo, writing about the Sainsbury Wing of London's National Gallery, thinks that the architects communicate '... not towards the masses but toward architects ...'.[8]

Faced with the monolithic Modern-Movement-satiated architectural profession, the baying masses are rather like an angry, disorganised crowd faced with a specially-equipped and highly organised squad of riot police. Right might be on the side of the crowd, but might is on the side of the police, and as so often, might is right. So what are they to do? As buildings are such permanent objects they can't just be 'got rid of', what can be done effectively or ineffectively? The resistance takes various forms; name-calling, writing articles and books, forming types of resistance groups and, in rather rare instances, getting the offending buildings demolished.

The easiest way for the public to show their displeasure at widely disliked buildings is to give them pejorative nicknames. During the building of Le Corbusier's iconic Unité,[9] it became known as the Madhouse; this was because a report had been produced that concluded that anyone who had to live there would go mad. Another of Corbu's buildings became (affectionately)[10] known as the Coal Bucket.

Known 'affectionately' as the coal bucket

Built in Firminy, home of one of the few 'other' Unités, the Coal Bucket was designed in 1960 but only completed in 2006. This was because, almost as soon as it was started, the Bishop of Lyons took against it and withdrew funding. Finally completed with some state funding, it cannot now be a church![11]

Several of Norman Foster's efforts in London have attracted nicknames, affectionate or otherwise. He has the new HQ of the London Assembly called the Headlamp or the Glass Testicle;[12] his Millennium Bridge across the

---

[6] Fletcher, 2001, p417.

[7] *Building Design*, 15 October 2004, p11.

[8] Ghirardo, 1996, p75.

[9] See pages 105–111 (Chapter 6).

[10] Architectural apologists often add the word 'affectionately' to the nickname. In this case it was Tom Dyckhoff in *The Times*, 19 December 2006.

[11] This is because French law forbids the state to spend money on churches.

[12] See pages 264–265 (Chapter 15).

Excitement for the visitors

So bloody tacky

Thames has become the Wobbly Bridge[13] and his office block for Swiss Re has famously become the Gherkin.

In the Isle of Wight, the architecturally 'exciting' entrance to a bang-up-to-date hospital obviously excited some in other ways, as it was christened Madonna's Tits.

Another amusing example (unless you live near it) of name-calling is the Bottle Bank built on the seafront of Porthcawl, the local baying masses think it is '... an abortion ... it's just stupid ... it's so bloody tacky, it's horrible',[14] and no doubt a lot more besides.

The architects '... thought very carefully about what was Porthcawl'. Apparently what was Porthcawl, according them, was '... the funfair, the sea-side, kiss-me-quick hats and all that' – and all that somehow got into the building with a childish hotchpotch of 'sea-side' elements like '... a façade like a ship's hull, apartments like ... beach look-out posts, plus [unbelievably] the ice cream cone columns.' What would they have designed if the building had been near a sewage farm? The mind boggles. But there is a 'wider problem when it comes to deciding what good architecture is.' How insightful. This is because 'the populace and the architects don't always seem to be on the same planet.' Too right, the populace are on overcrowded, globally-warmed planet Earth, whereas the architects seem to inhabit a planet where clouds and cuckoos must predominate.

A few people have gone one further than just name-calling and have taken the trouble to write disparagingly about Modern Movement architecture. One of the biggest selling books on architecture is *From Bauhaus to Our House* written by Tom Wolfe in 1981; 'A devastating and timely attack on the hideous follies of modern architecture' says the cover blurb.[15] In 1994, inventor and designer Stewart Brand wrote a book entitled, rather strangely, *How Buildings Learn.* The book is mainly concerned about how buildings are adapted over time, but apparently the book came into existence due to Brand's experience with modern architecture.[16] This was when he had to use the Wiesner Building at MIT designed by IM Pei (b1917).[17] Brand was shocked by the '... $45 million pretentious-

[13] See pages 197–200 (Chapter 11).

[14] *Arts Guardian*, 31 January 2007, p24 for these and subsequent quotations.

[15] Wolfe also wrote a book called *The Painted Word* which attacked the vacuity of abstract painting.

[16] Brand, 1994, p52.

[17] Considered in a 1991 poll to be 'the most influential living American architect'.

ness, ill-functionality and non-adaptability' and went on to discover that the building was '... not unusually bad. Its badness is the norm in new buildings overdesigned by architects'.[18]

Some architects have entered the fray. Peter Blake (1920–2006) for instance, who after pursuing a 'modernist' career suddenly went off the rails in 1977 by publishing a book called *Form Follows Fiasco: Why modern architecture hasn't worked*. This book seems to be unique as a direct attack on Modern Movement architecture by an architect.

Other architects have written books that attack 'modern' architecture, but this is not the sole purpose. These books try to show that there is another way, for instance Léon Krier's book with the rather odd title *Architecture: Choice or Fate* published in 1998. Although the book attacks Modern Movement architecture relentlessly, its main aim is to present an alternative to the modernist dream, in terms of buildings and in urban spaces. His vision is to get away from architecture as single sculptural objects, and to create urban spaces that people will enjoy using; one criterion being that everyone is within easy walking distance of all their desired amenities.

Architects rarely, if ever, appear in cartoons outside the ghetto press. But in the ghetto they are relentlessly lampooned by architect and cartoonist Louis Hellman (b1936); but his cartoons rarely, if ever, leave the ghetto. Perhaps they require too much inside knowledge to be appreciated by the baying masses – which is a great pity.

Shocking pretentiousness, ill-functionality and non-adaptability

A unique direct attack

How Krier sees the modern architect

An up-yours iconic building as seen by Hellman

---

[18] Brand, 1994, p53.

Perhaps the most effective book written, not directly criticising modern architecture, but criticising city planning based partially on Le Corbusier's vision of the city of tomorrow,[19] was *The Life and Death of Great American Cities* written in 1961 by journalist Jane Jacobs (1916–2006). Her book, which eulogised cities as a collection of friendly, diverse neighbourhoods, had a dramatic effect on the planning policies of the day, and her influence continues with people like Krier. But not everyone is so enthusiastic about her vision of the city, as modernist critics rubbish her quaint belief in human scale, saying that she 'argues for a way of life that, if it ever existed, had disappeared. She looks back to the vitality of urban neighbourhoods that she assumes were a vital part of the city ...'.[20]

Despite such magisterial put-downs from the modernist elite, attacks from non-architects pop up all over the place, often in the most unlikely publications. For example, in 1963 the Fabian Society produced a pamphlet called 'Architecture: art or social service?'[21]

The unlikely revolutionary

Technically almost perfect

The pamphlet attempts to outline a political policy towards architecture. The author, Paul Thompson, identifies two sorts of architects, those he called Functionalists by which he means architects whose '... overriding consideration is the need of the user ...' and those he terms Formalists who '... will base their design on aesthetic considerations'.[22] As an example of the latter he chooses Hunstanton Secondary Modern School designed by stars of the British architectural scene during the second half of the twentieth century, Alison (1928–1993) and Peter (1923–2003) Smithson. It was finished in 1954, and by 1963 it had been visited by over 3,000 architects – more than one a day on average. These visits were because the school was a ghetto icon; '... technically it was almost perfect. Aesthetically the most distinguished of buildings of the time', says modern architectural chronicler Dennis Sharp.[23] No doubt most of the architectural visitors came away with the same impression.

---

[19] See pages 92, 93 & 99 (Chapter 6).

[20] Sudjic, 1992, p23.

[21] This was a 'Young Fabian Pamphlet' written by Paul Thompson.

[22] ibid, p1.

[23] Sharp, 1972, p199. This building also appears without adverse criticism in many books on modern architecture – Frampton, 1980, p263, Gibberd, 1997, p168, Knobel, 1985, p129, and countless others. All the books mentioned were written long after 1963, so, one can assume that the multiple functional shortcomings of Hunstanton School were well-known by then; but this was of little interest to architectural writers who were solely interested to see how the icon complied with the Modern Movement belief system.

But were the teachers and pupils so chuffed? Far from it. Thompson, who is uninterested in aesthetics, notes that 'its disadvantages are numerous'[24] and goes on to list many of them:

... the door and window frames have twisted and the glass has split ...
... salt air has corroded the steelwork ...
... the classrooms are of minimum size ...
... there are ten staircases that act as drums ...
... there is no provision for several vital activities ...
... the details were equally unsatisfactory and have been extensively altered ...

and much much more. What is unusual about this publication, and there should certainly be many more of this type, is that it is a matter-of-fact report about the shortcomings of a Modern Movement icon.

But what about 'modern' architects being treated as a joke in popular culture? Modern architecture only appears in the popular press when there is something that can be described as a fiasco. As modern architectural projects frequently do end up as fiascos this is how they get portrayed. But the 'serious' press is another matter, many have 'architectural correspondents' who are fully paid-up members of the design ghetto. Their role is to 'explain' to the reader what is so good about modern architecture.[25] Other journalists on these 'serious' publications usually give things like modern architecture, or modern art for that matter, a wide berth, but an exception is Simon Jenkins (b1943). Jenkins is highly critical of modern architecture and attacks it frontally whenever the opportunity arises.

Reviewing an exhibition on Modernism[26] Jenkins opened with, 'Go at once. Take a young person to see the Modernism show at the V&A and feel fear. It is the most terrifying exhibition I have seen ...'.[27] When reviewing a book about housing estates Jenkins opined that 'The worst professional crime ever inflicted on Britain was the application of utopian modernism to the public-housing stock in the 1960s and 1970s. It dehumanised communities, spoilt landscapes and ruined lives.' and much more in the same vein, and accuses the Royal Institute of British Architects of remaining in '... total denial'.[28] Blimey, that's telling them.

But they'd been told before, in 1984 as it happens. This was when one of the most ferocious and sustained attacks on Modern Movement architecture came from a completely unexpected quarter – a member of the British royal family. Traditionally, at least during the twentieth century, members of the British royal family have kept a quiet aloofness. They undertake many public engagements during which they often make short speeches,

---

[24] See Thompson, 1963, p2 for all these quotes.

[25] Typical of these architectural correspondents and what they write is illustrated by Martin Pawley writing about architectural 'honesty' in the *Arts Guardian* – see pages 215–216 (Chapter 12).

[26] Held in 2006 at the Victoria and Albert Museum, London. The accompanying book, edited by C Wilk, is called *Modernism: Designing for a new world*.

[27] *Guardian*, 7 April 2006, p24.

[28] *Sunday Times*, 7 January 2007, p42.

always anodyne, pleasant platitudes such as, 'It give me great pleasure to be here today to open this wonderful hospital wing ... etc, etc.' So, when the heir to the throne Prince Charles attended the 150th anniversary banquet of the Royal Institute of British Architects on 30 May 1984, more of the same was expected. (Contrary to maybe some public opinion, the great and good of the architectural profession are far from pinko-radicals, and are as eager and willing to accept royal accolades as any other group.)

And so, as the great and the good leant back in their chairs, an expensive cigar in one hand and a jolly decent brandy in the other, it was to be the perfect end to the day – to be bathed in emollient praise from their royal patron. But the patronees were in for the shock of their lives. The Prince's speech started predictably enough – 'Ladies and gentlemen, it seems entirely appropriate in this anniversary year that the Royal Institute of British Architects should nominate Mr Charles Correa to the Queen to receive the Royal Gold Medal for Architecture. I have heard that he is a brilliant modern architect who has been responsible for splendidly brilliant and sensitive modern architecture, invariably of low cost ...'.

But gradually it appeared that HRH was not that enamoured with the architecture his hosts had produced; in fact he was wielding a knife, which he inserted into the profession as a whole. He said, 'For far too long, it seems to me, some planners and architects have consistently ignored the feelings and wishes of the mass of ordinary people in this country. Perhaps, when you think about it, it is hardly surprising as architects tend to have been trained to design buildings from scratch – to tear down and rebuild.' What was that? '... architects have consistently ignored the feelings and wishes of the mass of ordinary people ...'. No doubt many a smile became fixed or frozen in horror – their honoured guest and patron was turning on them! And worse was to come, he suddenly got seriously confrontational.

An architectural competition (oh no not another one) had been held recently for an extension to the National Gallery that is sited on the north side of the world famous Trafalgar Square. Predictably, a sore-thumb Modern-Movement-high-tech concoction had won. HRH couldn't bear it and he said so describing it memorably as 'like a monstrous carbuncle on the face of a much-loved and elegant friend ...'. This seems to be pushing it a bit as, anyone who knows Trafalgar Square is likely to agree that, it is hardly a beautiful or friendly piece of townscape; a large and rather arid stone square, surrounded by constant traffic and big, un-engaging, stone, neo-classical buildings, including the National Gallery.

He ended his extraordinary speech with, 'In this 150th anniversary year, which provides an opportunity for a fresh look at the path ahead and in which by now you are probably regretting having asked me to take part, may I express the earnest hope that the next 150 years will see a new harmony between imagination and taste and in the relationship between the architects and the people of this country.' A royal expressing an opinion in public was unheard of, let alone a specific attack. There was uproar.

There was also an immediately identifiable problem – what to do with the extension? After much to-ing and fro-ing it was 'generally agreed' that perhaps the winning scheme was not actually all that appropriate; so what to do? After even more to-ing and fro-ing an 'acceptable' scheme was elicited from Robert Venturi,[29] and this was built – round one to HRH.

[29] See page 219 (Chapter 12).

In 1987, Charles returned to the attack, this time more savagely. The occasion was the Corporation of London Planning and Communication Committee's Annual Dinner, and this time his main target was the proposed development next to St Paul's Cathedral; Paternoster Square. 'Nowhere is the problem more acute than in that special area around St Paul's Cathedral. What have we done, ladies and gentlemen, to St Paul's? What are we about to do to it now? Why in fact does St Paul's matter so much? Because it is our greatest national monument.'

Round one to HRH

Widening his attack, he compared the work of post-war British architects unfavourably with the rubble left behind after the World War II bombing by the Nazi airforce, the Luftwaffe, 'You have, ladies and gentlemen, to give this much to the Luftwaffe: when it knocked down our buildings, it didn't replace them with anything more offensive than rubble. We did that. Clausewitz called war the continuation of diplomacy by other means. Around St Paul's, planning turned out to be the continuation of war by other means.'[30] Subsequently a new and more appropriate design was built in Paternoster Square – round two to HRH.

Round two to HRH

But Charles was also a doer, and was willing to put his money where his mouth was. He organised a school of architecture which would teach the students how to design 'proper buildings'.[31] He made a television programme, and he wrote a book.[32] And he went even further.

---

[30] Actually HRH's adverse comparison of post-war architecture to Luftwaffe-produced rubble, shocking as it was, was not new. In 1945, Penguin Books published *The County of London Plan* and on page 77 it says, 'Once upon a time London – the beautiful city we have been destroying by our rebuilding faster than the blitz could do it'. What's all the more surprising was that a co-author was Ernö Goldfinger, a dedicated Modern Movement architect. Rather amusingly, AN Wilson regrets that when the Luftwaffe bombed Buckingham Palace they missed Aston Webb's façade. Wilson, 2003, p47.

[31] Initially called Prince of Wales's Institute of Architecture, it offered a Foundation Course and a Graduate Course, but never managed to turn itself into a school of architecture that would challenge the hegemony of the 'official' Modern Movement schools. The Institute closed in 2001. The organisation is now called the Prince's Foundation for the Built Environment, which promotes a number of activities related to non-Modern Movement architecture.

[32] The book was called *A Vision of Britain*.

He commissioned, from Léon Krier (b1946), a design for a whole suburb of a town; it was called Poundbury and was to be a new part of Dorchester.[33] And what's more he got it built. The project, which illustrates perfectly the 'architectural ghetto/baying masses' conflict deserves study. The architect chosen, Léon Krier, cuts a rather odd figure in the ghetto – because he is/was part of it. He gained street cred,[34] by working for the starry architect James Stirling,[35] known as 'Big Jim' in the biz.

But he didn't go on to design buildings using any of the three Modern Movement basic prototypes – the perfect glass box, the wonky box or the swirly thing. His designs incorporated 'normal' building elements such as pitched roofs and sensible-sized windows inserted into masonry walls; the entrances to his buildings were clear to everyone and there was no muddying of the interior with the exterior. His buildings were, what's the word – appropriate.

So Charles teamed up with Krier to design the 'notorious' new suburb of Dorchester called Poundbury. This, superficially at any rate, innocuous project drove members of the architectural ghetto to pour withering scorn on it and its perpetrators. Ghetto spokesman Stephen Bayley for example; 'Prince Charles's crude gropings in architecture have left us with Poundbury, a tart's boudoir of a model village Poundbury was a grave setback to intelligent building. Indeed, it was a grave setback to intelligence itself.'[36] Or, in a similar vein, Jonathan Glancey: '... tweedy architects sporting bird's nest haircuts and ancient polished brogues sat at the dainty feet of the Prince of Wales ... house and shops newly built to look

Part of the 'scuppered' plan

old-fashioned would doff their cornices to renaissance style piazzas'.[37] Glancey goes on, erroneously as it turns out, to console himself that it was a hopeless failure '... the bubble burst ... the reality of planning bye-laws and regulations helped to scupper the plan and so did a general lack of interest'.[38] None of this is true; the first phase of the project was built and was so successful that a second phase was started almost as soon as the first was finished. What's more the tourist office in Dorchester has endless requests from visitors for directions.

---

[33] Poundbury is often thought to be an isolated new ye olde village – which it isn't.

[34] For any aspiring star architect, it is essential that time is spent sitting at the feet of an acknowledged 'master'. This means that established star architects have an endless supply of cheap, and excessively willing, drawing-board (now computer-terminal) fodder. This also means that the star-architect's 'atelier' is stuffed with inexperienced 'students' with consequential results.

[35] See page 209 (Chapter 12).

[36] *The Observer*, 20 March 2005.

[37] Glancey, 2003, p68.

[38] ibid.

But it wasn't only ghetto members who attacked Prince Charles and Poundbury. Journalist, TV presenter and ex-architectural student, Janet Street-Porter (b1946), thinks that

Modern architecture gets a pretty rough ride in Britain without Prince Charles lobbing his tiara into the ring every time there's a chance to build something contemporary anywhere near anything ancient. This is the man responsible for the fake-Georgian horror of Poundbury, a Disney-like ghetto of twee stone houses near his estate.[39]

Which is quite funny really, as for many years 'klaxon-throated' Janet, as journalist Janet Abrams dubbed her,[40] lived in a 'gingerbread house'[41] designed for her by her friend, and architectural wit, Piers Gough (b1946).

Defenders of Poundbury also appeared in unlikely guises; *Newsweek* reporter Ray Sawhill for instance:

Part of the point, in fact, of the *New York Times* report about Poundbury was that visitors were surprised by how pleasant a place it's shaping up to be, because what had been predicted was a nightmare of kitsch and control – a miniature, right-wing version of that modernist disaster, Brasilia.[42]

Or according to Carolyn Torma

Some critics have dismissed Poundbury as hopelessly old-fashioned and dangerously romantic. Paul Goldberger writing in *The New Yorker* in July 1998,[43] pronounced all of Prince Charles's efforts 'A Royal Defeat.' But this view is too short sighted and much too focused on large-scale architectural commissions designed by major architects. Goldberger is probably correct in saying that Prince Charles has had limited influence on high-profile new architectural monuments in Great Britain. At the same time, however, Goldberger underestimates the importance of the choices that ordinary people make about where to live and how. It is in this arena that Poundbury succeeds.[44]

Janet's gingerbread house

---

[39] Quoted in http://www.channel4.com/life/microsites/D/demolition/demolish1.html (accessed October 2008).

[40] *The Independent*, 22 September 1988, p18.

[41] ibid.

[42] Quoted by Ray Sawhill in *SALON*, 29 October 1998.

[43] Paul Goldberger, 'A Royal Defeat', *The New Yorker*, 13 July 1998, p52–59.

[44] See 'Prince Charles builds a new town', in *The Commissioner*, Fall 1998/Winter 1999.

Maybe Prince Charles hasn't had the effect he had hoped for when he made his extraordinary speech in 1984, but on the other hand he has certainly not suffered 'A Royal Defeat'. In November 2005, he was awarded the Vincent Scully Prize by the National Building Museum of Washington USA. His intervention has been partly responsible for what is called the New Urbanism or Neo-traditionalism. But what his efforts at 'not putting up with it' also show is how resistant the architectural ghetto is to any view about architecture that doesn't coincide with their Modern Movement belief system, and that it is still oblivious to the desires of the baying masses.

But why didn't Charles come out on top? Mainly because he didn't get any significant support from other prominent figures. No politician will pronounce on any matter of taste: their heads are already too high above the parapet in the normal course of events. So who else could have helped? Well, anyway no-one did.

However, many people also feel uncomfortable with the alteration and/or demolition of non-Modern Movement inspired buildings. Many countries have official and non-official organisations to guard and conserve what they consider to be their 'architectural heritage'. These organisations aren't overtly against Modern Movement architecture but, with some exceptions, they could be seen as tacitly against it, because they want to preserve the buildings that the Modern Movement wanted to demolish.[45]

In Great Britain these organisations are numerous and somewhat complex. The idea of preserving or protecting buildings probably started with Queen Elizabeth I's 'Proclamation agaynst breaking or defacing Monumentes' in 1560, which led to the setting up of the College of Antiquaries in 1586. In 1707 the Society of Antiquaries was founded, and still exists today. Perhaps seminal was the establishment, in 1877, of The Society for the Protection of Ancient Buildings (SPAB). This was mainly the idea of the enemy of industrialisation William Morris, whose concern was that old buildings were being altered or restored 'incorrectly'.[46] In 1895 the National Trust was set up which was empowered by the 1907 National Trust Act. The Trust (now with over 3 million members) buys, maintains and opens to the public buildings and land that is thought to be part of Britain's heritage.

There followed a number of Acts of Parliament that gave rise to such concepts as 'Preservation Orders', 'Conservation Areas' and 'Listed Buildings'. The Acts also gave powers to authorites to attribute these concepts, and powers to prevent owners altering or demolishing Listed Buildings and what could, and could not, be built in Conservation Areas. Originally, the idea was to list buildings built before 1725, but many people felt that a lot of buildings built after this date should also be protected. This gave rise to the founding of the Georgian Group in 1937, and the Victorian Society in 1958. A turning point in the preservation of Britain's architectural heritage came in 1962 with a failure rather than a success. This was when, in spite of a high-profile 'Save the Arch' campaign, the Doric-columned arch that formed the entrance to the original Euston station was demol-

---

[45] For instance Le Corbusier wanted to knock down Paris – see page 99, and Manhattan come to that – see page 103.

[46] How an old building should be 'correctly' restored can be, and is, debated endlessly.

The arch that wasn't saved

Before the bomb

ished, along with the rest of the station, to make way for the present dreary and uninspired station concourse and buildings.[47]

But more organisations and societies were needed. In 1975 SAVE was set up as a pressure group to preserve threatened and abandoned buildings by, where possible, finding new uses for them. In 1983, English Heritage was set up to serve as the Government's statutory adviser on the historic environment. An interesting case history involving both SAVE and English Heritage was the fate of the Baltic Exchange. Built in 1903, it was severely damaged, in 1992, by an IRA bomb.[48]

The building was Grade II* listed, for which the governments guidelines state that the 'demolition of any Grade II* building should be wholly exceptional and require the strongest justification'. The site was sold to a developer on the understanding that any new building would incorporate the bomb-damaged Exchange Hall and the St Mary Axe façade. These parts were carefully, and expensively, dismantled and put into storage ready for becoming part of the new building. To cut a longish story short, the developer presented to the City of London Corporation a version of the Gherkin. English Heritage was consulted and they were against the scheme saying, amongst many unfavourable views, that '... the development ... would have a disastrous effect on near, medium and distant views ...'. That was in February 1999. By the time English Heritage Commissioners considered the application again (and finally) on 13 June 2000, the advice to the City and Government Office for London was that the 'remarkable quality' of the Gherkin outweighed 'the limited adverse impact of the proposal on the setting of a number of surrounding buildings and areas'. SAVE pushed for a public enquiry, but in July 2000 the

---

[47] One year later something similar happened in New York with the demolition of Penn Station – 'Any city gets what it admires, will pay for, and, ultimately, deserves. Even when we had Penn Station, we couldn't afford to keep it clean. We want and deserve tin-can architecture in a tinhorn culture. And we will probably be judged not by the monuments we build but by those we have destroyed'. 'Farewell to Penn Station', editorial of the *New York Times*, 30 October 1963.

[48] It killed three people: Paul Butt, 29, Baltic Exchange employee Thomas Casey, 49, and 15 year old Danielle Carter. The tragic consequences included the first ambulance man on the scene, he never recovered – five months later he killed his girlfriend with a shotgun and tried to kill himself – he is now in a secure psychiatric unit.

Mayor of London[49] wrote to the minister responsible[50] saying that the Article 14 Direction[51] should be lifted, that the 'quality of design was of the highest order,' and that the project had his 'full support'.[52]

At first sight, the Baltic Exchange/Gherkin story takes some believing. Part of Britain's architectural heritage, which had been officially protected for posterity, is badly damaged by an IRA bomb. The site is sold to a developer on the understanding that much of the damaged heritage would be reinstated. £4 million is spent on dismantling the precious parts and storing them ready for re-use. The developer presents a scheme that doesn't include any of the precious bits. English Heritage rejects it with a barrage of disparaging comments. The developer re-submits the scheme, still with no precious bits, but this time bigger and bolder and suddenly English Heritage just loves it. When protests are made and a public enquiry is demanded, the whole process is overridden by that expert on urban design, and 'man of the people' Two Jags John Prescott.

In 2005, the TV company Channel 4 ran a series of programmes called *Demolition*, where viewers were invited to vote for the building they'd most like to see demolished. The final list was of 12 buildings – the dirty dozen. All were built since World War II and all followed, one way or another, the edicts of the Modern Movement. Amongst the presenters of the programme was George Ferguson, who was at the time the president of the Royal Institute of British Architects. One of the dirty dozen was an embarrassment to him because the general public had selected for demolition the RIBA Stirling prize-winning project, the Scottish Parliament Building.[53] But Ferguson believed 'that to be a mischievous nomination'. But it's hard to understand why he should think that, as the building appeared as Britain's sixth worst building in a survey carried out in 2004.[54]

Another building nominated for demolition was Park Hill in Sheffield. Built in 1961 '... it may to the lay person appear harsh and uninviting, but this scheme represented a sincere attempt to break away from conventional local authority housing solutions,'[55] and 'Park Hill reveals its innermost secrets with the greatest architectual conviction ...'.[56] Oh really? Well the viewers want it knocked down even though it's Grade II listed, and Ferguson, perhaps in a 'truthful' phase of his cognative dissonance, thinks that 'The Park Hill estate in Sheffield is, amazingly, listed. To me, this was an indulgence and a mis-

---

[49] Mr Ken Livingstone MP, was known in a previous incarnation, while radical leader of the Greater London Council, as 'Red Ken'. On May 1, 2008, after eight years in office as Mayor, he failed to win re-election for a third term, being beaten by Tory MP Boris Johnson.

[50] The Rt. Hon John Prescott MP, known in the tabloid press, due to his ownership of several Jaguar cars, as 'Two Jags John' and later, after some sexual impropriety had become public, 'Two Shags John'.

[51] An Article 14 Direction is a term used in British planning law for a directive issued by the British Government which prevents a Local Planning Authority granting planning permission for a specific proposal. It has no time limit, so remains in force until explicitly lifted. It is typically used to allow a regional government office more time to consider proposals.

[52] For all this information about the Baltic Exchange go to www.savebritainsheritage.org/baltic.htm and follow the links (accessed in October 2008).

[53] *The Observer*, 20 March 2005.

[54] See press release by Cheltenham and Gloucester building society, dated October 2004.

[55] Sharp, 1972, p269.

[56] Banham, 1962, p143.

use of a system that should balance aesthetic quality with historic and social significance.'[57]

Although the general public – the users and the passers-by – generally restrict themselves to name-calling, the occasional letter to the press or voting in TV programmes, sometimes they are driven to demonstrate. This happened, for instance, in May 1981 when the tenants of houses designed by prize-winning architect Norman Foster had reached the end of their tether. Eventually the houses were modified, which included having the flat roofs replaced by pitched ones. Oh and the client received a '£3 million-plus settlement ...'[58] of which Foster paid about half.

Harsh and uninviting?

But some buildings did receive the ultimate accolade and got demolished because they weren't fit for purpose. These ranged from factories to housing estates, from schools to multi-storey blocks. James Stirling, another prize-winning architect, with his then partner James Gowan, designed a housing estate for Runcorn New Town (the houses were quickly nicknamed 'washing machines' by the tenants). The estate was problematic from the start, being 'Loved by architects ... hated by the residents...'.[59] By 1989 it was decided that the whole estate should be demolished. The architect claimed they weren't responsible as

Norman gets the thumbs down in 1981

Loved by architects...Hated by the residents

'... they had no choice but to comply with the government's social vision', but the chairperson of the resident's assocation thought that '"The architect either had a brainstorm or was suffering from acute depression" when designing the estate ...'.[60]

Schools can get knocked down too. Pimlico School, which predictably won 'a clutch of awards for its daring glass and concrete structure' but was 'reviled for the common drawbacks attached to these stylistic elements: floor to ceiling glass windows and large

[57] See http://www.channel4.com/life/microsites/D/demolition/worst2.html (accessed in October 2008).

[58] *Building Design*, 26 October 1984, p48.

[59] *Guardian*, 31 January 2007, p25.

[60] *Building Design*, March 1989.

An absolute eyesore of considerable architectural importance

Communal area friendliness - the fantasy

Communal area friendliness - the reality

expanses of bare, unadorned concrete means the school is a freezing cold box in winter and a sweltering greenhouse in summer', was demolished. Prize-winning architect Richard Rogers was against its demolition as it was of 'considerable architectural importance' whereas the chairman of the council planning committee thought it 'an absolute eyesore'.[61]

Perhaps the best known case of demolition was that of the Pruitt-Igoe estate, designed by Minoru Yamasaki (1912–2006). Built in St Louis Missouri between 1952 and 1955, it consisted of 33 11-storey blocks of flats with a total of 2,870 individual apartments.

It was, as ever, based on the social/architectural models of Le Corbuiser – tower blocks surrounded by greenery, the common areas a friendly bustle of childern playing, teenagers hanging out and neighbours passing the time of day, the usual fantasy – and of course the architects produced drawings showing how it all would be.

But none of this happened; the tenants became so unhappy with the architectual solution they'd been landed with, that they soon started taking it out on each other and the building. And the whole project was progressively vandalised.

After all else had failed,[62] in 1972 the extraordinary decision was taken to blow the whole of this Modern Movement-inspired, architectural masterpiece, to smithereens; and that's what happened, beginning on 16 March.

---

[61] *Time Out London*, 16/22 January 2008, p12.

[62] The failure of Pruitt-Igoe inspired Oscar Newman to come up with the idea of 'defensible space'. This became the influential book *Creating Defensible Space*. Pages 9–12 talk about Pruitt-Igoe.

Modern architecture blown to smithereens in 1972

There were many other cases, Cabrini-Green being one. A housing project built between 1942 and 1962 in Chicago, at one point it housed 20,000 people. By the 1990s the police were refusing to enter the project, and in 1999 it was scheduled for demolition, along with other Chicago housing projects. In 2006 demolition was still ongoing.[63] Since 1972, the demolition of individual tower blocks built for social housing has become commonplace throughout Europe and the United States: often blown up to the satisfaction of local residents.

So, rather oddly, the biggest group of people who got to live in buildings designed by Modern Movement architects were those without choice – tenants of social housing. And it was they who often got the power, one way or another, to have these buildings demolished. But whilst these buildings were designed, probably without exception, by architects who followed the beliefs of the Modern Movement, were their failings architectural? Obviously, people who don't like 'modern' architecture, which seems to be an awful lot, are only too pleased to take this view and point them up as being brilliant examples of the shortcomings of the Modern Movement mantra. But is this fair?

Supporters of modern architecture are quick to point out that the rich and the middle-class are able to live perfectly well in high-rise flats, and are even prepared to pay more the higher they go. As ghetto writer Deyan Sudjic puts it, 'Actually, the fact that Pruitt-Igoe turned out to be a disaster had nothing to do with the Modern Movement.'[64] Some of the ex-tenants seem to support him:

---

[63] But by the end of 2009, all 53 of Chicago's public housing high-rises will be gone.

[64] Sudjic, 1992, p181.

'Those were really some of the best years of my life,' says Herman King, who grew up on the Pruitt side. 'I've lived in Richmond Heights since 1971, but in the projects there was a sense of connectedness, a sense of closeness with your neighbors. In suburbia, it's just the opposite. I don't even know my neighbors' last names.'[65]

But the same source continues, in the next paragraph with:

History, however, tells a darker story of the Pruitt-Igoe experience ... the stark Modernist edifices live on as an icon of failure, one of the great public-policy blunders of the twentieth century. Even its ambitious young architect, Minoru Yamasaki ... regretted Pruitt-Igoe: 'It's a job I wish I hadn't done,' he conceded years ago.

The point at issue is that the people who get the opportunity to live in social housing are by definition not well-off. And the well-off, who pay for the social housing through taxes, are not that inclined to pay for social housing high-rises with manned, carpeted and well-appointed common areas which is where the problems start. After all, equally 'not-well-off' recipients of social housing, who end up in individual houses, with perhaps a bit of garden, do not in general set about destroying their environment.[66]

But the Modern Movement is at fault because their idealistic, or, rather, ideological vision was of segregated housing,[67] and the benefits of 'streets-in-the-sky' and 'towers-in-the-park' are core beliefs. The reality is that 'Modern architecture ... has let society down, and arrogance of too many architects who put dogma above utility and believe they know better than their clients how they should live ...'.[68] The *Demolition* TV programmes showed that people hate 'modern' architecture and want it destroyed; even if it's brand-spanking-new prize-winning modern architecture. And they don't want old buildings destroyed, even if they are 'new' old buildings like the extension to the National Gallery, the buildings in Paternoster Square, or even that architectural 'horror' Poundbury.

In 1971, four young men from the north-west of England were on holiday in Ireland and, after complaining about the way all British beer was starting to taste fizzy, decided to form a Campaign for Real Ale – CAMRA. Helped by Richard Boston (1938–2006), a columnist writing in the *Guardian*, the Campaign for Real Ale became (and remains) a force to be reckoned with in the brewing world, and was instrumental in radically improving the quality of English beer. Perhaps what is needed is an architectural equivalent, but so far no national or international Campaign for Real Architecture (CamRarch?) exists, or has even been suggested...

---

[65] See *It Was Just Like Beverly Hills* by Randall Roberts, published in the *St Louis News*, 1 June 2005.

[66] Contrary to some ghetto opinions, at their bête noir Poundbury, about 30% of the housing is in fact social housing – so far not destroyed by the tenants.

[67] Le Corbusier's view of the ideal town had the middle-class housed in a separate area to the working class – see page 92 (Chapter 6).

[68] Whitford, 1984, p200.

15. Who's right? Who's wrong?

What this book has shown is that modern architecture has turned out to be a failure for most people, while, at the same time has been a great success for many members of the architectural profession. That this is true is easily shown by considering what is perhaps the most basic building – the house – or as it was infamously dubbed by the high priest of modern architecture, Le Corbusier, a machine for living in. Perhaps this chapter could end here, because who would equate a house in which one would want to make a home with a machine? But no matter, what houses do the architectural ghetto see as icons? Here are four of the most iconic: the Villa Savoye by Le Corbusier, built in 1931, Fallingwater by Frank Lloyd Wright, built in 1937, the Wichita House by Buckminster Fuller, built in 1946, and the Farnsworth House by Mies van der Rohe, built in 1950. All were received panegyrically in the ghetto press and all were failures.

The Villa Savoye was so uncomfortable that every autumn there were 'cries of distress' from the owner. Whilst awaiting scheduled demolition, it was being used as a hay barn before being 'rescued' for posterity. Due to the interminable leaks, the owner of Fallingwater, Edgar Kaufmann, christened it Rising Mildew. Furthermore Wright, taking on the role of an expert structural engineer, proposed to use an entirely inadequate quantity of reinforcement in the 'stunning' cantilever beams; the contractor insisted on doubling the quantity, causing problems between him and Wright.[1] The structural problems were only resolved in 2002 after an $11.5 million restoration.[2] The Wichita House, that seemed to offer true machine living, was never used by anyone.[3] The Farnsworth House, which was never seen as a house in the normal sense, was, according to its owner Edith Farnsworth, too expensive and impractical in many ways. She unsuccessfully sued the architect for malpractice and later 'denounced' Mies as a menace to American architecture!

But apart from the technical failures, which were obviously due to the designer's incompetence, Savoye, Kaufmann and Farnsworth were all somewhat naïve to expect their houses to be places in which to live. According to the at-the-time Mies addict Peter Blake, 'All great houses by great architects tend to be somewhat impractical ... clients find that they are living in too expensive and too inefficient buildings.'[4] Writing about Fallingwater Jane Simley thinks that '... the house was meant as much to be seen and marvelled at as

---

[1] Like many architects, Wright thought of himself as an expert structural engineer. Actually not only had Wright got the quantity of reinforcement wrong so had the engineers, so double wasn't enough. When an investigation was undertaken in 1996 it was found that the cantilevers had been close to collapse since they had been built! *STRUCTURE* magazine, July/August 2001 and September 2005.

[2] One can't help wondering how many 70 year old 'normal' houses need multi-million dollar 'restorations'.

[3] The only original house still in existence was built into the end of a ranch-style house to be used as a playroom – not quite what Bucky had in mind. One is also on exhibition in the Henry Ford Museum.

[4] Blake, 1960[2], p88.

Iconic failures

it was to be lived in or enjoyed'.[5] And Edith Farnsworth was obviously deluded to think she was getting a family house, or probably a house at all because 'The Farnsworth house was meant to be, and succeeded in being, a clear and somewhat abstract expression of the architectural ideal ... the ultimate in objectivity and universality.'[6]

So when is a house not a house? When it's designed by an outstanding 'modern' architect. But these 'modern' architects can't, or apparently have no intention of, designing a house that can be used as one. So why should they be able to design any other sort of building that is anything other than a vehicle for them to achieve status in the blinkered world of the architectural ghetto? The answer is of course they can't. The list is endless and numerous examples have already been looked at: the Sydney Opera House that couldn't be used for opera; the Pompidou Centre that failed in its 'chief mission'[7] of staging art exhibitions; Hunstanton School with its multifarious failings; the Media Centre at Lord's where the papers blow off your desk; the Scottish Parliament... nuff said; the Ronchamp Chapel for which 'as a place for liturgy any barn would be better'; at Pruitt-Igoe, where 33 11-storey apartment blocks had to be blown-up; the architectural school in Mies' Crown Hall where the students couldn't study; and here's one more.

In 2000, a new organisation, the Greater London Authority, was set up to 'run' London. A grand spanking new modern headquarters was needed so Norman Foster was given a go. The result, a rather odd shaped glass lump, soon earned the sobriquet 'the Headlamp' which later became the more pejorative 'the Glass Testicle.'

---

[5] See Great Modern Buildings Supplement N°12 from the *Guardian*, October 2007.

[6] As footnote 4.

[7] See footnote 27 on page 146 (Chapter 9).

So what's it like to work in this up-to-date masterpiece of modern architecture? Not all that hot actually, well in the winter anyway, because, as one user reported: 'This building has not been a great success. Because there's so much glass it gets very hot in summer and cold in winter,' and '... you can't open any windows. Part of people being happy where they work is that they can control their environment, but you can't do that at all,' and '... because it gets so hot and people shut their blinds, we have a problem with there not being enough light,' and 'The other problem with this building is the almost constant window-washing operation',[8] and many more criticisms besides.

Why has all this happened? For the very basic reason that in rejecting the past the Modern Movement architects not only rejected willy-nilly the physical vestiges of the past – timber and brick was replaced by concrete and steel; windows were replaced by walls of glass; pitched roofs became flat. But this blanket rejection also meant that they lost the understanding of how buildings functioned as part of life.

This in turn was all part of the arrogance that is fundamental to Modernism in all its forms. Remember Duchamp and his urinal – if you don't or can't understand why this is art then piss off. This is precisely the attitude of Modern Movement architects – if you don't like the building I designed then you know what you can do, because you simply don't understand.

But it's the architects that simply don't understand. They don't understand how buildings need to function technically, hence the endless failures and extra expense.[9] When a public art gallery was provided with unnecessarily large and heavy doors for the main public entrance, the handles were designed by an architect.

A headlamp or testicle?

Not a great success?

A design that's difficult to grasp

---

[8] *Guardian*, 8 February 2006, p12.

[9] Remember the structural ladder at the Hongkong Bank that wrecked the budget (see pages 147–148) not to mention the Sydney Opera House and...

The design, which looks as if it came directly from a Bauhaus student workshop, has a thin, slightly curved, rod as the handle. As the doors are heavy, the largish force necessary to open them can cause discomfort if not actual pain.[10]

If a door handle is too difficult then a seaside promenade, in the hands of a Modern Movement architect, is unlikely to be a success. Prize-wining architect Eduardo Souto Moura (b1952), had a go in Matosinhos in the north of Portugal. Inaugurated in 2002, it runs besides a large sandy bay created by a rocky promontory to the south and by an extensive harbour wall to the north; in other words the perfect setting for a family outing to the sea.

So what did a dyed-in-the-wool Modern Movement architect produce? What was built was a half-mile long, barren expanse of grey granite paving that has all the charm of the deck of an aircraft carrier. There is nothing of visual interest; no flower beds, trees or bushes, in fact no plants of any sort. No comfortable benches, no shade from the sun, no play areas for small children, nowhere to park a bike, and even more surprisingly, only three accesses to the beach![11] All there is, is de Chirico-like grim-grey modernism.

de Chirico beside the seaside

Was the Modern Movement right to reject every aspect of the past, root and branch, in the way it did? Was there really no alternative, did it just have to be this way? While books on modern architecture are replete with damning comments about individual buildings, there is no blanket condemnation, no suggestion that the Modern Movement can be seen as a virus that infected the architectural profession globally. What most of these writers suggest is that, in retrospect, there are buildings or architects forming a bridge between the bad old architecture and the new; in reality, none of this can really be justified. Look again at the Red House, a favoured exemplar. Is it really, as Pevsner asserts, '... more prophetic of the coming twentieth century than anything in the field of domestic architecture in any country for 30 years ...'[12] Was it because of this house that 'Modern Architecture was born'? [13]

All because some bricks were left bare inside the house. Actually the Red House was '... part Gothic, part Georgian, part simply traditional.'[14] There is nothing in the work

---

[10] This happened because the designer took no account of the stress distribution. If a large force is concentrated on a small area a high stress results. Humans have a limit, which is why people injure themselves on sharp objects.

[11] So to access the ad hoc cafés erected on the beach, timber constructions have been built.

[12] Pevsner, 1968, p23.

[13] Hellman, 1986, p84.

[14] Andrews, 2001, p482.

The birth of Modern Architecture?

Next stop a white box?

of the designer Phillip Webb to suggest he was heading towards the Modern Movement.

Another popular harbinger is Charles Rennie Mackintosh (1868–1928), a regular link between traditional building and the perfect white boxes. Richards sees his buildings as '... having many qualities in common with modern architecture.'[15] Charles Marriott wrote in 1924 that 'the whole modernist movement derives from him.'[16] Talking about a balcony that he added to the house for Bassett-Lowke, Crawford considers that Mackintosh '... was as near ... [as] anyone in Britain to the cool, white rationalism of European Modern Movement.'[17] Again there is little in his work to suggest if he'd lived a little longer Corbu would be playing a secondary role.

Whilst certainly ambitious, Mackintosh appeared to be eager to please his clients, even at one point writing to a potential client that 'If you want a house in the Tudor or any other phase of English architecture, I promise you my best services'[18] (an accommodating and/or desperate architect?). When the Hill House – built for publisher Walter Blackie – was finished, Mackintosh said to Blackie, 'Here is the house ... it is a dwelling house' and Blackie considered that Mackintosh strove to '... serve the practical needs of the occupants.'[19] Not the approach one would expect from Corbu or Mies, for example. Many other linking figures such as Horta or Behrens are brought into play, to try and demonstrate the 'inevitability' of Modern Movement architecture becoming the true architecture of the twentieth century.

Yet there was a modern architecture of the twentieth century that spread all over the

---

[15] Richards, 1940, p68.

[16] Crawford, 1995, p192.

[17] ibid, p167. It's not clear if Crawford is using 'rationalist' because he thinks the Modern Movement is rational, or because that's how it's often described.

[18] Crawford, 1995, p135.

[19] For both quotations, Crawford, 1995, p102.

world. An architecture that has more or less been expunged from the history of the architecture of the twentieth century, or if not then only referred to sneeringly in passing – it was called Art Deco.[20] For example there is no reference to it in the seminal books of Reyner Banham,[21] Sigfried Giedion,[22] or Nikolaus Pevsner.[23] Charles Jenks has one reference to it in his book *Modern Movements in Architecture*, and Dennis Sharp's *Visual History of 20th Century Architecture*, has two references in passing. Bill Risebero's one reference notes that '… it seldom took the form of anything more than fashionable applied decoration … the streamlined shapes of Art Deco',[24] whilst Frampton refers to it as '… this highly synthetic style'.[25] Current website comment on the 1925 Paris Exposition des Arts Décoratif includes:

> It was the hope of the exposition organizers that the fair would bring about a truly new 'modern' style. Paul Géraldy, writing for *L'Illustration*, noted that the term 'modern' had been so widely and variously misappropriated by any and every group of artists that the word was falling out of favour.[26]

The start of Art Deco?

Art Deco never tried to be a 'movement'; no architect proclaimed him or herself an Art Deco architect, but many have been gathered under this convenient umbrella.

Essentially, Art Deco architecture was any ordinary building – house, shop, skyscraper or cinema for example – that had decoration that was geometric and/or stylised. 'Modern' materials like coloured mirror glass, chrome-plated metal and various types of plastics could be used as well as the more traditional ones. Whilst a style of the 1920s and 30s, it was seen more often in 'new' types of buildings – cinemas, garages, filling stations, cocktail bars and diners.[27] 'While there is no agreement on the first Art Deco building, consider Eliel Saarinen's train station at Helsinki (1904–1914). With its four giant figures, each holding a globe of light, it is the very essence of Art Deco.'[28]

---

[20] The origin of the term Art Deco seems unclear. Perhaps it had its origins in the 1925 Paris Exposition des Arts Décoratifs, the term was used mockingly by Le Corbusier in his mag *L'Espirit Nouveau*. It was also the part of title of a 1966 French exhibition and was the title of a book by Bevis Hillier in 1969.

[21] *Theory and Design in the First Machine Age.*

[22] *Space, Time and Architecture.*

[23] *Pioneers of Modern Design* and *The Sources of Modern Architecture and Design.*

[24] Risebero, 1979, p255.

[25] Frampton, 1980, p220.

[26] http://www.retropolis.net/exposition/artsofliving.html (accessed in October 2008).

[27] Here the word diner has the American use, i.e. a small building that is a café.

[28] See http://www.decopix.com/New%20Site/Pages/Directory%20Pages/Intro.html (accessed in October 2008).

For 'most people' in the 1920s, but perhaps more particularly in the 1930s, Art Deco – whether or not it had been labelled as such – was modern design. At that time few people had heard of the Modern Movement, the Bauhaus, Le Corbusier and the rest. And Art Deco was everywhere, from clocks and watches to furniture, domestic appliances and buildings – 'Luxurious, elegant and dramatic, Art Deco had it all, while still being accessible to ordinary folk' but, of course, 'usually derided by architectural critics.'[29]

Accessible to ordinary folk, derided by architectural critics

And not only was it accessible, it was also popular, in fact it was 'The only truly popular style.'[30] This was because '... human values of desire, warmth, sensuality and anecdotal incident were embodied in Art Deco ... buildings in a way that was excluded by Modernism.'[31] Gibberd, referring to some Art Deco doors, calls them 'well-mannered' and even regrets their passing as 'These doors go to show just how much has been lost in entrance architecture since World War II.'[32]

But because it was popular – the baying masses liked it – it was '... much frowned on by hard line modernists'.[33] In fact '... no aspect of architecture was held in more disdain than that of Art Deco ... it was either ignored ... or it was dismissed as an unfortunate, obviously misguided effort ...'.[34] This was because the baying masses were wrong and the Modern Movement architects were right.[35] But, in 1917, Mackintosh, who is considered by many as pointing the way to the Modern Movement, used a hard-edged, geometric style that actually points the way to Art Deco.

And Wright, when he wasn't designing failed icons for the Modern Movement, would often indulge in some Art Deco.

Well-mannered Art Deco

But whilst Mackintosh, amongst others, was according to some a precursor to the Modern Movement and Wright was a terrifying figure off stage, it wasn't these individuals

---

[29] ibid.

[30] Gibberd, 1997, p123.

[31] Benton, 2003, p259.

[32] Gibberd, 1997, p146. These doors no longer exist.

[33] ibid, p123.

[34] David Gebhard, quoted in Benton, 2003, p19.

[35] The demise of Art Deco is often attributed to the fact that due to post World War II austerity, everything had to be utilitarian and there was no space for something as frivolous as Art Deco. But it was after the war that the Modern Movement architects took power and it was '... much frowned on by hard line modernists'.

Next stop Art Deco?

Art Deco from Frank Lloyd Wright! In 1952!

that sent the architects down the Modern Movement blind alley; it was the éminence grise of the Modern Movement Adolf Loos. What really underpinned the whole dishonest enterprise was his 1908 essay *Ornament and Crime*.[36] As Trilling puts it,[37] Loos '... called openly for the rejection of all ornament. This was the real beginning of the modern movement in architecture and design',[38] and he goes on to note that '... the historical importance of Looshaus cannot be overestimated.'[39] According to Gibberd,[40] 'Loos said "ornament is a crime" ... and the foundations of true modernism were laid.' Because of this, the architectural profession came to suffer from a fear of ornamentation, and this is basically why the profession parted company with the baying masses.

What the baying masses wanted was not just decorated boxes, what they wanted, or in fact needed, was 'hierarchical complexity.' Whilst this need seems to be innate it is rarely explored in architectural literature. One book that discusses this in detail is *Theory of Architecture* by Nikos Salingaros. This unusual book attempts to discover precisely why 'modern' architecture is so unsatisfactory to 'most' people. He does this by using medical and psychological research to discover how people actually see and react. Basically what people want is 'hierarchical complexity',[41] not only in architecture but in general, and indeed this state predominates in many situations. If 'hierarchical complexity' is replaced by 'tedious simplicity' then boredom or depression ensues; if it is replaced by 'incomprehensible chaos' then the result is fear and anxiety – 'This explains why we built cathedrals as examples of organised complexity: because we cannot connect to objects or environments that are either too random, or too simple.'[42]

These situations can be observed in something as 'simple' as a tree. Trees are a pleasure for most people because there is a visual hierarchy of scales, which starts with the tree itself, and gradually steps down through branches, twigs and leaves to the veins in

---

[36] See pages 33–34 (Chapter 3).

[37] Trilling, 2001, p186.

[38] Actually Trilling argues, rather convolutedly, that Loos wasn't against ornamentation, just traditional ornamentation, so he re-invented ornament by finding it in ready made materials (like fair-faced concrete?). ibid, p190 et seq.

[39] ibid, p193. The Looshaus referred to here is the Goldman & Salatsch store – see page 33 (Chapter 3)

[40] Gibberd, 1997, p97.

[41] This is why, for tourists, '... signs to the historic centres ... draw them in'. *Guardian*, 6 November 2006, p12.

[42] Salingaros, 2006, p151.

Hierarchical complexity for all

Boring or what?

Dead beautiful

the leaves or the details of the bark. The complexity is enhanced by changes of colour or texture. In spite of its biological complexity a tree is readily 'understood' and enjoyed by most people.[43] Whereas a 'tree' constructed from uni-coloured poles (or fluorescent tubes) would seem boring. Even a dead tree that has been brutally pruned can still be beautiful. The most important aspect of the hierarchical scales is that there mustn't be too many, or too few, and the spacing between the units of the scales is related – Salingaros calls this the 'scaling factor' – which turns out to be around 2.7 to be satisfactory.

Salingaros goes on to describe a method that can be used to quantify some architectural qualities. Using the research that has been carried out on how humans react to various stimuli Saligaros aims to evaluate what he terms the 'architectural life' and the 'architectural complexity' of any building.[44] This is done by estimating values, between 0 and 2 for a number of factors. These are used to calculate the value of intermediate variables called the 'architectural temperature' and the 'architectural harmony'. Each of these has five components.[45] Salingaros carried out the calculations for a wide variety of well-known buildings. Unsurprisingly, Modern Movement buildings have low values for life whereas other buildings, from all ages have high values. The two extremes, of the examples given in the book, are the Hagia Sophia, in Istanbul, with a architectural life rating of 80% and the Salk Institute, in California, designed by Louis Kahn (1901–1974) with a rating of just 6% - photos bear out these findings.[46]

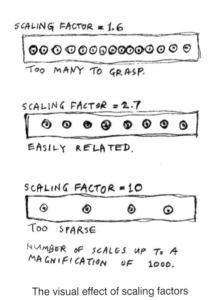

The visual effect of scaling factors

---

[43] Fractal geometry provides hierarchical complexity as well as being able to replicate much geometry from nature. It can, for instance, create a realistic tree. Lauwerier, 1987, p74.

[44] Salingaros, 2006, p107.

[45] ibid, p107–112.

[46] These few lines do not do justice to Salingaros' work which is detailed and wide ranging and based on research findings from an incredible diversity of sources – from fractal geometry to information processing, from chaos to neural networks.

80% alive   6% alive

The work of Christopher Alexander (b1936) is also relevant here. In 1977, his seminal work *A Pattern Language* was published. This vast tome shows how levels of complexity are necessary for a successful living environment, thus tacitly criticising 'modernism' for its simplistic approach that is central to the project of visual 'functionality'. For instance, Alexander examines the importance of the 'entrance transition'.

Abruptness/pain versus subtlety/pleasure

Like Salingaros, Alexander is also a gifted mathematician, but he doesn't try and quantify the required complexity for the design for successful living, his book shows how hierarchical complexity works at every level.[47] Unsurprisingly, for the Modern Movement architectural profession, Alexander's book was not seminal at all.

So who is right and who is wrong, the baying masses or the architectural ghetto? It all comes down to something quite simple, should buildings be designed for 'most' people, or should they be designed to please a small elitist group? 'How on earth did architects manage to paint themselves into this ridiculous corner?' asks renegade Modern Movement architect, the late Peter Blake,[48] answering with '... the real reason is clearly ... the Modern Movement, with its shining dogmas, its exciting slogans, and above all, with its absolute self-righteousness ...' and he goes on to assert that the Modern Movement is

---

[47] Superficially Alexander's work could be seen as a call to return to 'old ways' so it is interesting to note that his work proved to be of fundamental importance to the design of computer systems.

[48] Blake was a rare but not unique Modern Movement apostate. P Morton Shand, who was a personal friend of Walter Gropius and Le Corbusier, wrote evangellicaly about the Modern Movement in the *Architectural Review* in the 1930s. By 1958, he was writing to John Betjeman to say 'I have frightful nightmares ... for I ... helped to bring about ... Contemporary Architecture: ... the piling up of gigantic children's toy bricks in utterly dehumanized and meaningless forms ... it is frightening, all-invading menace.' Wilson, 2006, p88.

... quite clearly a religion as irrational as all others ... Like all religious cultists, the members of the sect treat their critics with patient condescension: those ... who don't know what's good for them; but the cultist, to whom the Truth has been revealed does know, and he or she will ram it down the non-believer's throats even if it chokes them.[49]

There is much evidence to support the view that Modern Movement architecture is a cult – Hudnut writing as early as 1931 that 'the dogma of functionalism has taken on an almost religious character'[50]. It has cult leaders, with quasi-religious status, such as Mies, Gropius and Corbu, who are inviolable[51] – for Gordon Bunshaft 'Corbu's books became our bible.'[52] There were edicts, such as Corbu's *Five Points of a New Architecture*,[53] which don't survive rational scrutiny. And there was an implied moral superiority in statements such as Mies' 'God is in the details,'[54] or Pawley that architecture '... hangs on the concept of honesty'[55] and, of course, Loos' claim that 'ornament is a crime'.[56] No wonder Arup thought that 'there is a lot of humbug in architects'.[57] 'Humbug', of course, is a word often associated with religious cults.[58]

People in sects, or who belong to cults, live, or partly live, in parallel universes. Some of these are apparently harmless, like those people obsessed with 'cult' TV series like *Startrek* or *Star Wars*. They dress up as their favourite characters and go to conventions, and probably know by heart the dialogues and plots from every episode.[59]

It would be no problem if the cultists in the architectural ghetto just kept their ideas in their parallel universe, the parallel universe of Sant'Elia's New City or Archigram's walking cities. They could meet and discuss things like the Blur Building.[60] This was to be a cloud that hovered above Lake Neuchâtel. Visitors would be able to enter the cloud, where they would be subjected to 'white noise' being emitted from the cloud making machinery.[61] To make the visit even more fun the visitors could go to the bar where people, dressed like dental nurses, would serve mineral water or mineral water or mineral water...

[49] Blake, 1977, p149.

[50] Bacon, 2001, p92.

[51] See Corbu cartoon on page 93, see page 238 for Gropius as 'a prophet', and page 239 for Mies being '... like Buddha'. According to Louis Hellman, Le Corbusier was, for architects, '... high priest, prophet and god in one'. Hellman, 1986, p134.

[52] Bacon, 2001, p97.

[53] See pages 95–96 (Chapter 6).

[54] See page 214 (Chapter 12).

[55] See pages 215–216 (Chapter 12).

[56] See page 215 (Chapter 12).

[57] See page 216 (Chapter 12).

[58] See for example http://inbobwetrust.net/religioushumbugkit.html (accessed in October 2008).

[59] Of course if these cultists spilled over into 'ordinary' life and dressed and spoke like their favourites, it would be tedious, to put it mildly, for everyone else.

[60] Jodidio, 2001, p82–83.

[61] Being subjected to white noise, a type of continuous hissing, is used by the SAS to break people during interrogation resistance training.

The Mekon's home from home

When a large building was erected in the centre of London it had obviously come from a parallel universe. Quickly nicknamed the Gherkin, it was clearly conceived with the Mekon[62] in mind rather than people from the universe of the baying masses.

But the Modern Movement cultists are uncompromising because they know that they *are* right, and one way or another everyone has to fit into their world, never mind whether it's what they want or whether they find it comfortable. In a meeting of leading architects, convened in 1946, it was noted that 'The general public generally have no knowledge of what they want'.[63]

There seems to be little, or no, evidence over the 80 years of the active life of Modern Movement architecture that it has struck, or ever will strike, a chord with the general public – one only has to glance at interior design magazines[64] or city travel guides to see why. But if you can afford to buy a new house, the builders know exactly what's wanted. Whereas architects certainly don't.

What the Modern Movement did was to produce an architectural profession whose arrogance is only equal to its ignorance.[65] Meanwhile, the baying masses have to accept resignedly the so-called and unwanted 'modern' architecture – '... the dreadful modern industrial city ... like a pile of discarded ... shoeboxes, twelve stories high',[66] so that 'Ugliness spreads like gangrene across the country,'[67] causing Gavin Stamp to lament that photographs of Victorian London show '... that almost every change that has taken place ... has been for the worse.'[68] Meanwhile in Tehran, tourism chiefs believe that '... behind the fumes and often characterless modern buildings lies a capital rich with architectural heritage.'[69]

But it's not just members of the general public that find modern architecture 'dreadful' and like 'gangrene', occasionally members of the ghetto realise, with horror, what

[62] The Mekon, an archetypal little green man, was Dan Dare's implacable enemy. Dan Dare was, of course, the hero of a strip in the *Eagle* comic – now a cult, and the subject of a major exhibition in 2008, *Dan Dare and the Birth of Hi-Tech Britain*, at the London Science Museum. For the influence of *Eagle* comic on the British Archigram group see pages 143–144 (Chapter 8).

[63] Kynaston, 2007, p167.

[64] For instance in the January 2008 edition of the popular design magazine *House & Garden*; its 200+ image-packed pages only contained 14 images that were of Modern Movement architecture or design.

[65] Which was also, inter alia, partially responsible for the de-skilling of the building industry and making sections of the engineering profession subservient.

[66] Bogarde, 1986, p253.

[67] Marchant, 2003, p249.

[68] Risebero, 1992, p39.

[69] *Guardian*, 27 May 2007, p15.

they're up to. The May 1977 edition of the prestigious ghetto mag, the *Architectural Review*, was largely devoted to the just completed, modern-architectural-icon-to-be, Pompidou Centre.[70] The introductory article, called 'The Pompidolium', ends with: 'To the architects and the French we offer awed congratulations.'[71] Before coming to that excited conclusion the writer notes that it is a 'menacing building ...'. But more extraordinarily goes on with '... but only contemplate what the centres of our cities would be like if they were chiefly composed of buildings of this kind and you would see what a repellent fix we would be in.'[72]

Why does one 'menacing building' deserve 'awed congratulations', when more than one would be 'repellent'. And if more than one Pompidou is repellent, then more than one of anything produced by the Modern Movement could equally be seen as repellent, couldn't it?

The great poet Victor Hugo was once asked to lend his support for the demolition of a thirteenth century tower that stood in the way of an architectural scheme; he wrote, 'Demolish the tower? No. Demolish the architect? Yes'.[73] Perhaps he had a point.

Entering the parallel universe of the Modern Movement

Just what's wanted

What no one wanted

---

[70] See pages 145–147 (Chapter 9).

[71] *Architectural Review*, May 1977, p272. No author is credited, but the editor at the time was Lance Wright.

[72] ibid.

[73] Robb, 1997, p516.

Bibliography

There are whole libraries devoted to books on architecture and associated subjects, but unfortunate[ly] few are of interest to the general reader. Bookshops often have sections dedicated to architectur[e] where most of the books are albums of 'architectural' photos of the work of currently fashionab[le] architects, with fawning and uninformative accompanying text – again of little interest.

Listed below are the books that have been referred to or been consulted. Two books that are sp[e]cially recommended are *The Story of Western Architecture* by Bill Risebero and *Architecture for Beginne[rs]* by Louis Hellman.

The following magazines were also consulted: *The Architect's Journal, Architectural Review, Architectur[e] Design, Building Design, The Structural Engineer, New Civil Engineer, Architectural Record, RIBA Journal,* [as] were architectural items in many daily newspapers.

Of course the best way to gain more knowledge about buildings is to use them and study them i[n] situ. This applies to all buildings and any buildings.

Ackerman, James S (1966) – *Palladio* – Penguin

Ackermann, Kurt (1991) – *Building for Industry* – Watermark Publications

Alberti, Leon (1988) – *On the Art of Building in Ten Books* – MIT Press

Alexander, Christopher (1977) – *Pattern Language* – Oxford University Press

Alexander, Christopher (1975) – *The Oregon Experiment* – Oxford University Press

Altet, Xavier Barral (1997) – *The Early Middle Ages* – Taschen

Ammann, Othmar et al (1941) – *The Failure of the Tacoma Narrows Bridge* – Federal Works Agency

Andrews, Peter et al (2001) – *The House Book* – Phaidon

Appignanesi, Richard & Garret (1995) – *Postmodernism* – Icon Books

Appleyard, Brian (1986) – *Richard Rogers* – Faber & Faber

Artigas, Isabel (2007) – *Gaudí: Complete Works* – Evergreen

Bacon, Mardges (2001) – *Le Corbusier in America* – MIT Press

Balcombe, George (1985) – *History of Building* – Batsford

Banham, Reyner (1960) – *Theory and Design in the First Machine Age* – Architectural Press

Banham, Reyner (1962) – *Age of the Masters* – Architectural Press

Bathurst, Bella (1999) – *The Lighthouse Stevensons* – Harper Collins

Bayer, Patricia (1992) – *Art Deco Architecture* – Thames & Hudson

Beaver, Patrick (1970) – *The Crystal Palace* – Hugh Evelyn

Bedell, Geraldine (2005) – *The Handmade House* – Penguin

Benjamin, Walter (1936) – *The Work of Art in the Age of Mechanical Reproduction*

Benton, Charlotte et al (2003) – *Art Deco 1910–1939* – V&A Publications

Benton, Tim (1987) – *The Villas of Le Corbusier 1920–1930* – Yale University Press

Beukers, Adriaan & Hunte, Ed van (2001) – *Lightness* – 010 Publishers

Bill, Max (1949) – *Robert Maillart: Bridges and Constructions* – Verlag für Architektur

Billington, David P (1979) – *Robert Maillart's Bridges* – Princeton University Press

Billington, David P (1985) – *The Tower and the Bridge* – Princeton University Press

Blake, Peter (1960[1]) – *Le Corbusier* – Penguin

Blake, Peter (1960[2]) – *Mies van der Roh[e]* – Penguin

Blake, Peter (1977) – *Form Follows Fiasc[o]* – Little, Brown & Co.

Boaga, Giorgio & Boni, Benito (1965) – *The Concrete Architecture of Riccad[o] Morandi* – Alec Tiranti

Boesiger, Willy et al (1998) – *Le Corbusier Complete Works: Oeuvre Complete* – Birkhauser

Bogarde, Dirk (1986) – *Backcloth* - Penguin

Brand, Stewart (1994) – *How Buildings Learn* – Viking

Briggs, Asa (1979) – *Iron Bridge to Crystal Palace* – Thames & Hudson

Britton, Karla (2001) – *Auguste Perret* – Phaidon

Buchanan, RA (1989) – *The Engineers* – Jessica Kingsley

Cantacuzino, Sherban (1966) – *Great Modern Architecture* – Studio Vista

Carey, John (1992) – *The Intellectuals and the Masses* – Faber & Faber

Caro, Robert A (1975) – *The Power Broker* – Vintage Books

Carter, Peter (1974) – *Mies van der Rohe at Work* – Praeger Publishers

Caygill, Howard et al (1998) – *Walter Benjamin* – Icon Books

Charles, Prince (1989) – *A Vision of Britain* – Doubleday

Charlton, TM (1982) – *A History of Theory of Structures in the 19th Century* – Cambridge University Press

Carter, EJ & Goldfinger, Ernö (1945) – *The County of London Plan* – Penguin

Chermayeff, Ivan (1972) – *Observations on American Architecture* – Viking

Clay, Jean (1980) – *Le Romantisme* – Hachette

Clifton-Taylor, Alec (1972) – *The Pattern of English Building* – Faber & Faber

Clifton-Taylor, Alec (1984) – *Another Six English Towns* – BBC Book

Cohen, Jean-Louis (2004) – *Le Corbusier* – Taschen

Collins, George (1979) – *Visionary Drawing and Planning of Architecture* – MIT Press

Conran, Terence (1994) – *The Essential House Book* – Conran Octopus

Cottam, D (1986) – *Owen Williams* – Architectural Association

Crawford, Alan (1995) – *Charles Rennie Mackintosh* – Thames & Hudson

Crinson, Mark & Lubbock, Jules (1994) – *Architecture: Art or Profession?* – Manchester University Press

Curtis, William JR (1983) – *Modern Architecture since 1900* – Phaidon

Curtis, William JR (1986) – *Le Corbusier* – Phaidon

Davies, Colin (1988) – *High Tech Architecture* – Thames & Hudson

Dale, Rodney (1985) – *The Sinclair Story* – Duckworth

Dawkins, Richard (2006) – *The God Delusion* – Bantam Press

Daza, Ricardo (2000) – *Looking for Mies* – Birkhauser

Dean, Andrea Oppenheimer (2002) – *Rural Studio: Samuel Mockbee and the Architecture of Decency* – Princeton Architectural Press

Desideri, Paolo et al (1979) – *Pier Luigi Nervi* – Gustavo Gilli

Dethier, Jean (1981) – *All Stations* – Thames & Hudson

Dethier, Jean (1986) – *Architectures de Terre* – Centre Pompidou

Dixon, Roger & Muthesius, Stefan (1978) – *Victorian Architecture* – Thames & Hudson

Drexler, Arthur (ed.) (1977) – *The Architecture of the Ecole des Beaux-Arts* – Secker & Warburg

Droste, Magdelena (1993) – *Bauhaus* – Taschen

Duncan, Alistair (1986) – *American Art Deco* – Abrams

Dunster, David (1985) – *Key Buildings of the Twentieth Century: Volume 1* – Architectural Press

Economakis, Richard (1993) – *Quinlan Terry: Selected Works* – Academy Editions

Elliot, Cecil D (1992) – *Technics & Architecture* – MIT Press

Evers, Bernd et al (2003) – *Architectural Theory* – Taschen

Faber, Colin (1962) – *Candela: The Shell Builder* – Architectural Press

Fiell, Charlotte & Peter (2000) – *Design of the 20th Century* – Taschen

Fitchen, John (1961) – *The Construction of Gothic Cathedrals* – University of Chicago Press

Fitchen, John (1988) – *Building Construction before Mechanisation* – MIT Press

Fletcher, Alan (2001) – *The Art of Looking Sideways* – Phaidon

Frampton, Kenneth (1980) – *Modern Architecture: A critical history* – Thames & Hudson

Frampton, Kenneth (2001) – *Le Corbusier* – Thames & Hudson

Fuchs, RH (1986) – *Dutch Painting* – Thames & Hudson

Galluzzi, Paolo (ed.) (1987) – *Leonardo da Vinci: Engineer & Architect* – Montreal Museum of Fine Arts

Gans, D (1991) – *Bridging the Gap* – Van Nostrand Rheinhold

Ghirardo, Diane (1996) - *Architecture After Modernism* – Thames & Hudson

Gibberd, Vernon (1997) – *Architecture Source Book* – Quantum Books

Gibbon, Edward (2003) – *The Decline and Fall of the Roman Empire*

(abridged) – The modern library

Giedion, Sigfried (1941) – *Space, Time & Architecture* – Harvard University Press

Girouard, Mark (1985) – *Cities & People* – Yale University Press

Glancey, Jonathan (2003) – *20th Century Architecture* – Carlton Books

Glover, Ian A & Kelly, Michael P (1987) – *Engineers in Britain* – Allen & Unwin

Goldberger, Paul (1979) – *The City Observed New York* – Penguin

Gordon, JE (1978) – *Structures: Why Things Don't Fall Down* - Penguin

Gössel, Peter (2005) – *Architecture of the Twentieth Century* – Taschen

Halpern, David (1995) – *Mental Health and the Built Environment* – Taylor & Francis

Hardy, Dennis (2006) – *Poundbury: The Town That Charles Built* – Town & Country Planning Association

Hawking, Stephen (1988) – *A brief history of time* – Bantam Books

Hellman, Louis (1986) – *Architecture for Beginners* – Unwin

Hennessy, Peter (2006) – *Having it so Good* – Allen Lane

Hensbergen, G van (2001) - *Gaudí* – Harper Collins

Hesketh, John (1980) – *Industrial Design* – Thames & Hudson

Heyman, Jacques (1999) – *The Science of Structural Engineering* – Imperial College Press

Hight, Eleanor M (1995) – *Picturing Modernism* – MIT Press

Hilton, Tim (2002) – *John Ruskin* – Yale University Press

Hitchcock, Henry-Russell & Johnson, Philip (1997) – *The International Style* – W. W. Norton & Company

Holgate. Alan (1986) – *The Art of Structural Design* – Oxford University Press

Jacobs, Jane (1961) – *The Life and Death of Great American Cities* – Penguin

Jaeger, LG (1969) – *Elementary Theory of Elastic Plates* – Pergamon Press

Jencks, Charles (1973[1]) – *Modern*

Movements in Architecture – Penguin

Jencks, Charles (1973²) – *Le Corbusier and the Tragic View of Architecture* – Harvard University Press

Jencks, Charles (1988) – *The Prince, the Architects and new wave monarchy* – Academy

Jodidio, Phillip (2001) – *Architecture Now* – Taschen

Jones, Peter (2006) – *Ove Arup* – Yale University Press

Karney, Robyn Ed. (1995) – *Chronicle of the Cinema* – Dorling Kindersley

Knobel, Lance (1985) – *The Faber Guide to Twentieth Century Architecture* – Faber & Faber

Krier, Léon & Larsson, Lars Olof (1985) – *Albert Speer: Architecture 1932-1942* – Archives d' architecture moderne, Bruxelles

Krier, Léon & Porphyrios, Demetri (1984) – *Houses, Palaces, Cities* – Academy Editions

Krier, Léon (1998) – *Architecture: Choice or Fate* - Papadakis

Kynaston, David (2007) – *Austerity Britain 1945-51* – Bloomsbury

Lambert, Phyliss (ed.) (2001) – *Mies in America* – Abrams

Larsen, Olga & Tyas, Andy (2003) – *Conceptual structural design* – Thomas Telford

Lauwerier, Hans (1987) – *Fractals* – Penguin

Lawson, Bryan (1980) – *How Designers Think* – Architectural Press

Lebrecht, Norman (2000) – *Covent Garden: The Untold Story* – Simon & Schuster

Le Corbusier (1910) – *Les voyages d'Allemagne* – Electraarchitecture

Le Corbusier (1927) – *Towards a New Architecture* – Architectural Press

Le Corbusier (1935) - *Aircraft* - Trefoil Publications

Leonhardt, Fritz (1984) – *Bridges* – MIT Press

Letts, Rosa Maria et al (1990) – *Futurism and the architecture of Sant'Elia* – Mazzotta

Lodder, Christina (1983) – *Russian Constructivism* – Yale University Press

Loyrette, Henri (1985) – *Gustave Eiffel* – Rizzoli

Lyall, Sutherland (2003) – *Masters of Structure* – Laurence King

Maguire, Robert & Murray, Keith (1965) – *Modern Churches of the World* –Studio Vista

Mainstone, Rowland (1975) – *The Development of Structural Form* - Penguin

Marchant, Ian (2003) – *Parallel Lines* – Michael Williams

Maré, Eric de (1975) – *Bridges of Britain* – Batsford

Matossian, Nouritza (1985) – *Xenakis* – Kahn & Averill

McAllister, G & EG (1941) – *Town and Country Planning* – Faber & Faber

McCullough, David (1972) – *The Great Bridge* – Simon & Schuster

Meller, J (ed.) (1979) – *The Buckminster Fuller Reader* – Jonathan Cape

Mikami, Yuzo (2001) – *Utzon's Sphere* – Shokokusha Publishing Co.

Millais, Malcolm (1997, 2005 2ⁿᵈ ed) – *Building Structures* – Spon Press

Molinari, Luca (2000) – *Santiago Calatrava* – Skira

Morton, Jane (1994) – *From Southgate to Hallwood Park* – Merseyside Improved Houses

Mumford, Lewis (1961) – *The City in History* – Penguin

Mumford, Lewis (1963) – *The Highway and the City* – Harcourt Brace

Murray, Peter (2004) – *The saga of the Sydney Opera House* – Spon Press

Nervi, Pier Luigi (1966) – *Aesthetics and Technology in Building* – Harvard University Press

Newman, Oscar (1972) – *Creating Defensible Space* – U.S. Department of Housing and Urban Development

Norman, Donald A – *The Design of Everyday Things* – MIT Press

Norton, John (1997) – *Building with Earth* – Intermediate Technology

Orton, Andrew (1988) – *The Way We Build Today* – Chapman & Hall

Pasley, Lt. Col CW (1826) – *Outline of a Course of Practical Architecture* – Donhead Ltd

Pawley, Martin (1990) – *Buckminster Fuller* – Trefoil Publications

Pearlman, Jill (1997) – *Joseph Hudnut's Other Modernism at the 'Harvard Bauhaus'* – JSAH December

Pearlman, Jill (2000) – *Joseph Hudnut and Post-modern Urbanism* – Planning Perspectives 15

Peters, Tom F (1996) – *Building the 19ᵗʰ Century* – MIT Press

Petroski, Henry (1996) – *Invention by Design* – Harvard University Press

Pevsner, Nikolaus (1960) – *Pioneers of Modern Design* – Penguin

Pevsner, Nikolaus (1968) – *The sources of modern architecture and design* – Thames & Hudson

Phaidon Editors (2008) – *Le Corbusier Le Grand* - Phaidon

Pollalis, Spiro N (1999) – *What is a bridge?* – MIT Press

Pugin, Augustus W (1856) – *Contrasts, or a parallel between the architecture of the 15ᵗʰ and 19ᵗʰ centuries* – http://books.google.pt/books?id=vKRWAAAAMAAJ

Read, Herbert (1959) – *A Concise History of Modern Art* – Thames & Hudson

Rees, William (1990) – *The Penguin Book of French Poetry 1820-1950* – Penguin

Restany, Pierre (2001) – *Hundertwasser* – Taschen

Richards, JM (1940) – *An introduction to Modern Architecture* –Penguin

Richards, JM (1958) – *The Functional Tradition* – Architectural Press

Richardson, Vicky (2001) – *New Vernacular Architecture* – Laurence King

Risebero, Bill (1979) – *The Story of Western Architecture* – Herbert Press

Risebero, Bill (1982) – *Modern Architecture and Design* – Herbert Press

Risebero, Bill (1992) – *Fantastic Form* – Herbert Press

Robb, Graham (1997) – *Victor Hugo* –

Picador

Robb, Graham (2007) – *The Discovery of France* – Picador

Rodgers, Nigel (2006) – *Roman Architecture* - Southwater

Rodrigues, Chris & Garratt, Chris – *Modernism* – Icon Books

Rolt, LTC (1970) – *Victorian Engineering* - Penguin

Rudofsky, Bernard (1964) – *Architecture Without Architects* – Academy Editions

Ruskin, John (1961) – *The Seven Lamps of Architecture* – The Noonday Press

Ruskin, John (2001) – *The Stones of Venice* – The Folio Society

Russell, Frank (ed.) (1985) – *Richard Rogers + Architects* – Papadakis

Safran, Yehuda E (2001) – *Mies Van der Rohe* – Gingko Press, Inc

Salingaros, Nikos A (2004) – *Anti-architecture & Deconstruction* – Umbau-Verlag

Salingaros, Nikos A (2006) – *A Theory of Architecture* – Umbau-Verlag

Sarnitz, August (2006) – *Otto Wagner* – Taschen

Sayle, Alexi (2002) – *The Dog Catcher* – Sceptre

Schiffer, Herbert (1979) – *Shaker Architecture* – Schiffer Publishing

Service, Alastair (1977) – *Edwardian Architecture* – Thames & Hudson

Sharp, Dennis (1972) – *A visual history of Twentieth Century Architecture* – Secker & Warburg

Shirley Smith, H (1953) – *The World's Greatest Bridges* – Phoenix

Sim, Stuart & Loon, Borin van (2001) – *Critical Theory* – Icon Books

Sinclair, Upton (1917) – *The Profits of Religion* – free at Project Gutenberg

Steele, James (1999) – *R.M.Schindler* – Taschen

Stern, Robert AM (ed.) (1995) – *New York 1960* – Monacelli Press

Stewart, Ian (1975) – *Concepts of Modern Mathematics* – Penguin

Stinton, Darrol (1983) – *The Design of the Aeroplane* – BSP Professional

Books

Sudjic, Deyan (1985) – *Cult Objects* – Paladin

Sudjic, Deyan et al (1988) – *English Extremists* – Blueprint

Sudjic, Deyan (1992) – *The 100 Mile City* – Harcourt Brace

Sullivan, Louis (1979) – *Kindergarten Chats and other writings* - Dover

Tavares, Domingos (2004[1]) – *Leon Baptista Alberti* – Dafne Editora

Tavares, Domingos (2004[2]) – *Philibert Delorme* – Dafne Editora

Taverne, Ed et al (1996) – *JJ Oud's Shell Building* – NAi Publishers

Thompson, D'Arcy (1961) – *On Growth and Form* – Cambridge University Press

Thompson, Paul (1963) – *Architecture: Art or Social Service* – Fabian Society

Thomson, Iain (2003) – *Frank Lloyd Wright Year by Year* – PRC Publishing

Timoshenko, Stephen P (1953) – *History of Strength of Materials* – Dover

Tinniswood, Adrian (2001) – *His Invention So Fertile* – Pimlico

Tisdall, Caroline & Bozzolla, Angelo (1977) – *Futurism* – Thames & Hudson

Torroja, Eduardo (1958) – *Philosophy of Structures* – University of California Press

Trieb, M (1996) – *Phillips Pavilion: Space calculated in seconds* – Princeton Press

Trigueiros, Luiz & Barata, Paulo Martins (ed.) (2000) – *Mies van der Rohe* – Blau

Trilling, James (2001) – *The Language of Ornament* – Thames & Hudson

Tzonis, Alexander (2001) – *Le Corbusier'* – Thames & Hudson

Vanderbilt, Tom (2002) – *Survival City* – Princeton Architectural Press

Venturi, Robert (1966) – *Complexity & Contradiction in Architecture* – Museum of Modern Art

Venturi, Robert et al (1972) – *Learning from Las Vegas* – MIT Press

Vitruvius (1960) – *The Ten Books on*

Architecture – Dover

Walther, René (1993) – *Construire en Béton* – Presses Polytechniques et Universitaires Romandes

Ward-Perkins, Bryan (2005) – *The Fall of Rome* – Oxford University Press

Watson, Anne (ed.) (2006) – *The Building of a Masterpiece: the Story of the Sydney Opera House* – Powerhouse Press

Weiss JH (1982) – *The Making of Technological Man* – MIT Press

White, Michael (2000) – *Leonardo: The First Scientist* – Abacus

Whitford, Frank (1984) – *Bauhaus* – Thames & Hudson

Wilk, Christopher (2006) – *Modernism* – V&A Publications

Williams, Stephanie (1989) – *Hongkong Bank* – Jonathan Cape

Willis, Carol (1995) – *Form Follows Finance* – Princeton Architectural Press

Wilson, AN (2003) – *After the Victorians* – Arrow Books

Wilson, AN (2006) – *Betjeman* – Arrow Books

Wolfe, Tom (1975) – *The Painted Word* – Picador

Wolfe, Tom (1981) – *From Bauhaus to Our House* – Picador

Wollen, Peter (1969) – *Signs and Meaning in the Cinema* – Secker and Warburg

Yeomans, John (1968) – *The Other Taj Mahal* – Longmans

Zeldin, Theodore (1997) – *The French* – Harvill Press

Illustrations

The illustrations used in the book are listed below in page order, together with the subjects and the source. Where more than one illustration appears in a page L and R are used after the page number to denote Left and Right, as is T, M and B for Top, Middle and Bottom.

All illustrations in the book by the Author may considered to be in the public domain.

All reasonable efforts have been made to trace and contact copyright holders of the illustrations used in this book. I apologise to anyone that I have been unable to contact.

Index

Some words such as architect, architecture, modern, functional and so on, appear frequently. Clearly it would not be useful to include in the index every reference, so for these words only a few entries are made. The term Modern Movement also appears frequently. The entries in the index refer to a point being made about the Modern Movement.

Entries that refer to illustrations have the page reference in italics. Where the illustration is of a specific building, the buildings name does not necessarily appear on the page referred to. In case of doubt, this can be cross-checked with the list of illustrations.

Where the entry refers to a footnote, an f is placed after the page number.